Austerity in Brita

Austerity in Britain

Rationing, Controls, and Consumption, 1939–1955

INA ZWEINIGER-BARGIELOWSKA

OXFORD
UNIVERSITY PRESS

*This book has been printed digitally and produced in a standard specification
in order to ensure its continuing availability*

OXFORD
UNIVERSITY PRESS

Great Clarendon Street, Oxford OX2 6DP

Oxford University Press is a department of the University of Oxford.
It furthers the University's objective of excellence in research, scholarship,
and education by publishing worldwide in

Oxford New York

Auckland Bangkok Buenos Aires Cape Town Chennai
Dar es Salaam Delhi Hong Kong Istanbul Karachi Kolkata
Kuala Lumpur Madrid Melbourne Mexico City Mumbai Nairobi
São Paulo Shanghai Taipei Tokyo Toronto

Oxford is a registered trade mark of Oxford University Press
in the UK and in certain other countries

Published in the United States
by Oxford University Press Inc., New York

© Ina Zweiniger-Bargielowska 2000

The moral rights of the author have been asserted

Database right Oxford University Press (maker)

Reprinted 2004

ISBN 0-19-925102-9

To

SONJA *and* GEOFFREY

Preface

My interest in rationing and austerity policies dates back to 1990 and this book is the outcome of ideas and research which I began to develop during my first year as a postdoctoral research fellow at Nuffield College, Oxford. *Austerity in Britain* in many ways builds on my interest in popular attitudes to government policy and the relationship between the state and society which I explored in my Ph.D. dissertation, 'Industrial Relationships and Nationalisation in the South Wales Coal Mining Industry' (Cambridge, 1990). Although this book also examines the complex relationship between the Attlee government and public opinion, *Austerity in Britain* amounts to a major departure from my doctoral research. This is exemplified by the shift in focus from economic and labour history to an emphasis on gender and consumption. While this change in perspective reflects wider intellectual and historiographical trends and fashions, the transition from coal-miners to housewives was above all inspired by personal experience. My daughter Sonja, born in spring 1990, fundamentally changed both my private life and my intellectual frame of reference. The experience of motherhood opened up a new world and raised many questions and issues addressed by feminists, women's, and gender historians. I have been greatly influenced by this work which has inspired me to examine the connections between gender, consumption, government policy, and party politics during the exceptional circumstances of the 1940s and early 1950s.

This research could not have been embarked upon, sustained, and completed without the support of a number of institutions and individuals to whom I am profoundly grateful. First of all, I would like to thank the warden and fellows of Nuffield College, Oxford, for their generous support during my period as research fellow at Nuffield College. I am grateful to the British Academy, the University of Wales, Aberystwyth, and the Department of History and Welsh History, UWA, for funding this research and granting me two semesters of sabbatical leave. A number of research grants have enabled me to undertake research at the Public Record Office, Kew, and at other archives, as well as to attend conferences where I had an opportunity to present my research at various stages during the last few years. My second period of sabbatical leave during the autumn of 1998 was particularly useful and gave me the time to finish the manuscript. I would like to express my gratitude to many colleagues and friends at Oxford, Aberystwyth, and elsewhere for reading draft chapters and commenting on conference and seminar papers. I have benefited greatly from numerous discussions and generous hospitality as well as intellectual encouragement and emotional support. I am particularly grateful to Paul Addison, Stephen Brooke, Sir David Cox, Charles Feinstein, Ewen Green, A. H. Halsey, Jose Harris, Aled Jones, Harriet Jones, Helen Jones, Maureen Jones, Avner Offer, John Ramsden, Michael Roberts, Neil Rollings, Miri Rubin, Peter Scott, John Stevenson, Gareth Stedman Jones, Barry Supple, Pat Thane, Nick Tiratsoo, and Jim Tomlinson. I am greatly indebted to Martin Francis who read and commented on various draft versions of the entire manuscript and whose friendship was invaluable during the last few years. I also want to thank Tony Morris, who as history editor at OUP commissioned the project as well as his successor, Ruth Parr, for seeing it through its final stages to publication. I want to dedicate this book to my daughter Sonja, who delightfully reminds me of what being a mother is all about and to Geoffrey Plank, whose love has helped me to retain my sanity in the process. Without Sonja I would never have become interested in housewives, mothers, and the domestic implications of the austerity policy and without Geoffrey this book might well never have been completed. I want to thank Geoffrey for his dedication and intellectual rigour in commenting on my writing during its final stages but, most of all, for filling my life with joy.

Ina Zweiniger-Bargielowska
Aberystwyth

Contents

List of Figures

List of Tables

Introduction

Rationing, austerity, and fair shares occupy a central place in British history during and after the Second World War, but there is no study which focuses on these policies throughout the entire episode from the outbreak of war in 1939 until the termination of rationing and controls in the mid–1950s. The purpose of this book is to explore this topic from a range of perspectives. Chapter 1 examines how rationing and controls were administered and assesses the implications of the policy on consumption and dietary trends. Subsequent chapters analyse the public response to the austerity policy by focusing on popular attitudes, women's experiences, and the black market. The continuation of austerity after the war became increasingly controversial, and the final chapter discusses the party political debate about post-war austerity and its electoral implications.

The austerity policy during and after the Second World War involved an exceptional degree of state involvement in the economy. Imports, production, distribution, and prices of consumer goods were extensively controlled, resulting in an unprecedented reduction in and regulation of consumption. While only a limited range of foodstuffs, clothing, and petrol were actually rationed, all consumer goods became subject to comprehensive regulations issued under emergency legislation and administered by a sizeable bureaucracy. As a result of rationing and controls, consumption of food, clothing, household goods, and private motoring was reduced dramatically as economic resources were channelled into the war effort. The post-war recovery policy prioritized exports, investment, and collective provision, and consumption continued to be curtailed. Consumption was not only reduced but also more evenly distributed between income groups as a result of the combined effect of rationing, price controls, and subsidies coupled with full employment and high taxes. This was true particularly with regard to food, which was the largest single category of consumer expenditure. Although total consumer spending had returned to pre-war levels by 1950, for many foodstuffs and consumer goods pre-war consumption levels were reached again only after the abolition of rationing and controls in the mid-1950s.

This book explores the connections between government policy, consumption, gender, and party politics in the exceptional circumstances of the 1940s and early 1950s. During this period, the regulation of consumption became a major element of the relationship between the state and British society. This development was not gender neutral. Men and women responded differently to the reduction in consumption since women in their role as housewives were primarily responsible for implementing the policy on a daily basis. The continuation and, indeed, intensification of rationing and austerity policies after the war were critical to the party political battle. Disaffection with austerity, particularly among women, undermined the popularity of the Labour government elected with a landslide majority in 1945, while the Conservatives' critique of austerity was instrumental to the Conservative electoral recovery and the party's victories in the general elections of 1951 and 1955.

This study is based on a range of primary sources such as government records, contemporary surveys, newspapers and periodicals, political pamphlets, and party propaganda material. The examination of these sources establishes how rationing, austerity, and fair shares intersected with many aspects of British experience during the middle decades of the twentieth century including consumption trends, diet and public health, the emergence and dismantling of administrative machinery, and the limitations of government regulation exemplified in the black market. This research qualifies the myth of the home front characterized by universal sacrifice, egalitarianism, and common purpose. While the notion of fair shares was a principal theme of wartime propaganda, popular attitudes to rationing and austerity were complex. The responses of different social groups were distinctive, and varied between particular policy initiatives. Personal experiences with regard to consumption were central determinants of the state of morale both during and after the war. Fair shares was a compelling slogan but at times there were widespread doubts whether sacrifice was in fact equally shared, and the principle of fair shares was bypassed in the black market. Moreover, attitudes changed over time and wartime acquiescence in civilian sacrifice was replaced by post-war discontent. This was true particularly among women who bore the brunt of the burden of post-war austerity and above all housewives' grievances became a major topic of debate after the war. The analysis of post-war austerity should be set alongside the customary emphasis on the Attlee government's achievements and underlines the absence of a party political consensus in a major policy area. The post-war debate about austerity, consumption, and living standards signified a fundamental conflict between Labour and the Conservatives with regard to the role of the state in the economy and society.

There is a growing interest in consumption among historians which amounts to a major departure from the traditional emphasis on production and the social relations of production. Much of this work focuses on earlier periods, above all the eighteenth century, while the twentieth century has been relatively neglected.[1] This is so despite the fact that the twentieth cen-

---

[1] N. McKendrick, J. Brewer, and J. H. Plumb, *The Birth of Consumer Society: The Commercialisation of Eighteenth-century England* (London, 1982); J. Brewer and R. Porter (eds.),

tury has witnessed the most dramatic rise in consumer expenditure interrupted only by world war and especially the Second World War and its
immediate aftermath. An examination of austerity is interesting since it
provides insight into the relationship between consumption and politics in
the sense that consumption was reduced for overtly political reasons—to
wage war—and this reduction was retained after the war as an integral part
of Labour's programme of post-war reconstruction. This study supports
Brewer and Porter's argument that 'the ultimate test of the viability of
regimes rests on their capacity, in the literal sense, to "deliver the goods"'.[2]
While this dictum was temporarily suspended in the exceptional circumstances of total war when Britain was governed by an all-party coalition and
normal political debate was set aside for the duration, it is doubtful whether
this situation could be maintained for long following the end of hostilities.
In the event, the continuation of austerity became the Attlee government's
principal predicament. The policy not only was difficult to defend politically but also weakened Labour's recovery policy, since shortages of food and
consumer goods provided little incentive for extra effort.

An emphasis on consumption draws attention to the importance of gender difference in roles, attitudes, and behaviour.[3] Many accounts of British
history during and after the Second World War focus on the public sphere
of work or politics and frequently ignore or marginalize women. A gendered analysis of austerity not merely rectifies this imbalance by adding
women to the discussion but alters the nature of the story fundamentally.
While men were of course also consumers and women producers, austerity
meant very different things for men and women. Women and above all
housewives, who accounted for the majority of the adult female population
even at the height of mobilization, were responsible for the management of
the household, family shopping, and the provision of meals on a daily basis.
Therefore, women were most directly affected by austerity while men
primarily benefited from full employment and higher earnings. Women
were disproportionately worried about post-war austerity and female
morale was low in contrast with wartime satisfaction. Although men and,
above all, manual workers were also dissatisfied with shortages, this was not
translated into disaffection with the Labour government—which retained

Consumption and the World of Goods (London, 1993); L. Weatherill, *Consumer Behaviour and
Material Culture in Britain, 1660–1760* (London, 1988); C. Shammas, *The Pre-industrial
Consumer in England and America* (Oxford, 1990); B. Fine and E. Leopold, *The World of
Consumption* (London, 1993). On the twentieth century see G. Cross, *Time and Money: The
Making of Consumer Culture* (London, 1993).

[2] Brewer and Porter, *Consumption and the World of Goods*, p. 1.
[3] J. W. Scott, *Gender and the Politics of History* (New York, 1988); V. de Grazia and E. Furlough
(eds.), *The Sex of Things: Gender and Consumption in Historical Perspective* (Berkeley and Los
Angeles, Calif., 1996).

overwhelming support among men and particularly manual workers. By contrast, female disillusionment with austerity was skilfully exploited by the Conservatives, whose appeal to consumers allowed the party to reconstruct an electoral majority which was supported disproportionately by women.

The post-war party political debate about austerity highlights the difficulties of restricting consumption in a parliamentary democracy in peacetime. Despite Britain's severe economic problems after the war there were genuine policy choices, and rationing and controls were not simply abolished as the supply situation improved. There was no consensus about the policy and both parties, influenced by their respective ideologies, had very different priorities with regard to consumption. Labour's continued commitment to socialist planning, economic controls and fair shares stood in stark contrast to Conservative advocacy of decontrol and a return to the free market. Labour achieved economic recovery, maintained full employment, and implemented social reform, but the government never fully addressed the implications of using wartime emergency legislation to control consumption in peacetime. While fair shares remained popular among Labour's core constituency, the continuation of shortages led to an erosion of support for the government and provided the key to the Conservative party recovery after 1945. The issue dominated political debate during the late 1940s and the electorate was deeply divided—as indicated by the close result of the 1950 and 1951 general elections. The ascendancy of the Conservative approach to consumption was only secure in 1955, after rationing and controls had been abolished and the post-war consumer boom was under way, when the party returned to power with an increased majority.

There is an extensive literature on British economic policy and performance during the 1940s and 1950s.[4] The following paragraphs briefly outline why rationing and direct controls were introduced and why the policy was retained until the mid–1950s. The austerity policy was central to the war economy as well as the post-war recovery. During the Second World War, Britain was transformed from an essentially free market economy into an economy distinguished by centralized control and economic planning.[5] The reduction of civilian consumption played a critical part in this conversion of the economy to the war effort by facilitating the reallocation of

---

[4] For general accounts of the period see J. C. R. Dow, *The Management of the British Economy, 1945–60* (Cambridge, 1965); N. F. R. Crafts and N. Woodward, *The British Economy since 1945* (Oxford, 1991); A. Cairncross, *The British Economy since 1945: Economic Policy and Performance 1945–90* (Oxford, 1992).

[5] P. Howlett, 'The Wartime Economy, 1939–1945', in R. Floud and D. McCloskey (eds.), *The Economic History of Britain since 1700*, 2nd edn. (Cambridge, 1994) vol. 3; W. K. Hancock and M. M. Gowing, *British War Economy* (London, 1949); D. N. Chester (ed.), *Lessons of the British War Economy* (Cambridge, 1951).

resources necessary for mobilization in a total war. Imports of food and raw materials were reduced drastically to economize on foreign exchange and shipping space while labour and factory space were freed for military requirements. The magnitude of this reallocation of resources is illustrated by the dramatic reduction of the share of consumption in net national expenditure from 87 per cent in 1938 to only 55 per cent in 1943, the peak year of mobilization, while military expenditure rose from 7 per cent to 55 per cent.[6] With the introduction of Lend-Lease in 1941, balance of payments considerations weighed less heavily but the combination of rationing, price controls, and subsidies was crucial to the stabilization policy introduced in 1941 and remained instrumental to anti-inflationary policy until the end of the decade.[7] At the end of the war, Britain was faced with exceptional economic problems, above all huge overseas debts, a balance of payments deficit, and the dollar shortage. Following the unexpectedly rapid cessation of Lend-Lease in August 1945 and particularly after the fuel and convertibility crises of 1947, the austerity policy contributed to dollar economy measures which were pursued in order to improve Britain's balance of payments position. This position remained precarious even after the introduction of Marshall Aid in 1948 and the devaluation of 1949.[8] These external considerations, coupled with Labour's primary policy commitment to maintain full employment and retain the greater social equality achieved during the war, were responsible for the continuation of rationing and controls throughout the Attlee government. The social wage—the combination of fair shares, price controls and subsidies on basic goods—buttressed a social contract between government and trade unions which was intended to forestall wage inflation under full employment.[9] For these reasons, planning, which effectively meant a continuation of wartime controls, was a central element of economic policy and Labour's conversion to Keynesianism

[6] Howlett, 'The Wartime Economy', p. 2, table 1.1. (The 1943 figures add up to more than 100 per cent because non-war capital formation was negative.)

[7] R. S. Sayers, *Financial Policy 1939–45* (London, 1956); F. H. Capie and G. E. Wood, 'Anatomy of Wartime Inflation: Britain 1939–45', in G. T. Mills and H. Rockoff (eds.), *The Sinews of War: Essays on the Economic History of World War II* (Ames, Ia., 1993); N. Rollings, 'The Control of Inflation in the Managed Economy: Britain, 1945–53', unpublished Ph.D. thesis, University of Bristol (1990).

[8] The leading accounts are A. Cairncross, *Years of Recovery: British Economic Policy, 1945–51* (London, 1985); J. Tomlinson, *Democratic Socialism and Economic Policy: The Attlee Years, 1945–51* (Cambridge, 1997). The earlier standard work is G. D. N. Worswick and P. H. Ady (eds.), *The British Economy, 1945–1950* (Oxford, 1952). See also J. Tomlinson, 'The Attlee Government and the Balance of Payments, 1945–51', *Twentieth Century British History* 2 (1991); J. Tomlinson, 'Marshall Aid and the "Shortage Economy" in Britain in the 1940s', Department of Government, Brunel University, Discussion Paper Series no. 97/2 (1997).

[9] N. Whiteside, 'The Politics of the "Social" and "Industrial" Wage, 1945–60', in H. Jones and M. Kandiah (eds.), *The Myth of Consensus: New Views on British History, 1945–64* (Basingstoke, 1996); N. Rollings, 'British Budgetary Policy 1945–1954: A "Keynesian Revolution"?', *Economic History Review* 41 (1988).

remained partial and ambivalent.[10] Indeed, the Attlee government in its final years envisaged direct controls as a permanent feature of economic policy, particularly of full employment policy, despite limited derationing and some relaxation—such as the so-called bonfire of controls of 1948.[11] There was general agreement about the need for rationing and economic controls during the war and the immediate transition period. However, the continuation of direct controls became controversial during the second half of the 1940s and ideological considerations came to the fore as Labour's policy of socialist planning clashed with Conservative calls for a return to the free market. The remobilization occasioned by the Korean War was of course important and both governments applied Keynesian demand management techniques. Nevertheless, Conservative rhetoric of decontrol was translated into policy and the wartime control apparatus was finally dismantled after 1951. The new Conservative government rejected permanent economic controls and abolished rationing along with controls on imports, raw materials, and prices before the 1955 general election.[12]

In sum, the austerity policy was never just a simple and straightforward response to scarcity. Rather, rationing and controls made a critical contribution to external and internal economic policy objectives which, after the war, came to be associated with a distinctive ideological perspective. The balance of payments and the dollar shortage dominated economic policy early on in the war and again after 1945. Rationing and controls held down imports, especially from the dollar area, and the curb on civilian consumption contributed towards channelling resources into investment and the export drive. Rationing, in conjunction with price controls and subsidies, was an integral element of anti-inflationary policy alongside fiscal policy instruments. The high weight of food and clothing in the cost-of-living index facilitated price stabilization after 1941, and stable prices of basic goods helped to contain inflation under full employment despite excess

---

[10] Tomlinson, *Democratic Socialism*, ch. 10, *passim*; Cairncross, *Years of Recovery*, ch. 11, *passim*; S. Brooke, *Labour's War: The Labour Party during the Second World War* (Oxford, 1992), ch. 6, *passim*; N. Rollings, '"Poor Mr Butskell: A Short Life, Wrecked by Schizophrenia"?', *Twentieth Century British History* 5 (1994); M. Francis, *Ideas and Policies under Labour, 1945–1951: Building a New Britain* (Manchester, 1997), pp. 37–49. On economic planning see B. W. E. Alford, R. Lowe, and N. Rollings, *Economic Planning 1943–1951: A Guide to the Documents in the Public Record Office* (London, 1992), pp. 1–21; S. Brooke, 'Problems of "Socialist Planning": Evan Durbin and the Labour Government of 1945', *Historical Journal* 34 (1991); J. Tomlinson, 'Planning: Debate and Policy in the 1940s', *Twentieth Century British History* 3 (1992).

[11] N. Rollings, ' "The Reichstag Method of Governing"? The Attlee Governments and Permanent Economic Controls', in H. Mercer, N. Rollings, and J. Tomlinson (eds.), *Labour Governments and Private Industry: The Experience of 1945–1951* (Edinburgh, 1992).

[12] See J. Tomlinson, ' "Liberty With Order": Conservative Economic Policy, 1951–64', in M. Francis and I. Zweiniger-Bargielowska (eds.), *The Conservatives and British Society, 1880–1990* (Cardiff, 1996); N. Rollings, 'Butskellism, the Postwar Consensus and the Managed Economy', in Jones and Kandiah, *Myth of Consensus*; G. D. N. Worswick and P. H. Ady (eds.), *The British Economy in the Nineteen-Fifties* (Oxford, 1962).

demand for consumer goods. Party ideology above all helps to explain why the policy was pursued until the early 1950s. The Labour government's continued commitment to controls was central to socialist ideology on a number of levels. Direct controls remained the principal tool of economic planning and an instrument of anti-inflationary policy under full employment. Rationing and subsidies helped to prevent a wage-price spiral through the social wage, and the maintenance of fair shares reflected Labour's ethical commitment to creating a more egalitarian society. By contrast, the Conservatives were hostile to economic planning, were less egalitarian, and favoured the restoration of free market prices as the central mechanism of resource allocation.

This book is divided into five chapters. Chapter 1 traces the evolution of food rationing policy during the 1930s, and describes the basic principles of rationing during the war, post-war changes, and decontrol. A discussion of ration levels and the range of control schemes is followed by an analysis of dietary trends. Wartime policy with regard to miscellaneous consumer goods included the introduction of clothes rationing, the utility schemes, and priority allocation. These policies were a consequence of drastic reductions in supplies which are illustrated by looking at consumption trends within a longer-term context. This chapter provides the background to the following three chapters which examine the public response to the austerity policy. Chapter 2 charts popular attitudes to austerity on the basis of a range of contemporary surveys. It highlights the significance of shortages, which are identified as a leading national and personal problem, and draws attention to the connection between morale and consumption. The discussion contrasts the range of responses of different social groups, namely classes, or more specifically income and occupational groups, as well as men and women. This analysis points towards the importance of gender differences and Chapter 3 examines the gendered implications of austerity by focusing on women's experiences and attitudes. Housewifery and motherhood acquired an enhanced sense of national importance since the successful implementation of rationing and other economy measures was vital in maintaining public health and morale. The chapter explores how housewives coped under austerity and discusses the introduction of additional rations and welfare foods for mothers and children. These formed an integral part of food policy and contributed towards improvements in vital statistics. Women's attitudes to austerity changed over time and wartime patriotic acquiescence gave way to discontent and disillusionment among many housewives during the late 1940s. Chapter 4 investigates the black market which casts doubt on the myth of shared sacrifice on the home front and indicates the limits of public co-operation in the austerity policy. The topic is explored from an administrative perspective and draws attention to extensive evasion of the control orders. The discussion highlights the growing division between public and private morality and traces the extent of the black market by focusing on a number of case studies, namely food, clothing, cosmetics, and petrol. Chapter 5 analyses the party political debate about post-war austerity from the end of the Second World War and Labour's landslide election victory until the Conservative victory in the 1955 general election. The debate about fair shares and consumer freedom, controls and decontrol, austerity and affluence, which continued with little modification for a decade following the end of the war, provided a focus for both parties to mobilize support and construct coalitions of interests. The analysis of electoral trends underlines the connections between consumption and gender as well as party policy and rhetoric since popular attitudes to austerity correspond neatly with changes in party popularity and voting behaviour.

I

Administration

During the Second World War civilian consumption of food, clothing, and miscellaneous goods was reduced drastically as economic resources were directed towards the war effort. In order to economize on raw materials, labour, and shipping space a comprehensive system of controls was introduced which regulated imports, production, and distribution, as well as demand. During this period of scarcity the price mechanism ceased to function and 'allocation was a mixture of price controls, rationing ... and uncontrolled black market prices. The extent to which any of these three methods prevailed determined the social experience of the war for most people'.[1] Controls were necessary to reduce personal consumption as well as to achieve a balanced redistribution of resources between military and civilian requirements which ensured that civilian efficiency was maintained. Rationing and controls were retained after the war in order to achieve anti-inflationary and dollar economy policy objectives and as part of Labour's wider commitment to economic planning and fair shares. After 1945 only the negative aspect of controls, that is the deliberate suppression of civilian consumption, remained and since 'government needs no longer took automatic precedence over those of the private sector'[2] the policy became increasingly controversial. The process of decontrol began under Labour in the late 1940s but decontrol proceeded steadily only from the early 1950s onwards, that is after the Conservative government—committed to a speedy ending of wartime controls—had been elected.

This chapter describes how rationing and controls were administered and examines the implications of the policy on consumption and dietary trends. The analysis begins with the introduction of rationing and the reduction of civilian consumption during the war and ends in the mid-1950s when all controls had come to an end and the post-war consumer boom was well under way. The focus is on consumption of food, clothing, and household goods, which accounts for about half of total consumer expenditure; food at 30 per cent of the total was the most important single category. The chapter explains the basic mechanics of rationing and controls, discussing food and miscellaneous consumer goods in turn. Consumers had to cope with all

---

[1] A. S. Milward, *War, Economy and Society 1939–1945* (London, 1977), p. 283.
[2] Cairncross, *Years of Recovery*, p. 343.

shortages simultaneously but a separate account allows for greater clarity particularly since the policies were administered by two separate ministries, the Ministry of Food and the Board of Trade. While the literature on the Second World War is extensive, very little has been written about post-war developments and decontrol in particular has been neglected.[3]

The trend of consumer expenditure during the middle decades of the twentieth century is summed up in Figure 1.1. The figure shows a rapid rise during the inter-war years and the severe reduction in the Second World War. In 1942 consumer spending had fallen by about 15 per cent and there was a shift 'towards goods and services with a low resource content'.[4] Expenditure on food was reduced by 15 per cent, expenditure on clothing stood at less than two-thirds of the pre-war level, the purchase of miscellaneous household goods had been cut by between one-quarter and three-quarters, and private motoring virtually disappeared.[5] Moreover, quality as well as variety of most foodstuffs declined while many consumer goods were subject to austerity and utility policies. Total consumer spending returned to pre-war levels in 1948 but consumption of furniture and other durables, clothing, and private motoring barely reached 1938 levels by 1950. Restrictions on food became more extensive after the war with the introduction of bread rationing in 1946, many rations were lower and more volatile, and pre-war consumption levels for many foodstuffs were not reached again until after the ending of rationing in 1954.

This reduction in consumption was unprecedented in modern British history in terms of magnitude and duration. According to Dow, 'the wartime system of controls was interlocking, self-reinforcing and, in total, almost all-extensive: demand not stopped at one point was stopped at another'.[6] Direct controls were an essential element of anti-inflationary policy since they helped to reduce total demand, buoyant due to full employment, and relieve pressure on those basic staple commodities for which there were no satisfactory substitutes such as meat or tea. Rationing, coupled with subsidies and price controls, promoted greater social equality, and consumption became more equal in contrast with the intense inequalities that existed during the inter-war years. The fair shares policy was critical in maintaining morale on the home front at a time when the share of personal

[3] Hancock and Gowing, *British War Economy*; R. J. Hammond, *Food Volume I: the Growth of Policy* (London, 1951); R. J. Hammond, *Food Volume II: Studies in Administration and Control* (London, 1956); R. J. Hammond, *Food Volume III: Studies in Administration and Control* (London, 1962); E. L. Hargreaves and M. M. Gowing, *Civil Industry and Trade* (London, 1952); Chester, *Lessons of the British War Economy*; R. J. Hammond, *Food and Agriculture in Britain 1939–45: Aspects of Wartime Control* (Stanford, Calif., 1954); Worswick and Ady, *The British Economy 1945–1950*; Worswick and Ady, *The British Economy in the Nineteen-Fifties*; Dow, *Management of the British Economy 1945–60*.
[4] Cairncross, *Years of Recovery*, p. 29.   [5] See Table 1.6.
[6] Dow, *Management of the British Economy*, p. 146.

FIG. 1.1. *Consumers' expenditure per capita at constant (1913) prices,*
1910–1960

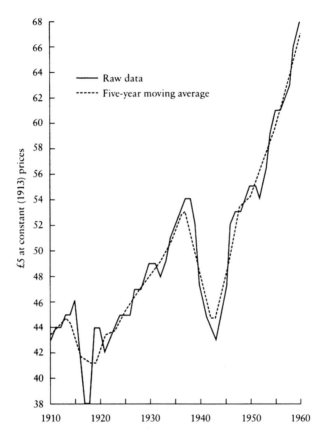

Source: R. Floud, K. Wachter, and A. Gregory, *Height, Health and History: Nutritional Status in the United*
Kingdom, 1750–1980 (Cambridge, 1990), p. 321, fig. 7.5, based on C. H. Feinstein, *National Income,*
Expenditure and Output in the United Kingdom, 1855–1965 (Cambridge, 1972), table 17.

consumption in national expenditure fell from about four-fifths in 1938 to
about half in 1944 while resources devoted to the war effort increased from
7 per cent to half the total.[7] Fair shares remained a cornerstone of Labour's
social policy after the war whereas the Conservatives were committed to a
return to the price mechanism.

This chapter is divided into three sections. Section 1.1 traces the evolution of rationing policy during the 1930s which built on experience gained

[7] Hancock and Gowing, *British War Economy*, p. 199.

in the First World War. The basic principles of rationing, post-war changes in rationing policy, and decontrol are discussed in turn. The second section examines ration levels and the range of control schemes within the context of wider food policy. This is followed by an analysis of dietary trends. The wartime system of rationing and food controls reduced long-standing class and income differentials in food consumption and nutrient intake. These inequalities, which were observed until the 1930s, did not return after decontrol in the mid-1950s—thereby contributing towards improvements in public health. Section 1.3 focuses on miscellaneous consumer goods, namely clothing, furniture, and other household goods. The twin objectives of controlling prices and limiting supplies gradually resulted in extensive controls such as clothes rationing, priority allocation of furniture, as well as austerity regulations and the utility policy. The final part of this section traces consumption trends from the 1930s until the 1960s in order to place the episode of wartime rationing and austerity within a longer-term context.

1.1. FOOD RATIONING AND CONTROLS, 1939–1955: GENERAL POLICY

Food policy during the Second World War was shaped by the precedent of the Great War and pre-war planners had little option but to take the success of the first experience of food control as a starting-point. This continuity is personified above all by Sir William Beveridge who was permanent secretary to the first Ministry of Food, author of *British Food Control*, a volume of the Carnegie Endowment history of the world war, and chairman of an influential subcommittee on rationing appointed in 1936.[8] The subcommittee effectively proposed to reproduce the system of food control which had worked well during the First World War. Many civil servants and food traders who had administered food control during the Great War were involved in discussions of wartime food policy during the 1930s.[9]

Food was not a major problem on the home front until December 1916 when a Food Controller was appointed in response to submarine warfare and growing shortages. These led to rising food prices and queues which were the leading cause of industrial unrest in 1917 and 1918. After June

[8] W. H. Beveridge, *British Food Control* (London and New Haven, Conn., 1928); Public Record Office, Kew (hereafter PRO), CAB 16/157, Committee of Imperial Defence (hereafter CID), Sub-Committee on Food Supply in Time of War, F. S. 13, Report of the Sub-Committee on Rationing, 5 Oct. 1936. See also T. G. Jones, *The Unbroken Front: Ministry of Food, 1916–1944* (London, 1944).
[9] Board of Trade, *Report of the Food (Defence Plans) Department for the Year ended 31st December, 1937* (London, 1938), p. 8.

1917 the government took complete control of imports and home production and the civilian population was 'catered for like an army'.[10] Rationing of sugar, fats, and meat was introduced in 1918 and continued until 1920. The Ministry of Food was abolished in the wake of decontrol in 1921. The rationing system was based on individual flat-rate rations, fair shares for all, and a consumer-retailer tie (that is each individual would register with a particular retailer who received supplies in proportion to registrations) as the main safeguard against fraud. Differential energy requirements were satisfied by bread, which was subsidized and freely available. Rationing was an 'immediate and almost unqualified success', public faith in food policy was restored, and the food queues quickly disappeared.[11] However, from an administrative point of view rationing policy had many weaknesses and was, in Beveridge's words, a 'supreme case of muddling through by brilliant improvisations'. The registration procedure required lengthy preparation and the system functioned mainly as a guarantee of supplies, which were more plentiful than on the Continent, 'but its efficiency as a means of restricting consumption to a level of real hardship was never tested'.[12]

In contrast with the call of 'business as usual' in August 1914, civil servants discussed the economic implications of a major war at some length during the inter-war years. These deliberations were conducted under the auspices of the Committee of Imperial Defence (CID). Under the ten-year rule of 1919, which presumed that there would be no major war for ten years, discussions were largely theoretical. A 1929 Treasury memorandum emphasized the problems of wartime shortages and inflation. It called for the 'fixation of wages and prices . . . strict control of imports and rationing of consumable goods so as to reduce possible objects of expenditure' as well as increased savings and taxes.[13] The ten-year rule, which had been renewed annually, was rescinded in March 1932 and a subcommittee was appointed by the CID to consider the issues raised by the Treasury memorandum. Since food was weighted at 60 per cent in the cost-of-living index, the subcommittee declared, 'If the problem of food can be met . . . the objects set out in our reference are in a fair way to attainment'.[14] Preparations accelerated after the establishment of a Sub-Committee on Food Supplies in Time of War and Beveridge was appointed to chair a subcommittee on rationing policy.[15] Its report stressed that successful rationing was only possible if each consumer was assured his or her share. This required comprehensive controls of supply and distribution and, in order to introduce rationing soon after the outbreak of war, a scheme would have to be prepared in

---

[10] Beveridge, *British Food Control*, p. 2.   [11] Ibid., pp. 206–7.   [12] Ibid., pp. 229–30.
[13] For details see Hancock and Gowing, *British War Economy*, pp. 47–52.   [14] Ibid., p. 51.
[15] PRO, CAB 16/156, CID, Sub-Committee on Food Supply in Time of War, Minutes of Meetings, 4 May and 20 July 1936; CAB 16/157, CID, Sub-Committee on Food Supply in Time of War, Reports, F. S. 2, Note by Secretary, F. S. 3, Report by Board of Trade.

advance.[16] These discussions led to the creation of the Board of Trade Food (Defence Plans) Department in December 1936, which was charged with formulating plans 'for the supply, control, distribution and movement of food'.[17]

The Food (Defence Plans) Department was the peacetime precursor of the second Ministry of Food which was expected to be established immediately after the outbreak of war. Two divisions dealt with the control of supplies and the regulation of consumers' demand respectively and rapid progress was made in planning both. In order to minimize disruption, normal trading would be replaced by wartime control within hours of the outbreak of hostilities. Following the precedent of the First World War, detailed control schemes for cereals, meat, sugar, fats, and tea were drawn up. The Ministry of Food would secure possession of bulk stocks, become sole owner of all subsequent imports and produce leaving farms, and negotiate long-term bulk contracts with overseas suppliers. Leading members of the food trade would act as government agents and shadow organizations, responsible for the regular flow of food to retailers and consumers, were set up. The country was divided into 19 divisions and local authorities cooperated in the establishment of some 1,400 local food control committees. In wartime, divisional food officers would be responsible for the smooth operation of food control and the local committees would deal directly with individual consumers, issue ration documents, supervise registration, allocate supplies, and enforce regulations.

With regard to the control of consumer demand, a comprehensive rationing policy was formulated so that 'every member of the public would be able to obtain a fair share of the national food supply at a reasonable price'.[18] Rationing was not just a restrictive device but also a guarantee of supplies and 'the cardinal point in any future system [was] that the British ration card should be as fully capable of being regarded as a guarantee in the next war as it was in the last'.[19] Rationing was inevitable for a number of reasons. First and foremost, rationing was intended to 'remedy an existing shortage or to prevent an expected shortage'. Further, it would 'check a rise in prices, . . . prevent the formation of food queues . . . economise certain commodities in order to create reserves . . . [and finally] ensure fair distribution among all classes of consumers'.[20] A general and prolonged shortage was always the most powerful argument in favour of rationing and

[16] PRO, CAB 16/157, CID, Sub-Committee on Food Supply in Time of War, Reports, F. S. 13, Report of Sub-Committee on Rationing, 5 Oct. 1936.
[17] PRO, MAF 72/534, Board of Trade Food (Defence Plans) Department, Note, 20 Feb. 1937.
[18] Board of Trade, *Report*, 1937, p. 10.
[19] PRO, MAF 72/598, Rationing, 4 Jan. 1937.   [20] Board of Trade, *Report*, 1937, pp. 25–6.

according to the Beveridge subcommittee only this would 'justify the elaborate and costly apparatus without which rationing is impossible'.[21]

Rationing during the Second World War was based on three postulates. First, there would be a flat-rate individual ration. Second, in order to ensure that each individual obtained his or her full share and no more, the consumer had to register with a retailer. Finally, acquisition of sufficient supplies and effective distribution required complete control.[22] The principle of a flat-rate ration for all, which ignored the diverse needs of heavy workers at one extreme and small children at the other, was justifiable since only a fraction of all foodstuffs were to be rationed. These were sugar, butter, bacon, and ham as well as meat, all of which were predominantly imported and had been rationed during the First World War. A so-called buffer of bread, potatoes, and restaurant or canteen meals was to be freely available to satisfy differential energy requirements.[23] Pre-war planners anticipated the possibility of differential rationing and supplementary ration books were prepared for adolescent boys and heavy workers who were to receive additional bacon and meat. These were never introduced and widespread doubts about the fairness of flat-rate rations became a major source of discontent during and after the war. The consumer-retailer tie, that is registration of consumers with individual retailers, was the 'kingpin' of rationing.[24] The system implied a certain loss of freedom on the part of the consumer but also provided him or her with the assurance of a guaranteed ration delivered to the chosen retailer. Ration books consisted of coupons and counterfoils. The latter were deposited with the retailer and it was this counterfoil or registration which served as a basis of stock replacement. Coupons played no part in the distribution of supplies. According to the Beveridge subcommittee, rationing had both negative and positive aspects.

[21] PRO, CAB 16/157, CID, Sub-Committee on Food Supply in Time of War, F. S. 13, Report of the Sub-Committee on Rationing, 5 Oct. 1936.

[22] For a useful discussion of the basic principles of rationing policy see W. B. Reddaway, 'Rationing', in Chester, *Lessons of the British War Economy*.

[23] Irrespective of this general policy, there were some differential elements. In the course of the war allowances were made for the additional requirements of particular groups, namely manual workers, pregnant women and nursing mothers, children, invalids, the elderly, and people adhering to special diets. The higher food requirements of workers were partly met by increasing the availability and use of industrial canteens, a special cheese ration was granted to workers who had no access to such facilities, and underground coal-miners were given an additional meat ration from 1946 onwards. Pregnant women and nursing mothers were entitled to supplementary food rations, welfare, and priority foods such as vitamin supplements, fresh eggs, fruit, and milk. Children and adolescents up to 18 years, in addition to receiving virtually the entire adult ration (except that there was less meat and no tea for the under-fives) had similar welfare and priority foods entitlements to pregnant women and nursing mothers. Certain specified groups of invalids were entitled to additional food and people over 70 years of age were given an extra allowance of tea from 1944 onwards. Finally, vegetarians, Jews, and Muslims forgoing their meat and/or bacon rations qualified for special cheese and vegetable cooking fats instead.

[24] Hammond, *Food and Agriculture*, p. 21.

The purpose of rationing policy was 'not merely [to] prevent people from buying more than the prescribed amount, but also to make certain that the prescribed amount is distributed to them. Rationing assumes control of supply and distribution.'[25]

Pre-war planning of food policy in a major war accelerated from 1936 onwards and the pace of preparations intensified especially after the Munich crisis of September 1938. The commodity schemes were ready to become operational, additional food stocks were being purchased, details of transport and storage policy were under discussion, and legislation to implement food control was being drafted.[26] In order to facilitate the early introduction of rationing 50 million ration books were printed in peace-time, a process which was completed in the summer of 1939.[27] In marked contrast with the First World War, the department heeded Beveridge's advice of 1936 that to 'think out in advance *and as a whole*, the civilian side of the next war is as important as to design measures of military attack and defence'.[28]

The second Ministry of Food was established a few days after the out-break of war in September 1939 and all powers relating to food exercised by the Board of Trade were transferred to the new ministry.[29] The supply side of the ministry was divided into a number of commodity divisions, each controlled by a director responsible for the commodity while it remained within the ministry's ownership. The regional divisions and local food control committees were responsible for the implementation of controls, supported by rationing, statistics, and intelligence as well as enforcement divisions. The ministry lacked cohesion since the commodity divisions, which grew out of the pre-war control schemes, were dispersed geographically. Another weakness was that pre-war preparations had been concerned primarily with control of supplies and distribution, that is the administration of food, and wider questions of food policy were usually dealt with by the war cabinet.

Rationing did not begin until January 1940, largely as a result of doubts and hesitations in cabinet. The widespread air attacks, feared by pre-war planners, did not materialize, the impact of the so-called phoney war on civilians was limited, and living standards were reduced little until after the fall of France. Nevertheless, the ministry, anxious to implement food

[25] PRO, CAB 16/157, CID, Sub-Committee on Food Supply in Time of War, F. S. 13, Report of the Sub-Committee on Rationing, 5 Oct. 1936.

[26] PRO, MAF 72/578, Board of Trade Food (Defence Plans) Department, Progress Report, 31 Mar. 1939.

[27] PRO, MAF 72/601, Board of Trade Food (Defence Plans) Department, Printing of Ration Documents.

[28] PRO, CAB 16/157, CID, Sub-Committee on Food Supply in Time of War, F. S. 13, Report of the Sub-Committee on Rationing, 5 Oct. 1936 (emphasis in original).

[29] Hammond, *Food I*, p. 51.

control, proposed the introduction of rationing from the beginning of November. The supply situation was not a crucial factor and it was thought that rationing 'might be necessary not because there was an actual or even an expected shortage of foodstuffs but as a matter of precaution or to ensure the equitable distribution of available supplies'.[30] The war cabinet now had to decide on the principle of differential rationing and the timing of the introduction of rationing. The question of extra meat for heavy workers and adolescent boys was examined by a subcommittee which noted that the Trades Union Congress (hereafter TUC) was 'strongly opposed to any differentiation between heavy workers and other classes of the community' due to 'the problem of identifying such workers'.[31] On the question of adolescents, it was argued that discrimination against girls would cause difficulties and that it was administratively simpler to have flat-rate rations for all except children under six who were entitled to only half the meat ration. It was also argued that the needs of adolescents were better met by increased milk consumption and, since the proposed meat ration was to be larger than that available in the Great War, the principle of flat-rate rations was recommended by the subcommittee and confirmed by the war cabinet.[32] The cabinet authorized butter and bacon rationing to begin in January 1940 but decided not to ration sugar and meat.[33] There were doubts whether public opinion would support the latter rationing schemes since there was no shortage, but the Colonial Office pointed out that Britain had purchased Empire sugar at a very favourable price and if the failure to introduce sugar rationing would require additional purchases at a higher price on the free market, colonial producers would have serious cause for complaint.[34] With rising consumption and uncertain supplies, the sugar and meat situation deteriorated and the subcommittee's recommendation to ration sugar and meat in order to economize on foreign exchange and shipping as well as to avoid price rises was finally endorsed by the war cabinet.[35] These deliberations illustrate that there were many reasons for rationing a commodity and that straightforward shortages of supply were not necessarily decisive.

Ration books were issued after National Registration in September

[30] PRO, MAF 72/635, Board of Trade Food (Defence Plans) Department, Memo, 4 Oct. 1939; this file also includes other timetables for the introduction of rationing in late Nov. or early Dec.

[31] PRO, CAB 75/27, War Cabinet: Home Policy Committee, Sub-Committee on Rationing, 21 Oct. 1939.

[32] Ibid.; PREM 1/295, Note from Minister of Health to Prime Minister, 16 Oct. 1939; CAB 65/1, WM 60 (39) 2, 25 Oct. 1939.

[33] PRO, CAB 65/1, WM 63 (39) 10, 28 Oct. 1939.

[34] PRO, PREM 1/295, Note from Minister of Health to Prime Minister, 16 Oct. 1939, Letter from Colonial Office to Prime Minister, 27 Oct. 1939.

[35] PRO, CAB 74/1, War Cabinet: Home Policy Committee, Ministerial Sub-Committee on Food Policy, Meeting, 1 Dec. 1939; CAB 65/4, WM 106 (39) 4, 6 Dec. 1939.

1939.[36] With about 44 million in circulation, the processing and distribution of ration books was a formidable task.[37] The buff-coloured R.B. 1 was issued to everybody above 6 years of age (the age later being reduced to 5) and young children received the green R.B. 2. This ration book also included extra allowances for pregnant and nursing mothers. There were special ration documents for travellers and seamen who could not be tied to a particular retailer. From 1943 onwards a Junior R.B. 4 (blue) was introduced for the 5 to 16 age group (extended to 18 from 1944). The introduction of bacon and ham and butter rationing was announced in November 1939 and consumers were told to register with retailers for these commodities as well as sugar. Sugar rationing was announced after Christmas 1939 when consumers were also told to register for meat. Rationing of bacon and ham, butter, and sugar started in January 1940 and that of meat in March. These four ration schemes proceeded smoothly and in July tea, margarine, and cooking fats were rationed. Rationing was extended to preserves and cheese in 1941, completing the gradual expansion of so-called straight rationing, that is rationing based on the consumer-retailer tie.

At the outset, the system placed a premium on economy of foodstuffs and laborious procedures paid little heed to administrative effort. The duration of retailers' permits, which provided the basis of their supplies, was short (only four weeks), supplies had to be allocated on a weekly basis in line with ration periods, and retailers were required to complete numerous returns on stocks and sales as well as to count coupons which were cut from ration books as proof of purchase. Coupons, which were returned to food offices, were intended as a check on retailers but limitations in manpower allowed for only a small sample to be counted. This practice was soon seen as a bluff and coupon cutting was abolished in January 1941. Subsequently, cancellation sufficed as proof of purchase, thereby eliminating an unnecessary administrative step. The administrators' intention to impose 'accuracy on a system whose principal merit was in being rough-and-ready'[38] had to be abandoned and rationing procedures were streamlined from as early as May 1940 onwards when permit periods were extended to eight weeks. After progressive relaxation permits were seen as a *'ceiling'* and had become *'continuing, composite* and *global'* by August 1942.[39] The *ceiling* level implied that a permit 'represented the retailer's maximum needs for his regular trade instead of an attempted assessment of his minimum needs'. The *continuing* permits were able to run until registrations changed by more than 5 per cent

[36] The following paragraph is largely based on Ministry of Food, *How Britain was Fed in Wartime: Food Control 1939-1945* (London 1946), pp. 56–7; and PRO, MAF 223/31 and MAF 83/3564, Rationing in the United Kingdom, various edns.

[37] PRO, MAF 223/102: in 1942 43,996,000 ration books were in circulation. On the format and printing of ration books see Hammond, *Food Volume II*, pp. 763–8.

[38] Ibid., p. 755.   [39] Ibid., pp. 625–6 (emphasis in original).

rather than being reissued every time. *Composite* permits eased the administrative burden by covering more than one commodity and their *global* nature allowed for an eight-week supply rather than a weekly quantity for each of the eight weeks.

Growing food shortages during the winter of 1940–1, the most difficult period of the war for Britain, led to public discontent with the unequal distribution of unrationed foods and demands for an extension of rationing. The foodstuffs in question, namely canned and processed foods and miscellaneous items such as dried fruits, rice, and biscuits, were unsuitable for straight rationing since demand was diverse and supplies were insufficient to guarantee a regular ration to each consumer. The ensuing debate about the extension of rationing to these foods was the most interesting aspect of rationing policy during the war, culminating in the launch of points rationing in December 1941. Points rationing involved repudiation of the basic principles of rationing policy, namely the guaranteed supply of a specific ration to each consumer and the consumer-retailer tie.

The demands of anti-inflationary policy and the desire to maintain fair shares of limited supplies sparked off a ferment of ideas within both the ministry and the Economic Section, largely composed of academic economists who worked as temporary civil servants during the war.[40] A host of different schemes was proposed including a household goods ration, tobacco rationing, and bread rationing. None of these was implemented since demand for household goods was irregular and any ration would be derisory, tobacco rationing was considered bad for morale and conflicted with the revenue-raising function of tobacco, and, finally, bread rationing would not result in appreciable savings.[41] The Ministry of Food was under growing pressure to extend rationing following the endorsement of the clothes rationing scheme in February 1941 and the Lord President's Committee called for an extension of rationing in March.[42] Given the Ministry of Food's traditions, and in view of the influence of the commodity directors, it is not surprising that the ministry defended the principle of being able to honour the ration at all costs. It was argued that rationing was only practicable if supply and distribution could be effectively controlled, if the food was not highly perishable, and if demand was relatively constant. The ministry proposed a number of so-called group ration schemes for canned meals; dried fruits; biscuits; pulses, rice, breakfast cereals, and other

[40] Hammond, *Food Volume II*, p. 572 and ch. 33, *passim*; A. Booth, 'Economists and Points Rationing in the Second World War', *Journal of European Economic History* 14 (1985), pp. 297–317; A. Cairncross and N. Watts, *The Economic Section 1939–1961: A Study in Economic Advising* (London, 1989).

[41] PRO, T 230/119 and 120, Economic Section: Rationing, General Policy.

[42] Hancock and Gowing, *British War Economy*, pp. 330–1; on clothes rationing policy see below.

cereal products; and chocolate and sugar confectionery.[43] This group
rationing scheme was a modification of straight rationing since it was based
on the same principles of a definite entitlement and the consumer-retailer tie
but instead of receiving a particular commodity the consumer was entitled
to one of a number of foods.

By contrast, the Economic Section, concerned about inflation and influenced by the German points system produced a radical alternative proposal,
namely points rationing.[44] This scheme, which had been adopted for clothes
in the summer of 1941, allowed an extension of rationing to non-perishable
commodities supplies of which were limited and demand for which was
infrequent. Points rationing, a coupon replacement scheme, could be seen as
the opposite of straight rationing since it required no registration with
retailers. Consumers received a number of points (or coupons) which could
be spent at any retailer and there was no guarantee of a fixed quantity of a
specified commodity. The only guarantee was that all points could be spent
on something. All foods were given a points price and consumers could
choose freely within each category. Points could be seen as an alternative
currency and demand for each item was regulated by adjusting points prices.
In contrast with ordinary rationing where coupons were merely cancelled,
coupons were cut and retailers' stocks were replaced by passing coupons
back along the chain of distribution. The scheme was intended to be self-
regulating and, after an initial period, stock replacement was based on past
performance of actual sales rather than an estimate of future demand as in
the registration system.

The argument raged during the late summer and the Ministry of Food
opposed points rationing because of its uncertainties, the need for high initial stocks, and the difficulties of coupon cutting and counting. The advantage of points rationing was its flexibility. This was in marked contrast with
the group rationing scheme which required six new registrations and far
more regimentation of retailers and consumers. The Lord President's committee finally pronounced in favour of points rationing because it 'allows
the consumer a greater liberty of individual choice of foods', consumers
were 'free to buy elsewhere', and the system did 'not impose any further limitation on the spirit of competition between retailers'.[45] The war cabinet
approved the recommendation with the proviso that, if 'a points system . . .
failed to achieve its object' a system of group rationing should be introduced, indicating some remaining doubts about points rationing of food.[46]

[43] PRO, T 230/118, Committee on the Machinery for Distribution of Unrationed Foodstuffs,
Final Report, 5 June 1941; T 230/119, Second Report of the Committee on Rationing, 30 July
1941.
[44] See PRO, T 230/119 and 120, Economic Section: Rationing, General Policy.
[45] PRO CAB 66/18, WP (41) 216, Memo by Lord President to War Cabinet, 9 Sept. 1941.
[46] PRO CAB 65/19, WM 92 (41) 10, 11 Sept. 1941.

Points rationing, initially restricted to canned foods, was launched in December 1941. The 'immediate popularity of the scheme exceeded expectations' and, according to Hancock and Gowing, it was one of 'the big home front successes of the war'.[47] Points rationing was gradually extended to many other foodstuffs. The commodity directors' opposition to points rationing may be seen as an illustration of their inability to grasp basic economic concepts[48] but it is important to remember that 'everything' about points rationing 'was alien to the tradition of food control'.[49] Building on the success of points rationing a separate scheme for chocolate and sugar confectionery was launched in the summer of 1942. These so-called personal points were detachable from ration books and distinguished from conventional points since they were intended as an individual ration rather than being consumed on a household basis. A coupon replacement scheme was again adopted to allow consumers freedom of choice between retailers.

There were many administrative strengths and weaknesses with regard to both straight rationing (a guaranteed ration, based on the consumer-retailer tie and registrations for stock replacements) and points rationing (a coupon replacement scheme where consumers could shop anywhere and retailers' stocks were replenished in proportion to coupons acquired). The consumer-retailer tie had a number of advantages such as a guaranteed entitlement to basic foods, relative ease of distribution, important particularly for perishable goods, and efficiency in the shops since no coupon cutting and counting was necessary. On the negative side, consumers disliked being tied to one particular retailer and straight rationing was only practicable for those commodities for which demand was regular and universal and where supplies were sufficient to allow a reasonable ration for everybody. The consumer-retailer tie originated as a loose substitute for rationing introduced in 1917 and since there were always some consumers who could not be registered, such as travellers or holders of temporary ration cards, retailers' supplies always had to exceed entitlement. There was also an assumption of 100 per cent uptake and, therefore, straight rationing could only function if supplies of a commodity were not particularly scarce.

The greatest weakness of straight rationing was the difficulty in maintaining an up-to-date record of registrations on which retailers' buying permits were based. A general re-registration was not undertaken every time ration books were issued and because of removals records were soon inaccurate. There were almost 35 million changes of address among the civilian population during the war, in addition to births and deaths as well as entries to and exits from the services. Theoretically these alterations should have

[47] Ministry of Food, *How Britain was Fed in Wartime*, p. 57; Hancock and Gowing, *British War Economy*, p. 332.

[48] Booth, 'Economists and Points Rationing', p. 315.

[49] Hammond, *Food and Agriculture*, p. 125.

been relatively simple to administer, and the new retailer could use supplementary permits to cope with additional demand until a new permit came into force. The difficulty was adjusting the permit of the old retailer or even tracing the correct trader. This could involve a number of food offices since individuals could register with different retailers for each of the rationed foods and many shopped at some distance from their place of residence. People were supposed to enter the name and address of each retailer in their ration books but a survey at one food office showed that 64 per cent of ration books submitted for notification of removals or cancellation did not contain retailers' names and addresses.[50] This problem resulted in considerable duplication and 'might probably mean in an extreme case that the ration for, say, bacon was reduced because the total liabilities to judge from the permit quantities appeared to be more than visible supplies'.[51] While retailers were quick to report additional customers, requests were seldom made for reductions in registrations and this inflationary tendency was a major shortcoming of straight rationing.

Points rationing had the great advantage of flexibility since coupons could flow along the regular trade channels to replace stocks. The system could cover a range of commodities simultaneously when supplies were not sufficient to ration an individual foodstuff and where demand might be irregular and variable. Points rationing was not suitable for perishable commodities, there was no guarantee of availability for any particular item, which might be a disadvantage if basic foods were included in the scheme, and it created extra work in the shops since coupons had to be cut and counted for each transaction. In practice, points rationing never lived up to the theoretical advantages of adjusting distribution to demand since restrictions on distribution, limitations of supply, and difficulties in fixing points values precisely meant that shortages of the most popular items persisted. The scheme:

always provided a guarantee that each consumer . . . would be able to spend all points on a reasonable variety of foods [but] it could never succeed in ensuring that he or she would be able to buy any particular food of their preference — or even their second or third preference. In fact, points never came near to achieving the power of money in drawing particular goods to the point where they were individually in demand.[52]

The analogy of points as an alternative currency breaks down in a number of ways. There was no free market since every consumer was guaranteed an equal supply, high demand could not increase production of the most popular lines, and there was no profit. Successful retailers could not increase

[50] PRO, MAF 99/927, Letter from Camberwell Food Executive Officer, 26 Feb. 1941.
[51] PRO, MAF 99/926, Memo, 28 Dec. 1940.
[52] PRO, MAF 75/64, Account of the Operation of Points Rationing, 1 Sept. 1950.

stock as it was only replaced as a result of sales whereas under straight rationing unsatisfactory retailers could be penalized by loss of registrations. It was difficult to fix appropriate point prices since changes could only be made in fairly large steps, usually of four points per pound, and national prices did not take into account local preferences. There were also political objections to allocating a commodity so large a number of points that one-person households could never obtain a share. Therefore, many goods were distributed along established lines and retailers were asked to reserve the most popular items for registered customers. Finally, points rationing created new problems of enforcement. Only small samples of coupons and vouchers, into which individual coupons were exchanged, could be counted by food offices. In order to avoid over-declaration and inconsistencies along the chain of distribution a points banking system was introduced in 1943. This system improved enforcement at the distribution end since coupons were now handled by the retailer only and all further transactions were conducted through these accounts. There were also weaknesses at the consumer end since stolen or lost ration books were frequently returned without the points and sweets coupons. This problem was never solved and straight rationing had definite advantages with regard to enforcement and security of ration documents.[53]

This outline has focused on general policy and excluded many exceptions and special cases which cannot be dealt with in any detail here. The administrative effort by the ministry frequently appeared out of all proportion to the size of the group, but:

Rationing, because it touched everyone, had to adjust itself to innumerable individual needs, from major categories such as expectant mothers and heavy workers, down to office teas and beekeepers. It could not turn aside from any *bona fide* food requirement, merely because the number of people concerned was small; in the last resort, for instance, invalids had to be treated as individual cases.[54]

Groups which caused particular problems were people who could not be tied to a retailer, such as seamen, gypsies, and other travellers, who were provided with a succession of special ration documents. Disruption of supplies and distribution due to enemy action, ranging from loss of shipping to bombed-out retailers and individuals who lost ration and identity documents after air raids, at times and particularly at a local level, caused severe difficulties. The complexities of most foodstuffs led to problems of control and standardization and a balance had to be struck between quantity, quality, and price. Self-suppliers provided a further challenge to administrators striving for the ideal of equal shares for all. The rationing policy which

---

[53] This issue is discussed in Chapter 4; the problem was particularly severe with regard to clothing coupons. [54] Hammond, *Food Volume II*, p. 754.

developed during the Second World War operated essentially unaltered until decontrol. However, the early post-war years witnessed three important changes, namely the introduction of bread rationing and a potato control scheme as well as a supplementary meat ration for coal-miners, which are discussed next.

Bread, which had remained unrestricted during the war, was rationed for two years from July 1946 and potatoes were controlled during the winter 1947–8. These policies conflicted with the underlying principle of rationing policy that a buffer of bread, potatoes, and restaurant or canteen meals was freely available. Without this buffer, which helped to satisfy differential calorie requirements, flat-rate rations were difficult to defend. For this reason bread rationing was controversial and the scheme introduced included differential allowances for different classes of consumer. Since the ration was generous, few savings of wheat were made and, as argued elsewhere, the policy can be understood only in the context of the post-war world food shortage, Britain's balance of payments problems, and Anglo-American relations during the inception of the cold war.[55] The potato crop of 1947 was 20 per cent below the previous crop due to a severe winter and in order to reduce consumption a loose control scheme operated from November 1947 until April 1948. Differential rationing was impracticable, ration books were simply marked, and the scheme was 'clearly far from satisfactory [since] it provided no guarantee of supplies to the individual, it took no account of varying nutritional needs, and enforcement would be virtually impossible'.[56]

The final innovation of post-war rationing policy was the introduction of an additional meat ration for underground coal-miners. This policy was contentious since it departed from the principle of flat-rate rations for all which had been endorsed by the TUC when rationing was introduced because it was impossible to distinguish between different classes of workers. Instead, workers' additional food requirements were addressed by increased industrial canteens and the introduction of a special cheese ration where canteens were impracticable. The special claim of underground miners was discussed on a number of occasions but in 1944 the TUC again defended 'the principle of no differential domestic rations'.[57] In the context of the impending coal crisis and problems of recruitment, the issue of extra rations for underground workers was raised again in February 1946.[58]

[55] I. Zweiniger-Bargielowska, 'Bread Rationing in Britain, July 1946–July 1948', *Twentieth Century British History* 4 (1993), pp. 57–85.

[56] PRO, CAB 128/10, CM 82 (47) 3, 23 Oct. 1947; CM 84 (47) 3, 3 Nov. 1947; CAB 129/22, CP (47) 295, 20 Oct. 1947; MAF 223/31, Rationing in the U.K., 1950 edn., pp. 20, 44.

[57] PRO, MAF 99/1239, Extract of TUC Advisory Meeting, 1 Mar. 1944.

[58] PRO, PREM 8/440, Minute Jay to PM, 16 Feb. 1946; Minute PM to Minister of Fuel and Power, 19 Feb. 1946.

Shinwell, the Minister of Fuel and Power, favoured extra meat, points, and fats for coal-miners since only a minority took a main meal at a canteen. This policy 'would bring home strikingly the exceptional and serious position of the Industry today'.[59] By contrast, Smith, the Minister of Food, was 'utterly opposed' to the policy which might result in lower basic rations and claims from other groups of workers. If the principle of equal rations were breached 'the whole rationing front would collapse' and the lowest class would be faced with 'a drastic cut' under a scheme of differential rations.[60] Attlee supported Shinwell's proposal and the Minister of Labour suggested that the TUC position had changed with regard to underground miners in view of the urgent coal situation. Nevertheless, Smith's arguments prevailed, that the miners' diet was substantial, in some cases exceeding 4,000 calories per day, that miners' claims were no greater than those of other heavy workers, and that basic rations might have to be cut, and it was decided to improve the provision of canteens instead.[61]

Against the background of an increasingly desperate coal situation the question of extra meat for underground miners was brought up once more during the summer of 1946. Strachey, the new Minister of Food, was prepared to accede to the proposal but only if TUC support was secured in advance and he warned 'that it would cause considerable dissatisfaction among other workers'.[62] It was considered more appropriate for the National Union of Mineworkers to negotiate directly with the TUC.[63]

When the matter was finally discussed, TUC representatives were 'profoundly disturbed at the way this matter had been handled' since there was 'no precedent' of a union consulting with a government department without prior consultation with the TUC, thereby presenting them with a *fait accompli*. They were 'profoundly disturbed by the suggestion to set up a privileged class of workers', particularly since many other groups of workers did not have access to canteens and their claims were equally justified. The TUC refused to accept responsibility for the matter and would not guarantee to refuse concessions to others.[64] The cabinet focused on TUC anger about procedure rather than the merits of the proposal and the additional meat for underground miners, which effectively doubled their meat ration, was finally agreed in October 1946.[65] There is ample evidence

[59] Ibid., Minute Minister of Fuel and Power to PM, 4 Mar. 1946.
[60] Ibid., Minute Minister of Food to PM, 1 Mar. 1946.
[61] Ibid, GEN 126/1, Cabinet: Extra Rations for Underground Miners, 3 Apr. 1946.
[62] Ibid., GEN 94/4, Cabinet: Lord President's Committee, Ministerial Committee on the Coal Situation during the Coming Winter, 1 Aug. 1946.
[63] PRO, MAF 99/1239, Correspondence, 15–20 Aug. 1946; PREM 8/440, GEN 94/5, Cabinet: Lord President's Committee, Ministerial Committee on the Coal Situation during the Coming Winter, 16 Sept. 1946.   [64] PRO, MAF 99/1239, TUC Advisory Committee, 24 Sept. 1946.
[65] PRO, CAB 128/6, CM 83 (46) 3, 26 Sept. 1946; CM 85 (46) 6, 10 Oct. 1946; MAF 99/1239, Meat for Miners, 27 Oct. 1950.

of continued TUC dissatisfaction. In January 1947 the TUC felt they 'had
been placed in considerable difficulty' but decided not to pursue claims
received in view of the supply situation. Minutes in the same file indicate
that the TUC did not even wish to discuss the matter, while a summary
account noted that other workers had 'to say the least been somewhat envi-
ous of the preferential treatment accorded to underground workers'.[66] Not
surprisingly, the suggestion by Strachey to provide the miners with extra
sugar, points, and fats in February 1947 was not pursued—particularly
since Shinwell doubted that these 'concessions would have the effect either
of attracting additional recruits . . . or of increasing the output of the existing labour force'.[67] Underground coal-miners retained this privilege, which
was never extended to any other group of workers, until the abolition of
meat rationing in 1954.

There was general agreement that wartime controls were necessary
during the transition period and the process of decontrol began under
Labour during the late 1940s. The conventional argument maintains that
decontrol was a continuous and inevitable process as the supply and balance
of payments situation improved.[68] This account of decontrol is misleading.
Labour and the Conservatives disagreed fundamentally about the continuation of wartime controls and the role of the state in economic
policy. Rollings, who first proposed this revisionist interpretation, maintains
that:

the Labour governments saw a continuing role for price control, as part of the continuation of some essential physical controls in the long term. In contrast, the
Conservative government after October 1951 did not and once the effects of the
Korean war and rearmament had dissipated actively carried out a policy of decontrol. In other words, the assumption that there was a natural and accepted trend
towards decontrol is false.[69]

Rollings focuses on price controls and draws attention to figures in
Dow which show that decontrol of prices did not really get under way
until after the 1951 general election.[70] Thus, Rollings concludes:

[66] PRO, MAF 99/1239, Meat for Miners, 27 Oct. 1950.
[67] PRO, CAB 128/9, CM 23 (47) 4, 18 Feb. 1947; CAB 129/17, CP (47) 61, 16 Feb. 1947.
The ineffectiveness of extra rations or supplies in mining areas is also noted in R. A.
Brady, *Crisis in Britain* (London, 1950), p. 21n.
[68] Dow, *Management of the British Economy*, pp. 164–7; Worswick, 'Direct Controls', in
Worswick and Ady, *The British Economy 1945–1950*, p. 284; Cairncross, *Years of Recovery*, pp.
335–6.
[69] Rollings, 'Control of Inflation', p. 109. See also Rollings, 'The Reichstag Method of Governing'?;
Rollings, 'Poor Mr. Butskell'.
[70] Rollings, 'Control of Inflation', p. 122; Dow, *Management of the British Economy*, pp. 165,
176.

there was a clear break in policy between the two governments and their attitudes towards price control were considerably different. The Labour governments were committed to the maintenance of some permanent economic controls, including ones over investment, prices and imports. These were seen to play a central role in the management of the economy in association with other less direct tools, such as budgetary policy and credit policy. In contrast, the Conservative government saw no role whatsoever for such permanent controls, relying solely on the more indirect tools.[1]

This difference in approach is illustrated by an examination of derationing of food, in which Labour's commitment to fair shares and reluctance to accept price rises stood in stark contrast with the Conservative policy to return to free market prices as an inevitable aspect of decontrol.

Sweets or personal points were derationed in April 1949. This was an administrative decision, urged by the trade and sanctioned by the Minister of Food and never discussed in cabinet although even changes in ration levels were usually endorsed at the highest level. The episode brings out neatly the difficulty of rationing as shortages subside. Sweets were rationed by weight and in 1948 the cheaper lines were no longer in short supply. As a result of trade pressure a partial derationing scheme was considered but rejected as impracticable since it would result in a lower ration for consumers who bought the more expensive lines, reduced turnover for retailers selling these, and difficulties in allocating unrationed supplies equitably.[2] Therefore it was decided to deration sweets, and extra sugar allocations were used to build up stocks. The policy proved to be a miscalculation, demand outstripped supply, and stocks were run down. With temporary supplies of about 6 oz. per head per week and demand at between 8 and 10 oz., sweets shortages became intense. The problem of allocation shifted to retailers, who were faced with queues resulting in empty shelves and under-the-counter sales. This high demand for sweets has to be understood against the background of extensive rationing of many other foodstuffs as well as suppressed inflation, but the obvious solution of raising the price of the more expensive lines was not considered. As Strachey put it in June:

if the present shop shortages go on indefinitely I am sure the whole country . . . will agree that by far the best thing to do is to reimpose rationing. We shall have no hesitation in doing that because our philosophy on these matters is very simple. We shall de-ration when we can meet demand at current prices, and if it is found that demand is well and persistently ahead of existing supplies at current prices I am

[1] Rollings, 'Control of Inflation', p. 123.
[2] PRO, MAF 75/63, Account of the Operation of Personal Points Rationing, 1942–1953, De-rationing of Sweets.

quite sure that everyone prefers to receive a regular ration than rely on a sort of improvised rationing by the shopkeeper which can never work properly.[73]

The possibility of reimposing rationing was considered in June, an announcement by the Chancellor of the Exchequer in July that sugar imports were to be cut proved to be decisive, and sweets rationing was reintroduced in August 1949.[74]

The zoning scheme, restricting distribution of food to economize on transport, ended in 1946 and during the late 1940s there were a range of minor relaxations. Derationing or decontrol of bread, potatoes, and preserves took place in 1948 and that of milk and soap in 1950.[75] The most interesting measure of decontrol was the termination of points rationing in 1950 which again illustrates the Labour government's ambivalence. With increased supplies the number of commodities covered by the scheme had been reduced substantially and stocks of the less popular items were accumulating in the shops, weakening the case for continued rationing. If these were removed from the scheme Webb, the Minister of Food, doubted 'that it would be practicable to maintain the present elaborate administrative apparatus in order to control the distribution of the few commodities that would then remain'.[76] He did not believe that ending the scheme which had become a 'source of irritation to housewives' would have serious consequences, the ration would amount to no more than one tin of the most popular items, and fair distribution of these could be achieved through price controls and controlled distribution to retailers. The administrative advantages had to be balanced against the risk that scarce foods would be 'shared out by "retailer's favour"'. Since this was already happening in any case Webb recommended termination of the scheme. During the discussion the majority of ministers were reluctant to take this decision because the government 'were deeply committed to a policy for the fair distribution of scarce commodities, and the abandonment of points rationing . . . might be regarded as inconsistent with that policy'. Under-the-counter allocation by retailers was not acceptable and the experience of sweets derationing was 'still fresh in the public mind'. It was assumed that the government would be blamed for inevitable shortages, and the cabinet therefore decided that it was premature to discontinue the scheme.[77] In May the Minister of Food again recommended withdrawing the scheme, which was now reduced to only a few commodities. Since points rationing was 'failing to secure equitable

[73] PRO, MAF 87/11, The Cocoa, Chocolate and Confectionery Alliance, Ltd. etc., Confectionery Trade Standing Committee, 22 June 1949, quoting from a statement made in the House of Commons, 3 June 1949.   [74] PRO, MAF 87/11, Minutes, 13 June 1949, 21 July 1949.
[75] See PRO, MAF 223/9, Changes in Administrative Controls, 1945–1951, Oct. 1951.
[76] PRO, CAB 128/17, CM 19 (50) 5, 6 Apr. 1950; CAB 129/39, CP (50) 59, 1 Apr. 1950.
[77] PRO, CAB 128/17, CM 20 (50) 1, 6 Apr. 1950.

distribution . . . its continuance was likely to bring into disrepute . . . the whole machinery of food rationing'. In discussion, the 'advantages and disadvantages of withdrawing the scheme were nicely balanced' but since it was no longer possible to ensure fair shares, the cabinet approved the termination of points rationing.[78]

The Conservative approach to decontrol was very different, although it is important to appreciate the wider economic context and particularly the balance of payments constraints which explain why rationing was not abolished sooner.[79] Indeed, in November 1951 the new government actually implemented a range of economy measures including cuts in imports of unrationed foods.[80] Food policy was set out clearly in a memorandum by the Minister of Food and the Lord President in December 1951.[81] While the cuts were accepted as an 'emergency measure', the ministers did 'not believe that the country can for long be contented and vigorous on the present and reduced import programme of food'. They were opposed to government bulk purchase and fixed prices, which reduced production, and the administrative burden of rationing. The aim of government policy should be, within the constraints of supply and finance, to achieve a 'full diet free from Government control'. Immediate steps were ending tea, sugar, and sweets rationing, raising the meat supply, and decontrolling feeding stuffs. While the ministers appreciated the 'difficulties, particularly in the short run, in the field of prices, wages, [and] subsidies . . . these views . . . [are] an indication of our approach to the problems of food supply . . . [in order] to release the people from some of the present controls and to fulfil our Election promises regarding food policy'. This policy was endorsed by the cabinet, and firm proposals were to be submitted early in 1952.[82]

The years 1952–4 witnessed the termination of all remaining rationing schemes and a host of controls of distribution, imports and the manufacture of food.[83] Simultaneously price controls, which accounted for about half of total expenditure on food in 1951, were reduced rapidly. In 1954 only a fifth of food expenditure was still price controlled, a figure which had fallen to less than 10 per cent by 1958.[84] Thus the critical difference between Labour and the Conservatives was the latters' acceptance of the need to return to market prices as an inevitable concomitant of decontrol

[78] PRO, CAB 128/17, CM 32 (50) 4, 18 May 1950; CAB 129/40, CP (50) 111, 15 May 1950.
[79] For decontrol under the Conservatives, see J. Ramsden, *The Age of Churchill and Eden, 1940–1957* (London, 1995), pp. 249–50; A. Seldon, *Churchill's Indian Summer: The Conservative Government, 1951–55* (London, 1981), pp. 207–13.
[80] PRO, CAB 128/23, CC 2 (51) 3, 1 Nov. 1951.
[81] PRO, CAB 129/48, C (51) 60, 24 Dec. 1951.
[82] PRO, CAB 128/23, CC 20 (51) 7, 28 Dec. 1951.
[83] See PRO, MAF 223/10, Changes in Administrative Control since November 1951, 14 June 1954.
[84] Dow, *Management of the British Economy*, p. 174, table.

despite concern about the potentially negative public response to rising prices.[85] In 1952 allocation of eggs was no longer satisfactory because eggs were:

escaping from control in quantities which make it impossible to secure equitable distribution of the whole supply. This unsatisfactory state of affairs can only be brought to an end and the consumer given access to all the eggs available by creating a market in eggs. . . . Some increase in price is inevitable if consumers are to be given better access to supplies.[86]

The cabinet decided to eliminate the subsidy of eggs, ended allocation and price control early in 1953, and authorized the Minister of Food to announce the policy in the House of Commons.[87] Similarly, 'Any shortage of sweets that still remains $7\frac{1}{2}$ years after the war is not enough to warrant our retaining a cumbrous and extravagant system for such a commodity'.[88] While the 'abortive attempt at derationing in 1949 was coupled with retention of price control', the simultaneous ending of price controls in the context of somewhat more plentiful supplies was an 'essential part' of derationing and 'should help to balance supply and demand'.[89] Accordingly, the cabinet decided to abolish rationing and price controls of sweets early in 1953.

Decontrol accelerated in 1953 stimulated by the reduction of food subsidies from £410 m. in 1951 to £250 m. in the 1952 budget and £220 m. in 1953.[90] Regardless of concern by the Minister of Labour about the cost of living, food prices were allowed to rise during 1953 as food subsidies were 'becoming less of a means of keeping down the price of food in the interest of consumers than a means of ensuring an adequate return to British farmers'.[91] During 1953 and 1954 negotiations with the National Union of Farmers, representing domestic producers, and the food trade about future marketing arrangements paved the way for derationing, lifting of price controls, and an end to state trading of those foods which were still rationed.[92] In 1954 only butter supplies still fell short of demand at current

[85] On the latter point see, e.g., PRO, CAB 128/25, CC 57 (52) 3, 29 May 1952; PREM 11/661, Minute PM to Minister of Food, 10 May 1954, Minute Minister of Food to PM, 11 May 1954.
[86] PRO, CAB 129/56, C (52) 389, Draft Statement by the Minister of Food in Memorandum by the Chancellor of the Exchequer: Marketing of Eggs, 4 Nov. 1952.
[87] PRO, CAB 128/25, CC 95 (52) 3, 11 Nov. 1952.
[88] PRO, CAB 129/57, C (52) 423, Memorandum by the Minister of Food: Decontrol of Sweets, 25 Nov. 1952.   [89] PRO, CAB 128/25, CC 101 (52) 8, 3 Dec. 1952.
[90] Rollings, 'Control of Inflation', pp. 128–9, 134–5, emphasizes differences in approach to food subsidies between the Labour and Conservative governments. See also, Rollings, 'British Budgetary Policy 1945–1954', pp. 283–98.
[91] PRO, CAB 128/26, CC 57 (53) 7, 13 Oct. 1953; see also CC 46 (53) 3, 28 July 1953; see also MAF 156/15, ES (53) 39, Cabinet: Economic Steering Committee, Note by the Minister of Food: Further Decontrol of Foodstuffs, 23 Sept. 1953.
[92] PRO, CAB 128/26, CC 59 (53) 6, 19 Oct. 1953; CC 60 (53) 8, 22 Oct. 1953; CC 61 (53) 4,

prices but 'we cannot maintain the necessarily elaborate rationing machinery for this one commodity' and the Minister of Food hoped that competition from high-quality margarine would prevent excessive price rises.[93] During the autumn of 1953 and the spring of 1954, sugar, bacon, and ham, as well as cheese, fats, and meat were finally derationed. Having terminated rationing and ended bulk purchasing, the Conservative policy of decontrol culminated in the abolition of the Ministry of Food, whose remaining functions were taken over by agriculture in a merged Ministry of Agriculture, Fisheries and Food in October 1954.[94]

1.2. FOOD RATION LEVELS AND DIETARY TRENDS, 1930S–1960S

During the period of control, there were three categories of foodstuffs. The first was rationed food, namely meat, bacon and ham, fats, cheese, and sugar and sugar products. This category accounted for about one-third of calories and the majority of animal protein, fats, and sugar.[95] Second, items such as milk and eggs were distributed under so-called quasi-rationing schemes which involved no definite entitlement and allowed additional purchases depending on supplies. Owing to limited quantities as well as seasonal and regional variations in supplies, perishable fresh foods such as fish, fruit, and vegetables were never rationed and only loosely controlled, despite continued public calls for a more equitable distribution of these foodstuffs.[96] Without rationing price controls were largely ineffective and these goods frequently disappeared under the counter. Finally, a so-called buffer of subsidized bread, potatoes, and restaurant or canteen meals was freely available and intended to prevent hunger by satisfying differential energy requirements. To economize on wheat the extraction rate of flour was raised, providing for a more nutritious national loaf. Even under bread rationing between 1946 and 1948 wheat consumption was not reduced significantly. In 1942 rationed and controlled foods accounted for more than half of total food expenditure. Straight rationed foods increased from

27 Oct. 1953; CC 62 (53) 7, 29 Oct. 1953; CC 36 (54) 6, 26 May 1954; see also Cmd. 8989, *Decontrol of Food and Marketing of Agricultural Produce* (London, Nov. 1953); Cmd. 9519, *Future Arrangements for the Marketing of Sugar* (London, July 1955).

[93] PRO, CAB 129/67, C (54) 143, 12 Apr. 1954.

[94] Seldon, *Churchill's Indian Summer*, pp. 212–13.

[95] PRO, MAF 83/3564, Teleprint, 30 Jan. 1943.

[96] Allocation of fresh fruit and vegetables did not involve registration with retailers. Rather, retailers simply marked ration books except for oranges, for which coupons were cancelled. Oranges, bananas from 1946, as well as other exotic fruit were distributed periodically when available and reserved for priority groups, although surplus oranges could be sold to any customer. Onions and other fresh vegetables were allocated according to similar principles but distributed evenly instead of being restricted to priority groups.

25 per cent in 1940 to about a third of total expenditure from 1942 onwards when points foods stood at 11–12 per cent and controlled distribution accounted for a further 15 per cent of expenditure on food.[97] Food rationing became more extensive after the war with the introduction of bread rationing in 1946 and the potato control scheme in November 1947. In 1947–8 about half of consumer expenditure on food was rationed; this proportion fell to a third in 1949 and in 1953 rationed food accounted for only a fifth of total expenditure.[98]

Figure 1.2 plots the changes in food ration levels throughout the period. The size of each ration obviously depended on supplies and the start of rationing did not necessarily imply a drastic reduction in consumption. Once the principle of rationing was established, a reduction in the size of the ration was more easily acceptable, especially during a period of national crisis. According to Hammond, 'Sugar, indeed, was the single staple food (if one counts butter and margarine as interchangeable) for which the ration represented a really severe cut in supplies. Rationing for other foods was largely necessary to restrict demand from rising as a result of war prosperity, and as an adjunct to price control.'[99] The figure shows that rations of fats, meat, and other sources of animal protein were lower and more volatile after 1945 than during the war. By contrast, the availability of sugar and sugar products was relatively well maintained but also highly erratic.

With falling supplies as a result of the reduction in imports to half the pre-war level, nutritional aspects of food policy received increased attention. The middle years of the war witnessed the emergence of a comprehensive nutrition policy which included fortification of margarine and flour with vitamins, the vitamin welfare scheme, and an expansion of communal feeding. Controlled distribution or quasi-rationing schemes for milk and eggs were launched in 1941. The main purpose was to raise the intake of animal protein, calcium, and vitamins among vulnerable groups such as expectant and nursing mothers, children, and adolescents, as well as invalids. In view of large seasonal and local variations in supply and the highly perishable nature of these foodstuffs controlled distribution schemes ensured supplies to the priority classes and no definite quantity was guaranteed to ordinary consumers.[100] As a result of the policy the priority

[97] Ministry of Food, *How Britain was Fed in Wartime*, p. 42. The following paragraphs draw on this source and PRO, MAF 223/31, Rationing in the UK, 1950.

[98] Dow, *Management of the British Economy*, p. 148.

[99] Hammond, *Food and Agriculture*, p. 230.

[100] PRO, MAF 223/31, Rationing in the UK, 1950; MAF 223/96, ABC of Rationing, 1951–1954, provide information on the quantities consumed. Non-priority consumers received between 2 and 4 pints of milk per week depending on seasonal availability while priority consumers received up to 7 pints of subsidized milk per week in addition to their ordinary entitlement. All restrictions on milk were lifted in January 1950. Shell egg allocations stood at about 30 per person per year during the war and gradually rose to about 100 by 1950 and all restrictions were lifted in

classes, accounting for about 30 per cent of consumers, received nearly half of the total milk supply. The vitamin welfare scheme was introduced in December 1941 to compensate for any possible shortfall in vitamin intake. Expectant and nursing mothers and children under 5 were entitled to free fruit juices and cod-liver oil or vitamin tablets.[101]

Communal feeding was expanded in order to provide for differential energy requirements as more and more foods were available only on flat-rate rations. The needs of industrial workers were catered for by a dramatic increase in canteens from 1,500 before the war to 18,486 in 1944 and workers, such as agricultural workers, for whom canteens were not practicable received a supplementary cheese ration. School meals increased from about 160,000 before the war to 1.6 million in 1945, when 40 per cent of children received a heavily subsidized school meal providing up to 1,000 calories a day.[102] The requirements of ordinary consumers were catered for by the development of British Restaurants. These began during the blitz and served more than 600,000 subsidized meals daily in over 2,000 restaurants by 1943. In April 1947 there were still 850 British Restaurants but government withdrawal of financial responsibility for communal feeding resulted in the gradual termination of the scheme. In total about 10 per cent of rationed food was consumed in catering establishments of all kinds and commercial restaurants and canteens accounted for about a third of these supplies. It is important not to exaggerate the impact of communal feeding since the overwhelming majority of food was eaten at home. The national food survey shows that on average only between 2.5 and 3 out of 27 meals per person per week were consumed outside the home.[103]

The British diet changed substantially in the century following the repeal of the Corn Laws in 1846.[104] In the early nineteenth century Britain was virtually self-sufficient, imports were discouraged by high duties, and the

March 1953. In addition, dried egg, available from 1942 onwards, became a staple of the diet until the late 1940s. Priority consumers received twice the amount of ordinary consumers.

[101] This issue is discussed in detail in Chapter 3, section 3.2.

[102] J. Burnett, 'The Rise and Decline of School Meals in Britain, 1860–1990', in J. Burnett and D. J. Oddy (eds.), *The Origins and Development of Food Policies in Europe* (London, 1994), p. 65.

[103] PRO, MAF 156/396–7. The detailed figures for the years 1943–7 show little difference between the social classes. Out of a total of 26.8 meals per week, the middle class consumed about 24 at home, 0.44 in canteens including schools and British Restaurants (0.04 in the latter), and 0.76 in commercial establishments. The figures for working-class consumers are 24.5 at home, 0.5 in canteens including schools and British Restaurants (0.04 in the latter), and 0.2 in commercial establishments.

[104] For a history of the British diet see J. Burnett, *Plenty and Want: A Social History of Diet in England from 1815 to the Present Day,* 2nd edn. (London, 1979); J. C. Drummond and A. Wilbraham, *The Englishman's Food: A History of Five Centuries of English Diet,* (London, 1957); rev. edn. D. J. Oddy and D. S. Miller (eds.), *Diet and Health in Modern Britain* (London, 1985); C. Geissler and D. J. Oddy (eds.), *Food, Diet and Economic Change Past and Present* (Leicester, 1993); D. J. Oddy, 'Food, Drink and Nutrition', in F. M. L. Thompson (ed.), *The Cambridge Social History of Britain 1750–1950* (Cambridge, 1990), vol. 2.

FIG. 1.2. *Weekly food rations in the United Kingdom, 1940–1954*

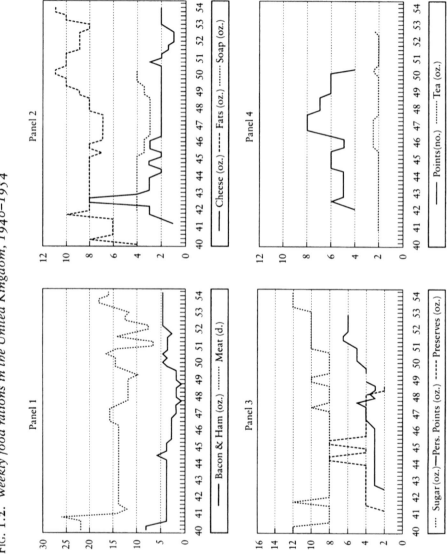

Notes: The data are presented on a quarterly basis. Rations frequently varied within quarters, in which case the prevailing level is cited in the graphs.

Bacon and ham were rationed in Jan. 1940, cooked gammon and ham were derationed in October 1952, and bacon was derationed in July 1954.

The meat ration includes beef, corned beef, veal, mutton, and pork. Meat was rationed by price rather than weight in order to maintain the customary choice between quantity and quality. Here the ration is calculated in pence (*d.*) (12*d.* = 1s.), thus the meat ration for much of the war was 1s. 2*d.* Meat was first rationed in March 1940 and from the end of this year until 1950 frequently 2–4*d.* worth of this ration had to be purchased as canned corned meat. Meat prices were raised in the second quarter of 1949 (PRO, CAB 128/15, CM (49) 34), the third quarter of 1950 (*Hansard*, 5th ser., vol. 490, c.214–15), and the third quarter of 1952 (*Hansard*, 5th ser., vol. 503, c.1304). The ration is presented at constant prices in the graph. Children under 5 were entitled to half a ration only; pregnant women received an additional half a meat ration from 1943; special rations for Christmas were issued from 1944, and underground coal-miners received a special meat ration from 1946. In May 1953 limited sales off the ration were permitted, and meat was derationed in July 1954.

Cheese was rationed in May 1941. In addition to the ordinary ration a special cheese ration of approx. 12 oz. per week was issued to a large number of workers, such as agricultural workers, for whom canteen facilities were impracticable. During 1953 there was some relaxation, limited sales off the ration were permitted, and cheese was derationed in May 1954.

Fats includes butter (rationed in Jan. 1940), margarine (rationed in July 1940), and cooking fats (rationed in Nov. 1941). The maximum quantity of butter was 2–4 oz. per week and the cooking fats ration stood at 2 oz. for most of the period. Extra rations for Christmas were issued from 1944 onwards, some off the ration sales were permitted in Jan. 1954, and fats were derationed in May 1954.

Soap was rationed in Feb. 1942 and the scheme was administered by the Ministry of Food since soap and margarine were based on the same raw materials. Shaving soap, scourers, shampoo powders, dental soap, and certain detergents were ration free. Many manual workers, infants, invalids, and expectant mothers received additional soap rations. Soap was derationed in Sept. 1950.

Sugar was rationed in Jan. 1940 and additional issues were granted during the Christmas period and from 1944 onwards during the summer months to encourage preserving. Between 1943 and 1945 the sugar ration could be exchanged for preserves. Sugar was derationed in September 1953.

Personal points, namely chocolates and sweets, were rationed in July 1942. The personal points ration was detachable from ration books and frequently used by individuals rather than purchased jointly for the entire household. After 1944 additional rations were issued to children under 18 and people over 70 years during the Christmas period. Sweets were derationed in April 1949. This policy proved to be a failure since demand far exceeded supply, rationing was reintroduced in Aug. 1949, and abolished in Feb. 1953.

Preserves were rationed in March 1941 and could be exchanged for sugar in order to encourage preserving from 1942 onwards. Categories of preserves included in the scheme varied since, after an initial influx, many were transferred to the points scheme after 1944. The majority of preserves were derationed in Aug. 1948 and rationing ended in Dec. 1948.

Tea was rationed in July 1940. From July 1942 children under 5 received no tea ration and people over 70 were granted an additional allowance from Dec. 1944 onwards. Tea was derationed in Oct. 1952.

Points rationing was introduced in Dec. 1941. The scheme covered processed foods such as canned fish, meat, beans, and fruit; biscuits; rice, oats, and other cereal products; cheese and condensed milk; dried fruit and pulses; and certain preserves. The scheme differed from so-called straight rationing since a number of food categories were included and consumers could choose freely between individual items. The number of points required for each item was adjusted frequently to equate supply and demand. The high number of points available between 1946 and 1949 was largely a consequence of the increased number of items included in the scheme; namely approximately 70 until the second quarter of 1945, 92 during the third quarter of 1946, 101 during the second quarter of 1947, a peak of 116 during the second quarter of 1948, and 75 during the second quarter of 1949. The scheme ended in May 1950.

Sources: PRO, MAF 223/31, Rationing in the United Kingdom, 1950; MAF 223/96, ABC of Rationing, 1951–4.

diet was dominated by bread grains. With rising living standards after 1850, the emergence of free trade and the development of long-distance transport the diet became increasingly plentiful. The consumption of wheat, sugar, meat, fats and dairy products as well as fruit rose rapidly and by the 1930s only a fraction of these foodstuffs were home produced. During the years 1934–8 imported food accounted for over two-thirds of calories and half of total protein consumed.[105] Food imports were halved from an average of 22 million tons before the war to between 10.6 and 11.5 million tons between 1942 and 1944. A combination of increased home production, conservation, regulation of distribution, and transformation of dietary patterns prevented starvation in these circumstances.

Tables 1.1 and 1.2 show that the wartime diet was characterized by an increase in the consumption of bread (which changed from white to brown), milk, and potatoes. Simultaneously, there was a reduction of butter and fats, sugar, meat, bacon, fish, and fruit, as well as fresh eggs. There was also a decline in quality since, for example, dried egg was not as palatable as fresh

TABLE 1.1. *Food supplies available per capita in the United Kingdom from 1934–1938 to 1960 (in pounds or pints)*

Date	Butter	Fish	Flour	Fresh fruit	Milk	Marg.	Meat[a]	Potatoes	Sugar	Tea
1934–8	24.7	25.3	194.5	78.5	N/A	8.7	129.3	181.9	102.9	9.3
1940	14.0	16.3	208.6	N/A	N/A	15.4	116.3	166.4	71.8	8.6
1941	10.2	14.7	237.1	N/A	N/A	17.5	99.3	188.2	67.4	8.1
1942	7.7	15.9	226.6	N/A	N/A	17.4	101.5	224.9	69.2	8.2
1943	7.6	17.3	230.2	28.7	231.8	17.0	98.5	248.8	69.3	7.0
1944	7.7	19.3	233.5	32.3	239.1	17.8	110.0	274.6	74.0	7.4
1945	8.5	23.6	240.7	35.9	243.8	17.1	100.4	260.2	70.8	8.2
1946	11.0	29.8	221.2	51.7	242.8	15.1	105.6	281.2	79.5	8.8
1947	11.2	31.3	224.9	68.0	237.6	15.0	95.6	285.9	83.8	8.5
1948	12.6	30.5	232.9	71.0	250.1	17.9	87.0	238.9	85.1	8.0
1949	13.9	26.7	222.2	64.0	263.9	18.4	88.0	258.3	93.1	8.3
1950	16.9	21.1	205.8	60.3	269.7	17.0	112.2	246.4	85.5	8.5
1951	14.6	23.3	203.6	68.3	268.0	18.7	89.8	234.7	95.0	8.1
1952	10.9	21.9	201.7	65.6	263.0	19.3	105.7	251.8	90.4	8.5
1953	13.2	19.7	192.7	68.5	255.8	17.8	116.1	245.3	98.7	9.5
1954	14.1	20.1	187.2	66.0	254.8	18.3	129.8	242.3	106.1	9.7
1955	14.7	20.6	182.5	66.5	251.8	17.9	136.7	234.2	108.8	9.3
1956	15.5	21.7	178.7	65.7	251.1	17.1	139.1	224.5	109.8	10.1
1958	20.0	22.0	171.5	64.0	247.6	13.7	143.3	212.0	115.5	9.9
1960	18.3	18.7	165.9	73.8	249.1	14.7	144.7	223.7	112.0	9.3

[a] Poultry meat is not included until 1952.
Source: B. R. Mitchell, *British Historical Statistics* (Cambridge, 1988), p. 713.

[105] Ministry of Food, *How Britain was Fed in Wartime*, p. 7.

TABLE 1.2. *Index of food supplies available per capita in the United Kingdom, from 1934–1938 to 1960*

Date	Butter	Fish	Flour	Fresh fruit	Milk[a]	Marg.	Meat[b]	Potatoes	Sugar	Tea
1934–8	100	100	100	100	100	100	100	100	100	100
1940	57	64	107	N/A	N/A	177	90	91	70	92
1941	41	58	122	N/A	N/A	201	77	103	65	87
1942	31	63	116	N/A	N/A	200	78	124	67	88
1943	31	68	118	36	127	195	76	137	67	75
1944	31	76	120	41	131	204	85	151	72	79
1945	34	93	124	46	134	196	78	143	69	88
1946	44	118	114	66	133	173	82	154	77	94
1947	45	124	116	87	130	172	74	157	81	91
1948	51	120	120	90	137	206	67	131	83	86
1949	56	105	114	81	145	211	68	142	90	89
1950	68	83	106	77	148	195	87	135	83	91
1951	59	92	105	87	147	215	69	129	92	87
1952	44	86	104	83	144	222	82	138	88	91
1953	53	78	99	87	140	204	90	135	96	102
1954	57	79	96	84	140	210	100	133	103	104
1955	59	81	94	85	138	206	106	129	106	100
1956	63	86	92	84	138	196	107	123	107	109
1958	81	87	88	81	136	157	111	116	112	106
1960	74	74	85	94	137	170	112	123	109	100

[a] 1934–8 data based on League of Nations consumption figure for 1930–1 (3.5 pints per head per week), Sir William Crawford and H. Broadley, *The People's Food* (London, 1938), p. 208.
[b] Poultry meat is not included until 1952.
Source: B. R. Mitchell, *British Historical Statistics* (Cambridge, 1988), p. 713.

egg, and the quality as well as the variety of biscuits, chocolates, and other manufactured foods was generally poorer. Without Lend-Lease supplies, which accounted for about a sixth of animal protein and 20 per cent of fats in 1943–4, the situation would have been even worse. This virtual peasant diet was nutritionally adequate and healthy but also dull and monotonous. The ministry's own account of wartime food policy admitted that there was a 'shortage of nearly all the more appetising and popular staple foods' and that people were 'compelled to satisfy their physical needs by filling up with larger quantities of the bulky and less attractive vegetable and cereal food-stuffs still obtainable'.[106]

The ending of Lend-Lease, the post-war world food shortage, and Britain's balance of payments problems resulted in reduced consumption of all foods, with the exception of fish, sugar, potatoes, and fruit in the urban working-class diet between 1946 and 1948.[107] Meat, bacon, cheese, and fats

[106] Ibid., p. 1.
[107] Ministry of Food, *The Urban Working-Class Household Diet 1940 to 1949* (London, 1951), pp. 58–9.

rations were low and, for instance, egg consumption fell to only 70 per cent of 1945 levels in 1947. With the exception of cheese and meat the diet had recovered to—or even exceeded—1945 levels by 1949. Following the termination of rationing in 1954 demand for rationed and controlled foods was high and intake increased for every item, with the sole exception of margarine.[108] Consumption of tea, sugar, cheese, and meat rose during the late 1950s and early 1960s and the increase in butter consumption was particularly steep as people moved away from margarine. Among controlled items only fish, consumption of which had been exceptionally high during the late 1940s, registered a decline, milk remained stable, and egg consumption rose sharply. Simultaneously, potato consumption fell by about 15 per cent and that of bread by nearly a third between 1954 and 1965. The most striking example of a change in consumption after the lifting of controls was the dramatic switch away from brown bread. After the abolition of National Wheatmeal Bread in 1956, consumption of brown bread dropped close to zero in a matter of months and the white loaf again became the principal bread eaten in Britain.[109]

Milward's analysis of wartime dietary trends in an international context cautions against comparing ration levels since rationing systems varied greatly between individual countries.[110] For instance, in Germany most foods were rationed under a differential system catering for the diverse requirements of specific classes of consumers whereas the British system was only partial and most rations were flat rate. Also in many countries rations were little more than targets whereas British rations were always honoured. Generally speaking, the British diet was more plentiful compared with much of the rest of the world and particularly occupied Europe during the war and Germany and Austria during the early post-war years. By contrast, British sacrifice in food consumption was well in excess of that of her allies and in 1943 British potato consumption was nearly 50 per cent higher than before the war and consumption of grain products had increased by 17 per cent. In the USA and Canada increased potato consumption remained in single figures and there was little change with regard to grain products. At the other extreme, whereas meat consumption declined by a fifth in Britain it actually increased in North America.[111] As a result of established trading relations, Britain retained a privileged position among food-

[108] D. H. Buss, 'The British Diet since the End of Food Rationing', in Geissler and Oddy, *Food, Diet and Economic Change*, pp. 121–32; see also Ministry of Agriculture, Fisheries and Food, *Annual Report of the National Food Survey Committee: Household Food Consumption and Expenditure 1990 with a Study of Trends over the Period 1940–1990* (London, 1991), app. c, table 2, pp. 94–8.   [109] Ibid., p. 35; Buss, 'British Diet', p. 125.
[110] Milward, *War, Economy and Society*, pp. 282, 287–8; Burnett, *Plenty and Want*, pp. 324–5.
[111] Ministry of Food, *Food Consumption Levels in the United States, Canada and the United Kingdom* (London, 1944), p. 12.

importing countries. This was especially important during the world food shortage of the early post-war years when Britain was the only food-importing country not to experience a significant reduction in consumption levels; in contrast, consumption in countries such as France and Belgium stood at 75–80 per cent of the pre-war level and that of Germany and Austria at 50–60 per cent.[112]

In order to appreciate the significance of wartime food policy in the history of the British diet it is necessary to go beyond averages and examine social class or income differences in food consumption. Burnett and Oddy emphasize the inequality in food consumed as well as nutrient intake which is a central and continuous theme in the history of the British diet until the late 1930s. These differentials disappeared with the introduction of rationing and food controls during the Second World War. Since the end of rationing the diet of rich and poor has remained fairly similar in terms of both quantity and nutrient intake and family size became increasingly important in determining expenditure on food per head.[113] During the 1930s there was an intense debate about the national diet within the context of concern about poverty and unemployment. Social investigators acknowledged that conditions had improved since the Edwardian period but a close link between diet and income persisted and rising affluence coincided with widespread poverty.[114] Boyd Orr noted that food expenditure per head ranged from 4s. to 14s. per week and the top groups consumed more of everything with the exception of margarine and condensed milk. He estimated that the diet of about half the population was deficient in some nutrients and that a third fell short of most requirements including calories, a finding confirmed by Crawford and Broadley's later study.[115]

Nelson's recent analysis of longer-term trends in differential food consumption from 1900 until 1980 illustrates this transformation. Drawing on data for the top and bottom 20 per cent in terms of income, his figures show that the large income differentials in the consumption of meat, fish, eggs, milk, fats, and sugar characteristic of the earlier period effectively disappeared after 1940.[116] Tables 1.3 and 1.4, which are based on the same

[112] Cmd. 6785, *The World Food Shortage* (London, 1946), p. 5; Cmd. 6879, *Second Review of the World Food Shortage* (London, 1946), p. 13.

[113] D. Hollingsworth, 'Rationing and Economic Constraints on Food Consumption in Britain since the Second World War', in Oddy and Miller, *Diet and Health in Modern Britain*, pp. 268–70. According to PRO, MAF 156/541, National Food Survey, Some Notes on Nutrition Policy in the United Kingdom, 1939–1955, August 1955, the diet was now 'satisfactory for nearly all groups of the population except those groups of households in which there were large numbers of children'.

[114] For a good summary of the debate see H. Perkin, *The Rise of Professional Society: England since 1880* (London, 1989), pp. 273–85.

[115] J. Boyd Orr, *Food, Health and Income* (London, 1936); W. Crawford and H. Broadley, *The People's Food* (London, 1938).

[116] M. Nelson, 'Social class trends in British diet, 1860–1980', in Geissler and Oddy, *Food, Diet and Economic Change*, pp. 106–9.

TABLE 1.3. *Weekly per capita food consumption in the United Kingdom by social class/income group from 1932–1935 to 1959*

Panel 1. Middle-class food consumption

Date	Butter (oz.)	Fats (total) (oz.)	Sugar, preserves (oz.)	Bever. (oz.)	Milk (total) (pt.)	Eggs (shell) (no.)	Eggs (dried) (no.)	Meat (rat.) (oz.)	Meat (other) (oz.)	Fish (oz.)	Potatoes (oz.)	Veg. (oz.)	Fruit (oz.)	Bread (oz.)	Flour, cereals (oz.)
1932–5	9.2	14.7	24.9	N/A	5.0	4.9	N/A	N/A	N/A	6.6	41.7	N/A	N/A	N/A	N/A
1936–7	10.5	15.0	24.8	3.9	4.6	5.6	N/A	(44.1)		9.7	65.3	N/A	N/A	49.4	N/A
1944	2.2	9.8	17.5	3.2	4.9	1.2	2.6	19.5	9.9	7.3	58.6	42.1	22.3	48.8	30.1
1945	2.4	9.5	17.5	3.2	5.1	1.7	2.5	18.5	8.4	10.5	57.3	42.9	27.1	47.9	31.3
1946	2.1	8.9	17.6	3.3	5.0	1.7	1.4	18.7	8.2	11.7	60.0	39.8	25.3	46.0	32.1
1947	2.3	8.6	18.0	3.3	5.1	1.9	1.1	17.5	8.3	12.4	55.5	36.4	36.0	45.9	30.4
1950	4.8	11.9	N/A	N/A	5.6	3.9	N/A	14.5	N/A	N/A	58.4	N/A	N/A	46.0	N/A
1951	N/A	11.9	18.6	N/A	5.7	3.9	N/A	12.4	13.1	7.4	59.1	32.1	34.9	46.0	31.0
1956	5.6	11.9	21.9	3.6	5.7	5.1	N/A	(37.6)		6.7	47.6	33.1	38.7	43.0	25.1
1959	6.9	12.5	22.2	3.6	5.9	5.2	N/A	(39.0)		6.2	47.1	33.6	43.3	40.4	25.1

TABLE 1.3 (continued)

Panel 2. Working-class food consumption

Date	Butter (oz.)	Fats (total) (oz.)	Sugar, preserves (oz.)	Bever. (oz.)	Milk (total) (pt.)	Eggs (shell) (no.)	Eggs (dried) (no.)	Meat (rat.) (oz.)	Meat (other) (oz.)	Fish (oz.)	Potatoes (oz.)	Veg. (oz.)	Fruit (oz.)	Bread (oz.)	Flour, cereals (oz.)
1932–5	6.6	13.3	22.8	N/A	2.7	3.5	N/A	N/A	N/A	3.7	54.1	N/A	N/A	N/A	N/A
1936–7	6.7	11.8	21.5	4.1	2.8	3.6	N/A	(33.8)		5.8	61.6	N/A	N/A	56.4	N/A
1944	2.1	9.3	15.2	2.7	4.4	0.9	2.0	18.8	9.6	6.5	71.4	37.3	13.9	59.9	23.4
1945	2.2	8.7	14.6	2.7	4.4	1.3	1.7	18.0	8.3	8.2	68.5	36.4	15.9	61.8	23.7
1946	2.8	8.3	15.0	2.9	4.4	1.4	1.1	18.2	8.5	9.6	73.8	34.6	15.7	59.9	22.6
1947	2.9	7.8	15.7	2.8	4.4	1.6	0.7	17.3	8.2	8.8	70.9	30.8	21.7	62.5	21.4
1950	4.5	11.6	N/A	N/A	4.6	3.3	N/A	13.7	N/A	N/A	65.3	30.8	N/A	57.3	N/A
1951	N/A	11.6	16.7	N/A	4.7	3.3	N/A	11.8	12.1	5.7	66.7	27.8	21.1	56.9	26.8
1956	4.4	11.7	21.5	3.7	4.9	4.2	N/A	(34.9)		5.8	60.9	30.6	24.5	53.1	24.2
1959	5.4	11.9	21.8	3.5	4.9	4.4	N/A	(34.2)		5.9	57.5	30.7	27.6	49.2	23.9

Notes: Bever. refers to tea, cocoa, and coffee, but in 1936–7 to tea and cocoa only. Milk includes cream, condensed and dried (equivalent pints) of milk. Dried eggs refers to the equivalent number. Rationed meat includes corned beef, fresh beef, veal, mutton, pork, ham (uncooked), and bacon. Unrationed meat includes offal, rabbit, poultry, game, sausages, and canned, cooked, and processed meat. Figures in brackets refer to all meat consumption prior to the introduction and after the abolition of rationing. Fish excludes canned fish until 1951, subsequently all fish is included. Potatoes excludes chips in 1932–5, subsequently chips are included, and crisps from 1950. Veg. refers to all vegetables except potatoes. Fruit includes fresh, canned, dried, and bottled fruit. Flour and cereals includes rolls, buns, cakes, etc., and all cereals and cereal products with the exception of bread until 1956 when rolls, muffins, and crumpets are included under bread consumption trends.

Samples vary and the 1932–5 data are based on 1,152 family budgets drawn during spring and early summer primarily in the north of England and Wales. The 1936–7 data are derived from a more extensive and representative survey of nearly 5,000 households between October 1936 and March 1937. The figures for 1944–7 are based on representative urban middle- and working-class samples covering the entire year except for 1947 (Jan.–Sept. only). Subsequently the figures derive from the fully representative National Food Survey (in 1951 Jan.–Feb. and Apr.–May only).

The two social classes are defined in terms of gross income of the chief earner in the household with the exception of 1932–5 (income per head per week). It was aimed to include approximately the top 20–25% of earners in the middle-class data but this was not always possible. In 1932–5 the middle-class figures were calculated on the basis of income groups V–VI (30% of the population), with the remainder included in the working-class data. In 1936–7 the middle class includes income groups A and B (24% of the population) and the working class, C and D (75% of the population). Between 1944 and 1947 two separate urban middle- and working-class samples were drawn by the National Food Survey. In 1950–1 the middle-class data are based on income groups A and B (16% and 31% of the population respectively) and the working-class data on income groups C and D (84% and 69% of the population respectively). Due to high inflation the B category expanded and became socially increasingly diverse and in 1956–9 the middle-class figures are based on the A group only (13% and 12% of the population respectively), with the remainder included in the working-class table. In 1951 working-class data excluded old age pensioner households and in 1956–9 D figures only were included.

The table refers to food purchased and consumed in the home only. It excludes all alcoholic beverages as well as sweets and sugar confectionery, i.e. personal points from 1942–53, which were not seen as part of the household budget. Tables analysing meals according to the place where eaten for both classes during 1943–7 suggest that there was relatively little difference between the classes. The average number of meals per person per week was 26.85 and 26.74 for middle and working class respectively. Of these the middle class consumed 24.01 at home, 0.44 in canteens, including schools and British Restaurants, and 0.76 in commercial establishments. The working-class figures are: 24.56 meals at home, 0.55 in canteens, etc., and 0.21 in commercial establishments (PRO, MAF 156/396–7).

Sources: 1932–5: J. Boyd Orr, *Food, Health and Income* (London, 1936), p. 65, table I (app. IV). 1936–7: W. Crawford and H. Broadley, *The People's Food* (London, 1938), various tables. 1944–7: Ministry of Food, *The Urban Working Class Household Diet 1940 to 1949* (London, 1951), pp. 109–10, app. B; Ministry of Agriculture, Fisheries and Food, *Studies in Urban Household Diets 1944–49* (London, 1956), p. 16, table 5; pp. 110–12, app. A, table I. 1950–9: Ministry of Food/Ministry of Agriculture, Fisheries and Food, *Domestic Food Consumption and Expenditure 1950, 1951, 1956 and 1959: Annual Report of the National Food Survey Committee* (London, 1952, 1953, 1958, and 1959), p. 37, table 26; p. 35, table 25; pp. 31–2, table 19; and pp. 35–6, table 20.

TABLE 1.4. *Middle-class food consumption as a percentage of working-class food consumption in the United Kingdom from 1932–1935 to 1959*

Date	Butter (oz.)	Fats (total) (oz.)	Sugar, preserves (oz.)	Bever. (oz.)	Milk (total) (pt.)	Eggs (shell) (no.)	Eggs (dried) (no.)	Meat (rat.) (oz.)	Meat (other) (oz.)	Fish (oz.)	Potatoes (oz.)	Veg. (oz.)	Fruit (oz.)	Bread (oz.)	Flour, cereals (oz.)
1932–5	139	110	109	N/A	185	140	N/A	N/A	N/A	178	77	N/A	N/A	N/A	N/A
1936–7	157	127	115	95	164	155	N/A	(130)		167	106	N/A	N/A	87	N/A
1944	105	105	115	118	111	134	131	104	103	112	82	113	160	81	129
1945	109	109	120	118	116	131	146	103	101	128	84	118	170	77	132
1946	75	107	117	114	114	126	131	103	96	122	81	115	161	77	142
1947	79	110	115	118	116	121	166	101	101	141	78	118	166	73	142
1950	107	102	N/A	N/A	112	118	N/A	106	N/A	N/A	89	N/A	N/A	80	N/A
1951	N/A	102	111	N/A	121	118	N/A	109	108	130	89	115	165	81	116
1956	127	102	102	97	116	121	N/A	(108)		115	78	108	158	81	104
1959	128	105	102	103	120	118	N/A	(114)		105	82	109	157	82	105

Notes and Sources: See Table 1.3.

sources but include the entire population, reveal the same trend. Although the middle class continued to consume more eggs and fruit while the working class ate greater quantities of potatoes and bread, income differentials in consumption of butter, milk, and meat declined substantially. With regard to nutrients, the large gap in calorie consumption disappeared, as indicated in Table 1.5 as well as Nelson's work.[117] For the first time ever income differences in protein and fat consumption were effectively eroded and the gap in vitamin and mineral intake also disappeared. Hence, rationing and food control 'revolutionised the social class distribution of the diet by redressing the imbalances which had been highlighted just prior to the war. Throughout the war and after, the income-group differences in diet were never as great as they had been before it.'[118]

The Second World War represented a major turning-point in the history of the British diet. The rise in consumption of brown bread, milk, and vegetables coupled with food fortification resulted in a healthier diet and no social group fell short of basic nutritional requirements. Middle-class food consumption standards undoubtedly deteriorated while the poorer sections of the working class were the main beneficiaries of the policy. Although food consumption after the end of rationing was by no means uniform differences were small compared with those of the pre-war years. Not only did wartime food policy narrow income differentials in consumption, but rations were deliberately targeted at large families and special allowances were provided for vulnerable groups such as pregnant women and children. The principle of flat-rate rations

was not only unequal in its incidence but designedly so . . . [because] it was felt that to give children the prescribed quantities of food was to weight rationing slightly in favour of the larger families on whom the cost of living would bear more hardly, and that the persons without children had generally more to spend on alternative and dearer foods.[119]

These dietary changes coincided with improvements in public health which is determined by the combined effects of nutrition and environmental factors.[120] Despite the strains and stresses of war, vital statistics and other sources show that the 'general health of the civilian was good throughout the period of war . . . [and the] fitness of babies and school children was particularly striking'.[121] This trend, which continued after the war, was the result of a 'powerful combination of influences—full employment, food

---

[117] Geissler and Oddy, *Food, Diet and Economic Change*, pp. 111–15.   [118] Ibid., p. 116.

[119] PRO, MAF 99/918, Memo, 16 Dec. 1940.

[120] D. J. Oddy, 'The Health of the People', in T. Barker and M. Drake (eds.), *Population and Society in Britain 1850–1980* (London, 1982); H. Jones, *Health and Society in Twentieth-Century Britain* (London, 1994), p. 99.

[121] Ministry of Food, *How Britain was Fed in Wartime*, p. 49. Maternal and infant mortality rates as well as anthropometric evidence are discussed in Chapter 3, section 3.2.

TABLE 1.5. *Calorie and protein intake in the United Kingdom by social class/income group, from 1932–1935 to 1959*

Date	Calories			Protein		
	Middle class	Working class	%	Middle class	Working class	%
1932–5	3,275	2,859	114	96	80	120
1936–7	3,159	2,557	123	89	70	127
1944	2,403	2,387	101	74	73	101
1945	2,402	2,375	101	77	76	101
1946	2,336	2,307	101	78	78	100
1947	2,307	2,308	100	77	77	100
1950	2,506	2,468	101	79	77	102
1951	2,510	2,463	102	78	76	103
1956	2,597	2,615	99	76	75	101
1959	2,636	2,564	103	77	73	105

Notes: The table shows the daily per capita consumption of calories (in kcals) and protein (in grams). The percentage columns show the percentage of middle-class to working-class intake; a figure above 100 indicates a higher middle-class intake.

See Table 1.3 for explanatory notes and sources.

subsidies, "fair shares", price control and the welfare food schemes'.[122] Jones accepts that public health improved, but her account is less celebratory than the official history since class or income inequalities in living standards and health persisted regardless of the introduction of the NHS after 1945.[123] Despite these limitations, food controls and especially the targeting of vulnerable groups contributed materially towards advances in public health. Nevertheless, a healthy diet is not necessarily popular and the complexity of attitudes to food policy is discussed in the next chapter.

1.3. CONSUMER GOODS RATIONING AND CONTROLS, 1939–1955

The reduction in supplies of and controls over miscellaneous consumer goods was administered by the Board of Trade. Clothing and footwear were rationed from 1941 onwards, but rationing proved impracticable with regard to goods such as furniture or hollowware, and distribution of the more necessary items was governed by priority schemes. During the Second World War the Board of Trade effectively became a production department administering increasingly tight controls over many goods, and production

[122] R. M. Titmuss, *Problems of Social Policy* (London, 1950), p. 533; see p. 524 for table on adult mortality trends and pp. 517–38 for a discussion of the implications of wartime social policy for public health. See also mortality data in Jones, *Health and Society*, pp. 196–7.

[123] Jones, *Health and Society*, pp. 112, 126; and table 5, p. 198.

of non-essential items such as jewellery was prohibited altogether. In contrast with the Ministry of Food, the Board of Trade never actually owned these products. Rather, controls were exercised by means of price regulation, limitation of supplies orders, and concentration of production, as well as licences and consumer rationing. This policy, which was intended to divert resources to the war effort and to prevent inflation, was accompanied by increasingly extensive and refined measures such as the utility schemes and austerity regulations. These involved the Board of Trade in production planning by specifying the allocation of raw materials and the design of output in many industries. There was no precedent for this interference in *Civil Industry and Trade* in the First World War and in 1939 the board 'was limited both in knowledge and preparations'.[124] This apparatus of controls was partially dismantled under the Labour government, and clothes rationing ended in 1949, but raw materials allocation, price controls, and the utility policy were abolished only under the Conservatives during the early 1950s.

The Board of Trade had three priorities on the outbreak of war. First, balance of payments requirements led to an export drive which ended following the Lend-Lease agreement of 1941. Second, raw materials, labour, and factory space were diverted from producing civilian consumer goods to the war effort, and, finally, prices had to be controlled in order to prevent inflation. The impact of war on the civilian economy was only gradual and the general standard of living was maintained during the first nine months but this situation changed quickly after the fall of France. Limitation of Supplies Orders, introduced in 1940, restricted the permitted sales of textiles and miscellaneous household goods to a fraction of the pre-war level. By spring 1941, supplies of textiles had been reduced to 20 and 40 per cent of the pre-war level for cotton and rayon respectively, while those of miscellaneous consumer goods had been cut by between one-third and three-quarters.[125] As a result of these restrictions, shortages of the more necessary commodities became severe since the cuts had been very much across the board.[126] Price control was first introduced with the Prices of Goods Act of 1939, which attempted to restrict price increases to those justified by increased costs and established central and local price regulation committees. This act was not working successfully and it soon became clear that effective price control required powers to fix maximum prices and margins; this called for control of production and supply. In the wake of the stabilization policy of April 1941, these powers were granted under the Goods and Services (Price Control) Act of July 1941, which enabled the

[124] Hargreaves and Gowing, *Civil Industry and Trade*, p. 14.
[125] Ibid., pp. 98, 102, 105–6, 108–9.
[126] Hancock and Gowing, *British War Economy*, pp. 322–4.

Board of Trade to fix maximum prices and to set maximum profit margins at all stages of manufacture and distribution.[127]

Clothes rationing is discussed below. With regard to miscellaneous goods there were further economies in 1942. The limitations of supplies orders were no longer suitable since they did not distinguish sufficiently between essential and non-essential goods. As the war dragged on, the Board of Trade had to strike a careful balance between economy and the impact of severe shortages of essential items on morale and efficiency. From 1941 onwards production of hollowware—pans, kettles, buckets, etc.—was permitted under licences which were only granted for essential items made to approved specifications. In 1942 this policy was extended to a wide range of consumer goods. Manufacture of pottery and pencils was controlled and many items such as floor coverings, domestic electric appliances, lighters, and umbrellas could be produced under licence only, with output frequently being standardized. Furniture production became subject to the utility policy and the manufacture of 'a long list of fripperies ranging through jewellery, metal toys, ornamental glassware, fancy goods and a miscellany of household gadgets' was prohibited.[128] There were inevitable problems of distribution but a general household ration was rejected as impracticable due to infrequent demand and because the total retail value of these goods amounted to less than half of the sweets ration. Over and above the actual cut in supplies, shortages were also due to uneven distribution. This was a consequence of the general practice of datum allocation of supplies, particularly when based on pre-war demand or population figures (some datum allocations were based on wartime data and, therefore, more accurate). However, the war not only resulted in exceptional mobility, but also led to changes in demand as a consequence of full employment. Many consumer goods continued to be distributed according to pre-war patterns resulting in great imbalances, for instance, in stock levels of prosperous and formerly depressed towns. The problem was addressed by the establishment of a Consumer Needs Branch which served as a 'most useful two-way channel of information between the Board and its distributing and consuming public' and helped to alleviate the worst shortages.[129] The central policy to counter the inequities of datum allocation was the priority dockets scheme. This scheme, which applied to furniture, mattresses, blankets and sheets, floor coverings and curtain materials, differed from rationing since only certain categories of people qualified for priority dockets. These were couples setting up home for the first time, families who needed furnishings for growing or additional children, and people who lost all or part of their

---

[127] Ibid., pp. 335–6; for details on price controls see Hargreaves and Gowing, *Civil Industry and Trade*, chs. 21 and 22, *passim*.   [128] Hancock and Gowing, *British War Economy*, p. 496.
[129] Hargreaves and Gowing, *Civil Industry and Trade*, p. 302; see pp. 298–302 for details.

possessions as a consequence of air attacks. The bulk of total supplies of priority goods (with the exception of furniture) was available for sale to the general public without restrictions and it was assumed that 'every housewife should gradually be able to make necessary replacements'.[130] For many household goods the priority scheme was impracticable and potential buyers had to compete with each other since 'the scramble of housewives . . . would probably produce as good a fit between real needs and actual purchases' as any scheme administered by the Board of Trade.[131]

Clothes rationing 'was not intended to restrict the quantity of clothing available for the public—that had already been done. The sole object of the scheme was to provide fair distribution of available supplies.'[132] There was no precedent for rationing consumer goods, and during the first year of war it was hoped that it could be avoided. The possibility of rationing was first discussed in autumn 1940 against a background of the inflationary danger of falling supplies coinciding with rising incomes. In January 1941 it was decided that rationing would be confined to clothing and footwear and based on quantity rather than price. Clothes were to be rationed under a points rationing scheme with coupons providing the basis of stock replacement along the chain of distribution. The next stage was to decide on the items to be included in the scheme, the size of the ration, and fixing of the points schedule. The scheme was to cover all clothing and footwear with certain exceptions such as headgear or workmen's overalls. Initially, household linen, furnishing fabrics, and blackout material were not rationed although household linen and furnishing fabrics were later brought within the scheme. Since few statistics were available setting the initial ration levels was difficult, and the ration was fixed at roughly two-thirds of pre-war consumption. This ration was then translated into points on a yardage basis, depending on the amount of material used, and with different points values for cotton and wool cloth. The scheme had to be fairly flexible since hosiery and footwear were also rationed and it was not possible to equate demand and supply. Large stocks proved to be invaluable in honouring the ration initially and subsequently supplies were more closely matched to available coupons by reducing the ration and changing the points value of individual items in line with stock levels.

Clothes rationing was discussed by the war cabinet in May 1941. Churchill in particular was doubtful about the scheme which was felt to be 'unnecessary, unpopular and unworkable'. These objections were overcome since only rationing would ensure fair distribution and prevent price rises in

---

[130] PRO, BT 64/1453, Memo, Priority Dockets for Household Furnishings, n.d. (approx. 1943).

[131] Hargreaves and Gowing, *Civil Industry and Trade*, p. 333. For housewives' shopping difficulties with regard to miscellaneous household goods, see Chapter 3, section 3.1.

[132] Hargreaves and Gowing, *Civil Industry and Trade*, pp. 312–13.

the context of growing shortages. Alternatively 'at least 200,000 additional tons of cotton and wool a year and at last 350,000 workers would have to be provided for civilian clothing'.[133] The decision to go ahead was announced on Whit Sunday, 1 June 1941. The policy had been kept secret in order to prevent panic buying and for this reason the unused margarine page in the food ration book provided the first instalment of 26 clothing coupons. Subsequently, a separate clothing ration book was issued and later clothing coupons were distributed in conjunction with food ration books.

In line with food rationing policy, the clothes ration was based on a flat-rate individual ration. However, special provision was made for children and manual workers. Children's clothes were pointed at a lower level than the equivalent adult clothes since they required less material and from 1942 onwards children received a supplement of 10 coupons. Industrial workers were the other major group with a claim to additional coupons since many trades required special clothes and manual work frequently caused exceptional wear and tear. The Board of Trade, lacking experience in this matter, over-hastily awarded 60 additional clothing coupons to underground coal-miners—not necessarily the heaviest users of clothing—causing great resentment and resulting in large claims by other groups of workers. In the second year of rationing these problems were avoided by issuing a general supplement of 10 coupons to all manual workers while a so-called iron ration administered by individual factories or works committees provided for certain heavy industries. This system was accepted as fair and easy to administer and proved to be extremely economical in coupon use. The clothes ration was reduced from 66 coupons a year, roughly two-thirds of pre-war consumption, to 60 coupons in 1942 and 48 coupons in 1943.[134] In the first year of peace the ration was cut further and briefly stood at a rate of 36 and then 42 coupons per annum. The ration was raised to 60 in September 1946, cut in two steps to 54 and 48 coupons after the fuel crisis. It remained at this level until August 1948. An additional 12 coupons became valid during the summer and from September 1948 the ration stood at 48 coupons again, although this was in fact more generous because it coincided with partial derationing of clothing and especially footwear.

In order to ensure that the ration could be honoured the clothing industries had to be controlled and detailed statistics were gathered on stocks and consumption in order to match coupons and supplies. Since the ration was

---

[133] Ibid.
[134] For changes in ration levels, see ibid., pp. 309–15; *Board of Trade Journal*, vol. 150 (1944), pp. 20, 275; vol. 151 (1945), p. 394; vol. 152 (1946), pp. 192, 781, 980; vol. 153 (1947), pp. 327, 559, 1618; vol. 154 (1948), pp. 227, 485; vol. 155 (1948), pp. 211, 2534; vol. 156 (1949), pp. 240, 570.

based on the yardage of cloth used, it was sufficient to control the large-scale and locally concentrated textile industries.

This method had the merit of avoiding the necessity for close official control or inspection of the clothing trade [which consisted of up to 25,000 firms]. Since makers-up had to pass back to cloth manufacturers as many coupons as corresponded to cloth supplied them, and as they could only obtain these coupons from the public, via retailers, they had no choice but to observe the scheme and pass on to the public as much cloth as they received.[135]

There were inevitable problems such as ensuring adequate supplies of large sizes or providing cloth for the manufacture of unrationed items such as mattresses. The difficulty was addressed by issuing extra coupons to the manufacturers concerned. A consumer panel for clothing, instituted in 1941, provided information on purchases by the public. Subsequently,

a comprehensive service of information [was] . . . gradually built up. On the supply side the Board now receive frequent statements of the total production . . . together with monthly records of sales, purchases and stocks of the principal type of cloth, clothing and footwear by a representative sample of whole-salers, and finally an index of retailers' sales and stocks of [these] . . . and a further index of the extent to which retailers are in or out of stock.[136]

This information provided a fairly accurate estimate of clothing available on which ration levels could be based.

A logical development of price controls and rationing was the need to specify production. The utility clothing scheme, launched in 1941, was the Board of Trade's central policy to ensure that adequate supplies of good quality clothing were produced particularly since rationing had resulted in trading up.[137] Utility cloth and clothes were distinguished by a distinctive utility mark, strictly price controlled, and produced according to detailed specifications, since price control could only be fully effective in the case of clearly defined goods. Moreover, utility goods were exempt from purchase tax, rated at $33\frac{1}{3}$ per cent for most consumer goods.[138] Utility cloth economized on labour and raw materials by encouraging long production runs and ultimately about 80 per cent of output was produced under the scheme. Utility was never intended to be cheap and aimed at a high standard. In order to give utility clothing the best possible start, the Board of Trade chose

---

[135] *Board of Trade Journal*, vol. 155, 21 Aug. 1948, 'How the Clothes Rationing Scheme is Operated', p. 354.   [136] Ibid.

[137] The following paragraph is based on Hargreaves and Gowing, *Civil Industry and Trade*, pp. 430–6; H. E. Wadsworth, 'Utility Cloth and Clothing Scheme', *Manchester Statistical Society* (1948), pp. 1–34; Worswick, 'Direct Controls', pp. 301–3; C. Sladen, *The Conscription of Fashion: Utility Cloth, Clothing and Footwear 1941–1952* (Aldershot, 1995).

[138] M. Hall, 'The Consumer Sector', in Worswick and Ady, *The British Economy in the Nineteen-Fifties*, p. 437, table 5.

top London fashion designers to create the first prototypes of utility clothes. While the cloth was produced according to strict specification, the clothes were not standardized and there was considerable scope for variation in colour and finish. Over and above the utility scheme, austerity regulations, which came into force in 1942, applied to all ready-made clothes to ensure simple, economical styles by banning trimmings such as embroidery and restricting pleats, buttons, and pockets along with the width of sleeves and collars.[139] During the war, utility schemes were introduced for footwear, hosiery and knitwear, bedding, and household textiles, as well as pottery, with further extensions to goods such as linen cloths and blankets after the war. All schemes laid down precise manufacturing specifications, production was usually restricted to a narrow range of austerity lines, and the control of furniture was the most comprehensive. Due to the need for strict economy of timber, specifications fixed not only minimum standards of construction but also design of furniture, with production limited to 22 essential items. Utility furniture, in particular, was part of the egalitarian ideology of 'war Socialism' and there was a paternalistic desire to guide the 'public towards making better aesthetic choices' in the direction of 'wholesome simplicity'.[140]

Labour initiated the process of decontrol of miscellaneous consumer goods, symbolized by the so-called bonfire of controls in 1948. Nevertheless, there were important differences in policy between Labour and the Conservatives and raw materials allocation, price controls, and the utility policy were abolished only after 1951. The austerity regulations on clothing ended in 1946, the priority scheme was abolished in 1948, and floor covering and household textiles were decontrolled in 1949.[141] Early in 1948, Wilson, the President of the Board of Trade, appointed a committee to make recommendations for the simplification and removal of controls; this led to the November bonfire of controls. Controls affecting some 60 commodities were relaxed and for some 25 categories including perambulators, toys, cutlery, and linoleum controls were ended altogether. However, many of the 200,000 licences abolished were of minor significance, the bonfire dealt with only a 'relatively small part of the control mechanism', and fewer than 40 civil service jobs disappeared as a result.[142] Although there were further relaxations, the Labour government did not intend to replace controls with budgetary management and leading cabinet ministers

---

[139] Hargreaves and Gowing, *Civil Industry and Trade*, pp. 436–7.

[140] H. Dover, *Home Front Furniture: British Utility Design 1941–1951* (Aldershot, 1991), pp. 3, 17, 20.

[141] Hargreaves and Gowing, *Civil Industry and Trade*, p. 439; *Board of Trade Journal*, vol. 154 (1948), p. 1204; vol. 155 (1948), p. 1026; vol. 156 (1949), pp. 42, 570.

[142] Worswick, 'Direct Controls', p. 285; Tomlinson, *Democratic Socialism*, pp. 230–1.

were united in their continued commitment to economic controls.[143] As Wilson stated in 1948, 'Apart from those basic controls which are essential for our economic recovery, for industrial efficiency or for full employment, it is our policy to maintain all those controls—and only those controls— which are essential to secure a proper distribution of materials which are still scarce'.[144]

These wider considerations are illustrated by Wilson's justification of the continuation of clothes rationing in the face of a campaign for derationing by clothes manufacturers, backed by the right-wing press, in 1948.[145] The policy was governed by three principles, first, the requirements of the export drive; second, shortages of supply and manpower; and finally, the desire to retain equitable distribution and avoid price rises. The government wanted to end clothes rationing 'as soon as circumstances permit' but was 'not prepared to take risks . . . with the fair distribution of essential clothing to the mass of people'. '[As] demand and supply come . . . into equilibrium for particular types of goods, we should deal with this not by a general increase in the ration but, wherever this can be done without affecting our export effort or increasing our import requirements, by taking goods off the ration or downpointing them.'[146] The policy of partial derationing began in September 1948 but clothes rationing was not abolished until May 1949.[147]

The difference in approach between Labour and the Conservatives is indicated by looking at raw materials and import and price controls, as well as the utility scheme. Dow sums up the situation, saying that, during the war:

almost all materials had been allocated. By the beginning of 1951, the coverage had been reduced to well under half . . . Reimposition of controls during the 'Korean' period increased their coverage to almost two thirds in 1952. But by 1954 these and most other controls had been removed: it was only coal allocations which kept the figure as high as a quarter until as late as 1958. In general, the degree of control over the allocation of materials followed very closely the degree of control over imports of materials.[148]

In view of the bonfire of controls it appears paradoxical that price controls were tightened in 1948 with the March price freeze.[149] There was no relaxation until 1949 and 1950 when hardware, ironmongery, and non-utility clothing were freed from price controls, but during the period of inflation that accompanied the Korean war there was a partial reintroduction and

[143] Tomlinson, *Democratic Socialism*, pp. 232–4.
[144] Quoted in Worswick, 'Direct Controls', p. 285.
[145] D. Smith, *Harold Wilson: A Critical Biography* (London, 1964), pp. 81–3.
[146] Statement made in the House of Commons, quoted in *Board of Trade Journal*, vol. 155, 7 Aug. 1948, p. 253.   [147] *Board of Trade Journal*, vol. 156, 5 Feb. 1949, p. 240; 19 Mar. 1949, p. 570.
[148] Dow, *Management of the British Economy*, p. 160.
[149] Worswick, 'Direct Controls', pp. 288–9.

price controls were finally dismantled in 1952 and 1953. With the termination of the utility scheme price controls over furniture and clothing ended in 1952 and the remaining price controls expired in 1953 with the repeal of the wartime legislation.[150] The Conservative government opposed the unfair tax advantage of the utility scheme, which was abolished in 1952 and replaced by a graduated tax system covering all consumer goods.[151]

The Second World War precipitated a dramatic reduction in supplies of consumer goods which is illustrated vividly by an examination of consumer expenditure trends during the twentieth century. Consumers' expenditure (at constant prices) increased about 3.5 times between 1900 and 1984.[152] This upward trend was interrupted significantly only by the world wars and particularly the Second World War and its immediate aftermath. Pre-war consumer expenditure was reached again in 1950 and during the 1950s there was a rapid expansion as the consumer boom got under way (see Figure 1.1). The reduction in consumption as well as changes in consumption patterns are summed up in Table 1.6. Total spending fell by about one-eighth during the war and there were significant changes in distribution with increased expenditure on travel, entertainment, and smoking and large reductions in spending on clothing, furniture, and miscellaneous household goods, as well as private motoring. These figures are of course crude and fail

TABLE 1.6. *Index of consumer spending on selected goods in the United Kingdom, 1938–1950 (1938 = 100)*

Category	1938	1940	1942	1944	1946	1948	1950
Food	100	87	85	87	94	102	109
Drink	100	96	93	96	95	92	92
Tobacco	100	100	116	115	131	112	109
Rent	100	102	101	102	104	108	112
Fuel and light	100	102	100	97	112	118	126
Furniture and hardware	100	70	29	25	61	79	98
Other household goods	100	95	76	73	83	92	111
Clothing	100	83	61	61	73	91	101
Private motoring	100	29	13	6	56	42	64
Total	100	90	85	86	98	101	106

Notes: From 1940 onwards there was full employment compared with about 10% unemployment in 1938. In addition to the changes in total consumption there were also changes in distribution between different income groups.
Sources: E. L. Hargreaves and M. M. Gowing, *Civil Industry and Trade* (London, 1952), p. 648, table 10; G. D.

[150] Dow, *Management of the British Economy*, pp. 164–6.
[151] Worswick, 'Direct Controls', pp. 302–6; *Board of Trade Journal*, vol. 162 (1952), pp. 594–5.
[152] A. Dilnot, 'The Economic Environment', in A. H. Halsey (ed.), *British Social Trends since 1900*, rev. edn. (London, 1988), p. 142.

TABLE 1.7. *Index of personal expenditure on certain classes of consumer goods, 1938–1943 (at 1938 prices, 1938 = 100)*

Date	Clothing	Footwear	Furniture and furnishings[a]	Hardware[b]	Private cars, bicycles etc.	Fuel and light	Other[c]
1938	100	100	100	100	100	100	100
1939	99	104	94	91	82	99	100
1940	82	93	69	74	24	93	81
1941	59	79	47	52	16	97	67
1942	58	77	32	35	10	98	54
1943	55	73	23	33	11	93	52

[a] Furniture, furnishings, household textiles, floor coverings, musical instruments (including wireless sets, gramophones, and accessories).
[b] Pottery and glassware, ironmongers' goods, electrical goods, heating and cooking appliances, and perambulators.
[c] Excluding food, drink, and tobacco but including chemists' wares, stationery, books and newspapers, fancy goods, jewellery, etc., travel goods, toys and sports goods, petrol and oil, soap, polishes, candles, and matches.
Source: Cmd. 6564, *Statistics Relating to the War Effort of the United Kingdom* (London, 1944), p. 27.

to 'take full account of changes in quality and . . . make no allowance for restrictions in consumers' choice'.[153] The official history sums up the wartime experience: 'in the six years of war, [civilians] had received less than four years' normal supply of clothing and less than three years' supply of household goods—to take at random two examples out of many. Private stocks of all civilian goods were low and clamoured for replenishment.'[154] Not surprisingly, demand was high, bolstered by large personal savings, but consumption during the early post-war years continued to be restricted in order to facilitate the export drive as well as investment in capital equipment. Although total consumption reached 1938 levels in 1948 and by 1950 was in excess of pre-war standards, it is important to appreciate that people were not able to spend their money as they wanted due to rationing and other shortages. Moreover, quality had frequently deteriorated and, according to Seers, 'the improvement since 1938 is somewhat overstated'.[155]

The striking reductions in expenditure on clothing and household goods during the war are illustrated in Table 1.7. By 1943, expenditure on furniture and hardware stood at just under one-quarter and one-third of the pre-war level respectively. Consumption of clothing, footwear, and miscellaneous goods held up somewhat better but private motoring effectively disappeared after 1941. The severity of civilian sacrifice is further demonstrated by comparing the British experience with that of her allies (see Table 1.8). Whereas total purchases in Britain *fell* by 16 per cent between 1938 and 1944—with much more severe reductions in the sub-

[153] Hancock and Gowing, *British War Economy*, p. 499.   [154] Ibid., p. 553.
[155] D. Seers, 'National Income, Production and Consumption', in Worswick and Ady, *The British Economy 1945–1950*, p. 49.

TABLE 1.8. *All consumer goods and services: percentage changes in per capita purchases by groups in the United Kingdom, USA, and Canada, 1938–1944*

Category	Per cent change, 1938–1944		
	UK	USA	Canada
Food[a]	−11	+8	+13
Alcohol and tobacco	+8	+33	+24
Clothing and footwear	−34	+23	+22
Housing[b]	+9	+14	[c]
Fuel and power	+2	+32	+28
Household goods (electrical and metal)[d]	−82[c]	−23	−13
Household goods (other)[d]	−51	+26	+15
Other personal effects	−37	+43	[c]
Reading matter[d]	+1	+24	+22
Amusements[d]	+10	+10	+53
Motor vehicles and their operation	−95	−52	−52
Public transport	+13	+87	+95
Postal etc. services	+8	+33	[c]
Miscellaneous services	−33	+19	+11
Total consumption	−16	+16	+16

Notes: Purchases are valued as far as possible at pre-war prices. Many of the figures relating to USA data are provisional only. Apart from alcohol and tobacco, the data are based on the civilian population.
[a] Including non-alcoholic beverages. The changes shown represent changes in the value of food consumption rather than of purchases.
[b] Rent, rates (in the UK), and water charges.
[c] These items are included in miscellaneous services as are some household goods, some amusements, and the value of room and board furnished to commercial employees. The percentage change is to 1943.
[d] The change is to 1943.
[e] The pre-war year is 1935.
Source: Treasury, *The Impact of the War on Civilian Consumption in the United Kingdom, the United States and Canada* (London, 1945), p. 26.

groups mentioned above—in the USA and Canada purchases actually *increased* by 16 per cent during the corresponding period. The civilian population in North America also suffered from reductions in expenditure on motoring and electrical household goods but these were more than compensated by considerable increases in spending on clothing, other household goods, and a range of services.

Table 1.9 shows that supplies of consumer goods to the home market rose rapidly after the war but in 1948, the last year for which these figures are available, supplies still fell well short of the pre-war level. According to Table 1.6, pre-war consumption levels were reached or even surpassed for all goods with the exception of private motoring in 1950. However, in view of the increase of the civilian population by 6 per cent during this period, 'the clothing and furniture bought in 1950 were still below

TABLE 1.9. *Index of new supplies for the home civilian market,*
1935–1949 (1945 = 100)

Date	Footwear	Clothing	Furniture and furnishings[a]	Hardware[b]
1935[c]	(175)	(200)	(350)	(200)
1945	100	100	100	100
1946	130	131	206	193
1947	151	143	231	184
1948	166	147	235	150
1949[d]	179	153	274	

[a] Includes household textiles, bedding, furniture, floor coverings, radio sets, and batteries.
[b] Includes electrical goods, lamp batteries, crockery, cutlery, glassware, hollowware, hearth furniture, and household brushes.
[c] Note that 1935 figures are only roughly comparable.
[d] Data for Jan. and Feb. only; with regard to clothing, furniture, and furnishings only provisional data are available.
Sources: Board of Trade Journal, vol. 151, 27 Oct. 1945, Special issue, 'Wartime Supplies of Consumer Goods to the Home Market', p. ii; *Board of Trade Journal,* vol. 156, 7 May 1949, p. 951.

1938, when measured as an average per head of population'.[156] The rapid growth of GDP during the period was not translated into significant increases in real consumption per head, and taking the mild redistribution of income after tax, relative price changes, and the subsidy policy into account, Seers concluded that 'the average wage could buy more in 1950 than in 1938' whereas salary-earners were 'on average considerably worse off'.[157]

The 1950s finally witnessed the emergence of a 'consumer economy', characterized by 'very substantial change' for consumers, including the end of shortages, rising real incomes, rapid growth in demand for durable goods, and the expansion of hire purchase facilities.[158] Especially:

after 1953 the face of the economy began to change rapidly and a new emphasis, hitherto characteristic of the American economy was seen: an emphasis on increased living standards for the mass of people and energetic attempts by industry to stimulate and channel consumer demand by advertising an ever-increasing range of mass-produced articles.[159]

These developments are summed up in Tables 1.10 and 1.11. Consumer expenditure increased rapidly from 1953 onwards and total expenditure was 27 per cent higher in 1960 than it had been a decade earlier. The rise was particularly steep for durable goods, sales of which rose rapidly after 1953 and consumption more than doubled during the ten-year period. New

[156] Worswick and Ady, *The British Economy 1945–1950,* p. 49.   [157] Ibid., pp. 59, 61.
[158] Hall, 'The Consumer Sector', p. 428.
[159] Ibid., p. 430.

TABLE 1.10. *Index of consumers' expenditure on selected goods,
1950–1960 (1950 = 100)*

Date	Total	Food	Drink and tobacco	Clothing and footwear	Durable goods[a]
1950	100	100	100	100	100
1951	98	98	103	90	99
1952	98	96	103	89	96
1953	102	101	105	91	122
1954	107	104	106	98	149
1955	111	107	110	105	164
1956	112	109	112	109	144
1957	114	111	114	112	159
1958	117	113	116	112	183
1959	122	115	119	117	217
1960	127	117	126	125	229

[a] Includes furniture, motor cars, television sets, and miscellaneous electrical appliances.
Source: M. Hall, 'The Consumer Sector', in G. D. N. Worswick and P. H. Ady (eds.), *The British Economy in the Nineteen-Fifties* (Oxford, 1962), p. 431.

TABLE 1.11. *Sales of selected consumer durable goods, 1938–1960*

Date	New car registrations[a] (nos.)	Motor cycles (nos.)	Domestic refrigerators (£'000)	Television sets (nos.)
1938	22,863	3,770	N/A	N/A
1948	9,312	6,178	215	N/A
1949	12,758	7,463	384	17,400
1950	11,117	11,085	445	42,400
1951	11,443	11,447	455	57,600
1952	15,702	11,322	231	65,300
1953	24,650	11,784	343	95,400
1954	32,273	14,060	515	104,200
1955	41,855	15,994	666	140,500
1956	33,411	12,327	538	119,400
1957	35,539	17,733	779	151,300
1958	46,371	15,939	1,370	168,300
1959	53,901	29,148	2,477	229,500
1960	67,218	22,821	2,550	151,400

[a] Excluding motor buses, trucks, etc. The data provide monthly averages of sales.
Source: M. Hall, 'The Consumer Sector', in G. D. N. Worswick and P. H. Ady (eds.), *The British Economy in the Nineteen-Fifties* (Oxford, 1962), p. 432.

car registrations indicate the revival of private motoring, with sales sur-
passing the pre-war level in 1953 and then roughly trebling in the next seven
years. Motor cycles became more popular than ever and sales of labour-
saving or recreational domestic durables such as refrigerators and television

sets rose very quickly during the decade. In sum, 'the mass diffusion of household appliances which began in America in the 1920s took off in Britain only in the 1950s'.[160]

The dramatic reduction in consumption of food, clothing, and miscellaneous household goods during the 1940s was a central component of the war effort and post-war reconstruction. In order to prevent inflation as well as to economize on foreign exchange, labour, and raw materials, an extensive system of controls was introduced and consumer rationing became the principal means by which to ensure fair shares and restrict demand in the context of full employment. The end of the war did not mark any relaxation and, indeed, food rationing during the late 1940s was more extensive and many ration levels were lower and more volatile than in wartime. Total pre-war consumption levels were reached again by the end of the decade, but for many foodstuffs and domestic consumer goods these were not achieved until the mid-1950s.

Food rationing policy, based on individual flat-rate rations and the consumer-retailer tie, closely followed the model introduced during the First World War but there was no precedent with regard to rationing and control of miscellaneous consumer goods. Rationing policy during the Second World War differed from that imposed during the First World War since food rationing was introduced at the outset, continued much longer, and was more extensive. Growing shortages resulted in the emergence of an alternative approach to rationing—namely the coupon-replacement scheme—which was applied to processed foods and sweets as well as clothing and footwear. Although rationing policy was generally based on the principle of flat-rate rations for all, special allowances were made for certain groups, namely manual workers and, above all, children and pregnant women who were the main beneficiaries of the welfare foods scheme. The combination of rationing, food subsidies, and full employment resulted in a narrowing of income differentials in food consumption and public health not only was maintained but actually improved, illustrated by the rapid reduction in mortality rates, particularly among infants. The Ministry of Food and Board of Trade were not only responsible for implementing a reduction in consumption but also charged with adjudicating between expendable luxuries and necessities which were indispensable in order to maintain morale in a prolonged war. The development of an acceptable minimum standard was a complex process which had to take account of established customs and values as well as questions of physical survival. For

---

[160] S. Bowden and A. Offer, 'Household Appliances and the Use of Time: the United States and Britain since the 1920s', *Economic History Review* 47 (1994), p. 730; see also J. Obelkevich, 'Consumption', in J. Obelkevich and P. Catterall (eds.), *Understanding Postwar British Society* (London, 1994), pp. 141–54.

example, food policy was not just based on nutritional needs, the diet had to retain sufficient amounts of familiar foodstuffs to permit the preparation of customary dishes, and propaganda aimed to popularize economical recipes and new foods.

The austerity policy altered the relationship between the state and the economy in the sense that the free market in consumer goods was replaced by extensive controls and regulation of imports, production, distribution, and exchange. As a result, the price mechanism lost its centrality and the great disparity in consumption standards between different social groups of the 1930s gave way to the political imperative of fair shares. This policy was introduced in the context of total war and equality of sacrifice was central to wartime propaganda. After 1945 the policy formed part of the Labour government's wider commitment to greater social equality. The continuation of rationing and austerity after the immediate transition period was not inevitable and there were significant differences in approach between Labour and the Conservatives. These raised fundamental questions about the role of the state in economic management which became a focus of party political debate. The equity of flat-rate rations, albeit tempered by special allowances for certain groups, was questionable since the policy took insufficient account of diverse needs, differential access to unrationed goods, and unequal distribution within the household. The aspiration of fair shares has to be qualified in view of the black market, which indicates the boundaries of popular consent in the regulation of consumption. These issues, and particularly the ambiguity of equality of sacrifice, are explored in the following chapters.

Popular Attitudes

The reduction of consumption was the most important consequence of the war for the civilian population alongside air raids, evacuation and disruption of family life. In contrast with air raids or evacuation, rationing and shortages affected everybody, and the end of the war did not put an end to austerity, which persisted until the early 1950s. Drawing on a range of contemporary surveys, this chapter shows that attitudes to rationing and austerity varied depending on the policy as well as between social groups. The austerity policy was generally accepted as a necessary sacrifice for the war effort and fair shares were popular, although the public was not always convinced that a particular scheme was fair. At times there was widespread discontent, especially with regard to certain aspects of food policy, but generally morale was maintained during the war. The continuation and, indeed, intensification of austerity after the war, in the face of expectations of improved consumption engendered by victory, depressed morale and contributed to growing disaffection with the Attlee government while the Conservative critique of austerity was instrumental to the party's recovery after 1945.

In order to facilitate the transfer of economic resources to the war effort, the cabinet determined in January 1940 that 'the needs of the home market must rank lowest in time of war' and concluded that it was 'essential to bring home to the public ... the magnitude of the effort required'.[1] Consequently, home front propaganda stressed the need for 'effort, suffering [and] sacrifice' which should be 'accepted willingly and proudly'.[2] Throughout the war, the public acquiesced in this policy. According to a Gallup poll conducted in February 1940, 51 per cent agreed that every person should buy as few goods as possible,[3] Home Intelligence noted that 'cuts in rations are apparently accepted philosophically as inevitable', and a later report observed a 'complete and expressed unwillingness to make voluntary

[1] PRO, CAB 65/5, WM (40) 21, 23 Jan. 1940.
[2] PRO, CAB 67/3, WP (G) (39) 162, 22 Dec. 1939; CAB 67/4, WP (G) (40) 20, 26 Jan. 1940.
[3] G. H. Gallup (ed.), The Gallup International Public Opinion Polls: Great Britain, 1937–1975, vol. I, 1937–1964 (New York, 1976) (hereafter Gallup Polls), p. 31; 34% disagreed and 15% registered no opinion.

sacrifices, but an apparent readiness to face compulsory sacrifices without undue grumbling'.[4] The end of the war did not result in a diminution of shortages and many rations were lower and more volatile than during the war. While the Labour government prided itself on the maintenance of fair shares after the war, it did not pay sufficient attention to the question of how far the public were prepared to tolerate this perpetuation of sacrifice after its erstwhile justification—winning the war—had been achieved. The issue was high on the political agenda and despite an unprecedented propaganda effort in peacetime,[5] the continuation of austerity contributed to the erosion in public support for the Attlee government.

The response to altered consumption patterns during and after the Second World War has received insufficient attention in the literature, which is relatively limited and predominantly anecdotal.[6] A close examination of popular attitudes towards rationing and austerity qualifies the myth of the home front characterized by universal sacrifice, egalitarianism, and common purpose[7] and highlights the importance of consumption to morale during and after the war.[8] The discussion complicates common stereotypes such as the image of a 'highly disciplined' British people who were 'used to receiving orders and to strict regulation' or the notion of a people characterized by a 'combination of hope and public purpose' who possessed if anything 'too much . . . faith in the possibilities of centrally conceived, nationally applied public policy as a bringer of beneficial change in the economic and social structure'.[9] The response to the persistence of shortages after the war was certainly more complex than Morgan's contention that the 'frustrations of rationing were borne without demur. After all, British

---

[4] PRO, INF 1/292, 5–12 Jan. and 11–18 May 1942.

[5] W. Crofts, *Coercion or Persuasion? Propaganda in Britain after 1945* (London, 1989).

[6] H. Hopkins, *The New Look: A Social History of the Forties and Fifties in Britain* (London, 1963); M. Sissons and P. French (eds.), *Age of Austerity* (London, 1963); A. Calder, *The People's War: Britain 1939–45* (London, 1969); N. Longmate, *How We Lived Then: A History of Everyday Life during the Second World War* (London, 1971); id., *The Home Front: An Anthology of Personal Experience 1938–1945* (London, 1981); P. Addison, *Now the War Is Over: A Social History of Britain 1945–1951* (London, 1985).

[7] For critiques of this myth see A. Calder, *The Myth of the Blitz* (London, 1991); N. Tiratsoo (ed.), *The Attlee Years* (London, 1991); J. Harris, 'War and Social History: Britain and the Home Front during the Second World War', *Contemporary European History* 1 (1992), pp. 17–35; S. Fielding, P. Thompson, and N. Tiratsoo, *England Arise! The Labour Party and Popular Politics in 1940s Britain* (Manchester, 1995); H. L. Smith (ed.), *Britain in the Second World War: A Social History* (Manchester, 1996).

[8] On morale see M. Balfour, *Propaganda in War 1939–1945: Organisations, Policies and Publics in Britain and Germany* (London, 1979); I. McLaine, *Ministry of Morale: Home Front Morale and the Ministry of Information in World War II* (London, 1979); T. Harrisson, *Living through the Blitz* (London, 1976).

[9] P. Hennessy, 'The Attlee Governments, 1945–1951', in P. Hennessy and A. Seldon (eds.), *Ruling Performance: British Governments from Attlee to Thatcher* (Oxford, 1987), p. 32; P. Hennessy, *Never Again: Britain 1945–1951* (London, 1992), p. 453.

people were happy enough to be alive at all in 1945.'[10] Keynes described
Britain's post-war economic problems as 'a financial Dunkirk'[11] but this was
never quite the same as the real thing and 'it was difficult to foresee how
readily the public would acquiesce in . . . the hardships that lay ahead'.[12] In
the event, the Ministry of Food and the Board of Trade suffered from a hostile press, were identified with a political doctrine, and the continuation of
controls became the focus of post-war political controversy.[13]

Opinion trends on rationing and austerity are analysed in this chapter
using a range of sources. Gallup polls and government social surveys, based
on large and representative samples, provide the bulk of the quantitative
data. Whereas Gallup polls are particularly useful for a brief snapshot of
attitudes at a national level, social surveys are more detailed and also
include many group differences in opinion. Wartime Home Intelligence
reports, compiled between October 1940 and December 1944, could be
seen as a hybrid between qualitative and quantitative data. Drawing on an
extensive network of sources, including their own regional information officers, press summaries, censorship reports, the police, the BBC, voluntary
organizations, and political parties, weekly reports attempted to gauge the
state of morale and track opinion on wartime inconveniences.[14] Mass-
Observation reports, based on small-scale surveys and a national panel of
observers, along with miscellaneous diaries and memoirs, illustrate popular
attitudes to these issues at the local and individual level. Most of the discussion is concerned with national trends and there are few references to
regional variations since the complex regional data, when available, defy
generalization. Group differences in attitudes distinguish between men and
women, age groups, and those with or without family responsibility.[15] The
discussion of class differences is complicated by the fact that the concept is
difficult to define[16] and contemporary Gallup polls and social surveys
divided the population into three income or economic groups. Even though
there was a broad overlap between occupation and income, the higher group
(frequently the top third) also included a number of the highest-paid manual workers and many low-paid clerical workers were excluded. There were
considerable differences in income and status within these strata, making it
virtually impossible to define the boundaries between middle and working

---

[10] K. O. Morgan, *Labour in Power 1945–1951* (Oxford, 1984), p. 327. Morgan's more recent
The People's Peace: British History 1945–1989 (Oxford, 1990), pp. 29–33, is more critical on this
point.
[11] Quoted in Cairncross, *Years of Recovery*, p. 10.   [12] Ibid., p. 11.
[13] Hammond, *Food and Agriculture in Britain*, p. 218; Hargreaves and Gowing, *Civil Industry
and Trade*, p. 637.
[14] PRO, INF 1/292. See also Balfour, *Propaganda in War*, pp. 72–3; McLaine, *Ministry of
Morale*, pp. 50–3.
[15] These are married and unmarried men, housewives, and 'other women'.
[16] See Chapter 5, pp. 251–2.

Fig. 2.1. *Main government or national problem, as reported in Gallup polls and social surveys, November 1940–January 1955 (per cent)*

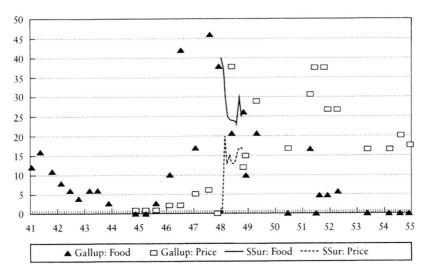

Notes: Food: Food supplies, food rationing, food shortages.
Price: Cost of living, rising prices.
From April 1951 fuel is included under 'food' in the Gallup polls.
   In the Gallup polls, food scored the highest percentage in Nov. 1940, June 1946, July 1947, and Nov. 1947; other important war problems were shipping losses, the second front, and war production; between 1945 and 1950 housing was the third major concern; in the 1950s foreign policy was the second most important problem.
   In the social surveys, food scored the highest percentage in Dec. 1947 and Jan. 1948; from February 1948 onwards housing was the most important single issue.
Sources: G. H. Gallup (ed.), *The Gallup International Public Opinion Polls: Great Britain, 1937–1975*, vol. 1, 1937–1964 (New York, 1976); PRO, RG 23/92, 94–6, 98–102, 105, Survey of Knowledge and Opinion about the Economic Situation.

class. The discussion of class differences in attitudes to rationing and austerity should be understood within these parameters.

   These surveys show that food and general shortages were a leading national and personal problem during the 1940s. Food shortages were the biggest single concern on the home front early on in the war, but as the supply situation stabilized during 1942 food worries became negligible (see Figure 2.1). The issue reappeared after the war and, as indicated by Figure 2.2, between 1946 and 1948 food shortages were a central, if not the most important, problem in the public mind. At the same time other shortages, queuing, and clothing difficulties also caused considerable concern (see Figure 2.3). During this period women and, especially, housewives worried more about food and other shortages than men. For instance 46 per cent of those questioned named food as their most important personal problem in December 1947, but the figure stood at only 38 per cent for men, 52 per cent for women, and 61 per cent for housewives. Among economic groups,

FIG. 2.2. *Main family problem, as reported in Gallup polls, April 1947–January 1955 (per cent)*

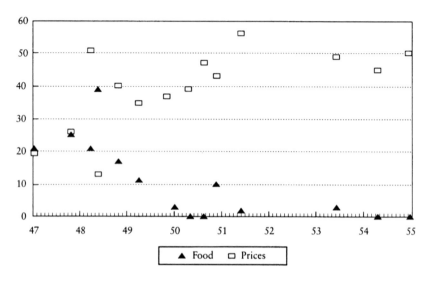

Notes: Food: food shortages or food difficulties.
Prices: cost of living, rising prices.
In Aug. 1948 'food' includes general shortages and from Jan 1951 fuel is included under 'food'. In Jan. and June 1948 clothing difficulties scored 11% and 9% respectively. Housing was the third main family problem during the period, and gradually replaced food and shortages.
Source: G. H. Gallup (ed.), *The Gallup International Public Opinion Polls: Great Britain, 1937–1975*, vol. 1, 1937–1964 (New York, 1976).

only 39 per cent of the higher group (the top third of the population) mentioned food while 49 per cent of the lower two-thirds did so.[17] Concern about post-war austerity was, therefore, not confined to the middle classes, and gender differences in attitudes were a critical factor. From 1949 onwards, food anxieties ebbed away, apart from a brief re-emergence early in 1951, and were gradually replaced by worries about rising prices which came to dominate the political agenda until the mid–1950s. Food worries correlated above all with the size of the meat ration and the re-emergence of the food issue early in 1951 was due to the exceptionally low meat ration at that time.[18]

An analysis of popular attitudes to austerity is important because of the close connection between consumption and morale. Civilian morale, the target of sustained bombing campaigns, was critical to the war effort and the focus of government propaganda during and after the war. Morale, a

[17] PRO, RG 23/92.
[18] PRO, RG 23/116. For changes in the meat ration see Figure 1.2; for the political debate about this reduction see Chapter 5, section 5.3.

FIG. 2.3. *Main personal problem, as reported in social surveys, December 1947–June 1951 (per cent)*

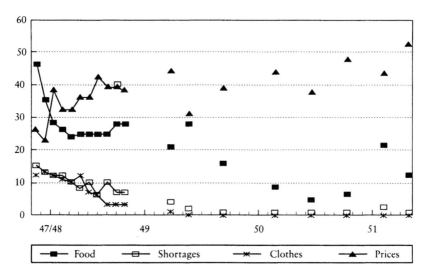

Notes: Food: food shortages and ration cuts.
Shortages: other shortages and queuing.
Clothes: clothing difficulties.
Prices: Cost of living, rising prices.
Housing, which became more important in 1949, was the other main personal problem during the period.
Sources: PRO, RG 23/92, 94–6, 98–102, 105–6, 108, 110, 112, 114, 116–17, Survey of Knowledge and Opinion about the Economic Situation.

'mishmash of fantasy and fact'[19] is virtually impossible to define and should be understood with regard to both behaviour and attitudes.[20] According to Home Intelligence, 'it has become increasingly noticeable that the morale of the civilian population depends more upon material factors, acutely involving their lives, than upon the ebb and flow of the events of war beyond these islands'.[21] A subsequent report distinguished between material and mental determinants of morale and again maintained that 'the material factors appear to be more important than the mental ones' because the British people were 'on the whole, practical and unimaginative'.[22] The most important material factor was food—'In severely blitzed populations, *hot* food has been found to be of great important [*sic*] in morale . . . in non-blitz times, inequalities of distribution, and wastage and profiteering, have proved to be

[19] Harrisson, *Living through the Blitz*, p. 282.
[20] McLaine, *Ministry of Morale*, pp. 7–10; Balfour, *Propaganda in War*, pp. 78–80; S. Nicholas, *The Echo of War: Home Front Propaganda and the Wartime BBC, 1939–45* (Manchester, 1996), pp. 3–4. For a general discussion of wartime public opinion see Fielding *et al.*, *England Arise*, ch. 2, *passim*.   [21] PRO, INF 1/292, 7–14 May 1941.
[22] PRO, INF 1/292, Home Morale and Public Opinion, 1 Oct. 1941.

the main foci of feeling'—followed by warmth, work, leisure, rest and sleep, a secure base, as well as safety and security for dependants. Mental determinants were the 'Belief that victory was possible', faith in 'equality of sacrifice', and that 'the war is a necessity and our cause just'. Popular attitudes were primarily based on personal experience; 'Air-raids, food shortages, shopping difficulties, queues, factory conditions, evacuees and hosts, these are the things about which the British public thinks and feels most'.[23]

During the war morale was promoted by the Ministry of Information, which soon learned that uplifting propaganda and exhortation had little effect, and focused instead on the provision of 'full and honest news'.[24] At the same time, the government successfully maintained a high and stable level of food rations once the system of food control was fully developed at the end of 1941. Morale was thought to be 'seriously menaced by discrepancies between government statements about the food situation and actual facts' and food queues were described as 'a bigger menace to public morale than several serious German air raids' in February 1941.[25] However, from 1942 onwards food rationing was perceived as the 'finest achievement of the war' and 'one of the chief causes of the excellent morale of the country'.[26] By contrast, the post-war Labour government's extensive propaganda campaign, exemplified by the slogan 'We work or want', ultimately failed.[27] Partly, this was a consequence of poor communication since it was easier for the public to identify with Churchill's call for 'blood, sweat and tears' than with Cripps's request of 'an export target of 140 per cent of 1938 by volume'.[28] More importantly, the continuation of shortages coupled with small and volatile food rations depressed morale after the war. According to the social survey 61 per cent thought things were going badly for Britain in March 1948. While pessimism gradually receded, 34 per cent still thought things were going badly in June 1951, with another 44 per cent giving a qualified answer.[29] An analysis of possible correlates found that 'feelings about food are more closely related to opinion as to whether things are going well or badly . . . than are opinions about unemployment or knowledge of our trade position'.[30] The social survey concluded that:

[21] PRO, INF 1/292, Home Morale and Public Opinion, 1 Oct. 1941 (emphasis in original); see also INF 1/292, Home Morale and Public Opinion, 9–16 Mar. 1942.

[24] McLaine, *Ministry of Morale*, p. 11. On the growth of government publicity during the interwar years and the pre-war planning of the Ministry of Information, see M. Grant, *Propaganda and the Role of the State in Interwar Britain* (Oxford, 1994).

[25] PRO, INF 1/292, 5–12 Feb. and 12–19 Feb. 1941.

[26] PRO, INF 1/292, 30 June–7 July and 8–15 Sept. 1942.

[27] Crofts, *Coercion or Persuasion?*, pp. 82–5, 250–5.   [28] Hopkins, *New Look*, p. 94.

[29] PRO, RG 23/95–6, 98–102, 104–6, 108, 110, 112, 114, 116–17.

[30] PRO, RG 23/100.

public opinion and feeling about the economic situation is influenced considerably more by personal experience of economic problems of a direct and obvious kind than by information about aspects of the crisis which are less concrete to the individual and affect him only indirectly. If there is an apparent contradiction between what is read in the papers and personal experience, the latter is more likely to be believed. It seems also that the public's interest in the situation cannot be centred on the methods being used to overcome the crisis, i.e. more production, increased exports, re-distribution of manpower, etc. For most people interest is centred on the objects for which these methods are used, to get food, houses, and ultimately a better standard of living.[31]

The continuation of austerity after the war contrasted sharply with immediate post-war expectations. Indeed, the very success of wartime food policy led to general confidence about the post-war situation. In three Gallup polls on the most urgent problem after the war conducted in December 1943 and April and August 1944, food supply and clothing scored only 7, 4, and 1 per cent respectively.[32] More specifically, with regard to food rations, people anticipated a degree of relaxation after the war. Only 9 per cent thought that rationing would be ended but 54 per cent expected an increase in rations during the first year of peace.[33] A Mass Observation survey of post-war buying plans indicates a high level of consumer demand after the war. Whereas men primarily coveted personal possessions such as a car, bicycle, radio, or camera, women longed for furnishings and other household goods as well as clothes and personal possessions.[34] Perhaps Mrs Milburn provided the best expression of middle-class post-war aspirations:

> When breakfast is a cheery meal with coffee rich and rare,
> And cream a-floating on the top and lashings still to spare,
>
> . . .
>
> When 'butter' bends before it breaks in winter's icy grip,
> When one may see without surprise the orange and its pip,
>
> . . .
>
> When shop assistants may be wrong—the customer be right,
> When milkmen pour out milk in quarts, the butcher brings the joints,
> And no one thinks of ration books, of coupons or of points.

[31] Ibid. (emphasis in original).   [32] *Gallup Polls*, pp. 85, 90, and 96.
[33] *Gallup Polls*, Nov. 1943, in PRO, INF 1/292, 30 Nov.–7 Dec. 1943; 18% thought that rations would be decreased and 19% registered no opinion.
[34] Mass-Observation extracts are reproduced with the permission of the trustees of the Mass-Observation Archive, University of Sussex (hereafter MO), File Report (hereafter FR), 2066, Postwar Buying, Apr. 1944.

. . .

When sugar's sweet and plentiful, and cakes are not a fluke,
When eggs are seldom mentioned, and Lord Woolton is a duke.[35]

These aspirations amounted to little more than a desire among a 'very large section of middle-class opinion . . . [to] return to the comforts of 1939'.[36] This dawn of affluence characterized by the introduction and rapid diffusion of many new consumer goods and a more plentiful diet was not confined to the middle classes but extended to substantial sections of the working classes, with average income rising by about a third in real terms during the interwar years.[37] Despite the image of the 1930s as a decade of mass unemployment, for those in work—the overwhelming majority— living standards increased due to a rise in real wages largely as a consequence of falling prices coupled with a demographic trend towards smaller families. These advances coincided with continuous relative poverty affecting about one-third of the working class or roughly 20 per cent of the population.[38] While unemployment was exceptionally high and persistent and most manual workers experienced at least a spell of unemployment, the problem was primarily structural, concentrated in the staple industries of the North and West and unemployment was high among the young, the old, and the unskilled.[39] There was a widespread desire for a return to the pre-war situation—albeit without the mass unemployment—few were prepared for an intensification of food shortages, and nobody expected that it would take the best part of a decade after VE day until pre-war consumption levels of many foodstuffs were reached again.

The remainder of this chapter is divided into two sections focusing on attitudes to food policy and clothes rationing along with miscellaneous shortages respectively. Section 2.1 begins by discussing the initial public response to the introduction of rationing and food control. This is followed by an exploration of general attitudes to wartime food policy, an analysis of surveys relating to the adequacy of the diet, and an examination of discontent with the distribution of unrationed foods, the persistence of luxury feeding, and queuing. Despite extensive grievances, food control was accepted during the war and morale remained high—a situation which

[35] Extracts from 'When', a poem by Clara Milburn, in P. Donnelly (ed.), *Mrs Milburn's Diaries: An English Woman's Day-to-Day Reflections, 1939–45* (London, 1979), facing front page.
[36] R. Lewis and A. Maude, *The English Middle Classes* (London, 1950), p. 92.
[37] J. Stevenson and C. Cook, *The Slump* (London, 1977); J. Stevenson, *British Society 1914–45* (London, 1984); Burnett, *Plenty and Want*.
[38] Perkin, *Rise of Professional Society*, pp. 276–80.
[39] M. Thomas, 'Labour Market Structure and the Nature of Unemployment in Interwar Britain', in B. Eichengreen and T. J. Hatton (eds.), *Interwar Unemployment in International Perspective* (London, 1988), pp. 97–145; see also W. R. Garside, *British Unemployment, 1919–1939: A Study in Public Policy* (Cambridge, 1990).

stands in stark contrast with the post-war period. The psychological impact of ration cuts and the introduction of bread rationing undermined public faith in post-war food policy and contributed to low food morale after the war. At the end of the 1940s rising prices became a major worry and in the early 1950s the public gave a cautious welcome to decontrol. Section 2.2 examines attitudes to clothes rationing, which received an initially favourable response despite doubts about the fairness of the scheme. Following cuts in ration levels there was widespread discontent during and after the war as clothing became increasingly threadbare. Despite high demand, the abolition of clothes rationing did not result in increased consumption in the face of high prices at the end of the 1940s. The final paragraphs of this section briefly discuss attitudes towards the utility schemes and shortages of miscellaneous consumer goods.

2.1. FOOD

In October 1939 the war cabinet considered the introduction of butter, bacon, meat, and sugar rationing. Discussion revolved around possible unrest and discontent and the expectation of widespread public opposition to rationing.[40] On the one hand, it was argued that a 'severe [meat] ration would have a most adverse effect on the morale of the country'.[41] On the other, in the Great War 'the most potent cause of industrial unrest had been maldistribution of foodstuffs, which had given rise to food queues. Public opinion would know that these injustices and inequalities could be avoided by the introduction of rationing'. The cabinet postponed a final decision until 'soundings of public opinion' had been taken.[42] Leading members of a number of bodies representative of various sections of public opinion were consulted. With the exception of the middle-class National Citizen's Union and the London Chamber of Commerce, the public, afraid of shortages and inequitable distribution, were prepared to accept rationing provided 'that the necessity for the measure has been clearly explained and brought home'.[43] At the next cabinet meeting the Minister of Food maintained that 'the home front would be strengthened by the institution of rationing'. But Churchill, then First Lord of the Admiralty, argued that there were 'signs in the Press . . . that public opinion was becoming increasingly critical of government control and interference with the liberty of the individual' and was prepared to countenance only bacon and butter rationing. Chamberlain opposed any further delay, stressed the need to show that rationing was the

[40] PRO, CAB 65, WM (39) 60, 25 Oct. 1939.
[41] PRO, CAB 75/27, War Cabinet Home Policy Committee, Sub-Committee on Rationing, 12 Oct. 1939.   [42] PRO, CAB 65, WM (39) 60, 25 Oct. 1939.
[43] PRO, CAB 67/2, WP (G) (39) 59, 27 Oct. 1939.

only means to ensure 'fair distribution' and the cabinet decided to ration butter and bacon but not to ration sugar and meat at present.[44] These latter rationing schemes were approved in December and subsequently the cabinet merely rubber-stamped further extensions of food rationing. During the autumn of 1939, the public were more worried about unfair distribution, hoarding, and favouritism among shopkeepers than potential infringements of civil liberties.[45] Mass-Observation rejected the anti-rationing press campaign as 'ill-founded' on the basis of a survey conducted early in November, which showed a small majority in favour of rationing.[46] This impression was confirmed by a simultaneous Gallup poll according to which 60 per cent thought that food rationing was necessary.[47]

While a majority was in favour of rationing and food control in principle, public support for these policies was by no means unconditional. A Gallup poll after the first wave of rationing, but prior to the introduction of meat rationing, showed only 36 per cent in favour of more rationing, with 54 per cent preferring voluntary reductions in consumption.[48] Moreover, in January 1941 only 44 per cent thought that the present rationing system worked fairly for everybody, another 19 per cent agreed with qualifications, and 31 per cent felt that the system was not fair.[49] Home Intelligence reports, from their inception in October 1940 onwards, provide ample evidence of widespread dissatisfaction with the food situation and, particularly, shortages of rationed and unrationed foods, high prices, and inequalities in distribution.[50] In January 1941, 42 per cent had difficulty in getting unrationed foods because there were none in the shops and another 16 per cent because prices were too high, and only 29 per cent had no problems in obtaining unrationed foods.[51]

This high level of discontent with the food situation, which persisted throughout the spring and summer of 1941, was alleviated with the gradual extension of food control. In February, a Mass-Observation report placed cheese at the top of food complaints and concluded that 'there is a tendency for foodstuffs about which the position is known and stable to be less mentioned than those about which it fluctuates'.[52] There were numerous objections to the introduction of the milk and egg distribution schemes

---

[44] PRO, CAB 65, WM (39) 63, 28 Oct. 1939.

[45] T. Harrisson and C. Madge (eds.), *War Begins at Home* (London, 1940), pp. 378–9; see also MO, Topic Collection (hereafter TC), Food, Box 1B, Introduction of Rationing: Autumn 1939.

[46] Harrisson and Madge, *War Begins at Home*, p. 380; the survey of 500 people in Fulham and Bolton found 53% men and 55% women in favour of rationing.

[47] *Gallup Polls*, p. 25; 28% thought it was unnecessary and 12% held no opinion.

[48] Ibid., p. 31; 10% held no opinion.

[49] Ibid., p. 40; 6% held no opinion.   [50] PRO, INF 1/292.

[51] *Gallup Polls*, p. 40; 13% did not know.

[52] MO, FR, 632, Food Tensions in late February, April 1941; the report is based on a survey of female members of the observer panel; cheese was rationed in May 1941.

along with anger about the scarcity of fresh fruit and vegetables and the ineffectiveness of price control.[53] Discontent with the unequal distribution of unrationed foodstuffs culminated in an 'increased demand for all-round rationing so as to avoid unfairness'.[54] The position improved from autumn 1941 onwards, when Home Intelligence observed greater satisfaction with the food situation[55] and a Gallup poll found that 40 per cent now had no difficulty in getting unrationed foodstuffs. Those who still had problems (43 per cent), mentioned particularly tinned foods, cereals, and dried fruits.[56] Hence, the points rationing scheme launched in December 1941, which ensured equitable distribution of these and other processed and packaged foods, became a turning-point in popular attitudes towards food control. The announcement of points rationing was welcomed as 'a fairer deal' and following its introduction the scheme was associated with praise and satisfaction.[57] American canned meats, newly available in Britain under Lend-Lease, contributed towards this success.[58] Subsequently, 60 per cent opposed any further extension of food rationing.[59] Nevertheless, the sweets or personal points rationing scheme, introduced in July 1942, was generally welcomed.[60]

The introduction of rationing and food control had a differential impact on social classes. Wartime

restrictions brought much smaller dietetic changes to *the poorer section of the community* than to the higher income groups. For poor people 'the acquisition of food ... has always been a major problem' ... there are indications that 'the poorer people themselves do not regard their food position as materially altered. It seems that so long as bread and potatoes are unrationed the position will be tenable'. . . . Among *higher-income groups* food is 'one of the chief topics of conversation'. It is noticeable that 'such persons, even where enabled by adequate funds to buy generously of non-rationed goods, and such luxuries as are available, have suffered a considerable reduction in their standard of living, though a far greater proportion of their income is now spent on food than in peace time'.[61]

[53] PRO, INF 1/292, e.g. 16–23 Apr., 14–25 May, 11–18 June, 25 June–2 July, and 16–23 July 1941; MO, FR, 704, Food and Rationing: An Observer's Report from Shotley Bridge, Newcastle; TC, Food, Box 3C, Overheards etc. on Food Rationing, Spring, Summer 1941.

[54] PRO, INF 1/292, 7–14 May 1941; see also 11–18 June 1941.

[55] Ibid., 29 Sept.–6 Oct. 1941 onwards.

[56] *Gallup Polls*, p. 48; 17% registered no opinion.

[57] PRO, INF 1/292, 27 Oct.–3 Nov. 1941; 1–8 Dec., and 22–29 Dec. 1941.

[58] Ibid., 15–22 Dec. 1941; MO, TC, Food, Box 3E, Attitudes to and Comments on American Tinned Foods, Dec. 1941.

[59] *Gallup Polls*, p. 50; 25% were in favour of further extension of rationing and 15% registered no opinion.

[60] PRO, INF 1/292, 21–8 July and 17–25 Aug. 1942. According to a Mass-Observation survey of 56 persons, MO, TC, Food, Box 3E, Questionnaire on Personal Points Rationing, 7 June 1942, 77% welcomed the scheme and only four people expected to be adversely affected by it.

[61] PRO, INF 1/292, 27 Aug.–3 Sept. 1941, quoting from a report by the Cambridge Regional Information Officer (emphasis in original).

Adjustment to the new eating patterns was difficult and, for example, complaints about food were a frequent topic in correspondence to *The Times* during 1940.[62] The prospect of butter rationing was greeted with trepidation by a middle-class housewife who 'didn't like margarine; [I] hate it; I'd rather have dripping' and a male manual worker protested about a 'quarter of a pound of f— bacon a week. Not a bloody square meal in it'.[63] A working-class housewife complained that rations were '*not* enuff [*sic*] for decent feeding'[64] and there was a general atmosphere of dearth. One report highlighted a 'Great scarcity of beef in town' and news that a 'local Co-op had salmon, tinned milk, cheese and chocolate' led to a 'raid' among local residents.[65] Onions and tomatoes were particularly coveted. One woman who obtained '*one* large onion . . . tied a piece of ribbon round it and placed it on the mantle shelf'[66] and the acquisition of 'half a pound of tomatoes [was] . . . Very exciting'.[67] 'Entertaining', according to a Cambridge University don, 'owing to . . . rationing, and reduced staff, has become next to impossible'[68] and a war diarist on one occasion could offer nothing but toast.[69] Formerly innocent pastimes such as feeding sparrows were now illegal, pets were not supposed to consume anything fit for human consumption, and it became a question of 'conscience that shipping space [should not be] taken for food for . . . animals'.[70]

By the end of 1941 a comprehensive system of food control, which continued essentially unchanged for the remainder of the war, was in place, the initial uncertainty had been overcome, and new eating habits had evolved. The earlier discontent gave way to satisfaction which was 'expressed in almost lyrical terms. "On the whole, . . . we are wonderfully well-fed, at this stage of the war" ' and 'only those who want to live at the prewar level have any grumbles now'.[71]

From 1942 onwards, rationing was 'accepted as a matter of course. The schemes [were] thought to be just and . . . functioning . . . surprisingly well. There is a real sense of gratitude for the abundance of food supplies so far'.[72] Only speculation about bread rationing in January 1943 produced a strong reaction 'ranging from "consternation" . . . to the view that

---

[62] A. Livesey (ed.), *Are We at War? Letters to The Times, 1939–45* (London, 1989).

[63] MO, TC, Food, Box 1B, Introduction of Rationing: Autumn 1939.

[64] MO, TC, Food, Box 2F, Directs on Rationing, Dec. 1940 (emphasis in original).

[65] Ibid.; see also MO, TC, Food, Box 3C, Overheards etc. on Food Rationing, Spring, Summer 1941.   [66] MO, TC, Food, Box 2F, Directs on Rationing: Dec. 1940 (emphasis in original).

[67] V. Hodgson, *Few Eggs and No Oranges* (London, 1976), p. 162; see also pp. 119, 130, and 168.   [68] A. F. S. Gow, *Letters from Cambridge* (London, 1945), p. 93.

[69] Hodgson, *Few Eggs and No Oranges*, p. 301.

[70] Longmate, *Home Front*, p. 157; C. Driver, *The British at Table, 1940–1980* (London, 1985), p. 36.   [71] PRO, INF 1/292, 29 Sept.–6 Oct. and 13–20 Oct. 1941.

[72] Ibid., 9–16 Mar. 1942; MO, FR, 1155, Food Tensions in Spring 1942 Compared with Spring 1941, based on a predominantly middle-class sample, observed a considerable reduction in food grumbles.

"people have such faith in rationing that they won't mind" '.[73] Opinion was almost evenly divided with 47 per cent backing a voluntary cut in consumption and 42 per cent in favour of bread rationing.[74] But support for rationing and food control was neither universal nor unqualified, as is indicated by social surveys conducted in 1942 and 1943. Table 2.1 shows that 54 per cent approved of rationing, another 27 per cent had no criticism, and only 14 per cent were dissatisfied. Approval of rationing was somewhat higher among women than men and in rural areas, but the most important differences in attitudes were between occupational groups. Rationing was most popular among white-collar workers, only a minority of manual workers approved of the policy, and almost a third of manual workers in heavy industry were dissatisfied. As discussed below, this was due to a widespread belief among manual workers that their diet was inadequate and that rationing was unfair. Regardless of this general support for rationing, there was extensive opposition to further food restrictions and smaller rations. According to Table 2.2, almost two-thirds

TABLE 2.1. *Attitudes to food rationing, 1942–1943* (per cent)

	Approve	No criticism	Dissatisfied
Total	54	27	14
Men	50	25	19
Women	57	28	11
Under 20	49	26	11
31–45	57	24	14
Over 65	48	28	18
Urban	53	27	15
Rural	62	25	9
Heavy industry[a]	37	30	30
Heavy industry[b]	43	22	29
Light industry	47	34	12
Clerical and distributive	66	21	8
Professional and managerial	68	21	7
Housewives	55	29	11
Retired and unoccupied	52	23	18

[a] Factories and shipyards.
[b] Agricultural, building and transport workers, and miners.
Notes: Respondents were asked, What do you think about food rationing? Percentages do not add to 100 due to a small percentage of miscellaneous answers and 'Don't knows'; 9% of under-20s did not know and another 4% gave miscellaneous answers.
   This survey is based on a sample of 2,047 people in representative proportions from the different occupational, regional, sex, and age groups, interviewed between 9 and 26 June 1942.
Source: Nuffield College Library, Oxford, Wartime Social Survey, Food I: Food Schemes: A Collection of Short Reports on Inquiries made by the Regional Organisation of the Wartime Social Survey, May 1942–Jan. 1943.

[73] PRO, INF 1/292, 12–19 Jan. 1943.
[74] *Gallup Polls*, p. 71; 11% registered no opinion.

TABLE 2.2. *Attitudes to possible extensions of food rationing in 1943 (per cent)*

	More rationing[a]	Ration Cuts[b]	Stricter rationing[c]
Yes	24	20	21
No	60	62	63
Don't know	15	18	16

[a] Do you think more sorts of foods should be rationed?
[b] Do you think any of the present rations could be cut down to make more room for war shipping?
[c] Do you think rationing should be made stricter in any way?
Notes: Percentages may not add to 100 because of rounding. This survey is based on a representative sample of 2,671 people interviewed between 18 Jan. and 8 Feb. 1943.
Source: Nuffield College Library, Oxford, Wartime Social Survey, Food I: Food Schemes: A Collection of Short Reports on Inquiries made by the Regional Organisation of the Wartime Social Survey, May 1942–January 1943.

were against more rationing, ration cuts, or stricter rationing at the beginning of 1943. As could be expected, white-collar workers were more in favour of an extension of rationing and ration cuts were particularly opposed by workers in heavy industries. Women, and especially housewives, were more reluctant than men to countenance ration cuts and further restrictions. These were also disproportionately opposed by people from rural areas.[75] With regard to other aspects of food control, in 1942 only about one in five had eaten at British Restaurants, which were popular with factory and clerical workers. Although only 5 per cent went regularly to these restaurants, the majority of responses was favourable.[76] By contrast, National Wheatmeal Bread, a brown loaf made compulsory to economize on wheat, remained unpopular. Although three-quarters accepted it 'under wartime conditions', two-thirds preferred white bread, and 63 per cent did not want National Wheatmeal Bread to be continued after the war.[77]

Wartime food discontent focused on a number of areas. First, there was widespread dissatisfaction among male manual workers who thought that their diet was inadequate. This was largely the result of the shortage of meat, which was highly prized as a marker of status and male privilege in the working class diet.[78] Tables 2.3 and 2.4 show that 42–45 per cent of

[75] Nuffield College Library, Oxford (hereafter NCL), Wartime Social Survey, Food I: Food Schemes: A Collection of Short Reports on Inquiries Made by the Regional Organisation of the Wartime Social Survey, May 1942–January 1943; PRO, RG 23/9A.
[76] NCL, Wartime Social Survey, Food I: Food Schemes: A Collection of Short Reports on Inquiries Made by the Regional Organisation of the Wartime Social Survey, May 1942–January 1943.
[77] PRO, RG 23/61, Wartime Social Survey, National Wheatmeal Bread, Apr. 1944. The survey was based on a representative sample of 2,858 people.
[78] L. Oren, 'The Welfare of Women in Laboring Families: England, 1860–1950', *Feminist Studies* 1 (1973), pp. 107–25; E. Ross, *Love and Toil: Motherhood in Outcast London, 1870–1918* (New York, 1993), pp. 30–4.

TABLE 2.3. *Attitudes to the adequacy of the diet among selected groups in 1942 (per cent)*

	Men		Women	
	Heavy industry	Light industry	Light industry	Housewives
Enough food to keep fit[a]				
Yes	58	55	68	78
No	42	45	32	22
Reasons given[b]				
Insufficient				
—Meat	56	37	23	23
—Fats	29	14	19	37
—Eggs	25	13	16	25
—Sugar	32	14	10	28
—Tea	20	12	7	24
—Bacon	27	10	6	11
—Vegetables	3	3	3	4
—Fruit	9	9	25	18
Not enough	72	62	54	58
Difficulties[c]	3	8	20	7

[a] Do you consider the food you are getting at the moment enough to keep you fit?
[b] Reasons given as a cause for the inadequacy of the diet. More than one answer was possible.
[c] Shopping difficulties, irregular mealtimes etc.
The table is based on three inquiries carried out between 30 April and 11 July 1942: 4,139 men and women in light industry, 1,989 heavy workers, and 1,948 housewives were interviewed.
Source: Nuffield College, Oxford, Wartime Social Survey, Food: An Inquiry into a Typical Day's Meals and Attitudes to Wartime Food in Selected Groups of the English Working Population, n.s. 16 and 19, 1942–3.

male manual workers felt they were not getting enough food to keep fit in the spring and summer of 1942. The situation deteriorated and in February 1943 50 per cent of male manual workers considered that they did not have sufficient food to keep fit and another 11 per cent were doubtful. Among women and the under-20s satisfaction was higher, but female manual workers were more dissatisfied than housewives and discontent was greater in 1943. This trend may have been influenced by seasonal factors since 'a winter's hard work, the black-out and bad weather probably all tended to make [people] feel run-down'.[79] Home Intelligence noted an 'increasing tendency to attribute "the general debility from which so many people are suffering" to "the poor food and lack of nourishment"' in April 1943 and similar comments were made at the beginning of 1944.[80] Regarding the causes of dissatisfaction, there were conspicuous gender differences. A majority in all

[79] NCL, Wartime Social Survey, Food: An Inquiry into (i) A Day's Meals, and (ii) Attitudes to Wartime Food in Selected Groups of British Workers, n.s. 32, June 1943.
[80] PRO, INF 1/292, 13–20 Apr. 1943; see also 2–9 Nov. 1943, 1–8 Feb., and 29 Feb.–7 Mar. 1944.

TABLE 2.4. *Attitudes to the adequacy of the diet among selected groups of workers in 1943 (per cent)*

	Men	Women	Total	Under 20s
Enough food to keep fit[a]				
Yes	39	58	46	75
No	50	31	43	15
Uncertain	11	11	11	9
Reasons given[b]				
Insufficient				
—Meat, bacon	64	29	55	32
—Fat, butter	25	29	26	30
—Eggs	25	24	25	23
—Sugar, sweets	28	17	25	19
—Vegetables	4	3	4	6
—Fruit	7	20	11	23

[a] Do you consider the food you are getting at the moment is enough to keep you fit?
[b] If not enough, what is lacking? More than one answer was possible.
The table is based on a survey conducted during Feb. 1943 of 2,970 men and 1,520 women in selected occupations, viz. docks, shipyards, mining, iron and steel, public utility and transport, distributive, clerical, light engineering, leather and textile, and building industries.
Source: Nuffield College, Oxford, Wartime Social Survey, Food: An Inquiry into (i) A Day's Meals, and (ii) Attitudes to Wartime Food in Selected Groups of British Workers, n.s. 32, June 1943.

groups considered their diet to be inadequate but dissatisfaction was greatest among men in heavy industry, 72 per cent of whom thought that their diet was generally inadequate, largely as a consequence of flat-rate rations. These made no allowance for differential energy requirements, and account for much of the discontent. This problem was partly addressed by the expansion of canteens and British Restaurants, which reached a peak during 1943 and 1944, and the introduction of a special cheese ration for workers who could not be catered for in canteens.[81] By contrast, working women stand out as the only group significantly affected by shopping difficulties. With regard to individual food items, men and, above all, manual workers repeatedly named meat and bacon shortages as their most important grievance. Female tastes were more diverse and whereas fats and sugar were missed most among housewives, other women also missed meat, eggs, and fruit. Meat was the most politically sensitive of all rationed foods and Bevin, the Minister of Labour, considered the low meat ration in 1941 to be a 'serious danger' to morale. He drew attention to workers' belief that they 'are not getting enough to eat so long as so little meat is available to them' and argued that an 'increase in the supply of meat ... would have a very great effect on morale'.[82]

[81] Hammond, *Food Volume II*, fig. 4, p. 394; PRO, MAF 223/31, Rationing in the United Kingdom, 1950.   [82] PRO, CAB 67/9, WP (G) (41) 51, 21 May 1941.

Second, wartime discontent was caused by the inadequacy of rations, high prices, and the uneven distribution of unrationed foods. War diaries and memoirs provide ample evidence and the Home Intelligence monthly summary of constant topics illustrates the severity of these grievances.[83] Fats, mentioned regularly in up to 6 out of 13 regions in 1944, were exceptional as the only *straight* ration considered inadequate. Discontent about the shortage of dried fruit, rationed under the points scheme, was high before Christmas and eggs and milk were a recurring problem. The most persistent grievance concerned shortages, high prices, and the uneven distribution of fish and fresh fruit, two highly perishable foodstuffs, which were not rationed and distribution of which was only partially and ineffectively controlled. Discontent about fish was expressed continuously and at times covered almost the entire country, with complaints in up to 11 regions. Similarly, fresh fruit, including tomatoes, were mentioned in up to 10 regions. It was virtually impossible to prevent extortionate prices and unfair distribution of these foods and price control without rationing was thought to be 'worse than useless' since the food disappeared under the counter.[84] An example is a 'tomato ramp' which occurred in 1941. Prices, which had stood at about 3s. per pound, were controlled at between 1s.4d. and 1s.7d. from Monday, 23 June 1941; the 'previous week . . . tomatoes were plentiful . . . but on Monday morning none were to be found' leaving housewives astonished at this 'sudden and complete famine'.[85]

A third persistent wartime grievance was queuing, along with other shopping difficulties. According to Home Intelligence, queues were thought to weaken morale, with 'complaints of "peace talks being fostered in queues", . . . "growing anger" of working women who cannot queue' and they could be ' "hot-beds of anti-Semitism" [in the] belief, very generally held, that Jews "always manage to get hold of more food than other people". . . . "Opinion is steadily forming . . . that queues are an unhealthy symptom, and inconsistent with the underlying principles of rationing"'.[86] A Mass-Observer captures the heady atmosphere of a queue; being told that 'tabs' and 'chocolate' were available, he 'was off as quickly as he could on his bike. The shop was full, crowds waiting at both counters'. Having obtained twenty Players and two chocolate bars he left; 'A long queue formed outside the shop . . . about 100 people . . . gathered in a few minutes. . . . As he went out . . . he heard some remarks: "Oh Players!!" "Lucky, isn't he?" "20, by

[83] PRO, INF 1/292, Monthly summary of constant topics: general shortages, August 1942–December 1944. See also Longmate, *Home Front*, pp. 148–58; Hodgson, *Few Eggs and No Oranges*, pp. 379–80.   [84] PRO, INF 1/292, 14–21 May 1941.
[85] MO, TC, Food Box 3C, Note on Tomato Ramp, 25 June 1941.
[86] PRO, INF 1/292, 16–23 July 1941. Queuing and shopping difficulties, which of course persisted after the war, are discussed in more detail in Chapter 3, section 3.1.

Christ, they're well stocked!"[87] Wartime shortages resulted in at times acute tension between retailers and customers as well as widespread discontent among retailers who were the butt of much criticism but unable to control the situation.[88] Retailers were accused of 'preferential treatment', particularly of the "'favoured few who can place orders'", 'conditional sales', and other 'malpractices', such as 'articles going off the market as soon as the controlled price, point or coupon value is reduced'.[89]

Finally, wartime discontent centred on the continuation of so-called luxury feeding. There is plenty of evidence and, for example, the diaries of Harold Nicolson and Sir Henry Channon contain numerous references to luncheons and dinners in hotels, restaurants, and clubs.[90] Owing to limited supplies, luxury foods such as shellfish or game were never rationed and could be obtained at exorbitant prices throughout the period. Class tension during the war was embodied in widespread resentment of lavish eating by the rich as exemplified in a poem by columnist 'Sagittarius':

> 'The Passionate Profiteer to his Love'
>
> Come feed with me and be my love,
> And pleasures of the table prove,
> Where *Prunier* and *The Ivy* yield,
> Choice dainties of the stream and field.
>
> . . .
>
> On caviare my love shall graze,
> And plump on salmon mayonnaise,
> And browse at *Scott's* beside thy swain,
> On Lobster Newburg with champagne.
>
> . . .
>
> Come share at the *Savoy* with me,
> The menu of austerity.[91]

Home Intelligence noted 'ill-feeling about the advantage of the rich over the poor in the matter of "feeding out" ' and in October 1941 a majority (55 per cent) favoured giving up coupons for rationed foods eaten in restaurants.[92] In March 1942 there was a growing feeling that:

---

[87] MO, TC, Food, Box 3C, Shotley Bridge, Newcastle, Food Rationing and Supply Report, II, 21 June 1941.   [88] MO, FR, 581, Food Retailers' Reactions to Rationing, Feb. 1941.
[89] PRO, INF 1/292, 29 June–9 July and 2–9 Nov. 1943.
[90] R. Rhodes James (ed.), *Chips: The Diaries of Sir Henry Channon* (London, 1967); pp. 272, 325; H. Nicolson, *Diaries and Letters 1939–1945* (London, 1967), pp. 138, 249; see also Driver, *British at Table*, pp. 33–5; J. L. Hodson, *Home Front* (London, 1944), p. 25.
[91] After Christopher Marlowe, 'The Passionate Shepherd to his Love', Sagittarius, pseud. (Olga Katzin), *Quivers' Choice* (London, 1945) quoted in A. Sinclair, *The War Decade: An Anthology of the 1940s* (London, 1989), p. 220. Compare with a version about the post-war black market, see Chapter 4, pp. 158–9.
[92] PRO, INF 1/292, 13–20 Aug. 1941, see also 23 Feb.–3 Mar. 1942; *Gallup Polls*, p. 48; 32% were opposed and 13% registered no opinion.

'everything is not fair and equal and that therefore our sacrifices are not worth while'. In particular, there is some belief that the rich are less hit by rationing than 'ordinary people' for the following reasons:

(a) They can eat at expensive restaurants.
(b) They can afford to buy high priced goods . . . such as salmon and game.
(c) They can spend more on clothes and therefore use their coupons more advantageously.
(d) They receive preferential treatment in shops, as 'people giving large orders are favoured and the poorer people wanting "little bits" are refused'.[93]

In a Gallup poll, 76 per cent approved of the '"promise of a ruling restricting the cost of restaurant meals" [in] view of the feeling that "luxury feeding of all kinds should be controlled"'.[94] The Ministry of Food, concerned about morale, considered but rejected as impracticable rationing of restaurant meals, but a 5s. price limit on restaurant meals was introduced in 1942.[95] The effectiveness of this policy is doubtful, it was 'said to arouse "sarcastic comment"', there is no evidence that luxury feeding ceased, and resentment persisted.[96]

Wartime grievances essentially consisted of disagreements about the interpretation of fairness and the extent to which sacrifice could ever be equal. Fair shares and common hardship were central to propaganda and home front morale. Support for rationing along with public acceptance of food control depended on the degree to which these policies were thought to be fair. Fair shares was a compelling slogan and the 'Ministry of Food prided itself . . . on having achieved fair distribution of food'[97] but the public was not always convinced that the system was in fact fair. This is illustrated by discontent with the uneven distribution of unrationed foods, luxury feeding, and flat-rate rationing among manual workers. These grievances exposed a fundamental weakness in wartime food policy since, according to a Ministry of Food memorandum, '"Rationing is essentially inequitable; it provides the same quantity of an article for each person without any consideration of their needs or habits or of their capacity to secure alternatives"'.[98] To some extent 'rationing bore most heavily on those living alone [and] least upon those families whose capacity for mutual adjustment was greatest'.[99] However, the situation was complicated by the fact that single

[93] PRO, INF 1/292, 16–23 Mar. 1942.
[94] *Gallup Polls*, p. 56; 13% disapproved of a maximum price for restaurant meals and 11% registered no opinion; PRO, INF 1/292, 6–13 Apr. 1942.
[95] Hammond, *Food Volume I*, pp. 288–93.
[96] PRO, INF 1/292, 26 May–2 June 1942; see Hodson, *Home Front*, p. 25; Driver, *British at Table*, p. 33; PRO, INF 1/292, 9–16 June 1942.
[97] Hammond, *Food and Agriculture*, p. 232.
[98] This quotation is cited in ibid., pp. 232–3; and Hammond, *Food Volume I*, p. 125.
[99] Hammond, *Food and Agriculture*, p. 233.

people frequently had more money to spend on unrationed foods and whereas the system advantaged families with young children, flat-rate rations were not generous with regard to adolescent needs. Ready access to restaurant or canteen meals or the possibility to keep livestock and dig for victory could augment rations considerably. 'To some extent these various inequalities and privileges ... cancelled each other out'[100] since the urban population benefited from the former whereas rural areas primarily took advantage of the latter. Moreover, fair shares were of course bypassed in the black market, which is discussed in Chapter 4.

Despite these difficulties, rationing and food control were on the whole popular and discontent was eclipsed by general satisfaction. This contentment was reinforced by the fact that most ration levels remained stable from 1942 onwards and Lord Woolton, the Minister of Food, was immensely popular. In May 1942, 79 per cent thought he was doing a good job and he was regularly showered with 'bouquets for his handling of the food situation'.[101] According to one correspondent, quoted by postal censorship; 'if ever a man deserved a halo, it is Lord Woolton'.[102] Ultimately, food morale was maintained during the war, even though two-thirds thought that food quality was worse in 1944 than before the war, because people accepted the necessity of sacrifice for the duration.[103]

By contrast, after the war discontent was extensive and the food situation became a major topic of public debate. There was a clash between widespread feelings of deprivation and evidence suggesting that the nation was better fed and healthier than ever before. The magnitude of discontent is illustrated by surveys of attitudes regarding the adequacy of the diet. Whereas between 40 per cent and 50 per cent of male manual workers thought that they did not have enough food to keep fit in 1942–3,[104] Table 2.5 shows that the majority of the entire population felt that their diet was inadequate to keep in good health during 1948. This high percentage was observed when the general level of discontent about food was declining and after the worst shortages were over.[105] During 1948 there were no statistically relevant gender or economic differences but the middle age group was considerably more dissatisfied. In April and June 59–62 per cent of 40–59 year-olds believed that they did not have enough to eat and in March 1949 47 per cent of women (51 per cent of housewives) but only 42 per cent of men deemed that their diet was insufficient.[106] In line with earlier

[100] Hammond, *Food and Agriculture*, p. 234.
[101] *Gallup Polls*, p. 60; 12% did not think so and 9% registered no opinion; PRO, INF 1/292, 11–18 May 1942.   [102] PRO, INF 1/292, 8–15 Sept. 1942.
[103] *Gallup Polls*, p. 87; 9% thought that the quality of their family's food was better and 24% considered it to be the same.   [104] See Tables 2.3 and 2.4.
[105] See Figures 2.1 and 2.3; and Figure 1.2, Table 1.1, and Table 1.2.
[106] Only 34% of other women thought this. PRO, RG 23/96, 98, 100, 102, 105.

TABLE 2.5. *Attitudes to the adequacy of the diet, 1948–1949 (per cent)*

	Yes	No	Doubtful
Apr. 1948	36	55	7
June 1948	36	53	9
Aug. 1948	40	48	10
Oct. 1948	38	51	9
Mar. 1949	45	45	8

Notes: Respondents were asked: Do you feel you are getting enough food to keep you in good health? During each survey 2% were in poor health anyway. The table is based on random samples of 1,800–2,000 people per survey.
Sources: PRO, RG 23/96, 98, 100, 102, 105, Survey of Knowledge and Opinion about the Economic Situation.

findings, meat was mentioned most frequently by men whereas women mainly missed fats. Table 2.6 displays group differences in respect of the impact of the diet upon the ability to work. In accordance with wartime findings, more manual workers felt that an inadequate diet impaired their work, and housewives' attitudes were now closer to those of manual workers, indicating a substantial deterioration compared with wartime findings. These attitudes may well have impeded the post-war recovery. As the social survey concluded, the opinions were 'subjective and do not tell us whether people's ability to work hard is in fact being limited by lack of food, but whether this is so or not a widespread feeling that food is inadequate for a maximum effort cannot but have its effect on production'.[107]

According to contemporary surveys, the population was better fed and healthier than ever before. Even though consumption patterns changed, the nutrient content of the post-war diet actually improved in some instances and was well within British Medical Association (hereafter BMA) recommendations for most items.[108] While the proportion of total calories obtained from potatoes and grain products increased from 34 per cent before the war to 42 per cent in 1946 and the diet 'deteriorated in variety and palatability . . . supplies of calories have been well maintained and those of most nutrients increased'.[109] With the intensification of rationing income differentials in food intake were reduced and large families, precisely those who had been most vulnerable during the inter-war years, were supported most.[110] According to the BMA committee on nutrition, which reported in 1950, 'it would appear to be a fair conclusion that the health of the population as a whole, despite the trials and tribulations of recent years, has been well maintained' and vital

---

[107] PRO, RG 23/96.

[108] Ministry of Food, *The Urban Working-class Household Diet*, pp. 58–60; Ministry of Agriculture, Fisheries and Food, *Studies in Urban Household Diets*, pp. 19–22.

[109] British Medical Association, *Report of the Committee on Nutrition* (London, 1950), pp. 50, 52.

[110] See Hollingsworth, 'Rationing and Economic Constraints', pp. 262–6.

TABLE 2.6. *Attitudes to the relationship between diet and the ability to work, 1948 and 1949 (per cent)*

	Work harder	No difference	Doubtful
Total[a]			
Apr. 1948	59	36	5
Mar. 1949	52	42	6
Manual workers			
Apr. 1948	66	30	4
Mar. 1949	56	41	3
Non-manual workers			
Apr. 1948	52	44	4
Mar. 1949	46	49	5
Housewives			
Apr. 1948	59	34	7
Mar. 1949	53	38	9

[a] All working, excluding the retired and unoccupied.

Notes: Respondents were asked: If you personally could have more food or more variety in your food than you do now, do you feel you would be able to work harder, or would it make no difference to your work? The table is based on random samples of 1,743 and 1,804 people interviewed in Apr. 1948 and Mar. 1948.

Sources: PRO, RG 23/96, 105, Survey of Knowledge and Opinion about the Economic Situation.

statistics showed a continuous improvement throughout the period.[111] This trend was a consequence of the 'powerful combination of . . . full employment, food subsidies, "fair shares", price control and the welfare food schemes',[112] which formed a corner-stone of Labour's social policy.

The dilemma can be resolved by distinguishing objective evidence and subjective attitudes. Whereas there was little, if any, evidence of undernourishment or even starvation, *perceived deprivation* was intense, particularly during 1947 when the adequacy of the diet was extensively debated.[113] The overwhelming majority were dissatisfied with the post-war diet and, for instance, 75 per cent of the population thought that their present diet was worse than it had been just before the war with another 9 per cent doubtful in March 1949. There were few differences between economic groups and the social survey concluded:

So far as the objective situation is concerned there is little doubt that the effect of price control and rationing, in equalising the distribution of food, has been to increase the number of calories and nutrient value of the diet of the poorer section of the working class. So far as people's opinions are concerned, however, it is unlikely that such an advantage would offset the disadvantage of lack of variety in food or of limited choice.[114]

[111] BMA, *Report on Nutrition*, p. 91. For a discussion of vital statistics, see Chapter 3, section 3.2.   [112] Titmuss, *Problems of Social Policy*, p. 533.
[113] See Chapter 5, section 5.2; on housewives' problems see Chapter 3, section 3.1.
[114] PRO, RG 23/105; only 8% thought that their diet was better than before the war and another 8% that it was the same.

Grievances centred on the perceived deficiency in animal protein and fats. The post-war world food shortage coupled with Britain's balance of payments problems led to a deterioration in consumption of most popular foods and many rations were low and erratic.[115] Most people had expected rations to be increased after the war and there was little readiness among the public to tolerate further reductions, particularly of meat, eggs, and fats. Ration cuts of these foodstuffs were hardest to bear in 1945[116] and in April 1946 Sir Jack Drummond, government nutritional adviser, warned about the psychological effects of more reductions:

There are limits in regard to the supply of meat, fats, cheese, etc., below which it becomes so difficult for the housewife to provide palatable meals that ill-effects may be caused. I regard the current ration of meat, cheese and fats as representing about that level and it is probable that any further cuts may be reflected by loss of weight of adults ... simply because meals have become so much more unattractive that people will not eat sufficient to provide their daily energy requirements.[117]

Regardless of his opinion, rations were reduced further and it is this psychological context which provides the key to understanding post-war food discontent. In 1949 demand still focused on protein foods and fats,[118] but as the supply situation improved a growing proportion denied that there actually was a food shortage.[119] Subsequently matters deteriorated again. In spring 1951, following the reduction in the meat ration, there was a sharp increase in concern about food shortages and cuts in the meat ration were the most unpopular among food economies introduced in March 1951.[120] The uncertain international situation culminating in the outbreak of the Korean war postponed a return of confidence in the food situation before these surveys were discontinued.

In addition to the ration cuts the post-war period witnessed two highly controversial extensions, viz. bread rationing, operational from July 1946 until July 1948, and the control of potatoes during the winter and spring of 1947–8. The entire system of food control was based on ample supplies of these so-called buffer foods and any restrictions had been avoided at all costs during the war. Bread rationing represented the height of post-war austerity and the policy dealt a 'symbolic blow to civilian morale'.[121] The

[115] See Figure 1.2, and Tables 1.1 and 1.2.
[116] *Gallup Polls*, pp. 108, 112: reporting on two surveys of attitudes to potential and actual ration cuts. [117] PRO, MAF 99/1237, letter, 9 Apr. 1946.
[118] PRO, RG 23/105.
[119] This figure increased from 4% in May 1949 to 25% in July 1950, PRO, RG 23/106, 108, 110, 112.
[120] In March 1951, only 5% still denied the existence of the food shortage, PRO, RG 23/116; *Gallup Polls*, p. 243.
[121] Harris, 'War and Social History', p. 23.

introduction of bread rationing, the most politically motivated and contentious extension of food control, was vociferously debated and opposed by the Conservative party, the right-wing press, as well as housewives and bakers.[122] Initially, public opinion was divided, with 50 per cent disapproving and 41 per cent approving of the prospect of bread rationing in April.[123] According to a Mass-Observation survey of women only, 59 per cent opposed bread rationing, 21 per cent were in favour, and opposition was strongest among the unskilled working class.[124] After some weeks of intense debate opinion had shifted considerably. In July, just prior to the introduction of the policy, 40 per cent disapproved, with a third neutral, and 20 per cent in favour. Opposition was now strongest among the middle classes, the 40-plus age group, and men.[125] Following the introduction of bread rationing, support increased to one-third, with 41 per cent disapproving and 28 per cent neutral. Opposition remained concentrated among the middle classes, older people, and men. Women and the under-40s were evenly divided between approval, neutrality, and dislike and the unskilled working class now supported the policy.[126] Attitudes were more favourable after the introduction of the policy because generous ration levels meant that consumption was barely altered. A survey of housewives showed that 87 per cent had 'no difficulties whatsoever' with bread rationing.[127] Similarly, a Gallup poll found that 76 per cent managed very or fairly well in August and bread consumption among the Mass-Observation panel during the second week of rationing was identical to the prerationing level.[128]

Ironically, the first major attempt to relax food control, namely the abolition of personal points rationing in April 1949, also resulted in frustration and discontent. This was a consequence of a miscalculation of demand which was expected to be about 5 oz. per head per week after derationing compared with a weekly ration of 4 oz. According to a Gallup poll conducted in March only 39 per cent planned to buy more sweets after derationing with 45 per cent intending to buy the same amount.[129] In the event, 'consumer demand for chocolate and sugar confectionery far exceeded the supply, . . . the rush . . . by the general public was unprecedented in the

[122] See Chapter 5, section 5.2.   [123] *Gallup Polls*, p. 131; 9% registered no opinion.
[124] MO, TC, Food, Box 6B; Bread Rationing Survey of 106 Women in 5 London Boroughs, 28 June 1946.
[125] MO, TC, Food, Box 6C; Bread Rationing Survey of 62 People in 4 London Boroughs, 17–18 July 1946.
[126] MO, TC, Food, Box 6D; Bread Rationing Survey of 101 People in 4 London Boroughs, 14–16 Aug. 1946.   [127] PRO, MAF 156/274, Bread Survey Report, 17 Aug. 1946.
[128] *Gallup Polls*, p. 136; 18% managed with difficulty and only 6% managed badly;–MO, Mass-Observation Bulletin, n.s. No 3, July–Aug. 1946, based on 150 replies.
[129] *Gallup Polls*, p. 195; 9% intended to buy less sweets and 7% did not know the amount.

history of the trade ... and stocks ... were soon denuded'.[130] Shortages became severe, sweets disappeared under the counter, in June only 8 per cent were able to buy more whereas 57 per cent obtained less, and 66 per cent disapproved of derationing.[131] The ration was reintroduced at the former level in August. This episode illustrated the effects of premature deregulation and thereby enhanced the legitimacy of food rationing. Accordingly, the social survey concluded that the fiasco helped 'to lessen very substantially the frequency with which people complain about food shortages'.[132]

Finally, dissatisfaction focused on rising prices which should be set alongside small rations as a major food grievance during the late 1940s. In 1948 over 70 per cent found it more difficult to make ends meet than a year earlier. Worry about money was greater among housewives and married men than among other women and unmarried men.[133] For example, high food prices were mentioned by 49 per cent in February 1948, followed by anxiety about clothing and coal prices. However, 61 per cent of housewives named food prices, which scored only 23 per cent among unmarried men, 47 per cent of whom mentioned cigarette and tobacco prices. These figures show that 'the increased cost of living bears most heavily on those with family responsibilities and ... that unmarried men are the group least seriously affected by high prices'. Unmarried men's concern about the cost of cigarettes and tobacco was exceptional since the data were generally clear that 'complaints about the rising cost of living arise from difficulties in paying for necessities and are not due to a desire for luxury spending'.[134] A further question aimed to establish the significance of rationing and price constraints by asking whether people would be able to afford more at present prices if there were plenty to buy in the shops. In December 1947 just under two-thirds could not afford more and nearly three-quarters could not in March 1949.[135] Again those with family responsibilities and the lowest income group were least able to buy more, with the middle group (the bulk of the working class) only marginally behind. The higher-income group (the middle and highest-paid working class) possessed considerably more spending power with only 57 per cent unable to buy more in December 1947 but this position deteriorated and in March 1949 67 per cent could not afford more. Despite this growing concern about prices, a Gallup poll of March 1950 found that small rations were still the most important food grievance (32 per cent), followed by lack of variety (20 per cent), and high prices (19 per cent).[136]

[130] PRO, MAF 75/63, Account of the Operation of Personal Points Rationing 1942–1953.
[131] *Gallup Polls*, p. 201; 14% bought the same amount, 4% none, and 17% had not bothered or did not know; 26% approved of derationing and 8% registered no opinion.
[132] PRO, RG 23/108, Sept. 1949.
[133] PRO, RG 23/94–6, 98–102; see Figures 2.1–2.3.   [134] PRO, RG 23/94.
[135] PRO, RG 23/92, 94–6, 98–102, 105.   [136] *Gallup Polls*, p. 218.

Low food morale after the war was a consequence of frequent changes and volatile rations which amounted to a traumatic and disruptive experience in contrast with wartime stability. Rations of protein foods and fats dropped below the already sparse wartime levels, the psychological effect of this undermined faith in the adequacy of the diet among the majority of the population, and food became a central and contentious issue for the public. Middle-class expectations of a gradual return to pre-war standards were dashed but disillusionment extended far beyond the middle classes, and discontent among male manual workers was high. Many who benefited in objective nutritional terms under post-war food control were equally frustrated and in March 1949 only 8 per cent thought that their present diet was better than that before the war.[137] The middle-aged and those with family responsibilities were most dissatisfied, in contrast with the young and single who had few memories of pre-war life and limited responsibilities. Gender was a more important determinant of attitudes than class; and housewives in particular, who bore a disproportionate share of the burden of post-war austerity, emerged as one of the most disaffected sections of society.

Decontrol of food began in the late 1940s, but despite this relaxation ration take-up continued to be high and there were signs of penned-up demand. In 1950 over 90 per cent bought all of their rations and in June a majority (62 per cent and 57 per cent respectively) planned to buy more butter and meat if these foods came off the ration.[138] In May 1952 there was still little room for manoeuvre, take-up of sugar, tea, butter, and meat stood at over 90 per cent, that of bacon and margarine at over 80 per cent, and only sweets take-up was fairly low at 76 per cent. Moreover, 50 per cent hoped to buy more if these items came off the ration.[139] The second phase of decontrol began in autumn 1952 with derationing of tea, ham, and gammon, the abolition of the personal points scheme, and the lifting of controls on eggs in spring 1953. In the summer approximately 90 per cent still bought their entire sugar and butter ration, but only three-quarters took all their margarine and meat, and two-thirds all the bacon.[140] Sugar, fats, meat, and bacon were finally derationed between September 1953 and July 1954. After derationing, consumption increased for every item, with the sole exception of margarine, and intake of bread and potatoes declined as people switched to those foods they had missed most during the 1940s.

The evidence on attitudes towards decontrol as shortages receded at the

---

[137] PRO, RG 23/105.

[138] PRO, MAF 156/564, Estimated percentage take-up of rationed foods, March 1950–March 1951; *Gallup Polls*, p. 222.

[139] *Gallup Polls*, p. 270; 38% planned to buy the same, 4% less, and 8% did not know.

[140] Ibid., p. 304.

beginning of the 1950s is limited. The social survey suggested in March 1950 that:

A general improvement in the supply of consumer goods especially of food, has made people less inclined to view the domestic situation as one requiring special effort. . . . At the same time the appearance of more, and more varied, goods in the shops—although partly the *result* of rationing by the purse—has made people more conscious of what they are missing, and thus more inclined to *resent* rationing by the purse. This has contributed to increasing uncertainty about the wages issue, and to the steady shift of emphasis on to prices and the cost of living. The reasons for retaining controls have become less apparent as the existence of shortages has become less obvious, and this has resulted in an increase in suggestions for decontrol.[141]

A number of Gallup polls illustrate attitudes towards decontrol. After the lifting of controls on fish in May 1950, 27 per cent thought that choice was better but one in four also found that prices were higher. However, nearly half were unable to say and a fifth thought that there was no change. None the less, almost two-thirds did not want to see controls reintroduced.[142] In March 1953 opinion was almost evenly divided on the gradual disappearance of rationing and the return of the price mechanism—47 per cent were in favour of the policy while 43 per cent disagreed.[143] A year later only 28 per cent were opposed to derationing of fats and 59 per cent welcomed the prospect despite the expectation that butter prices would increase at the same time.[144] In January 1955, some months after all foodstuffs had been derationed, just over half were able to buy better food despite the fact that prices had gone up; however 40 per cent could not afford to buy the better food at the higher prices. Nevertheless, even among the minority who could not afford better food, almost three-quarters were opposed to a return of rationing and only 8 per cent of the population wanted rationing to be reintroduced.[145] During the early 1950s, when the need for rationing became less obvious, popular attitudes moved increasingly in favour of deregulation, more choice, and better quality of food, even if this was accompanied by higher prices.

2.2. CLOTHING AND MISCELLANEOUS CONSUMER GOODS

Civilian consumption of clothing, rationed from 1941 to 1949, and miscellaneous consumer goods was reduced dramatically during the Second

---

[141] PRO, RG 23/110 (emphasis in original).
[142] *Gallup Polls*, p. 220; with regard to choice, 7% thought it was worse, 46% did not know, 15% noted that prices were lower, and 40% were unable to say.
[143] Ibid., p. 290; 10% did not know.　　[144] Ibid., p. 314; 13% did not know.
[145] Ibid., pp. 341–2; 9% did not know whether they had bought better food.

World War and shortages especially of clothing were a persistent grievance throughout the 1940s.[146] The announcement of clothes rationing, in June 1941, 'came as a complete shock and surprise' but the initial public response was favourable.[147] According to a Mass-Observation survey 70 per cent approved of the policy[148] and people were 'willing to put up with it as . . . an essential part of the war effort'.[149] Those who had 'had enough money and foresight to lay in a good supply' greeted it with '"smug satisfaction"' and there was no delay in spotting 'methods of evading the payment of coupons'.[150] Indeed, illegal practices with regard to clothing coupons were extensive, particularly during the first year of rationing and the black market in clothing coupons was an endemic problem.[151] Mass-Observation found that 58–64 per cent were not affected by clothes rationing and only 4–8 per cent expected to be affected a lot. However, there were some notable gender and age differences; whereas 67 per cent of men thought they would be unaffected, only 54 per cent of women felt this. The figure was lowest among women under 30 (43 per cent) and highest among men under 30 (71 per cent).[152] Women were also three times more likely to be critical, anticipated stocking difficulties, and considered clothes rationing to be unfair to children and expectant mothers.[153]

Early criticism of clothes rationing questioned the fairness of the scheme. From the outset, there was 'a feeling that the advantage will tend to lie with those who can afford to buy a garment of good quality which requires the same number of coupons as a cheap article, but which will last twice as long'.[154] This absence of a link between quantity and quality led to class tension. A typical working-class comment was that 'all government plans are unfair to people with a limited income', and the issue was raised as one example of unequal sacrifice in spring 1942.[155] Consequently, boasts by government ministers Hugh Dalton, the President of the Board of Trade, and Ellen Wilkinson that they had not spent any coupons were greeted with derision: '"Will people in high places ever realise that poor people can't afford clothes that last for years and years?"'[156] The policy of flat-rate

---

[146] See Chapter 1, section 1.3, and Tables 1.6, 1.7, 1.9, and 1.10.

[147] Mass-Observation, *Clothes Rationing Survey: An Interim Report Prepared for the Advertising Service Guild* (London, 1941), p. 7.   [148] Ibid., p. 8.

[149] PRO, INF 1/292, 28 May–4 June 1941.

[150] Ibid., 28 May–4 June and 4–11 June 1941; see also MO, FR, 756, Clothes Rationing: First Reactions, June 1941; MO, FR, 791, Clothes Rationing: Based on War Diaries, July 1941.

[151] See Chapter 4, section 4.2.

[152] Mass-Observation, *Clothes Rationing Survey*, pp. 68–9; the surveys were conducted in Worcester, London, and Bolton and based on samples of 300 each.

[153] Ibid., p. 61; PRO, INF 1/292, 4–11 June 1941; MO, FR, 756.

[154] PRO, INF 1/292, 28 May–4 June 1941.

[155] Mass-Observation, *Clothes Rationing Survey*, p. 63; PRO, INF 1/292, 16–23 Mar. 1942 (see note 93 above).

[156] PRO, INF 1/292, 2–9 Mar., 13–20 Apr. 1943.

individual rations caused unprecedented problems for public dignitaries and indeed anybody who required special clothes for work. Doctors and medical students voiced their concern immediately but apart from civilian uniform wearers such as members of the Civil Defence Services, fire services, or police there were few concessions.[157] Newly appointed High Court judges and senior clergy received additional coupons and initially mayors and may-oresses were also granted concessions. Requests could be substantial and in August 1943 the mayor-elect of Blackpool asked for an additional 328 coupons for himself (equivalent to nearly seven years' consumption at 48 coupons per annum) and 178 for his wife (nearly four years' consumption), while others asked for a few extra shirts, gloves, and stockings. From the summer of 1943 all requests were rejected 'owing to the increasing strin-gency of supplies' in a standard reply:

The only two classes in the civilian population for whom special provision can be made are the children . . . and the industrial workers . . . In time of war a relaxation of conventional standards of dress is accepted by all, and Mayors and Mayoresses, many of whom have only limited supplies of clothing, are making do with what they have and are performing their duties most willingly.[158]

The administration of supplementary coupons for industrial workers ini-tially caused tension within the working class. During the first year of rationing a generous issue of supplementary coupons to underground coal-miners generated 'strong discontent' among other groups of workers.[159] Subsequently, all manual workers received a supplement of 10 coupons, with an additional coupon pool administered by works committees. This system was accepted as fair and discontent subsided.[160] Although children were also granted supplementary coupons and other concessions, mothers' difficulties with children's clothes and particularly footwear became a per-sistent grievance under rationing.[161]

Furthermore, there were widespread complaints about clothes rationing following the cut in ration levels and the inclusion of household linen within the rationing scheme in autumn 1942. In stark contrast with Dalton's exhortation that 'Any sacrifice of comfort or appearance, which clothes rationing may bring to any of us, will, I am sure, be cheerfully borne, in order that victory may come sooner', the Home Intelligence monthly sum-mary of constant topics observed perpetual and extensive discontent with

[157] PRO, INF 1/292, 4–11 June 1941; Hargreaves and Gowing, *Civil Industry and Trade*, pp. 322–3.

[158] PRO, BT 64/1444, Applications for Supplementary Clothing Coupons from Public Dignitaries. [159] PRO, INF 1/292, 9–16 June 1942.

[160] Hargreaves and Gowing, *Civil Industry and Trade*, pp. 318–20.

[161] See Chapter 3, section 3.2.

clothes rationing.[162] Between autumn 1942 and December 1944 complaints
about the inadequacy of clothing coupons and demands for additional
coupons for household linen were mentioned regularly in 8–12 out of 13
regions. These complaints were less vociferous only in the winter of
1942–3, and during 1944 the issue was raised in 10 or more regions
throughout most of the year. While satisfaction with food rationing
increased from mid-war onwards as ration levels stabilized, there was no
shift towards contentment with regard to the clothing situation in Home
Intelligence weekly morale reports. In October 1942, rationing of towels
was described as 'the last word' and housewives from nine regions were dissatisfied. 'Furnishing material on clothing coupons is reported to have been
rather a "sore point all along", but towels is "really a heavy blow". There is
an increased demand for household ration cards'.[163] These grievances were
repeated over and over again. For instance in April 1943, housewives who
'"loyally economised in the early days of the war" feel that if they had spent
the money three years ago they would not now have to surrender coupons
to replenish stocks, while people who had then bought heavily are "sitting
pretty"'.[164] In the summer, Dalton's suggestion of further ration cuts was
greeted with 'consternation' since the 'minimum has already been reached'
and 'Contrasts [were] drawn between the Government's handling of the
food and clothing situations'.[165] Regardless of this, the ration was cut further in September 1943 and clothing difficulties continued to be a major
topic on the home front. For example in July 1944, people were 'finding it
"increasingly difficult to keep themselves even respectable"'. Housewives
from 11 regions demanded a 'special coupon allowance for household
replacements'. Nine regions reported the shortage of 'reasonably priced
sheets' and some women were 'said to have been trying to buy sheets for two
years'.[166] The problem was particularly severe among the poorer sections of
the working class whose stocks of clothing and household linen were well
below those of higher-income groups.[167] The added burden placed on
women by rationing was indicated by the fact that, after shoes and
stockings, 42 per cent mentioned towels and 35 per cent curtains as the item
they would buy if rationing were to end, with even higher proportions
among poorer working-class women, but men only mentioned clothing for
themselves.[168]
    Male and female attitudes towards clothes rationing and clothing
economies diverged, not only because women were primarily responsible for

---

[162] Foreword, Board of Trade, *Clothing Coupon Quiz* (4th edn., London, 1943); PRO, INF 1/292,
Home Intelligence Monthly Summary of Constant Topics: Clothing Difficulties, Aug. 1942–Dec.
1944.
[163] PRO, INF 1/292, 6–13 Oct., 27 Oct.–3 Nov. 1942.   [164] Ibid., 13–20 Apr. 1943.
[165] Ibid., 13–20 July 1943.   [166] Ibid., 18–20 July 1944.   [167] PRO, BT 64/4084, 4086.
[168] PRO, BT 64/4084.

household linen and children's clothes, but more importantly because women tended to be more concerned about their appearance.[169] Female demand for fashionable clothes and beauty products, stimulated by women's magazines and the cinema, was high on the eve of war. As a result of rising living standards coupled with falling prices due to the spread of mass production and simpler styles, these products were within reach of ever wider social groups, and age rather than income became the most important determinant of consumption.[170] During the war the 'beauty as duty' discourse of the 1930s became elevated as a critical element in the maintenance of morale among both women and men, including those fighting abroad.[171] Women responded enthusiastically and the widespread aspiration of an attractive, fashionable appearance is illustrated for example by the extensive use of cosmetics. According to a wartime social survey, two-thirds of all women applied cosmetics. They were used by 90 per cent of the under-30s but only 37 per cent of women over 45. Regular use of cosmetics was high among clerical and distributive workers (85 per cent), somewhat lower among factory workers (75 per cent), and lowest among housewives, the retired, and unoccupied women (55 per cent).[172] During the war demand for cosmetics was not only high but rising and, with output restricted, cosmetics became subject to extensive black market dealings despite continuous efforts by the Board of Trade to curtail illegal practices.[173] Demand for cosmetics was high since women focused on elaborate make-up, inventive hairstyles, and coupon-free accessories to counterbalance the limitations of their wardrobe. Wartime style, distinguished by short skirts and a severe, square silhouette—in contrast with the glamour of the 1930s—was influenced by a military look and economical in design. A Mass-Observation report of 1943 noted that female acquiescence in these restrictions was a temporary phenomenon. Wartime clothing economies had resulted in:

a tendency to wear older, shabbier clothes. But while women are very clear that, once restrictions are removed, they will return to buying clothes similar to those bought before the war, and will be little affected by newly acquired liking of simpler,

[169] P. Kirkham, 'Fashioning the Feminine: Dress, Appearance and Femininity in Wartime Britain', in C. Gledhill and G. Swanson (eds.), *Nationalising Femininity: Culture, Sexuality and British Cinema in the Second World War* (Manchester, 1996), pp. 152–74.

[170] These issues are discussed in more detail in I. Zweiniger-Bargielowska, 'Women under Austerity: Fashion in Britain during the 1940s', in M. Donald and L. Hurcombe (eds.), *Gender and Material Culture: Representations of Gender from Prehistory to the Present* (Macmillan, 1999).

[171] P. Kirkham, 'Beauty and Duty: Keeping up the Home Front', in P. Kirkham and D. Thoms (eds.), *War Culture: Social Change and Changing Experience in World War Two Britain* (London, 1995), pp. 13–14.

[172] PRO, RG 23/17, Wartime Social Survey: Retail Services and Shortages, May 1942–Mar. 1943.

[173] See Chapter 4, section 4.3.

more informal clothes, men welcome the release from compulsory smartness. They hope, when they speak about it, that it has come to stay.[174]

The depth of female disaffection is illustrated by the rapid adoption of the New Look, characterized by long, flowing skirts, in the face of official condemnation in the late 1940s. While rationing and high prices precluded extensive purchases, women altered their existing clothes by adding waistbands or dropping hems in order to acquire the New Look which was perceived as a 'symbol of a more decorative, more leisured [and] more feminine way of life'.[175]

Despite a more relaxed attitude, men were by no means immune to the dictates of fashion, as demonstrated by the controversy over trouser turn-ups. The simplified styles prescribed by austerity regulations, introduced to save labour and materials in spring 1942, included a prohibition of trouser turn-ups.[176] Confronting 'some grumbling' in March 1943 Dalton highlighted the contribution of this measure which had saved 'millions of square feet [of material] a year'. He went on:

There are no turn-ups in either the Army, Navy or Air Force and I should have thought a style that was good enough for the Fighting Forces should have been good enough for civilians in wartime. . . . There can be no equality of sacrifice in this war. Some must lose their lives and limbs; others only the turn-ups on their trousers.[177]

The policy was difficult to enforce and evasion was common, particularly 'in bespoke tailoring . . . [since] trousers could be made longer than necessary and then turned up at home'.[178] Lyttelton, the previous president, described it as 'ineffective and vexatious'.[179] In fact, men who had risked their lives were not prepared to sacrifice their trouser turn-ups and in February 1944 all austerity restrictions on men's outer clothes were removed because 'it was decided that the demobilised soldiers could not be offered civilian clothing in austerity styles'.[180] Austerity suits sold poorly and in 'order to clear stocks [they] had to be down-pointed and some were sold to the Ministry of Supply for relief purposes'.[181]

Gender differences in attitudes to clothes are again illustrated with regard to post-war expectations. Among women there was a strong desire to 'buy

[174] MO, FR, 1867, Mass-Observation Bulletin: Rationing and Changed Clothing Habits: Men, July 1943; see also MO, FR, 1866, Mass-Observation Bulletin: Rationing and Changed Clothing Habits: Women, July 1943.   [175] MO, FR, 3095, New Look: Panel Reactions, March 1949.
[176] Hargreaves and Gowing, *Civil Industry and Trade*, pp. 436–40; Longmate, *Home Front*, p. 158.   [177] H. Dalton, *The Fateful Years: Memoirs 1931–1945* (London, 1957), p. 410.
[178] Hargreaves and Gowing, *Civil Industry and Trade*, p. 439.
[179] O. Lyttelton (Viscount Chandos), *The Memoirs of Lord Chandos* (London, 1962), p. 206.
[180] Hargreaves and Gowing, *Civil Industry and Trade*, p. 439.
[181] Ibid.; restrictions on men's socks and other hosiery were removed at the end of 1945 and in early 1946 but all restrictions on women's clothes continued until March and April 1946.

new clothes in large quantities', at least among Mass-Observation's mainly middle and artisan class sample. A typical response was, 'after the war is over I would like to scrap all my clothing and get a brand new outfit'.[182] Men were generally less interested in the topic, there is no evidence of extensive buying plans, and the tendency was towards 'making clothes last longer, buying better quality, and wearing simpler clothes'.[183] Clothing occupied a prominent place on women's post-war shopping list.[184] In the event, expectations of a post-war spending spree were disappointed, particularly during the first year of peace when the clothes ration reached its lowest ever level. As stocks became exhausted and clothes increasingly threadbare, clothing difficulties scored over 10 per cent as a main family or personal problem in 1948 and even men became concerned.[185] As one man, who like many 'never did worry much about clothes', put it, 'as I economised on them in the early days of the war I am now getting very shabby'.[186]

In September 1948 footwear, children's clothes, and some miscellaneous items were derationed, there was a further relaxation in March 1949, and clothes rationing was finally abolished in May. Demand for clothes was certainly high and according to three Gallup polls conducted in October of 1947, 1949, and 1950 clothing topped the list as the first item people wanted to buy for their own use.[187] In practice clothes purchases were prevented by high prices and in June 1948 lack of money was already a more important factor than the shortage of coupons, as indicated in Table 2.7. High prices bore most heavily upon housewives and the lower economic group, whereas single people and the higher group were still considerably affected by coupon restrictions. In January 1949 nearly three-quarters were prevented from buying clothes by high prices and housewives and the lowest economic group rated prices even higher. Consequently, in March 1949 85 per cent were unable to buy any clothes as a result of recent rationing relaxations, 53 per cent claimed they would buy more if purchase tax were removed or reduced, and clothes again topped the list of items which people wanted to buy.[188] Hence, the dream of a new post-war wardrobe was shattered in the face of rising prices and high taxes at the end of the 1940s.

Over and above clothes rationing and the austerity regulations, civilian clothing was controlled under the utility scheme introduced in 1941 in order to save labour and materials by encouraging long production runs.

---

[182] MO, FR, 1866, Mass-Observation Bulletin: Rationing and Changed Clothing Habits: Women, July 1943; see also MO, FR, 2046, Women's Clothes in Chester, Mar. 1944.

[183] MO, FR, 1867, Mass-Observation Bulletin: Rationing and Changed Clothing Habits: Men, July 1943.

[184] MO, FR, 2066, Post-war Buying, Apr. 1944.   [185] See Figures 2.2 and 2.3.

[186] MO, FR, 2502, Clothes Buying and Wearing: Use of Coupons and Effect of Rationing, July 1947.   [187] *Gallup Polls*, pp. 162–3, 210, 232.

[188] Ibid., p. 195; 15% bought additional clothes, 29% were unaffected by purchase tax, and 18% did not know whether they would buy more if it were reduced or removed.

TABLE 2.7. *Attitudes to clothes buying, June 1948–January 1949 (per cent)*

	Coupons	Money
Total		
June 1948	35	47
July 1948	31	53
Aug. 1948	22	60
Oct. 1948	14	68
Jan. 1949	14	73
Men		
All July 1948	32	50
Oct. 1948	17	63
Married July 1948	30	52
Single July 1948	37	43
Women		
All July 1948	30	55
Oct. 1948	12	71
Housewives July 1948	27	57
Jan. 1949	N/A	77
Others July 1948	39	46
Jan. 1949	N/A	66
Economic group		
Lower July 1948	20	58
Aug. 1948	14	67
Jan. 1949	N/A	79
Middle July 1948	28	57
Aug. 1948	21	64
Jan. 1949	N/A	71
Higher July 1948	38	47
Aug. 1948	25	56
Jan. 1949	N/A	55

Notes: Respondents were asked: In getting the clothes you want, is your main trouble too few coupons or not enough money? The percentages do not add to 100 because a small number were either doubtful or able to get all the clothes they wanted. The lower economic group consists mainly of old-age pensioners and the low paid, the bulk of the working class is included in the middle group, and the higher group includes the middle class and highest-paid working class. The table is based on a random sample of just under 2,000 people per survey.
Sources: PRO, RG 23/98–100, 102, 104, Survey of Knowledge and Opinion about the Economic Situation.

Utility clothes, which were price controlled and exempt from purchase tax, accounted for about four-fifths of clothes produced during and after the war and detailed specifications were intended to ensure that quality was maintained or even improved. Despite an apparently favourable initial response,[189] complaints about the '"poor quality" and "shoddiness" of some utility clothes' were frequent throughout the war.[190] For example, utility stockings were said 'to be shapeless and absolutely to be lacking in

---

[189] MO, FR, 1143, Utility Clothing Scheme, Mar. 1942; TC, Personal Appearance and Clothes, Box 4/E, Utility Clothes, Mar. 1942.   [190] PRO, INF 1/292, 22–9 Sept. 1942.

reasonable durability. The popular view is that they are just a waste of coupons'.[191] Home Intelligence reported in April 1943 that at 'first people were prepared to trust the utility mark—now they fight shy of it' and the severity of discontent is indicated by the monthly summary of constant topics.[192] In the second half of 1943 and throughout 1944 complaints about utility clothing were frequently mentioned in between four and six regions and, occasionally, in eight or nine out of 13 regions. Not surprisingly, although 80 per cent had bought some utility clothes in August 1944, two-thirds did not want the policy to be continued after the war.[193] The utility scheme was extended to furniture and other household items. In contrast with clothing, utility furniture was popular, between half and two-thirds of housewives who owned or had ordered utility furniture expressed 'unqualified satisfaction', and about two-thirds considered it 'well designed for its functional purpose'.[194] In the face of rising prices utility furniture remained popular and 60 per cent were in favour of continuing the scheme, primarily because prices were controlled in 1950.[195] At the same time, attitudes towards utility clothes became more favourable. In two surveys conducted in 1948 and 1950 half supported an increase in utility clothes and the percentage wanting less declined from 28 to 15 per cent. There was little difference between economic groups and utility clothes were more popular among women and married men, precisely those groups most affected by high prices.[196] Irrespective of this increase in public approval, the utility schemes were abolished by the new Conservative government in 1952.

During this period shortages of furniture and miscellaneous consumer goods were intense and demand exceeded supply throughout the 1940s. Whereas the allocation of furniture, household textiles, and carpets was governed by a priority scheme, with regard to miscellaneous consumer goods any form of rationing was impracticable and consumers essentially had to compete with each other for whatever supplies were available. It is not surprising that discontent about miscellaneous shortages featured prominently among Home Intelligence constant topics. A typical list included 'crockery, glass-ware and hardware, hot-water bottles, elastic and everything made of rubber, prams, bicycles and type-writers, blankets, sanitary towels, hair pins, combs, . . . cigarettes, tobacco, matches, flints,

---

[191] Ibid. Similar grievances were mentioned regularly; see also MO, FR, 2046, Women's Clothes in Chester, Mar. 1944.

[192] PRO, INF 1/292, 8–15 Dec. 1942; ibid., Monthly Summary of Constant Topics: Clothing Difficulties, June 1943–Dec. 1944.

[193] *Gallup Polls*, pp. 93–4; 19% had not bought any utility clothes (excluding stockings), 1% did not know, and 33% wanted the policy to be continued after the war.

[194] NCL, The Social Survey, Furniture: An Inquiry Made for the Board of Trade, n.s. 63, May 1945.   [195] RG 23/164, Utility and the Public, Oct. 1950.

[196] PRO, RG 23/99, July 1948; RG 23/164, Utility and the Public, Oct. 1950.

lighters and torch batteries [and] razor blades'.[197] Between August 1942 and December 1944 there were continuous and occasionally widespread grumbles about the unavailability of crockery, glass, and kitchenware. Again and again there were complaints about shortages ranging from matches and lighters, torch batteries, razor blades, and alarm clocks to shoe polish, toilet paper, combs, and toothbrushes. These shortages certainly added to the housewife's burdens and there was little improvement until the end of the 1940s. Demand for furniture was high, especially among women who placed furnishings on the top of their post-war shopping list.[198] In October 1947 furniture and household equipment occupied second place, after clothing, on the list of things people wanted to buy. Women mentioned furniture nearly three times more frequently than men did.[199] This high level of demand was often unsatisfied and in spring 1947 a small majority expected that they would be unable to get anything.[200] The priority scheme was abolished in 1948 and floor coverings and household textiles were decontrolled in 1949. Despite decontrol, in 1950 there was still a major discrepancy between what people needed and what they were able to buy, 37 per cent thought they would be unable to get anything, and high prices had replaced shortages as the major limiting factor.[201] As in the case of clothing, there was no post-war spending spree on furniture and household goods, and pre-war consumption levels were surpassed only in the mid-1950s.

During the war the public approved of rationing and controls of consumption as the best method to ensure fair shares. The fair shares policy was welcomed in principle, but support for rationing was neither universal nor unqualified. Most people were opposed to further restrictions as well as an extension of rationing and attitudes varied between different schemes. With regard to food control, initial discontent gave way to general satisfaction from 1942 onwards. By contrast, first responses to clothes rationing were favourable but as stocks were exhausted and the ration was reduced the issue became a major wartime grumble.

Universal sacrifice and egalitarianism are central to the myth of the home front, but in the event sacrifice was uneven and, at times, substantial social groups did not consider the system to be fair. The ambitious claims of wartime propaganda based around the theme of fair shares stood in stark contrast with a more equivocal experience provided by the implementation of rationing policy. The equity of this policy was in many ways questionable since it took insufficient account of diversity with regard to stocks, access to unrationed goods, as well as varying requirements between different social groups. These shortcomings are illustrated by endemic discontent among

---

[197] PRO, INF 1/292, 19–26 Jan. 1942.   [198] MO, FR, 2066, Post-war Buying, Apr. 1944.
[199] *Gallup Polls*, pp. 162–3, 30% of women and 11% of men mentioned furniture and household equipment.   [200] Ibid., p. 156, May 1947.
[201] Ibid., p. 230.

male manual workers who felt discriminated against by flat-rate rations, and the expansion of industrial canteens was not sufficient to compensate for this grievance. Among women wartime grievances focused on the unfairness of clothes rationing. Class tension was exemplified by resentment against luxury feeding, high prices, and the uneven distribution of unrationed food, along with the failure of clothes rationing to distinguish between quality and quantity. The notion of common purpose on the home front has to be qualified in view of the widely held opinion that sacrifice affected some more than others and that the rich could still get what they wanted. The middle class and better-off working class gave up most, and income differentials in consumption patterns were reduced. However, these did not disappear and consumption standards were never genuinely equal. The rich who possessed large stocks and could afford high-priced unrationed goods and frequent restaurant meals were least affected by reductions in consumption. By contrast, although the diet of the poorest improved in terms of basic nutrients, austerity also hit the poor. With low stocks and limited funds, they were least able to buy the more desirable unrationed foods as well as high-quality clothing economical in coupons or a range of household goods in short supply.

Despite these areas of discontent illustrating the complexity of wartime attitudes, consumption never fell below a certain minimum and the population generally acquiesced in the need for sacrifice for the duration. Ultimately, morale on the home front was of course maintained and Britain won the war. Post-war demand for food and consumer goods was high and victory only served to reinforce expectations of a gradual return to pre-war consumption standards. These expectations were undermined by the continuation and indeed intensification of rationing and austerity after the war coupled with unprecedented levels of taxation in peacetime. When the shortages receded at the end of the decade remaining hopes of a return to the comfortable living of the interwar years were finally dashed by the high rate of inflation in the late 1940s and early 1950s. A return to affluence was only achieved from the mid–1950s onwards after inflation had been reduced and when wartime controls on personal consumption were finally abolished.

Disillusionment with the post-war situation was high among the middle classes who suffered as much from actual as perceived deprivation expressed in the 'magic, nostalgia-laden phrase, "before the war"'.[202] This 'plight of the middle classes'[203] was summed up well by a middle-class housewife as the loss of 'things that made life gracious in the past'.[204] However, resentment against the continuation of austerity went well beyond the middle class.

---

[202] Hopkins, *New Look*, p. 154. [203] Ibid., p. 153.
[204] MO, FR, 3037, Middle Class: Why?, Dec. 1948.

Wide sections of the working class were equally frustrated by the persistence of restrictions on personal consumption. According to a Gallup poll conducted in November 1947, 62 per cent preferred their lifestyle before the war to the present.[205] This general disillusionment with post-war life contributed to low morale during the late 1940s and discontent progressively focused on the Labour government. Despite Labour's achievement of full employment and the creation of the welfare state, the continuation of controls on consumption alienated many, including some of the government's erstwhile supporters. Since the principal justification for sacrifice—winning the war—no longer applied, the wartime political consensus on austerity was replaced by fierce controversy which was central to the party political battle during the post-war years.

In many ways gender and marital status differences in attitudes towards rationing and austerity were more significant than variations between social classes. Anxiety about the post-war situation was consistently higher among women and also among the middle aged and married, in other words, those with family responsibilities. Disillusionment was highest among housewives, who were very much at the receiving end of austerity. They did most of the queuing and it was their responsibility to manage the household and provide meals for the family. After the war there was little readiness to tolerate further hardship but housewives' position was made more arduous by ration cuts and the continuation of shortages. Women's experience of and attitudes towards austerity, including the plight of housewives after the war, are discussed next and the political implications of popular discontent with post-war austerity are explored in Chapter 5.

[205] *Gallup Polls*, p. 165; 31% preferred the present and 7% registered no opinion.

3
Women

The discussion of popular attitudes has highlighted gender differences and the purpose of this chapter is to examine the gendered implications of the austerity policy by focusing on women's experiences and attitudes. Women in their role as housewives and mothers were primarily responsible for implementing the policy on a daily basis. Rationing and shortages of food and miscellaneous consumer goods added to the housewife's burdens while the introduction of welfare foods contributed towards improving the health of mothers and children. During the 1940s housewifery and motherhood acquired an enhanced sense of national importance since the successful implementation of rationing and other economy measures was vital in maintaining public health and morale. Housewifery was no longer regarded as a private concern but rather as a central component of the war effort and post-war reconstruction. Thus the housewife's battle on the kitchen front was as critical to victory as that of the soldier or the worker in essential industry. This pivotal female contribution was recognized by the government, resulting in an unprecedented outpouring of propaganda aimed to help women to adapt their housewifery skills and child-rearing techniques to wartime conditions as well as to raise standards generally. For example, a Ministry of Information pamphlet declared that housewives' 'part in the war is no mean one. Many vital decisions for the home front have been taken by Ministers of the Crown for the whole nation, but the housewives have had the task of translating national economy into domestic practice'. According to Woolton:

'When I was given the responsibility for this work of keeping the nation fed during the war . . . I knew that failure . . . meant that all the heroism and sacrifice of brave men would be in vain.' That sacrifice was not demanded largely owing to 'the understanding and fortitude of the housewives of this country'.[1]

Women were not passive recipients of government policy and propaganda and attitudes varied depending on the policy as well as the income group. Moreover, women's attitudes towards austerity changed over time and wartime patriotic acceptance gave way to disillusionment and discontent among many housewives during the late 1940s.

---

[1] PRO, INF 2/5, Ministry of Information, *British Women at War* (London, 1944).

Housewifery and motherhood during and after the Second World War was a popular aspiration for many women and should not necessarily be perceived as passive acquiescence in their traditional role prescribed by patriarchy and gilded by a mindless consumerism from the 1950s onwards. As a result of women's principal role in the austerity policy domesticity became a site of political and economic power and a basis of female citizenship. Housewives became a major political force after the war and their discontent with the continuation of austerity had important political and electoral consequences. Housewives were courted by both Labour and the Conservatives, and the women's vote was crucial in determining the outcome of the early post-war general elections.

There is a considerable literature on women during the 1940s, but little has been written about housewives.[2] The focus is on female employment and particularly changing participation rates, conscription, and the post-war recruitment drive.[3] A related issue is the debate about equal pay, which has implications for women's political allegiance and gender differences in voting behaviour.[4] Recent accounts have explored shifting gender roles and identities as well as the construction of memory.[5] Finally, women's appearance, fashion, and the cultural and political implications of the New Look

---

[2] The obvious exceptions are social histories including: Longmate, *How We lived Then*; Addison, *Now the War is Over*; S. Cooper, 'Snoek Piquante', in M. Sissons and P. French, *Age of Austerity* (London, 1963); and contemporary diaries, such as R. Broad and S. Flemming (eds.), *Nella Last's War: A Mother's Diary 1939–45* (Bristol, 1981); Donnelly, *Mrs Milburn's Diaries*. Recent studies are D. Morgan and M. Evans, *The Battle for Britain: Citizenship and Ideology in the Second World War* (London, 1993); E. McCarty, 'Attitudes to Women and Domesticity in England, c.1939–1955', unpublished D.Phil. thesis, University of Oxford (1994).

[3] P. Summerfield, *Women Workers in the Second World War: Production and Patriarchy in Conflict* (London, 1984); G. Braybon and P. Summerfield, *Out of the Cage: Women's Experiences in Two World Wars* (London, 1987); M. Pugh, *Women and the Women's Movement in Britain 1914–1959* (London, 1992); H. L. Smith, 'The Womanpower Problem in Britain during the Second World War', *Historical Journal* 27 (1984); H. L. Smith, 'The Effect of War on the Status of Women', in H. L. Smith (ed.), *War and Social Change: British Society and the Second World War* (Manchester, 1986); Tomlinson, *Democratic Socialism and Economic Policy*; S. L. Carruthers, '"Manning the Factories": Propaganda and Policy on the Employment of Women 1939–1947', *History* 75 (1990); Crofts, *Coercion or Persuasion?*; S. Bruley, '"A very Happy Crowd": Women in Industry in South London in World War Two', *History Workshop Journal* 44 (1997), pp. 58–76.

[4] H. L. Smith, 'The Politics of Conservative Reform: The Equal Pay for Equal Work Issue, 1945–1955', *Historical Journal* 35 (1992); B. Campbell, *The Iron Ladies: Why Do Women Vote Tory?* (London, 1987); J. Hinton, 'Women and the Labour Vote, 1945–50', *Labour History Review* 57 (1992); J. Hinton, 'Militant Housewives: The British Housewives' League and the Attlee Government', *History Workshop Journal* 38 (1994); I. Zweiniger-Bargielowska, 'Explaining the Gender Gap: The Conservative Party and the Women's Vote, 1945–1964', in M. Francis and I. Zweiniger-Bargielowska (eds.), *The Conservatives and British Society, 1880–1990* (Cardiff, 1996).

[5] J. G. de Groot, '"I Love the Scent of Cordite in Your Hair": Gender Dynamics in Mixed Anti-Aircraft Batteries during the Second World War', *History* 82 (1997), pp. 73–92; P. Summerfield, *Reconstructing Women's Wartime Lives: Discourse and Subjectivity in Oral Histories of the Second World War* (Manchester, 1998); L. Noakes, *War and the British: Gender, Memory and National Identity, 1939–1991* (London, 1998).

have received attention.[6] The neglect of housewives is somewhat surprising given the fact that even at the height of mobilization they still accounted for the majority of women.[7] This indifference, criticized by those scholars who have focused on the topic, is not confined to 1940s Britain notwithstanding that women throughout history have spent much of their lives in the domestic context of housewifery and child rearing. Davidoff, writing in the 1970s, deplored the fact that housework 'was not only neglected but, on all levels, treated with contempt. The idea of asking serious questions about housework seemed unthinkable.' Davidoff cites the example of one woman's attempt to discuss the issue which resulted in her husband's comment, 'Housework? Oh my God, how trivial can you get. A paper about housework!'[8]

This chapter, which aims to redress this imbalance, uses a range of neglected sources generated in the exceptional circumstances of total war when the:

state was dependent upon the willing co-operation of households ... To secure this co-operation it became necessary for the state to demonstrate a close interest in the ordinary domestic lives of its citizens, both male and female. Thus women became the target of an extraordinary barrage of government advice, which took the form of information about diet, child care, the care of the home and those endless other issues that can be related to domestic life.[9]

In addition to the propaganda and information literature that was targeted at housewives and mothers, social surveys monitored their experiences relating to rationing, shortages, shopping difficulties, and special provision for mothers and children. Social surveys and Home Intelligence weekly morale reports during the war also explore attitudes towards the austerity policy as well as female morale more generally. Mass-Observation surveys and Gallup polls provide a useful supplement to government sources. Finally, women's magazines and contemporary advice manuals aimed at housewives and mothers are of some interest but have to be treated

[6] Kirkham, 'Beauty and Duty', pp. 13–28; Gledhill and Swanson, *Nationalising Femininity*; A. Partington, 'The Days of the New Look: Consumer Culture and Working-class Affluence', in J. Fyrth (ed.), *Labour's Promised Land? Culture and Society in Labour Britain, 1945–51* (London, 1995); Zweiniger-Bargielowska, 'Women under Austerity'.

[7] Smith, 'The Effect of War on the Status of Women', p. 210.

[8] Quoted in L. Davidoff, 'The Rationalisation of Housework', in L. Davidoff, *Worlds Between: Historical Perspectives on Gender and Class* (Cambridge, 1995), p. 73, reprint of a chapter first published in D. Leonard Barker and S. Allen (eds.), *Dependence and Exploitation in Work and Marriage* (London, 1976). See also A. Oakley, *Housewife* (London, 1974), p. 6; C. Davidson, *A Woman's Work is Never Done: A History of Housework in the British Isles, 1650–1950* (London, 1982), p. 1; C. Hall, 'The History of the Housewife', in C. Hall, *White, Male and Middle-class: Explorations in Feminism and History* (Cambridge, 1992), p. 43.

[9] Morgan and Evans, *Battle for Britain*, p. 71.

with care since they may well give more information about the concerns and priorities of editors and authors rather than represent the experiences and opinions of their readership.[10]

The discussion is divided into two sections dealing with housewifery and motherhood respectively. The first section begins by defining housewives and discusses the literature on women and domesticity during the period. This is followed by a description of the housewife's day and environment. Austerity altered culinary traditions and the kitchen front was central to propaganda on the home front. Sustained by a uniform propaganda message, housewives co-operated in the war effort and wartime food policy was generally popular. However, shopping difficulties and queuing, in particular, added to housewives' burdens; attitudes towards clothes rationing were rather more critical while the Board of Trade's 'Make do and mend' campaign largely backfired. In the face of high post-war demand, the continuation of austerity was unpopular and ration cuts contributed to low morale and housewives' discontent. Section 3.2 focuses on motherhood and child rearing, aspects of women's life which changed considerably during the period. There were many gains, above all special rations and welfare foods for mothers and children; and vital statistics indicate notable improvements in maternal and infant mortality rates. While there is little doubt about the improved health of babies and young children under flat-rate rations, feeding of adolescents was at times difficult and rationing caused severe problems in clothing children. Similarly, mothers had to contend with shortages of nursery equipment, toys, and treats which contributed towards the spartan nature of 1940s Christmases.

3.1. HOUSEWIFERY

At the height of mobilization in 1943 there were approximately 16 million women of working age of whom 7.25 million were in the Forces, civil defence, or industry, amounting to an increase of just under 2.5 million in female employment since 1939. This included up to 90 per cent of single women and 80 per cent of married women or widows without young children. Despite this massive transformation, the majority of women,

---

[10] J. Mechling, 'Advice to Historians on Advice to Mothers', *Journal of Social History* 9 (1975/76). The sheer success of women's magazines, sales of which expanded rapidly after 1945 and reached an all-time high in the early 1950s, is beyond doubt but whether their advice was generally followed or whether the magazines were read as escapism is debatable. On women's magazines see C. L. White, *Women's Magazines 1693–1968* (London, 1970); M. Ferguson, *Forever Feminine: Women's Magazines and the Cult of Femininity* (London, 1983); R. Ballaster *et al.*, *Women's Worlds: Ideology, Femininity and the Woman's Magazine* (Basingstoke, 1991); J. Waller and M. Vaughan-Rees, *Women in Wartime: The Role of Women's Magazines 1939–1945* (London, 1987).

approximately 8.75 million, were full-time housewives.[11] In 1951 female participation rates effectively returned to pre-war levels, with women accounting for about 30 per cent of the labour force and about two-thirds of women aged 20–64 were full-time housewives. Subsequently female participation rates increased, primarily due to the expansion of part-time employment among married women, a trend which can be observed from 1951 onwards.[12] The overwhelming majority of housewives were married women caring for children under 14 and managing a household on a full-time basis. However, the picture was more complicated, particularly during wartime conditions when many working women were also housewives. Mothers of children aged over 2 were encouraged to take up war work and a number of part-time employment schemes were developed. Full-time housewives were faced with new responsibilities and affected by wartime disruption such as the absence of husbands in the Forces, evacuation of children, or providing a billet to evacuees. Not all housewives were married and some kept house for other relatives such as aged parents and well over one million were engaged in essential voluntary work in addition to their domestic duties.[13] This disruption of established employment patterns threatened traditional family structures and gender identities but 'wartime policies were mediated through the domestic ideal'.[14] With regard to female mobilization, married women, even if they had no children and their husbands were away, were treated as 'immobile' workers since women's presence was perceived as essential in maintaining a home. Domestic duties which could exempt women from conscription included looking after a man, such as a widowed father. By contrast, women caring for female relatives did not qualify. Allen concludes that the domestic ideal was essentially preserved and housewives were 'women [who] were identified with, and seen as necessary for, the continuation of a "home", [but] a woman alone could not constitute a "home". Neither could men by themselves, make a "home". Home-making was shown basically to be something which women did for men or children'.[15]

In contrast with an older literature, written by second-wave feminists who emphasized housewives' low status, boredom, social isolation, and the demeaning nature of housework, it is possible to paint a positive picture of

[11] Cmd. 7225, Ministry of Labour and National Service, *Report for the Years 1939–1946* (London, 1947), pp. 2–3.
[12] J. Bourke, *Working-class Cultures in Britain, 1890–1960: Gender, Class and Ethnicity* (London, 1994), pp. 100–1; J. Lewis, *Women in England 1870–1950: Sexual Divisions and Social Change* (Brighton, 1984), pp. 146–9; J. Lewis, *Women in Britain since 1945* (Oxford, 1992), pp. 65–6.
[13] M. Allen, 'The Domestic Ideal and the Mobilisation of Womanpower in World War II', *Women's Studies International Forum* 6 (1983), p. 402.
[14] Ibid., p. 404.   [15] Ibid., p. 411.

housewifery[16] Davidoff highlights the significance of housework's basic concern 'with creating and maintaining order in the immediate environment, making meaningful patterns of activites, people and materials'. Cooking, 'the transformation of raw ingredients into a new substance . . . [was] used in family or social ritual' in the sense that 'proper' meals had to adhere to 'ritually prescribed patterns' and their consumption demarcated 'the boundaries of the household, of friendship patterns, of kindship gradations'. Cleaning played a similar role in marking boundaries by imposing and maintaining order. Women's housework, therefore, imposed 'cultural patterns upon the natural waork' in an attempt to '"generate and sustain systems of meaningful forms (symbols, artefacts, etc.) by means of which humanity transcends the givens of natural existence, bends them to its purposes, controls them in its interests"'.[17] Roberts stresses the contribution of housewifery skills in raising family living standards and the high status in family and community that working-class women derived from their success in making ends meet although this was eroded with rising prosperity in the middle decades of the twentieth century.[18] Indeed, womens's domestic role was critical in holding the family together as well as defining and maintaining social status.[19] While Zweig's earlier research had 'shattered [his] idea of "economic man"', his study of women restored his faith in human rationality:

the 'economic man' exists, but 'he' is female. . . . Every penny is used with a plan and a forethought. While working automatically with their hands, women think about the food they are going to prepare and about their shopping, what is the best way of spending and saving, and how to economise on this and that. They are the ones who are responsible for the survival of their families.[20]

Similarly, Bourke criticizes both feminist scholarship and conventional economic history which undervalues housewives as supposedly non-productive by stressing the significance of housewifery in converting cash into domestic comforts. Women's transition towards full-time housewifery from the late nineteenth century onwards was a popular aspiration and a rational choice which contributed towards raising family living standards and defining social status. Full-time housewifery was a power base since husbands

---

[16] B. Friedan, *The Feminine Mystique* (London, 1963); Oakley, *Housewife*; A. Oakley, *The Sociology of Housework* (Oxford, 1974).

[17] Davidoff, *Worlds Between*, pp. 75–6.

[18] E. Roberts, *A Woman's Place: An Oral History of Working-class Women, 1890–1940* (Oxford, 1984); E. Roberts, *Women and Families: An Oral History, 1940–1970* (Oxford, 1995).

[19] Ross, *Love and Toil*; M. Stacey, *Tradition and Change: A Study of Banbury* (Oxford, 1960); F. Zweig, *Women's Life and Labour* (London, 1952).

[20] Zweig, *Women's Life and Labour*, pp. 9–10.

were as dependent on female domestic skills as women were on male earnings.[21] Finally, Giles argues that the popular aspiration of a 'home of one's own' should not be understood as one-dimensional acquisitiveness but as a means by which women could make sense of themselves. The 'ordinary housewife' who emerged in the twentieth century at least superficially transcended class boundaries since femininity was redefined in terms of women's home-making skills.[22] Informed by this literature, this chapter highlights the significance of women's housewifery skills in preserving customary domestic comforts and providing palatable meals for their families during the exceptional circumstances of wartime and post-war austerity.

This perspective makes it easier to understand why most women perceived employment, especially in low-paid manual jobs, as a temporary necessity during the war and why domesticity was the predominant female aspiration in the early post-war years.[23] This was summed up well by a typical WAAF: 'My plans are simple and ordinary. My aim is to return to . . . normality in an England at peace . . . I want to marry . . . I want children . . . I aspire to being a good cook and housewife, one who makes a house a *home*.'[24] The decline in female employment and the post-war marriage and baby boom show that these aspirations were widely shared. Post-war official policy towards women was contradictory, combining pro-natalism and the desire to rebuild the family along traditional lines with female recruitment drives. The contradiction can, however, be partly resolved since recruitment drives were not aimed at mothers of very young children, and the expansion of part-time jobs enabled some women to reconcile employment with domestic duties.[25] Indeed, the argument that increased employment during the war resulted in women's liberation is difficult to sustain and Riley disposes of the 'vague but hardy feminist folk-myth' that after the war 'the government wanted women off the labour market and back to the home' by closing nurseries and propagating psychological theories about the close

[21] J. Bourke, *Husbandry to Housewifery: Women, Economic Change and Housework in Ireland, 1890–1914* (Oxford, 1993); Bourke, *Working-class Cultures in Britain*, ch. 3; J. Bourke, 'Housewifery in Working-class England 1860–1914', *Past and Present* 143 (1994), pp. 167–97.

[22] J. Giles, 'A Home of One's Own: Women and Domesticity in England 1918–1950', *Women's Studies International Forum* 16 (1993).

[23] Smith, 'The Effect of War on the Status of Women', pp. 213–18; Summerfield, *Women Workers in the Second World War*, pp. 187–90.

[24] Quoted from a woman's magazine in Waller and Vaughan-Rees, *Women in Wartime*, p. 124 (emphasis in original). In contrast with earlier generations, the WAAF envisaged a companionate marriage, a home full of labour-saving devices, and a part-time clerical job to fit around child care and domestic commitments. See also D. White, *D for Doris, V for Victory* (Milton Keynes, 1980), the autobiography of a wartime engineering worker who left her job never to return when she got married towards the end of the war; Roberts, *Women and Families*, pp. 51–8, 117–33 on female aspirations and attitudes towards employment.

[25] Lewis, *Women in Britain since 1945*, pp. 16–26; Tomlinson, *Democratic Socialism and Economic Policy*, pp. 189–99.

relationship between mothers and young children.[26] The conventional argument holds that feminism reached a nadir in the middle decades of the twentieth century as a direct consequence of the resurgence of domestic ideology celebrated in, or manufactured by, women's magazines and the commercial interests of manufacturers of domestic appliances.[27] McCarty rejects the simple dichotomy between feminism and domesticity, which is derived from ahistorical assumptions about the inherently emancipatory power of paid work and the inherently repressive nature of domesticity, since it fails to acknowledge the diversity of female attitudes towards domesticity and its relationship with the public sphere.[28] As argued above, the picture was certainly more complex, employment did not necessarily result in female liberation or greater equality, and full-time housewifery was a locus of female power both within the family and in wider society.

The housewives' environment was transformed considerably with rising living standards during the middle decades of the twentieth century. On average, income per head increased dramatically as a result of rising real wages coupled with smaller families due to the decline in fertility. These developments coincided with improvements in housing quality due to extensive house building. While suburban houses for middle-class owner occupation were predominant in the interwar years, after the war the bulk of new houses were built by local authorities for working-class tenants.[29] Piped water was generally available, even if shared, in towns before the First World War but almost a third of the rural population did not have access to piped water during the Second World War. However, according to the 1951 census 80 per cent of households in England and Wales had exclusive use of their own water supplies.[30] About two-thirds of households were wired for electricity in 1938, a figure which rose to 86 per cent by 1949 when four out of five households had gas supplies and two-thirds of households had both, with only 3 per cent in remote rural areas having neither mains electricity

[26] D. Riley, 'War in the Nursery', *Feminist Review* 2 (1979), p. 82; D. Riley, *War in the Nursery: Theories of Child and Mother* (London, 1983).

[27] See e.g. M. Pugh, 'Domesticity and the Decline of Feminism 1930–1950', in H. L. Smith (ed.), *British Feminism in the Twentieth Century* (Manchester, 1990); O. Banks, *Faces of Feminism: A Study of Feminism as a Social Movement* (Oxford, 1981). In his later book, Pugh acknowledges that this view is a 'considerable exaggeration', Pugh, *Women and the Women's Movement*, p. 284. For a critique of this view, see also C. Blackford, 'Wives and Citizens and Watchdogs of Equality: Post-war British Feminists', in Fyrth, *Labour's Promised Land?* pp. 58–72.

[28] McCarty, 'Attitudes to Women and Domesticity', pp. 9–30.

[29] J. Parker and C. Mirlees, 'Housing', in A. H. Halsey (ed.), *British Social Trends since 1900: A Guide to the Changing Social Structure of Britain*, rev. edn. (London, 1988); J. Burnett, *A Social History of Housing 1815–1970* (Newton Abbot, 1978); A. E. Holmans, *Housing Policy in Britain: A History* (London, 1986).

[30] M. J. Daunton, 'Housing', in Thompson, *The Cambridge Social History of Britain 1750–1950*, vol. 2, pp. 195–250; Davidson, *A Woman's Work is Never Done*, pp. 31–2.

nor gas supplies.[31] As a result of these developments, coupled with the expansion of mass-production techniques and hire purchase facilities, the middle decades of the century witnessed a revolution in domestic interior design that transformed kitchens and bathrooms as well as lighting and space heating.[32] The range of new so-called labour-saving devices such as gas or electric cookers and heaters as well as vacuum cleaners, washing machines, and refrigerators were marketed as reducing the housewives' burdens particularly in the new middle-class servantless home. The appearance of these appliances coincided with a reduction in the number of servants, a topic much discussed in the interwar years. Glucksmann stresses the link between the two factors since working-class women who had traditionally worked as servants in middle-class households now worked in domestic appliance factories which produced consumer goods purchased by middle-class women.[33] According to advertisements, these appliances transformed the housewife into a home technician who merely had to operate the new machinery by pushing a few buttons instead of spending long hours on demanding jobs such as washing, cooking, or cleaning. In practice, labour-saving appliances fell well short of this claim since their introduction tended to lead to rising standards as well as the withdrawal of domestic help by other family members such as children. As Schwarz Cowan put it, there is:

more work for a mother to do in a modern home because there is no one left to help her with it . . . although the work is more productive (more services are performed, and more goods are produced for every hour of work) and less laborious than it used to be, for most housewives it is just as time consuming and just as demanding.[34]

Whatever the merits of modern domestic technology, the overwhelming majority of women in 1940s Britain had to do without. Although most households were wired up for electricity and three-quarters of households possessed gas cookers, only lighting, radios, and perhaps electrical irons were widely available on the eve of war and the diffusion of washing machines, refrigerators, and vacuum cleaners as well as water and space heaters took off in Britain only in the 1950s.[35] During the 1940s and early

---

[31] T. A. B. Corley, *Domestic Electrical Appliances* (London, 1966), p. 19; Davidson, *A Woman's Work is Never Done*, p. 43.

[32] For details of changes in interior design and domestic technology see A. Forty, *Objects of Desire: Design and Society, 1750–1980* (London, 1986); C. Hardyment, *From Mangle to Microwave: The Mechanization of Household Work* (Cambridge, 1988); R. Schwarz Cowan, *More Work for Mother: The Ironies of Household Technology from the Open Hearth to the Microwave* (New York, 1983).

[33] M. Glucksmann, *Women Assemble: Women Workers and the New Industries in Interwar Britain* (London, 1990).

[34] Schwarz Cowan, *More Work for Mother*, p. 201.

[35] Davidson, *A Woman's Work is Never Done*, pp. 68–71, 100; Corley, *Domestic Electrical Appliances*, p. 16; Bowden and Offer, 'Household Appliances and the Use of Time', pp. 745–6; S. Bowden and A. Offer, 'The Technical Revolution that Never Was: Gender, Class and the Diffusion

1950s, with full employment, high taxation, rationing, and miscellaneous shortages, class differentials narrowed and most housewives did the bulk of their own housework. This applied also to middle-class women, who in contrast with their mothers and grandmothers had to manage without servants apart perhaps from a daily help among the more prosperous. It is interesting to note that the home management books published by the Good Housekeeping Institute (GHI) after the war, addressed mainly at a middle-class readership, assumed that the housewife would do virtually all housework herself.[36]

There is no doubt about the arduous and time-consuming nature of housework during this period. A good contemporary source is a Mass-Observation survey of married working-class housewives in the London suburbs conducted during spring 1951.[37] This showed that housewives spent between 10 and 11 hours a day (8 on Sundays) engaged in domestic duties, with about four hours a day (6 on Sundays) accounted for by personal toilet, leisure, and other activities outside the home. Using slightly different criteria, Gershuny's time-budget analysis between 1937 and 1961 highlights the convergence of working- and middle-class women's domestic duties. For 'middle-class women, the household workloads almost doubled during these years, from about 250 to 450 minutes a day. For working-class women, after rising from less than 500 minutes in 1937 to more than 500 in 1952, time spent in housework declined to about 450 minutes in 1961, the same level as middle-class women.'[38] The major single activity for most housewives was cooking, eating, and cleaning up after meals, which took between four and five hours a day and typically involved a cooked breakfast and mid-day meal as well as tea and supper. This was followed by between two and three hours a day (less on Sundays) making beds, cleaning, and dusting, indicating that many housewives followed the elaborate cleaning routines advised in women's magazines and household manuals. Laundry, ironing, and mending came next, with between one and a half and two hours a day but more on Mondays, the traditional washday. Based on oral evidence, Zmroczek provides a vivid account of the 'weekly wash', during

of Household Appliances in Interwar England', in V. de Grazia and E. Furlough (eds.), *The Sex of Things: Gender and Consumption in Historical Perspective* (Berkeley and Los Angeles, Calif., 1996), pp. 244–74.

[36] See, e.g., GHI, *ABC of Good Housekeeping* (London, 1947); id., *The Happy Home: A Universal Guide to Household Management* (London, 1955); id., *The Book of Good Housekeeping* (London, 1956).

[37] Mass-Observation Bulletin No. 42, *The Housewife's Day: Pattern of Work* (London, May–June 1951). The survey is based on 700 daily diaries, 100 per day, compiled during the week commencing 30 April 1951. The remainder of this paragraph is largely based on this source.

[38] J. I. Gershuny, 'Time Budgets as Social Indicators', *Journal of Public Policy* 9 (1989), p. 422; id., 'Are We Running Out of Time?', *Futures* (Jan./Feb. 1992), pp. 15–16, quoted in Bowden and Offer, 'Household Appliances and the Use of Time', p. 734.

which water was carried and heated in a copper, laundry was boiled, mangled between rinses, elaborately starched, and ironed.[39] Shopping took about an hour a day on average, with rather more on the popular shopping days, Fridays, Saturdays, and Tuesdays. Housewives were responsible for purchasing not only all the food consumed by the household, but also the bulk of miscellaneous household goods, including clothing, for themselves and other family members.[40] Shopping was more time-consuming during the 1940s when housewives spent a considerable amount of time queuing and searching for items in short supply. Finally, childcare was arranged around these activities, with a great deal of variation in the time devoted exclusively to children depending on the number of children and perhaps more importantly their age.

The remainder of this section explores the impact of austerity on housewives along with their attitudes towards the policy. The dietary changes generated by rationing and shortages altered culinary traditions as recipes were adapted to wartime conditions, and many new dishes were developed. The general aim was to economize on foods such as meat, eggs, fats, or sugar and to make the most of plentiful bread, flour, potatoes, or seasonal fruit and vegetables. An avalanche of official propaganda, bolstered by advice in women's magazines, was intended to help housewives cope and aimed to raise their awareness of the significance of domestic economies and the maintenance of family health and morale to the wider war effort. A Ministry of Food leaflet declared:

The line of Food Defence runs through all our homes. . . . It may seem so simple, this urgent duty, that we may tend to overlook its full meaning. A little saving here and there—how can that really help us to win the war? A little here and there, with our 45 million people all contributing, becomes an immense amount. . . . *The woman with the basket* has a vital part to play in home defence. By saving food you may be saving lives.[41]

Similarly, *Good Housekeeping* eulogized the housewife's contribution:

Yours is a full-time job, but not a spectacular one. You wear no uniform, much of your work is taken for granted and goes unheralded and unsung, yet on you depends so much. Not only must you bring up your children to be healthy and strong, look after your husband or other war-workers so they may be fit and alert, but you must contrive to do so with less help, less money, and less ingredients than ever before. In the way you tend your family, especially, your skill—and your good citizenship—are tested. Thoughtlessness, waste, a minor extravagance on your part may mean lives

[39] C. Zmroczek, 'The Weekly Wash', in S. Oldfield (ed.), *This Working-day World: Women's Lives and Culture(s) in Britain 1914–45* (London, 1994).

[40] MO, FR A17, Clothes, 22 Apr. 1939; PRO, RG 23/211, Consumer Expenditure Survey: Expenditure on Clothing, 1950; R. Scott, *The Female Consumer* (London, 1976).

[41] Ministry of Food, *Wise Housekeeping in War-time*, n.d. [approx. 1940], in MO, TC Food, Box 2C (emphasis in original).

lost at sea, or a cargo of vitally-needed bombers sacrificed for one of food that should have been unnecessary. . . . We leave it to you, the Good Housekeepers of Britain, with complete confidence.[42]

Apart from information about rationing, food propaganda focused on two themes. On the one hand, there was general advice on economies and basic principles of nutrition. On the other, new recipes were designed to help the housewife provide palatable and varied meals, which were easy and quick to prepare, saved on fuel, and made the most of available supplies.

Food propaganda was disseminated in leaflets, booklets, cookery demonstrations, posters, 'food flashes' screened in cinemas, and above all through the radio. The prominence given to the BBC's *Kitchen Front* programme, which broadcast daily immediately after the morning news bulletin, illustrates the significance attached to food in home front propaganda. Newspapers and especially women's magazines provided a further outlet for government-sponsored advertisements. Moreover, features on housekeeping or cookery, and particularly recipes, frequently emphasized official sanction and, for example, the Good Housekeeping Institute published its own, Ministry of Food approved, recipe booklets. According to Nicholas, the radio 'was central', since 'the BBC not only reached everyone but could tailor particular messages to particular audiences with far more precision than any other medium'.[43] The *Kitchen Front* suggested best buys, always included at least one recipe, and introduced new foods such as dried egg or Lend-Lease haricot beans and fat bacon. The programme advised on all aspects of food policy and once a week Charles Hill, the 'Radio Doctor', gave general nutritional advice and discussed specialist diets.[44] Judging by listening figures, the *Kitchen Front* was 'a remarkable success, attracting some five million listeners, 15 per cent of the available audience, and four times the audience of any other daytime talk'.[45]

This multi-media propaganda campaign repeated the same topics and issues over and over again. For example, *Wise Housekeeping in War-time* advised housewives to plan shopping and cooking carefully to avoid waste. Fuel should be saved by steaming, cooking a number of dishes in the oven simultaneously, or not filling the kettle more than necessary. Further, vegetables should be shred finely, boiled with very little water, and potatoes left in their skin. Left-over fat should be strained and used again, meat off-cuts should be used for stock or flavouring soup, and the latter was a useful way of processing left-overs. Nutritional advice focused on promoting a

[42] *Good Housekeeping*, Aug. 1941.
[43] Nicholas, *The Echo of War*, p. 71.
[44] The Ministry of Food published some of these talks: C. Hill, *Wise Eating in Wartime* (London, 1943).
[45] Nicholas, *The Echo of War*, p. 82.

balanced diet based on daily consumption of some items from each of four food groups. These were 'body building foods' (milk, cheese, eggs, meat, and fish); 'energy foods' (foods rich in fats and sugar, as well as cereals and potatoes), and finally groups 3 and 4, the 'protective foods' (dairy products, fish, offal, and fresh fruit and vegetables).[46] The same message was promoted in the *ABC of Cookery*, published in 1945, which stressed 'rules for good meal planning' emphasising economy, labour saving, as well as attractive and varied meals. A typical day's menu, suggesting a substantial and fairly stodgy diet, consisted of breakfast (porridge, cooked dish, bread with butter or margarine and marmalade or jam), dinner (soup, meat, fish or vegetarian alternative, fresh vegetables, potatoes, baked or steamed pudding or fruit with milk or custard), tea (bread with butter or margarine, a sandwich spread or filling, cakes, biscuits, or scones), and supper (main dish of cheese, fish, or egg, vegetables or salad, potatoes, bread with butter or margarine and jam or other spread), all accompanied by tea and milk or cocoa for children.[47]

This advice was often patronizing in tone and perhaps little more than common sense, especially for housewives used to managing on a tight budget.[48] According to a Home Intelligence special report on housewives' attitudes towards official campaigns and instructions conducted in 1943, food propaganda was generally welcomed. There was:

little evidence of either confusion or annoyance, beyond 'good natured grumbling' . . . On the whole, housewives seem very willing to comply with official instructions and advice, for some of which, notably in Ministry of Food publicity, there is said to be considerable appreciation. Reports from four Regions suggest, however, that housewives are now impervious to 'the flood of official propaganda' and that they select from it only the information that seems essential to them.

Salvage or fuel economy campaigns were more frequently ignored than Ministry of Food propaganda and, for example, the 'Radio Doctor's' talks were '"specially commended"'.

Three reports suggest that working class housewives are . . . more receptive to the Government's appeals and publicity than are women of other classes. But some of the economies that have been suggested are regarded as 'piffling' by working class women, on whom such forms of thrift have long been imposed by necessity. Opinions seem to vary as to the best or most popular medium of propaganda. On the whole, the radio and cinema seem to be liked rather better than the press; neither posters nor leaflets are thought 'to cut much ice', and are considered by some

---

[46] Ministry of Food, *Our Food To-day: How to Eat Wisely in Wartime* (London, n.d. [approx. 1940]), in MO, TC Food, Box 2C.

[47] Ministry of Food, *The ABC of Cookery* (London, 1945), pp. 68–71.

[48] See for example, Broad and Flemming, *Nella Last's War*, which includes frequent references to economical recipes and more generally, Roberts, *Women and Families*.

housewives to be a waste of paper . . . except for leaflets giving food recipes or gardening hints.[49]

With regard to the aim of inculcating healthier eating habits and greater nutritional awareness, food propaganda was relatively ineffective. For example, National Wheatmeal Bread remained unpopular, uptake of welfare foods was relatively low, and a survey of nutritional knowledge concluded that 'large numbers of people have no scientific knowledge of dietetic food values. They consider the foods which make up their traditional diets as those which are good for them'.[50]

The shortage of many conventional foodstuffs coupled with a desire for variety resulted in the emergence of many new recipes such as 'mock' dishes, vegetarian main courses, and the promotion of substitutes which aimed to adapt new and unconventional foods to the British palate.[51] For example, 'mock duck' included sausage meat while 'mock goose' consisted of potatoes, cooking apples, and cheese. 'Mock cream' was made with milk, margarine, and cornflour, parsnips laced with flavouring provided the basis for pineapple or banana spread and an 'eggless sponge' used custard powder as a substitute for eggs. Vegetarian main courses acquired prominence, most famously the 'Woolton pie', which consisted of mixed vegetables and oatmeal topped with potato pastry or mashed potatoes. Among new foods above all dried egg was a great success, used in a host of recipes throughout the 1940s. By contrast, other novelties such as salted cod, whale meat, or the infamous snoek, which appeared after the war, failed to win approval and the latter was apparently sold as cat food.[52] Also prominently featured were off-ration offal and rabbits, as well as nuts, berries, crab apples, and elderberries. There was no change after the war and *100 ideas for supper*, published in 1947 by the GHI, was designed around the four key themes of saving fuel, advance preparation, general economy, and off-ration dishes. Above all the meat shortage remained a key theme in recipe books published until the end of the decade. This changed only from the mid–1950s onwards when roasts again held a prominent place, farmhouse or dairy-rich cookery was promoted, and frozen food as well as slimming recipes appeared for the first time.[53]

    [49] PRO, INF 1/293, Home Intelligence Special Report No. 44, Housewives' Attitudes towards Official Campaigns and Instructions, 14 May 1943.
    [50] PRO, RG 23/9A, Wartime Social Survey, Food during the War, Feb. 1942–Oct. 1943.
    [51] The following examples are based on M. Patten, *We'll Eat Again: A Collection of Recipes from the War Years* (Twickenham, 1985); J. Davies, *The Wartime Kitchen and Garden: The Home Front 1939–45* (London, 1993).
    [52] Cooper, 'Snoek Piquante', pp. 50–2. Snoek was an apparently unpalatable southern African fish which possessed the advantage of being imported from within the sterling area.
    [53] GHI, *The Book of 100 Ideas for Supper* (London, 1947); id., *Five Hundred Recipes for Today* (London, 1949); id., *Picture Cookery* (London, 1950). For example id., *Cookery Book*, 2nd edn. (London, 1954) includes a large number of meat dishes, the few remaining wartime economy

Housewives were more concerned about the food situation than any other social group and while rationing was generally popular support for other food schemes was more qualified. Attitudes also changed over time and initial worry and discontent was replaced by acceptance in mid-war as the food situation stabilized and women adapted to wartime conditions. Dissatisfaction increased again during the late 1940s when many rations were smaller and more volatile than during the war and housewives' food morale was low, as indicated, above all, by the considerable deterioration compared to the war in their attitudes towards the adequacy of their diet.

According to a Mass-Observation survey of 400 London working-class housewives conducted in spring 1940, there was a 'good deal of worry and tension' and the 'downward change in their standard of living had been rapid and had left them bewildered'.[54] A Mass-Observation diarist made the point succinctly: 'Before commencing this diary I invariably say to my wife, "Well, what do your friends say about the war?" To which she always replies, "Nothing, they don't discuss it. They are more concerned about what to get for tea."—which is, I suppose, after all a war topic.'[55] Likewise, an investigator noted that:

Innumerable conversations and discussions between housewives have shown that the food question, the difficulty of eking out rations with unrationed foodstuffs, the high prices, particularly of perishable foods, shortages and the consequent queues, occupy *the first place* in the average working woman's present-day life. However, it is beginning to become a major worry and topic of conversation with the men too, who are involved from the economic aspect, as well as the direct impact of having less to eat . . . and food discussions have been heard both between men and women that *lasted up to an hour.*[56]

Home Intelligence weekly morale reports, discussed in the previous chapter, show that discontent was most intense early on in the war and satisfaction increased from 1942 onwards although food grumbles were a persistent problem on the home front.

Wartime social surveys provide the best evidence of housewives' attitudes towards rationing and food policy. Table 3.1 shows that, above all, rationing and points rationing were supported overwhelmingly as both fair and necessary. The few critics mainly disliked the small size of rations. The milk scheme was popular, especially among younger women and mothers of

recipes are relegated to the back, dried egg had disappeared, and vegetarian dishes assume choice rather than necessity. See also id., *Farmhouse Cookery* (London, 1955); id., *Every Day Dairy Recipes* (London, 1959); id., *Frozen Food Cookery* (London, n.d. [appprox. late 1950s]); id., *Eat and Keep Slim* (London, 1957).

[54] MO, FR 93, The Housewife's War, May 1940.
[55] MO, TC Food Box 2F, extract from diary by a male clerk, 24 Nov. 1940.
[56] MO, FR 704, Food and Rationing: An Observer's Report from Shotley Bridge, Newcastle, May 1941 (emphasis in original).

TABLE 3.1. *Housewives' attitudes to rationing and food control in 1942 (per cent)*

	Approve	Disapprove	No opinion
Rationing	91	4	5
Points rationing	86	7	7
National and priority milk	77	8	15
Price control	80	6	14
British Restaurants	40	4	56
National Wheatmeal Bread	52	35	13
Scheme for selling oranges first to people with children under 5	47	39	14

Notes: Percentages may not add to 100 because of rounding. This survey is based on a representative sample of 2,530 housewives interviewed between 24 June and 11 July 1942. Housewives were asked whether they approved, or disapproved, of each of the food schemes specifically named.
Sources: PRO, RG 23/9A; Nuffield College Library, Oxford, Wartime Social Survey, Food I: Food Schemes: A Collection of Short Reports on Inquiries Made by the Regional Organisation of the Wartime Social Survey, May 1942–Jan. 1943.

children under 5 as well as the lower income groups who also strongly favoured price control. The popularity of these food schemes stands in contrast with the remainder. While few disapproved of British Restaurants, a majority of housewives had no opinion. This is not surprising since only 1.3 per cent of housewives had actually eaten a midday meal at a British Restaurant, either because none were available or within easy reach but also because they preferred to eat at home which was cheaper, more convenient, and did not require queuing.[57] National Wheatmeal Bread was widely disliked, especially among older and working-class housewives. Finally, the priority given to young children in the distribution of oranges was unpopular not only among housewives with no children or older children but also among those with children under 5, a quarter of whom disliked it, perhaps because it was 'the only scheme which [was] not made watertight by clear regulations' and, therefore, likely to cause resentment.[58] This generally strong support of food controls was conditional upon the special circumstances of war and barely half wanted rationing to continue after the war (see Table 3.2). Indifference towards British Restaurants and the unpopularity of National Wheatmeal Bread are again illustrated. Post-war rationing was most popular among the middle and more affluent working class and opposition was strongest among the very rich and the poorest as

[57] Nuffield College, Oxford, Wartime Social Survey, Food: An Inquiry into a Typical Day's Meals and Attitudes to Wartime Food in Selected Groups of the English Working Population, n.s. 16 and 19; based on a survey of 1,948 housewives interviewed between 30 Apr. and 11 July 1942.
[58] PRO, RG 23/9A.

TABLE 3.2. *Housewives' opinion on the continuation of rationing and food control after the war (per cent)*

	Continued	Not continued	Don't know
Rationing	49	36	15
Points rationing	50	35	15
National and priority milk	61	14	25
Price control	82	4	14
British Restaurants	37	9	54
National Wheatmeal Bread	31	55	14

Notes: Percentages may not add to 100 because of rounding. This survey is based on a representative sample of 2,944 housewives interviewed between 14 May and 6 June 1942. Housewives were asked which of these food schemes they would like to be continued after the war.
Source: PRO, RG 23/9A, Wartime Social Survey, Food During the War: A Summary of Studies on the Subject of Food Made by the Wartime Social Survey between Feb. 1942 and Oct. 1943.

well as older housewives. The latter, poor, older women, were also most critical of the continuation of price controls, which was the only policy supported by an overwhelming majority.

Despite perpetual food difficulties, the overwhelming majority of housewives (78 per cent) considered themselves to be well fed, a finding which stands in stark contrast to male attitudes, particularly among manual workers.[59] Among the dissatisfied, the majority thought food generally to be insufficient and, above all, missed fats and sugar followed by a range of other foodstuffs. Detailed analysis of food consumption and sleeping habits suggests that housewives' greater satisfaction may be due to the fact that they tended to eat less and sleep more than male manual workers but the question 'whether [housewives] feel satisfied because they need less or because their standard is lower cannot be decided here'. It is also interesting to note that when housewives were asked about the adequacy of the diet in relation to their children only 68.9 per cent (as opposed to 78 per cent) were satisfied.[60]

The continuation and, indeed, intensification of austerity after the war was unpopular and housewives were more worried about food shortages and the difficulties of making ends meet than the rest of the population.[61] Following the general trend in the supply situation, food worries were most

[59] See Table 2.3.
[60] Nuffield College, Oxford, Wartime Social Survey, Food: An Inquiry into a Typical Day's Meals and Attitudes to Wartime Food in Selected Groups of the English Working Population, n.s. 16 and 19.
[61] PRO, RG 23/92–117, Survey of Knowledge and Opinion about the Economic Situation, which dealt with a range of economic issues including attitudes to shortages, prices, and rationing and was conducted on a regular basis between Dec. 1947 and June 1951. The remainder of this paragraph draws heavily on this source.

intense between 1946 and 1948 and matters improved somewhat from 1949 onwards, although rising prices caused a great deal of concern towards the end of the decade. When details of gender differences are available, women responded more pessimistically than men to the question whether things were going well or badly. For example, in March 1948 two-thirds of women but only 56 per cent among men thought things were going badly and this gender gap persisted in later surveys. Among housewives, 86 per cent found it more difficult in December 1947 to make ends meet than a year ago, a figure which declined to 76 per cent in October 1948. This trend was similar among married men and other women. By contrast, among single men only just over half were concerned about rising prices. Similarly, housewives disproportionately mentioned rationing, food, and other shortages, as well as high prices, as their most important personal problem caused by the economic situation or crisis. For instance, in December 1947, 61 per cent of housewives mentioned food shortages, 24 per cent general shortages, and 14 per cent clothes rationing. Among men, the corresponding figures were only 38 per cent, 8 per cent, and 8 per cent respectively and a similar gender gap was observed in later surveys. Housewives' food worries were caused by the inadequacy of rations and above all the meat ration, high prices, and the scarcity of unrationed foods.

A good indication of housewives' low food morale after the war are surveys on the adequacy of their diet, which reveal a considerable deterioration compared with wartime findings. When asked whether more food or greater variety in the diet affected their ability to work in April 1948 and March 1949, 59 per cent and 53 per cent of housewives maintained that they could work harder on a more plentiful diet. Just over a third felt it would make no difference and less than 10 per cent were doubtful.[62] Housewives' attitudes were now closer to those of manual workers than non-manual workers whereas in the war housewives had been more satisfied than all other groups of workers. This evidence is confirmed by a Mass-Observation survey conducted during 1946, according to which 78 per cent among women and only 56 per cent among men did not consider that they were getting enough of the essential foodstuffs.[63] A Mass-Observation Bulletin highlighted the low food morale after the war, noting that the 'dominant feeling is a resigned one', and concluded:

When people were asked whether or not they thought they were getting enough of the essential foodstuffs, about two-thirds replied that they were not. This question has been asked at intervals since summer 1941, and . . . the number of people saying

---

[62] See Table 2.6.
[63] MO, TC Food Box 6A, survey based on 120 persons from the London area questioned on 18 Feb. 1946.

they are not getting enough has risen pretty steadily over the whole period, from rather more than a fifth in 1941 to about two-thirds in 1946.[64]

According to a survey of London middle-class housewives in 1949, attitudes towards rationing were characterized by 'fatalistic resignation' and only a third felt they were getting enough of the essential foodstuffs. Again, especially meat, as well as fats and eggs, were missed most, and dissatisfaction was greatest among women over 40 and those without children among whom three-quarters considered their diet to be inadequate.[65] From the autumn of 1949 onwards, there was a steady and substantial decline in concern about food shortages and a shift on to money problems. For instance, in March 1950 only 12 per cent among women and 7 per cent of men considered food to be their most serious problem, just under half of both men and women now mentioned money, and 21 per cent actually denied that there was a food shortage.[66]

Inevitable consequences of shortages were queues and empty shelves, which made shopping more time consuming as well as frustrating. The brunt of this added burden was borne by women. Summerfield analyses the shopping difficulties of working women, focusing on the partial and largely ineffective official attempts to deal with this problem, which was a leading cause of absenteeism among female workers.[67] The following discussion focuses on housewives, many of whom were forced to spend a considerable amount of time queuing both for rationed foods such as meat in order to obtain more desirable cuts and, above all, for unrationed foods such as fish, cake, or fresh fruit and vegetables, which were generally only available on a first-come, first-served basis. A Mass-Observation report sums up the situation:

To a great extent queues have been the trial of the women rather than the men. Men have felt the lack of variety of food at the dinner table, but they have not gone through the tiring ordeal of queuing, for what there is in front of them. Queues are so numerous everywhere that many housewives have almost accepted them as a very tiring but a usual part of their shopping. Many housewives feel that they could put up with queues to some extent if they could be sure of getting what they wanted after their waiting, but in so many cases a housewife arrives at the beginning of a queue to find that their [sic] is nothing left that she wants, and from there she has to join another queue and start all over again.[68]

---

[64] MO, Bulletin, Future Outlooks 1946, n.s. No. 1, Mar.–Apr. 1946.
[65] MO, FR 3160, The London Middle-class Housewife and her Food Problems, Sept. 1949.
[66] PRO, RG 23/110 (Mar. 1950); see also RG 23/112, 114, 116.
[67] Summerfield, *Women Workers in the Second World War*, ch. 5, *passim*; P. Summerfield, 'Women, Work and Welfare: A Study of Child Care and Shopping in Britain in the Second World War', *Journal of Social History* 17 (1983/84), pp. 249–69.
[68] MO, TC Food Box 3C, Report on the Food Situation, 14–20 July 1941.

Queues were mentioned regularly in Home Intelligence weekly morale reports and resented particularly by 'war-workers, mothers with babies, and the old and infirm [who were] unable to compete'.[69] In June 1941 queues starting at 6 a.m. were reported, housewives' early shopping trips caused transport congestion, and 'much police time [was] said to be occupied with the control of queues'.[70] The widespread nature of the problem is confirmed by a Gallup poll, according to which 45 per cent of women had difficulty in finding time to do their shopping. Women under 29 (51 per cent) and women in employment (58 per cent) were most affected.[71] Food queues and shopping difficulties were an unremitting problem on the home front, mentioned in up to nine (out of 13) regions at the end of 1942 and again in the summer of 1943 when complaints were observed in up to 11 regions.[72]

Yet again, social surveys provide the best quantitatively representative evidence of housewives' experience of and attitudes towards queuing. Table 3.3 shows that the incidence of queuing increased between February and June 1942 when almost a third had queued during the previous week and the same percentage still queued regularly in 1949. At this time only 11 per cent of men and 20 per cent of other women queued regularly. Between February and June 1942 queuing, which was most prevalent among working-class housewives, increased among all income groups, with the greatest rise among the rich. In 1949 housewives in the higher income groups queued most frequently and only a quarter of poor housewives queued regularly. The pattern remained remarkably persistent between 1942 and 1949.[73] On average, housewives queued for between 15 and 30 minutes in order to buy fish, groceries, and meat, although cakes, confectionery, and biscuits were also frequently queued for during the war. In 1942, just over a third of housewives did not need to queue and about one in ten would not queue. Strong criticism and disapproval were expressed by about 20 per cent, while a small number either thought that queues were fair and could not be helped or blamed other queuers for queues. According to a Gallup poll of April 1947, 46 per cent had queued during the previous week, primarily for food.[74] Of the queuers, most had spent between one and two and a half hours queuing, with some spending over three hours, and only one in five queuing for less than one hour. A Mass-Observation survey conveys the irritation provoked by queues: there was 'no other current topic that arouses such immediate and fierce reaction . . . as the subject of queues . . . which clearly to many is the symbol of all the frustrations of this post war era'.

[69] PRO, INF 1/292, 4–11 June 1941.   [70] Ibid., 11–18 June 1941.

[71] Cited in ibid., 15–22 Dec. 1941. See also Table 2.3.

[72] Ibid., Home Intelligence Monthly Summary of Constant Topics, Aug. 1942–Dec. 1944.

[73] PRO, RG 23/7, 18; National Library of Wales, Social Survey, Consumer Expenditure Surveys: Expenditure on Meals in Catering Establishments, Reports of 4 Inquiries Carried Out in 1949 (2), 1951, 1956, and 1961.   [74] *Gallup Polls*, p. 155.

TABLE 3.3. *Incidence of queuing among housewives, February and June 1942, April–May 1949 (per cent)*

Date	Total	Income group			
		A	B	C	D
Feb. 1942	20.6	6.2	18.9	20.3	24.3
June 1942	31.8	25.2	26.3	34.1	32.8
		Over £10	£7.10–£10	£5–£7.10	£3–£5	Up to £3
Apr.–May 1949	33	37	40	36	31	25

Notes: In 1942 housewives were asked whether they had queued in the last seven days, in 1949 whether they had spent any time queuing when shopping. The bases for the income groups are as follows: during the war, A (top 5.2%), B (next 20.2%), C (38.9%), D (35.7%); after the war, according to weekly household income, viz. over £10 (top 5.6%), B (next 9.2%), £7.10–£10 (next 9.2%), £5–£7.10 (41.1%), £3–£5 (25.1%), up to £3 (15.1%).
Sources: PRO, RG 23/7, 18; National Library of Wales, Aberystwyth, Social Survey, Consumer Expenditure Surveys: Expenditure on Meals in Catering Establishments, Reports of 4 Inquiries Carried out 1949 (2), 1951, 1956, and 1961.

Most members of the national panel of observers queued but the 'brunt of all queuing still falls largely on women'. As one man put it succinctly, '"I don't queue; my wife does that" '. While a few did not mind queuing or were merely resigned to it, 'the feeling of irritation rising to full blooded hate or disgust is most wide spread. The majority queue because of dire necessity, and this compulsion adds to the mere irksomeness of waiting'. '"I detest", "I loathe", "disgusting", "murderous" . . . [were] recurrent epithets' and frustration was frequently directed at other queuers.[5] Queues did not cause the breakdown of female morale during the war but they certainly exacerbated housewives' grievances, especially during the late 1940s. It is interesting to note that the British Housewives' League (BHL), a post-war housewives' protest organization, emerged from an anti-queuing protest in 1945 and the interminable shopping difficulties under austerity contributed towards the pessimism, fatigue, and low morale among housewives after the war.[6]

Austerity was not confined to food, and the following paragraphs briefly discuss housewives' experience of and attitudes towards shortages of miscellaneous consumer goods which were administered by the Board of Trade. A wartime propaganda leaflet maintained that 'the housewife has the warm satisfaction of knowing how directly her sacrifices of energy and triumphs of ingenious make-shift contribute to the war' such as the saving provided by one additional clothing coupon, which released sufficient labour and raw

[5] MO, FR 3036, Queuing: Panel Replies on Feelings About Queues, Sept. 1948.
[6] Hinton, 'Militant Housewives', p. 132.

materials to equip half a million soldiers.[77] However, in the event these policies generated continued dissatisfaction, suggesting that the Board of Trade
lacked the flair for public relations exhibited by the Ministry of Food.
Housewives' discontent with cuts in the clothes ration and the inclusion of
household linen in the ration were discussed in the previous chapter and
the focus here is on the 'make do and mend' campaign and miscellaneous
shortages.

The 'make do and mend' campaign was the Board of Trade's central propaganda effort directed at housewives. It gave advice on preservation, renovation, and repair of clothing and other household goods. Although the
campaign was originally launched with the slogan, 'Mend and Make-Do to
save buying new',[78] 'make do and mend' has become one of the catch-
phrases of the Second World War on a par with 'kitchen front' or 'dig for
victory'. Following the precedent of food propaganda, the 'need for a
national campaign to stimulate the public to remake, mend and renovate'
was discussed in 1941.[79] The campaign, launched in the summer of 1942
with the advice and help of women's groups, was 'based on the fact that a
nation's wardrobe is one of the most important of its resources in
wartime'.[80] 'Make do and mend', driving home the point that '"clothes-
carelessness is Sabotage"', was a multi-media campaign publicized in newspapers, women's magazines, leaflets, films screened in cinemas, and BBC
broadcasts, as well as exhibitions, advice centres, and 12,000 formal
classes.[81]

The 'high spot' of Board of Trade publications was a 1943 booklet, 'literally crammed with information about everything from how to beat the
moth to how to launder shirts; from getting grease stains out to turning two
old coats into one new one'.[82] Dalton, in his foreword, thanked the public
for accepting clothes rationing, which 'has saved much-needed shipping
space, manpower and materials, and so assisted our war effort' and hoped
that the hints 'intended to help you to get the last possible ounce of wear
out of all your clothes and household things' would 'prove useful'.[83] The
advice, which was frequently time consuming and laborious ranged from
common sense to bizarre and impracticable. Weak places such as elbows or
underarms should always be reinforced, old clothes could be remade into
new garments by unpicking, turning, and cutting to size—remembering
to use 'your up-to-date measurements', and woollens could be unravelled to
knit a new item. Washing hints included advice on not mixing whites and

[77] PRO, INF 2/5, Ministry of Information, *British Women at War* (London, 1944).
[78] PRO, INF 2/72.   [79] PRO, BT 64/3023, Memo, 2 July 1941.
[80] Ibid., Memo, June 1943.
[81] Ibid., Memo, June 1943, Memos, n.d. [1943] and 27 Oct. 1943.
[82] Ibid., Memo, June 1943.
[83] Board of Trade, *Make Do and Mend* (London, 1943).

colours or saving on (heated) washing water by washing least dirty items first then washing other items in the same water. Clothes should not be thrown 'down in a heap', but brushed and aired 'in the sun if possible—taking care to turn out pockets and look behind collars and seams for dust and fluff and moth eggs'. Avoiding damp places, they should be hung or folded carefully—'put bunched-up newspaper between the folds to prevent creases'. Clothes and footwear should be worn on alternate days 'as a rest does them good'. It is perhaps not surprising that housewives' response to the campaign was predominantly negative according to a Home Intelligence special report compiled about five months after the campaign was launched.[84] In seven out of 12 regions:

the campaign appears to have 'passed unnoticed by a very large number of people'. The minority who have been aware of it are said to appreciate the advertisements and 'to look forward to all the hints they can get'. Three main reasons are suggested for the campaign's apparent failure to attract more attention:-
(i)   'Most women have little time nowadays for elaborate mending and making do' (six Regions).
(ii) To the majority of working class housewives, 'mending and making do is nothing new'; while among the poorest families, the quality of clothes bought, which are mostly secondhand [sic], does not 'warrant the time spent on elaborate mending' (four Regions).
(iii) 'Women's papers [a major source of publicity] are hard to come by now for the casual purchaser who has not got a standing order'.

Practical hints were also criticized because they lacked detail such as patterns for remaking clothes. Some were 'thought to be "unpractical because they need a lot of time spent on them, which most people are unable to spare nowadays"; others [were] thought to be too well known and "already used by hundreds of women"'. It is impossible to speculate on later attitudes although the criticism of the campaign's uneasy combination of impracticability and common-sense advice is unlikely to have altered dramatically during the remainder of the 1940s.

As a result of the drastic reduction in supplies, shopping difficulties with regard to miscellaneous household goods were a continuous source of irritation throughout the period. Shopping difficulties were investigated in social surveys of 3,000 housewives each conducted regularly between April 1943 and January 1945 for the Board of Trade's consumer needs department.[85] With regard to a host of household items, housewives were

---

[84] PRO, INF 1/293, Home Intelligence Special Report, no. 35, The 'Mend and Make Do' Campaign, 3 Dec. 1942.
[85] Nuffield College Library, Oxford, Social Survey, *Wartime Shortages of Consumer Goods: A Report on a Series of Inquiries Made by the Social Survey for the Board of Trade, April 1943–January 1945* (by K. Box) (London, 1945).

asked whether they tried to buy these and whether they actually bought any. A summary table highlights particularly shortages of hardware (kettles and pans, mixing bowls, brooms, and brushes). Between less than half and less than one-quarter succeeded in buying these items and only one in ten was able to purchase a kettle not made of tin. Detailed analysis of the figures over time shows a high level of stability suggesting chronic shortages. The supply situation was rather better with regard to crockery since about two-thirds of housewives were able to purchase the items they needed and this was also the case for miscellaneous items such as needles or toothbrushes. The other area of severe shortage was household linen. While two-thirds or more were able to purchase the towels they needed, the figure dropped to one-third for pillow cases and only 15 and 8 per cent respectively were able to purchase flannelette and cotton or linen sheets. About two out of three women who had failed to purchase what they needed visited three or more shops and the most common reason given, particularly with regard to hardware, was that the item in question was not available. Crockery caused difficulty because the available stock was frequently the 'wrong' type and household linen stands out because purchase was discouraged by the high number of coupons or dockets required as well as high prices. The survey's conclusion with regard to income groups is interesting because it belies the notion that shortages primarily hit the middle class. Among two economic groups, the lower 75 per cent

tend to show higher proportions trying to buy, no doubt because cheaper articles in general need more frequent replacement, and because . . . stocks . . . would probably be smaller when shortages began. The proportion of all housewives succeeding in buying in the two economic groups do not however differ very much. . . . It is clear that shortages are harder in their effect on the poor than the rich.[86]

This frustrating, time-consuming, and dispiriting experience of shopping probably continued largely unchanged after the war, as illustrated by Orwell's evocative, if fictional, account of housewives' scramble for cheap, low-quality saucepans. Winston Smith, wandering the streets of London heard

a great formidable cry of anger and despair, a deep, loud 'Oh-o-o-oh!' that went humming on like the reverberation of a bell. His heart had leapt. It's started! He had thought. A riot! The proles are breaking loose at last! When he had reached the spot it was to see a mob of two or three hundred women crowding round the stalls of a street market, with faces as tragic as though they had been the doomed passengers on a sinking ship. But at this moment the general despair broke down into a multitude of individual quarrels. It appeared that one of the stalls had been selling tin saucepans. They were wretched, flimsy things, but cooking-pots of any kind were

[86] Nuffield College Library, Oxford, Social Survey, *Wartime Shortages of Consumer Goods*, p. 6.

always difficult to get. Now the supply had unexpectedly given out. The successful women, bumped and jostled by the rest, were trying to make off with their saucepans while dozens of others clamoured round the stall, accusing the stall-keeper of favouritism and of having more saucepans somewhere in reserve. There was a fresh outburst of yells. Two bloated women . . . had got hold of the same saucepan and were trying to tear it out of one another's hands. For a moment they were both tugging, and then the handle came off. Winston watched them disgustedly. And yet, just for a moment, what almost frightening power had sounded in that cry from only a few hundred throats! Why was it that they could never shout like that about anything that mattered?'[*]

Rather more prosaically, a middle-aged country housewife described her weekly shopping in 1949: 'I glance through fruit shops (in case citrus fruits are in), may look in at . . . ironmonger's for some small item—inquiring meanwhile for goods in short supply . . . Watch other people's shopping baskets and glance in at grocers'. Similarly a young town housewife looked 'round the shops with an eye to a bargain or something to put away for Christmas or birthdays. I visit Smith's and ask for books like Beatrix Potter's, which have to be asked for regularly. I wander along to the furniture shop to ask after Utility carpets'.[88] Although supplies of course improved after the war, for many household items they remained below pre-war levels until the end of the 1940s when erstwhile hopes of a post-war spending spree were dashed in the face of rising prices and high taxes.

There is little doubt about the high level of post-war female demand for consumer goods as well as women's growing realization, especially from 1947 onwards, that this demand was unlikely to be satisfied. Furnishings and household goods stood at the top of women's post-war shopping list among Mass-Observation's panel of observers while men overwhelmingly favoured personal possessions.[89] As a result of wear and tear and minimal replacement, stocks of many household goods were low at the end of the war. For example, about a quarter of households fell below the Board of Trade's minimum standard with regard to furniture possession and shortages were greatest among the lower income groups and large families.[90] Similarly, about 50 per cent of working-class households had no carpets at all and four-fifths of working-class housewives wanted to buy a carpet if any were available at a suitable price.[91] In 1947 demand for crockery was 'considerably greater than in wartime, but there has been no rise in the

[*] G. Orwell, *1984* (London, 1949), pp. 64–5 [Penguin, Harmondsworth, 1983 edition].

[88] MO, reprint of article published in *News Review*, 27 Jan. 1949.

[89] MO, FR 2066, Post-war Buying, Apr. 1944.

[90] Nuffield College Library, Oxford, Social Survey, Furniture: An Inquiry Made for the Board of Trade, n.s. no. 63, May 1945.

[91] Nuffield College Library, Oxford, Social Survey, Carpets: An Inquiry into the Present Use of and Future Demand for Carpets in Working-class Households Made for the Carpets Working Party of the Board of Trade, n.s. no. 82, Oct. 1946.

proportion of successful shoppers . . . Thus, from the consumer's point of view there is a greater shortage of crockery today than there was during the war.' Most housewives were unable to buy the items they needed because they were 'simply not available in the shops'.[92] According to this survey, four-fifths of housewives badly needed some household goods they were unable to buy, with curtains and furnishing fabrics, household linen, and floor covering mentioned most frequently. This evidence is confirmed by a Gallup poll of May 1947 in which the overwhelming majority felt that their homes needed household textiles, floor coverings, as well as repairs and fittings, but 54 per cent thought that they would be unable to get anything.[93] A similar poll in 1950 still showed a high level of demand for these items as well as furniture, but over a third thought they would be unable to get them primarily due to high prices.[94] These surveys clearly indicate the effect of continued shortages of household goods until the end of the 1940s. Consumer demand after the war did not focus on luxuries such as electrical appliances, which were rarely mentioned; nor was it predominantly a middle-class phenomenon. Indeed, working-class housewives whose stocks were lower and who had less money to spend were worst affected by shortages. The frequently frustrated desire to brighten up the home was demoralizing at a time when many housewives were literally trying to create or re-create a home following the end of the wartime dislocation of family life.

Food shortages were of much greater significance. Housewives' low food morale after the war and their general pessimism—in stark contrast with the wartime experience—have been discussed above. The ration cuts of 1946–8 bore particularly heavily on housewives who, in contrast with many men and schoolchildren, were almost entirely dependent on rations and rarely consumed meals outside the home. Government critics in the 'calorie' debate of 1947 claimed that while average calorie consumption might be adequate many housewives were likely to fall below the average.[95] According to a Gallup poll of July 1947, a third of mothers but only 12 per cent among fathers deliberately gave up some of their bacon, egg, fats, and meat rations to other members of the family.[96] A survey, conducted between February 1947 and May 1948, investigated the impact of ration cuts as well as bread and potato rationing on adolescents and their mothers who 'might have deprived [themselves] in favour of [their] offspring'. While adolescents did well, their mothers were identified as 'the most vulnerable' group yet examined and the proportions classed as 'fair' (10.9 per cent) and 'poor'

[92] PRO, RG 23/528, Social Survey: Domestic Crockery Survey. A Report on Domestic Crockery Stocks and on the Demand for Household Crockery Prepared by the Social Survey for the Statistics and Consumer Needs Division of the Board of Trade, n.s. no. 99, July 1947.
[93] *Gallup Polls*, p. 156.   [94] Ibid., p. 230.
[95] On the 'calorie' debate, see Chapter 5, section 5.2.   [96] *Gallup Polls*, p. 160.

(1.7 per cent) were higher than in any other group.[97] Similarly, a survey of 61 Brighton housewives in 1948 noted that the diet of 47 was inadequate. This was 'never attributable to lack of money' but the result of bad eating habits coupled with the fact that 'many women gave up their own rations to the family . . . [whose members] always fared much better than she did'. Not surprisingly, the 'outstanding impression made by these housewives was their look of fatigue'. Many suffered from anxiety and 'Several of them dreamed regularly of cooking, shopping, and standing in a queue. A few admitted to waking up at intervals during the night and planning the next day's meals.'[98]

A BMA report, *Report of the Committee on Nutrition*, provides further evidence which is worth quoting at some length.[99] A series of studies between 1941 and 1948 aimed to measure the cost of the diet and the availability of food for a standard family consisting of husband, wife, and three children aged 5, 7, and 12.

Throughout the war the 'housewife' of the 'standard' family would have had little difficulty in obtaining the 'human needs' diet. . . . In the Spring of 1945, however, . . . although the diet could be purchased without any difficulty, 'only a housewife who was a moderately skilled cook and also had a fair knowledge of nutritional values and requirements would have been able to provide a satisfactory diet for her family at the cost stated.' The picture changed somewhat in Spring, 1946, for although the diet could still be obtained without much difficulty, it is suggested that the shortage of fats made it difficult for adults to obtain a sufficient calorie intake without considerable strain on the digestion, this being the cause of the 'recurrent complaints' that 'people have not enough to eat'. The same point is made in regard to the survey in Spring, 1947. At that time cheap fish, meat and vegetables were scarce and bread and flour were rationed, but two fairly inexpensive calorie foods, oatmeal and barley flakes, could be bought freely. 'It was therefore possible for a housewife to obtain enough food to prevent her family from going hungry, although sometimes it may have been difficult to induce everyone to eat his full share of the meals she was able to prepare with the foods that were available.' . . . [Similarly in 1948] the 'various important changes in rationing necessitated a large number of adjustments in the planning of the family diet that were difficult to make, in particular when they had to be procured at the lowest possible cost'.

These surveys suggest that after the end of the war the difficulties facing housewives in obtaining a sufficient and appetizing diet for their families were increased, owing not so much to an actual shortage of food as to an insufficiency of the more palatable foods. Those especially affected were families who could not afford to

[97] *Monthly Bulletin of the Ministry of Health and the Emergency Public Health Service* 7 (1948), pp. 153–4.

[98] S. Instone, 'The Welfare of the Housewife', *The Lancet*, 4 Dec. 1948, pp. 899–901.

[99] BMA, *Report of the Committee on Nutrition*, pp. 46–7, 90, 97–9. The remainder of this paragraph is based on this source.

spend much on food . . . [and] a woman working at home may have difficulty in getting more than her bare rations.

The psychological effect of shortages was examined in the concluding sections of the report. Complaints after the war were very often a reaction to the erosion of many elements of the traditional British diet. The provision of acceptable meals was an immense strain for many housewives if we may judge by comments collected through the Women's Voluntary Service (WVS) at the beginning of 1948. With rationing of both bread and potatoes,

especially for families who could not take meals out, there was difficulty in obtaining sufficient unrationed foods to provide, with the rations, really adequate meals. It was pointed out that tinned foods were costly in points and that the high prices of fruit and vegetables made them luxuries for many households. As regards shortages of individual foods, the restricted supply of fat (including cooking fat) was said to be a serious problem. There were complaints, too, of insufficient milk, of a shortage of sausages, and of the poor quality of some meat and offal. Finally, it was clear from the comments received that the necessity of standing for long periods in queues, and carrying heavy shopping baskets home, contributed greatly to the fatigue and irritation suffered by those people responsible for family catering.

Although the report did not accept all these complaints at face value and welcomed that some sections of the population were fed rather better than before the war,

there can be little doubt that the continuing difficulties associated with the procuring and preparation of food in the post-war period have tended to depress the morale of many members of the community. The monotony in the diet which has resulted from the restricted choice of foods has added to the unattractiveness of meals; in some cases it may be impracticable for the busy housewife to add variety by using the recipes for made-up dishes recommended by the Ministry of Food, as the preparation of many of these dishes occupies much time. . . . The physical and mental strain imposed upon the housewife may be increased as a result of her consuming less than her proper proportion of the rations. A devoted wife or mother may sacrifice her own share of the more appetizing foods for the sake of a hardworking husband or a growing child, in which case her nutrition may suffer. . . . It need hardly be said that to catalogue the tribulations of those who are responsible for providing present-day meals is not to disparage in any way the achievements of the Ministry of Food. The Committee is concerned solely to point out the fact, perhaps obvious enough, that dissatisfaction with monotonous and unappetizing, even if adequately nutritious food, and the constant mental irritation of the housewife's daily catering task, cannot but have a depressing effect on the national morale.

This evidence suggests that especially under post-war austerity women's traditional role as a buffer in the family economy during periods of economic crisis acquired renewed significance despite the Welfare State and full employment. While welfare policy, including food subsidies, largely benefited women, the gains of full employment and higher wages were not shared equally within the household since many men failed to adjust house-keeping allowances in line with rising earnings. The effect of this custom was exacerbated by the high rate of inflation during the late 1940s.[100] Oren's conclusion, although based on an earlier period and different focus, helps us to appreciate the gendered consequences of post-war austerity: 'to reduce the pressures, both physical and mental, on the husband's standard of liv-ing', the wife 'absorbed the blows of an insecure existence and provided the necessary margin . . . out of her own and the children's standard of living. . . . The wife's elastic standard of living served as a buffer of the larger eco-nomic system as well'.[101] During the 1940s, this traditional response to eco-nomic crisis was transformed in two ways. On the one hand, children's experience was now more akin to that of fathers rather than mothers and, on the other, female sacrifice in the family economy extended well beyond the poorest income groups. With regard to the national economy women's buffer role still applied since a disproportionate share of the burden result-ing from the post-war recovery policy, characterized by domestic austerity and the export drive, was borne by women and particularly housewives.

Not surprisingly, there is a general agreement in the literature that 'life was hard and cheerless for women in the second half of the 1940s'.[102] Women responded with a mixture of despondency and protest. A good example of the former is Mrs Jones, a typical, if fictional, housewife in *Picture Post*'s special issue on the economic crisis:[103]

Mrs Jones doesn't care a damn for economics. To her, political theories, costs of liv-ing, trade pacts, imports and exports are just so many words . . . She is too busy with the urgent considerations of living to care about theories. She is absorbed every hour of the day in the task of feeding her family, keeping her house clean, keeping the children decent, shopping, scrubbing, cooking, mending—and making the money go round. And she finds the job a hard one. Harder than before the war. Harder, even, than during the war. She is utterly weary. So she grumbles. Yes, her prevailing mood is one of profound disappointment. We won the war. We expected an easier time. Why is it so much worse? Why are we so short? She finds there is less food for the family . . . that there are less goods in the shops. . . . She is fed up with queuing . . . And she hates the rudeness, the drabness she meets everywhere . . . This is her general attitude to life today.

[100] M. Young, 'Distribution of Income within the Family', *British Journal of Sociology* 3 (1952), pp. 305–21.
[101] Oren, 'The Welfare of Women in Laboring Families', p. 121. See also S. Nicholas and D. Oxley, 'The Living Standard of Women During the Industrial Revolution, 1795–1820', *Economic History Review* 46 (1993), pp. 723–49; Ross, *Love and Toil*, ch. 2, *passim*.
[102] Braybon and Summerfield, *Out of the Cage*, p. 277; see also Addison, *Now the War is Over*, pp. 29–40.   [103] *Picture Post*, 19 Apr. 1947.

While Mrs Jones did not necessarily blame the government, she resented 'being told that she is the best-fed housewife in Europe, and better fed than before the war. It may be true but she doesn't believe it.' In conclusion, Mrs Jones 'wants more leisure and more colour, as well as more food and clothes and less wearying work. But most of all she wants hope. That is why she is sadder now than during the war. Then there was always a target, Victory. Today, no one has tried to show her how and when the break may come.' A well-known example of housewives' protest was the BHL, whose membership was probably never very large, but which received considerable attention in public debate and acquired front-page notoriety particularly in the right-wing press. However, female frustration and discontent had significant political implications much beyond the nuisance value of the BHL. Because of housewives' central role in the austerity policy, housewives were a key political category during the late 1940s and early 1950s, heavily courted by Labour and the Conservatives whose battle over consumption during the general elections of the period was directed particularly at female voters.

3.2. MOTHERHOOD AND CHILD REARING

Motherhood and child rearing were changed considerably during the 1940s. Benefits such as special rations and welfare foods for mothers and children coincided with new difficulties such as shortages of infants' and children's clothes or nursery equipment. In the context of full employment, food subsidies, better maternity care, and particularly the introduction of the Welfare State and National Health Service after the war, vital statistics registered significant improvements from 1941 onwards.[104] These policies were aimed at the lowest income groups and especially working-class women, whose health was frequently poor before the war since most women were not covered by health insurance schemes. However, the redistributive effect of these reforms is debatable and the structure of the Welfare State in which wives were classed as dependants has been criticized by feminist scholars.[105] More specifically, as a result of redistribution within the family, mothers did not necessarily consume the extra rations to which they were entitled, the uptake of welfare foods was low, particularly among the lower income groups, and class differentials in vital statistics persisted. Feeding adolescents on flat-rate rations could be difficult and the effect of clothes

---

[104] See Titmuss, *Problems of Social Policy*; R. Lowe, *The Welfare State in Britain since 1945* (Basingstoke, 1993); Lewis, *Women in England*; A. Digby, 'Poverty, Health and the Politics of Gender in Britain, 1870–1948', in A. Digby and M. J. Stewart (eds.), *Gender, Health and Welfare* (London, 1996).

[105] E. Wilson, *Women and the Welfare State* (London, 1977); Lewis, *Women in Britain since 1945*, pp. 92–5. This debate is summed up in Lowe, *The Welfare State*, pp. 33–5.

rationing on children, especially shortages of children's shoes, caused frustration throughout the period.

There are many important issues concerning mothers and children during the 1940s which cannot be dealt with in any detail here. Both debate and policy regarding women's role in the family were contradictory. While married women were excluded from conscription and wartime and post-war recruitment drives were not primarily aimed at mothers of young children, many mothers of young children did work, and inadequate childcare provision forced the majority to rely on private arrangements.[106] Evacuation disrupted family life and, for instance, 826,926 unaccompanied school-children and 523,670 mothers with pre-school children, as well as over 12,000 expectant mothers, were evacuated in September 1939.[107] Most returned home within months but there were further waves of evacuation during 1940 and 1944 as well as private arrangements. As a result, during the war many women became either evacuees or hostesses of evacuees. Despite these policies, official debate about the family and especially the need to reconstruct it after the war focused on the conventional nuclear family in which the mother's role was central and pro-natalist concerns were further heightened by the low fertility rate before the war.[108]

The 1940s and 1950s witnessed important changes in demographic trends and above all a post-war baby boom reversing the decline in fertility which could be observed from the late nineteenth century onwards.[109] After a reduction in the inter-war years, the popularity of marriage increased again and there was a marriage boom during the early years of the war and particularly the late 1940s. With earlier marriage, longer life expectancy for both sexes, and low divorce rates—apart from a brief post-war rise—'marriages enjoyed a stability without precedent in history'.[110] The reversal of declining fertility, which stood below the replacement level of 2.1 births per woman in the 1930s, from the late 1940s until the early 1960s was,

[106] Summerfield, 'Women, Work and Welfare', p. 250.

[107] J. Macnicol, 'The Evacuation of Schoolchildren', in Smith, *War and Social Change*, p. 6. Macnicol criticizes Titmuss' hypothesis in *Problems of Social Policy* that evacuation, in revealing urban poverty and deprivation to rural middle-class opinion, provided a catalyst for post-war welfare reforms. Welshman's recent study is more sympathetic to this argument; see J. Welshman, 'Evacuation and Social Policy during the Second World War: Myth and Reality', *Twentieth Century British History* 9 (1998), pp. 28–53.

[108] Morgan and Evans, *Battle for Britain*, ch. 3, *passim*; on the reconstruction of the family see Lewis, *Women in Britain since 1945*, pp. 16–26; on the wider social policy debate and family allowances see G. Bock and P. Thane (eds.), *Maternity and Gender Policies: Women and the Rise of the European Welfare States, 1880s–1950s* (London, 1991); V. Fildes, J. Marks, and H. Marland (eds.), *Women and Children First: International Maternal and Infant Welfare, 1870–1945* (London, 1992).

[109] See D. A. Coleman, 'Population', in Halsey, *British Social Trends*, pp. 39–49; J. M. Winter, 'The Demographic Consequences of the War', in Smith, *War and Social Change*, pp. 151–78; Lewis, *Women in England*, pp. 3–7.   [110] Coleman, 'Population', p. 75.

according to Winter, a 'fundamental change in demographic behaviour' brought about by a 'broad cultural reaction to the disturbances of 1939–45 which marked the outlook and aspirations of an entire generation' in Britain and elsewhere.[111] High post-war fertility was not just due to deferred fertility or higher illegitimacy which, despite a rise owing to wartime dislocation preventing many marriages taking place, remained low. While full employment and the Welfare State made childbearing economically more attractive, for Winter cultural factors and above all the perception of the family as a '"haven in a heartless world"' are central in explaining why the generation of women born during the interwar years and marrying after the war opted for marriage, domesticity, and motherhood, in contrast with both their mothers' and their daughters' generation.[112]

The following paragraphs examine those aspects of rationing and austerity policies which were directed at mothers and children, along with mothers' attitudes towards and the implications of these policies. The discussion of special rations for expectant and nursing mothers is followed by an evaluation of these policies with regard to maternal mortality and women's health. Children's diet improved with additional rations, the introduction of welfare foods, as well as the expansion of school meals and school milk. During the period infant mortality declined considerably, while anthropometric evidence points towards continued improvements in child health. With regard to miscellaneous consumer goods, the discussion focuses on mothers' difficulties with children's clothing and footwear, soap rationing, and shortages of nursery equipment as well as toys and treats. The lack of the latter items led to discontent especially during the Christmas period.

There is little doubt about the beneficial effects of rationing on expectant and nursing mothers. Over and above the general principle of fair shares for all, food policy provided for the particular needs of certain groups, namely manual workers, expectant and nursing mothers, and children. Details of entitlement changed somewhat throughout the period but essentially pregnant women and new mothers received extra rations and priority supplies of eggs, milk, and vitamins under the welfare foods scheme. The supplementary ration book issued to expectant mothers advised that:

All the extras provided . . . are essential for you in addition to the full share of your ordinary rations. You should also visit your doctor or local clinic regularly. If you do so and follow the advice given and also take all the extra food and vitamin supplements provided by this book, you are doing all you can to ensure your health and that of your child.[113]

[111] Winter, 'The Demographic Consequences of the War', pp. 153, 172.
[112] Ibid., p. 172.
[113] PRO, MAF 75/68, quoted from sample ration book for expectant mothers.

From 1943 onwards pregnant women received an additional half a meat ration and mothers were supposed to benefit from the half meat ration to which new-born babies were entitled.[114] While fresh fruit was not rationed due to limited and sporadic supplies, expectant mothers and children received priority in the allocation of oranges and bananas when available. Under bread rationing between 1946 and 1948, expectant mothers were entitled to 11 bread units compared with 9 for normal adults. Until 1943 pregnant women and mothers of babies under one year received priority in the allocation of eggs, effectively doubling their entitlement, and subsequently expectant mothers received one egg in addition to normal supplies as well as a double allocation of dried eggs. Perhaps the most important policy was the National Milk Scheme, introduced in 1940, under which pregnant women and mothers of babies under one year received 7 pints of subsidized or free milk a week in addition to their normal entitlement. Finally, from 1942 onwards expectant mothers were entitled to cheap or free orange juice, cod-liver oil, or Vitamin A and D tablets and after 1947 these were supplied for up to 30 weeks after confinement.

Any attempt at assessing the effect of this policy on mothers' diet is problematic, due to income differentials in the diet before the war, frequently low uptake, and the possibility that extra rations and milk were used for general family consumption. The limited evidence suggests, not surprisingly, that mothers ate less sugar, meat, and fruit than before the war but more bread and potatoes.[115] With regard to calorie and protein consumption there was little change on average but pregnant and nursing women were the only group who consumed more animal protein (compared with a fall of between 17 and 40 per cent among adults) during and after the war. According to two surveys, animal protein consumption was either equal to or greater than that of the richest two groups before the war. Milk consumption of almost two-thirds of pregnant women in Shoreditch was higher than that of the richest group during the 1930s. However, in Edinburgh in 1946, 'only 4 out of 35 pregnant women drank a pint of milk a day . . . Only 15 of these 35 women were taking orange juice and only 23 [were] taking cod-liver oil'. In Bristol in 1948, 'about two-thirds of pregnant women were getting 14 or more oz. of milk a day, and the average amount consumed was 17.6 oz. a day. However, 80 per cent were not taking their full allowance.' In London, again in 1948, '40 per cent of women in the first

---

[114] PRO, MAF 223/31 Ministry of Food, *Rationing in the United Kingdom*, 1950 edn.; Ministry of Food, *Urban Working-class Household Diet 1940 to 1949: First Report of the National Food Survey Committee* (London, 1951). These sources provide the information on all special entitlements. On milk and the welfare food scheme, see also Titmuss, *Problems of Social Policy*, pp. 511–14.

[115] BMA, *Report of the Committee on Nutrition*, pp. 42–3. The following sentences also rely on this source.

half of pregnancy and 52 per cent in the second half were taking a pint or more of milk per day'. Similarly, uptake of vitamin tablets was relatively low with only 51 and 18 per cent of expectant and nursing mothers respectively taking the tablets in 1950.[116] Nevertheless, a BMA report concluded that 'all the data relating to expectant mothers point to the maintenance of a high level of nutrition. The increased rates of improvement, compared with those found before the war, in neo-natal mortality and still births support this conclusion'.[117]

After 1939 female mortality rates fell, including a dramatic decline in the maternal mortality rate, but the question of overall female health is more ambiguous. The beneficial effect of dietary changes have to be viewed within the wider context of full employment and the introduction of the National Health Service as well as the wartime extension of female access to medical care. The reduction in the female mortality rate during and after the Second World War was part of the long-term decline in mortality since the mid-nineteenth century.[118] Between 1940 and 1951 standardized female mortality declined in England and Wales by 26.3 per cent, exceeding the reduction registered during the First World War.[119] This decline was due above all to the lower death rate of infants, children, and young women; much smaller gains occurred after the age of 40. For Winter, the key factors explaining these advances were the 'chemotherapeutic revolution' especially of the late 1940s coupled with 'several generations of improvements in nutrition and overall living standards', a long-term trend which was further accelerated by wartime and post-war policies.

The most striking advance was the rapid reduction in maternal mortality which had shown no improvement between the turn of the century and the mid-1930s.[120] The rate stood at 5.29 per 1,000 births in 1935, 3.99 in 1939, and 1.15 in 1950, amounting to a reduction in the risks associated with childbirth by 75 per cent in one decade.[121] Both Loudon and Winter explain these advances as a result of the combined effects of improved and more comprehensive maternity care coupled with a better diet due to rationing and welfare foods. While causality was complex since

[116] PRO, MAF 256/213, Memo, 5 Dec. 1950.
[117] BMA, *Report of the Committee on Nutrition*, p. 90.
[118] D. Coleman and J. Salt, *The British Population: Patterns, Trends, and Processes* (Oxford, 1992), p. 239, fig 7.1; B. Harrison, 'Women's Health and the Women's Movement in Britain: 1840–1940', in C. Webster (ed.), *Biology, Medicine and Society 1840–1940* (Cambridge, 1981), p. 15.
[119] Winter, 'The Demographic Consequences of the War', p. 166; Winter's discussion on pp. 165–70 is summarized in the following sentences.
[120] I. Loudon, *Death in Childbirth: An International Study of Maternal Care and Maternal Mortality 1800–1950* (Oxford, 1992), pp. 254–5.
[121] Winter, 'The Demographic Consequences of the War', pp. 154–7, 170–2.

many factors affect infant and maternal mortality rates, among these being social status, age and parity of the mother and advances in obstetric skill. All authorities, however, agree that satisfactory nutrition is important in lowering these mortality rates and it is evident that since the inception of the Welfare Foods Service the infant and maternal mortality rates have continued to fall.[122]

Winter maintains that women from the lowest income groups (semi-skilled and unskilled workers) benefited most,[123] but other evidence suggests a more complicated picture. For example, Marks shows that the East End of London, despite extensive poverty, registered a below-average maternal mortality rate before the war as a result of very high quality maternity care provision around the teaching hospitals as well as integrated charitable community services.[124] Moreover, with regard to still births and neo-natal mortality (under one month), both closely related to maternal health, class differences not only persisted but actually increased between 1939 and 1945. This apparent paradox was partly a consequence of the fact that 'priority rationing during pregnancy could not be expected to overcome differences in maternal physique, which may date from childhood or adolescence'.[125]

Prior to discussing infants' and children's diets and mortality, we look briefly at female morbidity. Before the war, the standard of female health was frequently appalling, judging by Spring Rice's survey of 1,250 working-class housewives and mothers during the late 1930s.[126] Until the 1940s most women were denied easy access to medical care. Child and maternal welfare policy was essentially voluntaristic and limited, based on the principle of a social minimum rather than optimum standards for all, and an emphasis on self-help and education of mothers rather than amelioration of poverty. Lewis concludes that between 1900 and 1939 these policies 'showed remarkable consistency . . . Perhaps not surprisingly the reality of women's health needs remained constant as well. Social surveys published during the 1930s echoed the findings of the Women's Cooperative Guild fifteen years before.'[127] The Second World War undoubtedly paved the way for major improvements with full access to medical care, despite the pressures on housewives' post-war diet discussed above. There is little evidence on maternal

[122] PRO, MAF 156/541, Some notes on nutrition policy in the United Kingdom, 1939–1955, Aug. 1955; see also BMA, *Report of the Committee on Nutrition*, pp. 73–4.

[123] Winter, 'The Demographic Consequences of the War', p. 172.

[124] L. Marks, 'Mothers, Babies and Hospitals: "The London" and the Provision of Maternity Care in East London, 1870–1939', in Fildes *et al., Women and Children First*, pp. 48–73.

[125] BMA, *Report of the Committee on Nutrition*, p. 73; on the significance of generational effects and cohort patterns of perinatal mortality see J. Winter, 'Unemployment, Nutrition and Infant Mortality in Britain, 1920–50', in J. M. Winter (ed.), *The Working Class in Modern British History* (Cambridge, 1983), pp. 254–5.

[126] M. Spring Rice, *Working-class Wives: Their Health and Conditions* (London, 1939).

[127] J. Lewis, *The Politics of Motherhood: Child and Maternal Welfare in England, 1900–1939* (London, 1980), p. 225.

or female health beyond vital statistics. For example, deaths due to tuberculosis among women aged between 20 and 35 declined during the war but
increased again in 1946–7.[128] More encouraging were haemoglobin level
surveys which noted improvements during and after the war indicating a
decline in anaemia, which had been 'relatively common in the distressed
areas before the war'.[129] In sum, the health of pregnant women and new
mothers improved markedly during the 1940s although the picture with
regard to female health generally is perhaps a little more ambiguous.

Food policy prioritized children but whereas the flat-rate rationing system
was generous to small children, there was little extra for adolescents, especially after they left school. Yet again entitlement varied slightly throughout
the period but essentially there were three kinds of special arrangement:
'first, special provision of certain foods for the individual child; second, the
provision of higher allowances for meals served to day-scholars in schools
. . . and third, the provision of rationed or controlled food for clubs, centres,
camps and similar institutions for young people'.[130] All children received the
same rations as adults apart from only half the meat ration and no tea for
those under 5. Under bread rationing from 1946 to 1948, children 4–11
years were entitled to the normal adult ration of 9 bread units, with less (5
bread units) for those under 4 and more (13 bread units) for 11–18 year-
olds. Oranges, when available, were reserved for children under 18 (with
double the allocation for those under 5) and after the war bananas were distributed to children under 18 years old. Children between 6 and 18 months
(24 months from 1945 onwards) received priority in the allocation of eggs
with three per week when the normal allocation stood at about one a week,
or less, until the very late 1940s. Children under 5 also received roughly
double the normal allocation of dried egg. Perhaps the most important
dietary advantage enjoyed by children was the allocation of milk as well as
vitamin supplements under the welfare foods scheme. Children under 5
were entitled to 7 pints a week of subsidized or free milk and children aged
5–18 received 3.5 pints per week. This reduction was based on the assumption of school milk, and those children unable to attend school received 5
pints per week. From 1942 onwards, children under 5 were entitled to

[128] BMA, *Report of the Committee on Nutrition*, p. 75.
[129] PRO, MAF 156/541, Some Notes on Nutrition Policy in the United Kingdom, 1939–1955,
Aug. 1955.
[130] PRO, MAF 223/29, Ministry of Food, *The Feeding of Children and Young People* (London,
1943); see also PRO, MAF 223/31 Ministry of Food, Rationing in the United Kingdom, 1950;
Ministry of Food, *Urban working-class Household Diet 1940 to 1949: First Report of the
National Food Survey Committee* (London, 1951). These sources provide information of special
entitlements. On milk, welfare foods, and school meals, see also Titmuss, *Problems of Social Policy*,
pp. 511–14; C. Webster, 'Government Policy on School Meal and Welfare Foods 1939–1970', in
D. F. Smith (ed.), *Nutrition in Britain: Science, Scientists and Politics in the Twentieth Century*
(London, 1997), pp. 190–213.

subsidized or free orange juice and cod-liver oil and after the war children up to 10 received orange juice and cod-liver oil which was provided free of charge for all from 1946 onwards.

Communal provision for children focused on the substantial extension of school meals as well as the milk-in-schools scheme. Compared with only 4 per cent before the war, by 1945 '40 per cent of schoolchildren in England and Wales were eating school dinners, either free or subsidised, which provided around 1,000 kcals, at least one-third of their energy requirements'.[131] Not only did the quality of meals improve but school dinners lost their pre-war association with poverty and became an integral part of school routine. For example, while two-thirds of meals were free before the war, in 1942 only one out of ten meals was free. Consumption rose further after the war and 42 per cent of children in 1946 and 45 per cent in 1953 took school dinners.[132] At the same time, the milk-in-schools scheme, introduced in the 1930s, expanded rapidly. Under the scheme children were entitled to one-third of a pint of milk per day, either subsidized or free until 1946 when milk became free for all. While just over half of all children took milk before the war, the figure increased from 57 to 76 per cent between 1941 and 1944 and rose further after the war to 85 and 92 per cent respectively in 1946 and 1948. These figures indicate the manifest success of policies intended to augment the rations of schoolchildren but similar policies aimed at adolescents achieved little. To follow on from school milk, Natmilco (National Milk Cocoa) was made available to young workers and later students up to the age of 18 (21 after 1944) as well as youth organizations. The scheme 'did not, however, prove popular and very few adolescents took advantage of it'.[133] There was little alternative but to provide cheap canteen meals for juvenile workers as well as extra allowances of rationed and controlled foods to residential students and youth organizations.

A number of surveys suggest that children's diets during and after the war were not only maintained but better than those of the pre-war period. Milk consumption in particular increased and, for example, children from industrial towns consumed as much milk during the war as children from high income groups in the 1930s.[134] Nutritional requirements varied greatly between age groups and a 1947 study stressed that:

rations of children under 5 years old supplied more calories than are needed; children from 5 to 10 years get about as much as they need from rationed foods alone.

[131] Burnett, 'The Rise and Decline of School Meals', p. 55; BMA, *Report of the Committee on Nutrition*, pp. 48–9; PRO, MAF 156/541, Some Notes on Nutrition Policy in the United Kingdom, 1939–1955, Aug. 1955.
[132] For detailed statistics see B. Harris, *The Health of the Schoolchild: A History of the School Medical Service in England and Wales* (Buckingham, 1995), pp. 155–60, 195–200.
[133] PRO, MAF 156/541, Some Notes on Nutrition Policy in the United Kingdom, 1939–1955, Aug. 1955.   [134] BMA, *Report of the Committee on Nutrition*, pp. 42–3, 48, 51.

But adolescents, normal adult males, pregnant women and manual workers, with high calorie requirements would have real difficulty in getting enough ... unless they got meals in canteens or restaurants or ate prodigious quantities of potatoes.[135]

The problem of feeding adolescents increased when rations were cut further at the end of 1947. While the authorities were concerned about adolescents, surveys of young factory workers and grammar school boys between 1942 and 1948 suggest that the nutritional state of the overwhelming majority (95 per cent or more) was considered to be good and less than 1 per cent were classed as poor.[136] As argued above, it was mothers rather than children themselves who bore the brunt of food shortages after the war. The nutritional state of schoolchildren resembled that of adolescents, with 86 per cent assessed as good during and just after the war, and the figure rose to 95 per cent between February 1947 and May 1948.[137] According to the BMA report, 'good provision is made for the school child' with school milk and school meals; 'It seems unsatisfactory, however, that during the school holidays the nutrition of the child is in some cases maintained only by sacrifice on the part of the parents'.[138] In theory, milk continued to be available in schools but few children actually took it during the holidays and it was suggested that this milk should be made available as part of the child's individual ration. The only evidence regarding pre-school children's diet is a social survey, conducted in 1951, which concluded that the nutritional level of a representative sample of children was 'as good as [the] pre-war nutritional level of middle class children'.[139] Pre-school children also benefited from vitamin supplements in the form of orange juice and cod-liver oil. Table 3.4 shows that uptake of these vitamin products rarely exceeded a third of potential demand, with the exception of orange juice between 1943 and 1947, and cod-liver oil was unpopular especially during the war. A range of surveys suggest that uptake was influenced above all by income group, education, and age of the mother, all pointing towards significantly higher uptake among the middle classes.[140] Consumption of vitamin products declined among older children, cod-liver oil was discontinued since children disliked it, orange juice was frequently shared among

[135] BMA, *Report of the Committee on Nutrition.*, p. 46. See Ministry of Food, *Manual of Nutrition* (London, 1945), p. 43 for differential nutritional requirements based on American wartime data and used during the 1940s.

[136] *Monthly Bulletin of the Ministry of Health and the Emergency Public Health Service 7* (1948), p. 154.   [137] Ibid., p. 155.

[138] BMA, *Report of the Committee on Nutrition*, p. 99.

[139] National Library of Wales, The Social Survey, The Diets of Young Children, n.s. 169/2, 1952, p. 36.

[140] PRO, MAF 98/60, Welfare Food Scheme: Distribution of Cod-liver Oil; Nuffield College Library, Oxford, Wartime Social Survey, Food supplements: An Inquiry for the Ministry of Food into the Use of Fruit Juices and Cod-liver Oil, 1944; Social Survey, The Uptake of Welfare Foods: Report of an Inquiry Carried Out by the Social Survey in April 1951 for the Ministry of Food, Sept. 1951.

TABLE 3.4. *Annual uptake of vitamin products in the United Kingdom as a percentage of maximum potential demand, 1942–1951 (per cent)*

Date	Orange juice	Cod-liver oil	Vitamin A & D tablets
1942[a]	23.5	14.8	N/A
1943[b]	37.9	19.9	31.8
1944	52.5	22.1	37.3
1945	45.0	12.4	33.2
1946[c]	41.2	24.7	42.5
1947	39.6	32.3	40.8
1948	35.9	32.8	37.3
1949	33.7	30.2	35.9
1951	27.0	26.0	N/A

[a] Orange juice and cod-liver oil were introduced on 1 Apr. 1942.
[b] Vitamin A & D tablets were introduced on 1 Apr. 1943.
[c] From 21 July 1946, cod-liver oil and vitamin tablets were issued free of cost to beneficiaries.
Sources: PRO, MAF 75/89; Nuffield College Library, Oxford, Social Survey, The Uptake of Welfare Foods: Report of an Inquiry Carried out by the Social Survey in April 1951 for the Ministry of Food, Sept. 1951.

all children, and uptake also depended on the location of clinics where welfare foods could be obtained.

These nutritional policies coincided with dramatic improvements in vital statistics, and the post-war Labour government highlighted the image of healthy, well-fed, and well-dressed children of the late 1940s, for example on the front cover of *Proud Heritage*, published in 1949. In contrast with unemployment, misery, and poverty during the interwar years, 'in spite of shortages, the children are rosy-cheeked, well-clothed . . . They are taller, heavier and healthier than before the war.'[141] While the reduction in infant and child mortality as well as gains in height and weight were part of a longer-term trend during the twentieth century, this trend certainly accelerated during the 1940s and 1950s. The greatest gains in mortality rates during the twentieth century were achieved by infants and children and, for example, life expectancy at birth increased by one decade between 1931 and 1961.[142] Similarly, Winter's analysis of female mortality rates between 1940 and 1951 emphasizes the disproportionate gains made especially by children—the death rate of girls aged 5–9 fell by 75 per cent—as well as young adults.[143] The infant mortality rate declined throughout the century and, apart from a temporary increase in 1940–1, the reduction was

[141] Labour Party, *Proud Heritage* (London, 1949); see also Central Office of Information, *Something Done: British Achievement 1945–47* (London, 1948); *Picture Post*, 24 Apr. 1948, special issue on children, which contrasts hunger and neglect in continental Europe with Britain's 'lucky babies' who had a 'better chance of good health than in any country in the world'.
[142] Coleman and Salt, *The British Population*, p. 239, fig. 7.1; pp. 242–3.
[143] Winter, 'The Demographic Consequences of the War', p. 168, p. 166, table 7.

particularly rapid during the 1940s. The infant mortality rate in England and Wales fell from 51 per 1,000 in 1939 to 46 in 1945, and stood at only 27 in 1953.[144] The greatest reduction occurred in the post-neonatal mortality rate (between one and 12 months), pointing towards improvements in environmental factors, whereas the neonatal mortality rate (under one month) is associated primarily with problems during pregnancy and childbirth.[145] These advances were shared by all social groups but income differentials persisted. The excess mortality rate among babies from Registrar-General Class V (the poorest), which was more than double the rate of Class I, remained 'virtually the same' between 1939 and 1951.[146] Whereas 'many people have consequently dismissed nutrition as unimportant', a Ministry of Food memorandum maintained that 'there is a flaw in this argument because . . . the higher social classes used vitamin supplements more than others . . . and this may have offset the equalising effect of rationing'.[147] Dietary policy undoubtedly contributed towards these dramatic improvements in infants' and children's survival chances but the policy failed to eliminate class differences. Despite the fair shares policy and equal rations for all, environmental factors as well as the differential uptake of welfare foods help to explain why infant survival chances still varied between classes in the early 1950s.

Mortality is a rather crude indicator of subtle changes in social conditions, and data on morbidity as well as height and weight arguably provide a better indication of the impact of dietary changes on children. Unfortunately, evidence on morbidity is limited but, for example, haemoglobin level studies of schoolchildren and adolescents during and after the war 'indicated that anaemia was less prevalent in . . . children than before the war'.[148] The BMA report was rather more ambiguous and noted a deterioration in the child death rate from respiratory tuberculosis in the early post-war years especially among pre-school children. In conclusion, this was considered

a disturbing feature; and there are still some cases of rickets. There can be no doubt that for school children the pre-war fall in mortality from respiratory tuberculosis has been slowed down since 1939. Although physique improved up to 1945 and the state of nutrition as judged by the rapid nutrition surveys was good, the reduction

[144] Winter, *The Demographic Consequences of the War*, pp. 154–6, tables 2–3; I. Loudon, 'On Maternal and Infant Mortality 1900–1960', *Social History of Medicine* 4 (1991), p. 38, fig. 3; PRO, MAF 156/541, Some Notes on Nutrition Policy in the United Kingdom, 1939–1955, Aug. 1955.

[145] Winter, 'The Demographic Consequences of the War', pp. 154–6, tables 2 and 3; Loudon, 'On Maternal and Infant Mortality 1900–1960', pp. 36–8, fig. 3; Winter, 'Unemployment, Nutrition and Infant Mortality in Britain, 1920–1950', p. 236, fig. 3.

[146] Winter, 'Unemployment, Nutrition and Infant Mortality in Britain, 1920–1950', p. 246, table 3.   [147] PRO, MAF 256/213, Notes on Welfare Foods, n.d. [approx. 1947].

[148] PRO, MAF 156/541, Some Notes on Nutrition Policy in the United Kingdom, 1939–1955, Aug. 1955.

in growth-rates between 1945 and 1947, considered in conjunction with the trends in the mortality from tuberculosis, raises the question whether some adverse factors may be operating.[149]

Anthropometric evidence clearly points towards improvements during the 1940s and 1950s, despite the persistence of class differentials. Height is a useful indicator of nutritional status or a biological standard of living.[150] Due to rapid growth in the womb, during infancy, childhood, and adolescence, studies of children are particularly suggestive of changes in diet and environmental factors. Malnutrition during these periods delays growth and also results in a lower terminal height in adults. Schoolchildren were measured and weighed regularly following the introduction of school medical inspections before the First World War and there is no doubt about the upward trend on average in both height and weight until the 1950s and beyond. For example, de V. Weir's study of London schoolboys aged between 5–13 shows an increase in mean height of 7.46 cm. (almost 3 in.) and weight of 4.09 kg (about 9 lb.) between 1905–12 and 1949.[151] Oddy and Floud *et al.* emphasize an acceleration in the trend during the Second World War and especially between 1945 and 1953 'when heights continued to increase while weights "rose steeply"'.[152] Similarly, Harris notes a 'substantial improvement' in child health during the period reflected in mortality and height data as well as the 'virtual elimination of many of the extreme forms of physical disability which had disfigured the lives of earlier generations'.[153] The BMA report endorses the wartime advances. After small regressions in some areas during 1940–2, in 1944 boys and girls on average had gained between $\frac{1}{4}$ and $\frac{1}{2}$ in. in height and between $1\frac{1}{2}$ and 2 lb. in weight compared with pre-war figures. Nevertheless, 'the annual reports of school medical officers for the years 1945 and 1947 indicate that, on the whole, there was a slight falling away in rates of growth during 1945–7'.[154] Again, Ministry of Food sources suggest variations in trend—in line with food supplies—and after improvements in 1948–50 weights tended 'to

[149] BMA, *Report of the Committee on Nutrition*, pp. 73, 90.

[150] B. Harris, 'Health, Height and History: An Overview of Recent Developments in Anthropometric History', *Social History of Medicine* 7 (1994) is a useful introduction to the anthropometric approach; see also Floud *et al.*, *Height, Health and History*; J. Komlos (ed.), *Stature, Living Standards, and Economic Development: Essays in Anthropometric History* (Chicago, 1994).

[151] J. B. de V. Weir, 'The Assessment of the Growth of Schoolchildren with Special Reference to Secular Changes', *British Journal of Nutrition* 6 (1952), p. 21, table 1.

[152] Oddy, 'The Health of the People', in Barker and Drake, *Population and Society in Britain*, p. 130, quoting from A. W. Byone, F. C. Aitken, and I. Leitch, 'Secular Changes in Height and Weight of British Children, Including an Analysis of Measurements of English Children in Primary Schools, 1911–1953', *Nutrition Abstracts and Reviews* 27 (1957), pp. 1–18; Floud *et al.*, *Height, Health and History*, p. 181.

[153] Harris, *The Health of the Schoolchild*, p. 200, and see pp. 165–71, 200–5 for wartime and post-war statistics.   [154] BMA, *Report of the Committee on Nutrition*, p. 79.

decrease slightly between 1950 and 1953, particularly in children under eight years of age. ... children from small families tend to be of better physique than those from large ones, especially from those in the lowest social groups (Registrar-General's Social Groups IV and V)—a fact which has been known for a long time'.[155]

Despite these short-term fluctuations, the final comment draws attention to the greater significance of class and regional differentials. These are emphasized by Harris, whose study of the interwar years concludes that in the more prosperous areas 'the average height of children was already close to modern standards by the end of the 1930s, but the height of children in other areas [worst affected by the depression] was well below the height of children today. The differences ... may well have increased during the period'.[156] Hence it is perhaps not surprising that de V. Weir's London sample, a relatively prosperous region, showed less improvement during the 1940s in contrast with the Glasgow data where a considerable acceleration in height and weight gain points towards the beneficial effect of wartime nutrition policies. In 1947 even East End children registered only slight improvements compared with pre-war data but children from poor districts of Liverpool showed disproportionate gains in weight while boys from affluent districts gained little and girls actually lost weight.[157] In the 1950s, London's exceptional record was again illustrated. Whereas the School Medical Officer of the London County Council noted in 1954 that 'within his school population differences in heights and weights by area had "largely disappeared"', studies from Liverpool, Sheffield, and Newcastle during the late 1940s and early 1950s emphasized the persistence of social gradients in height and weight of children.[158] In line with vital statistics, anthropometric evidence suggests that rationing and fair shares contributed towards improvements in children's physique on average but failed to eliminate class differentials—yet again illustrating the limitations of the policy.

It remains to examine how rationing and shortages of miscellaneous consumer goods affected mothers and their children. With the exception of clothing and footwear difficulties, which led to widespread and continuous grumbling, the irritation caused by shortages was relatively minor, apart from the Christmas period, as mothers resorted to alternatives such as the second-hand market and home-made furniture, bedding, or toys.

Clothes-rationing policy provided no additional allowances for maternity wear and the Board of Trade advised women to 'avoid spending coupons on

---

[155] PRO, MAF 156/541, Some Notes on Nutrition Policy in the United Kingdom, 1939–1955, Aug. 1955.

[156] B. Harris, 'The Height of Schoolchildren in Britain, 1900–1950', in Komlos, *Stature, Living Standards, and Economic Development*, p. 38.

[157] BMA, *Report of the Committee on Nutrition*, p. 80.

[158] Quoted in Oddy, 'The Health of the People', pp. 133–5.

special maternity clothes. Almost all your existing clothes can be altered easily so that you can wear them comfortably until the baby is born, and you can wear them again afterwards'.[159] During pregnancy women on average spent 25 coupons on clothes for themselves but this was not considered to be a problem since when they were 'wearing these garments, they [were] not wearing others. This means that at least some of the 25 coupons can justifiably be regarded as taken out of the mother's own ration'.[160] Women continued to improvise, adapt clothes, or buy second-hand until the end of the decade. For instance, the GHI approved of second-hand maternity corsets and advised on how to make a maternity belt as well as how to alter clothes, urging women in 1946 'to avoid any suggestion of dowdiness—nothing is so destructive of self-confidence'.[161] Nothing had changed by 1949 but in 1953 new undergarments were to be bought and 'attractive maternity dresses at reasonable prices [were] now much more readily available'.[162] There is no evidence of discontent with shortages of maternity wear and women apparently accepted the situation with equanimity, in stark contrast with constant and at times intense complaints about the difficulties of clothing children.

Although baby clothes were initially coupon free, from August 1941 they were incorporated into the rationing scheme and pregnant women were issued 50 (later 60) coupons to purchase a baby's layette or the materials required for it since many women preferred to make their own clothes. From birth babies were entitled to the full ration, allowing for further purchases. This change in policy caused some resentment, particularly in view of the high coupon price of nappies, approximately 24 coupons, but again mothers soon adapted to the situation.[163] While *Good Housekeeping* lamented the disappearance of the 'old carefree days' of the 1930s, 'baby's 60 coupons will suffice—if you follow the "Two Layers of Wool, One of Fine Flannel" Plan'.[164] Not surprisingly middle-class mothers found it more difficult to manage than working-class mothers who seemed 'better able to forecast their baby's needs', and complaints focused on the 'insufficiency of coupons to cover the necessary number of napkins'. The Board of Trade showed little sympathy according to an internal comment; the 'shortage of napkins may sorely afflict the infant, but it looks as though this always has

[159] Quoted in Longmate, *How We Lived Then*, p. 175.

[160] PRO, BT 64/1370, Report on Coupon Expenditure of Expectant Mothers and Mothers with Newly Born Babies, November 1941–January 1942, Memo, 23 Apr. 1942.

[161] GHI, *Baby Book*, 7th edn. (London, 1946), pp. 14–17.

[162] GHI, *Baby Book*, 9th edn. (London, 1953), p. 30.

[163] PRO, INF 1/292, Home Intelligence Weekly Morale Reports, 3–10 and 8–15 Sept. 1941.

[164] *Good Housekeeping*, Oct. 1942. Of course not everybody shared in these 'carefree days' and poorer mothers found it difficult to purchase the range of recommended baby requisites during the interwar years; see E. Peretz, 'The Costs of Modern Motherhood to Low Income Families in Interwar Britain', in Fildes *et al.*, *Women and Children First*, pp. 257–80.

been one of the penalties of infancy'.[165] Later in the war the Board was concerned that the 'official' layette was 'undefended', that is, if there were public protests because of the shortage of coupon-free muslin nappies the Ministry of Health would not back up the Board of Trade, but since protest was muted or non-existent the issue was no longer discussed.[166] In 1947–8 supplies of infant wear and nappies were considered adequate despite some local shortages, and throughout the 1940s 'present-day conditions' forced mothers to focus on the essential items and juggle coupons since, for example, coupon economy on nappies might result in laundry difficulties.[167] At least for middle-class mothers, nostalgia about former largesse in contrast with present 'sterner times' remained a motif until the end of the decade.[168] Only from the early 1950s onwards did recommended layettes become more elaborate, distinguishing between summer and winter wear and advising on new clothes after four months, in stark contrast with earlier advice on making garments last up to 18 months.[169]

Apart from manual workers, children were the only major group receiving preferential treatment under clothes rationing. Children's clothes were pointed at a lower level and from 1942 onwards all children qualified for 10 supplementary coupons per year with up to 20 further coupons for adolescents and 'outsize' children, those under 13 who were exceptionally tall or heavy for their age. More than two million children were weighed and measured at school to qualify for the additional coupons.[170] Despite these concessions, difficulties with children's clothing and footwear developed into an acute problem on the home front, if we may judge by Home Intelligence morale reports. The inadequacy of the clothes ration for growing children as well as the high price and poor quality of clothes was first raised in the summer of 1942 and in November the shoe shortage was mentioned in five regions as '"harrass[ed] mothers"' feared that '"serious foot deformities may result"'.[171] The shoe shortage was again highlighted in the winter, 'said to be affecting school attendance' in some regions, and 'many children have no change of shoes at all or [were] wearing wrong sizes'.[172] In the spring of 1943, the reduction of the clothes ration was 'received with some dismay,

[165] PRO, BT 64/1370, Report on Coupon Expenditure of Expectant Mothers and Mothers with Newly Born Babies, November 1941–January 1942, Memo, 23 Apr. 1942.

[166] Ibid., Minutes, 23 Nov. 1944, 19 Feb., and 30 May 1945.

[167] PRO, BT 64/2024; GHI, *Baby Book*, 7th edn. (London, 1946), editor's note, pp. 27–31.

[168] *Good Housekeeping*, Apr. 1948.

[169] GHI, *Baby Book*, 9th edn. (London, 1953), p. 34; GHI, *Baby Book*, 10th edn. (London, 1955), pp. 54–5, 60–1.

[170] Hargreaves and Gowing, *Civil Industry and Trade*, pp. 317–18; Board of Trade, *Clothing Coupon Quiz*, 1st edn. (London, Aug. 1941); PRO, BT 64/1517, Circular, *Extra Clothing Coupons for the Under 18's*, 23 Aug. 1946.

[171] PRO, INF 1/292, Home Intelligence weekly morale reports, 16–23 June, 7–14 July, and 10–17 Nov. 1942.   [172] Ibid., 15–22 Dec. 1942; 5–12 Jan. 1943.

especially by mothers of growing children'.[173] In the summer, shortages of children's shoes were '"said to be acute and becoming a real anxiety to mothers." There is some criticism of the Board of Trade statement . . . that three pairs of shoes are provided for each child a year. "Does anyone seriously think that growing children need only three pairs of shoes a year?"'[174] In July there was intense resentment at the Board's handling of the situation and the government was

felt, particularly, to show 'no sign whatever of understanding the difficulties of the growing child'; 'it would be interesting to know whether there are any real family men in the administration of this sphere'. Mothers who have already been sacrificing their coupons for their children's clothing 'have no idea how they will manage in the future'. . . . Footwear difficulties . . . [were] a 'major problem' (All Regions). 'Shoes are responsible for more parental worries and grey hairs than all the air raids.' Children are being kept from school . . . [and] in Newcastle 'they are to be seen running barefoot in the streets, after a lapse of twenty years'.[175]

In August, the problem was again a 'major topic on the home front' and similar complaints persisted for the remainder of the year as well as during 1944.[176] In the later years of the war, demand for children's clothes—held down by rationing—roughly equalled supply but footwear presented serious difficulties and many mothers were unable to buy shoes since those available were frequently the wrong type or size despite the fact that most mothers had visited three or more shops.[177] The GHI, which advised three pairs of shoes at any one time rather than for a whole year, hardly needed to remind mothers that it was 'most important . . . that a child should never wear badly fitting footwear: shoes that are either too small or too big definitely harm the feet and should not be allowed'.[178] This context helps in understanding why the shortage of children's shoes acquired political significance after the war and why the so-called 'barefoot' episode tarnished the reputation of Harold Wilson when he was President of the Board of Trade.[179]

Mothers had to cope with the situation, of course, and a number of

[173] Ibid., 16–23 Mar. and 4–11 May 1943.
[174] Ibid., 15–22 June 1943.   [175] Ibid., 13–20 July 1943.
[176] Ibid., 31 Aug.–7 Sept. 1943. There are numerous further references on this topic in 1943 and 1944.
[177] Nuffield College Library, Oxford, Social Survey, *Wartime Shortages of Consumer Goods: A Report on a Series of Inquiries Made by the Social Survey for the Board of Trade, April 1943–January 1945* (by K. Box) (London, 1945), pp. 28, 31–3, 69, 71, and 74.
[178] GHI, *Parents' Book: Your Children from Five to Fifteen* (London, 1947), p. 56.
[179] Wilson, rejecting complaints about shortages, maintained that the situation in 1948 was a dramatic improvement on the interwar years when many working-class children were barefoot. This led to a flood of denials from former headmasters and medical officers acquainted with conditions in working-class districts during the 1920s and 1930s. This episode contributed to allegations that Wilson was a liar and untrustworthy and the issue was raised again, for instance, in the 1960s; see B. Pimlott, *Harold Wilson* (London, 1992), pp. 122–4, 577.

strategies were adopted to minimize the impact of shortages. From 1943 onwards the WVS organized clothing exchanges where mothers could swap good quality children's clothes with the help of a points price given to individual items since no money was to be involved.[180] The Board of Trade supported the initiative since children '*do* get through their clothes and coupons at a great rate' and mothers who had run out of coupons were advised to exchange 'outgrown but not outworn clothes and shoes' at one of the hundreds of exchanges started all over the country.[181] At the same time, women's magazines as well as 'Make Do and Mend' leaflets provided interminable advice on how to repair children's clothes to maximize wear as well as how to make children's clothes out of adult or older children's cast-offs. The theme persisted well into the late 1940s, causing growing frustration in the GHI's literature. In 1947, under the headline '*Down with Drabness!*', mothers of girls were urged 'to make some effort to do away with this feeling of eternal drabness'. The 'considerable ingenuity' required was justifiable since it 'cannot be too strongly emphasised that efforts made by the mother to dress a small girl prettily and suitably are of inestimable value in later life' because it helped girls to develop into 'a poised, well-groomed and suitably-dressed person, which means a great deal in any woman's life'.[182] After the termination of clothes rationing, matters improved and, for instance, in 1950 simplicity was still preferred in toddlers' clothes, but home sewing used new materials and the availability of well-fitting shoes was taken for granted.[183]

Soap was rationed in 1942 but shampoos, shaving soaps, and soap-free detergents, as well as soda-based products, remained ration free. The scheme was administered by the Ministry of Food since soap and margarine were produced using the same raw materials.[184] Initially, soap rationing caused 'very little resentment or surprise' and the ration was thought to be adequate except for 'those in very dirty work, mothers of babies, small children, those who cannot afford laundry and those in very hard water areas'.[185] Provided that the 20 per cent cut in soap deliveries aimed at by the Ministry of Food was achieved, the ministry was not too concerned about detail and in order to economize on manpower a loose rationing scheme in which there was no link between allocation of supplies and consumption was introduced. This presumably helped consumers in hard water areas

---

[180] For a description of WVS clothing exchanges, see PRO, INF 1/292, Home Intelligence weekly morale report, 16–23 Feb. 1943; *Picture Post*, 2 Oct. 1943.
[181] Board of Trade, *Clothing Coupon Quiz*, 6th edn. (London, 1946), p. xxi (emphasis in original).   [182] GHI, *Parents' Book*, pp. 54–6.
[183] GHI, *Toddlers' Book* (London, 1950), pp. 103–5; compare with GHI, *Toddlers' Book* (London, 1945), pp. 62–4 which includes a long list of examples of how to make toddlers' clothes out of larger cast-offs.
[184] See Figure 1.2 for ration levels and Hammond, *Food Volume III*, pp. 492–504 for details.
[185] PRO, INF 1/292, Home Intelligence Weekly Morale Report, 9–16 Feb. 1942.

(which received additional supplies) as well as those with extra need like mothers of young children who received no additional rations. From the autumn of 1945 onwards, in the wake of growing shortages of oils and fats, the rationing scheme was recast on the basis of coupon-replacement and ration levels were also cut. Apart from manual workers and invalids, children under 5 years were exempted from these cuts, expectant mothers now received a one-off additional ration for their confinement, and an extra ration was granted to children under 2 years. There was renewed concern about the adequacy of the ration, illustrated by an article in *Good Housekeeping* entitled, 'Your soap ration is ample if you know these things', which advised women to soften water and make full use of off-the-ration cleaners.[186] Post-war shortages of soap do not appear to have caused any major difficulties at a time when so many other consumer goods were in short supply—there is little comment on the topic—and soap rationing was abolished in 1950.

With regard to nursery equipment—ranging from baby bottles and teats to cots and prams or push chairs—demand greatly exceeded supply especially during the late 1940s when tight supply policies coincided with a rapid increase in the birth rate. For example, in August 1944 there were complaints about the '"acute"' shortage of teats for babies' bottles:

the position is thought to be very grave and is causing disquiet; mothers are particularly bitter. In some cases they have to buy bottles they do not need in order to get a single teat. Anger is all the greater because 'they ask us to increase the population', and because of the plentiful supplies of contraceptives.[187]

The shortage, which was mentioned regularly in between 6 and 10 out of 13 regions in Home Intelligence constant topics during the second half of 1944, was addressed by the Board of Trade's consumer needs section. Despite some improvements, supplies were still short during the first half of 1945, the 'main grouse is that teats are still getting into the *black market*' and, therefore, 'supplies *at a price* [were] fairly unlimited'.[188] Subsequent surveys suggested 'adequate to good' stocks despite 'concern about possible shortages in the future'.[189]

At the same time there was great concern in the Board of Trade about the 'acute shortage of cots and nursery furniture', supplies of which had been cut as a result of a reduction in the timber allocation after the war.[190] Although about three-quarters of babies were expected to use cots passed down by older siblings or purchased second-hand, demand was intense, particularly since 'baby production' greatly exceeded expectations.[191]

[186] *Good Housekeeping*, Jan. 1946.   [187] PRO, INF 1/292, 9–15 Aug. 1944.
[188] PRO, BT 13/182, report 10/1254, 12 Apr. 1945 (emphasis in original).
[189] PRO, BT 64/1999, Reports of Regional Distribution Officers, 28 Feb. and 6–7 Mar. 1947.
[190] PRO, BT 64/2090, Memo, 15 Aug. 1947.   [191] Ibid., Memo, 14 May 1947.

Consumer needs reports indicated intense shortages. For example, in one region 'three out of five stockists . . . had been without stocks for over three weeks. One other retailer had one cot only' and in another region most outlets 'had been without supply during the past 3 months, and had a considerable waiting list for Cots'.[192] The Board responded by increasing the production of cots which returned to 1945 levels in 1948, partly at the expense of other nursery furniture, but subsequently civilian consumption of nursery furniture remained below 1945 levels until the end of 1951.[193]

The story of prams was similar. Only a limited number of strictly price-controlled models were produced.[194] While postwar output was comparable to that of the mid-1930s (when the birth rate was low), apart from a brief rise in 1947, production was held down until the beginning of 1952.[195] Not surprisingly, *Good Housekeeping* condemned profiteering from second-hand pram sales citing an example of a sale at more than double the original purchase price in January 1945, and the 1946 edition of the GHI's *Baby Book* considered second-hand equipment the likely option under 'present-day restrictions'.[196] In contrast with working-class mothers who had always relied on improvisation and second-hand equipment, in the late 1940s for the first time most middle-class mothers also had to cope with shortages and without a nanny, help which many of their mothers would have taken for granted. Mothers from all income groups were lucky to obtain often 'battered and rather down-at-heel equipment' on the second-hand market. This could however be improved 'beyond recognition' with time-consuming and elaborate renovation.[197] There was little change in 1949 when high prices rather than shortages were the main problem, whereas in 1953 it 'was a matter of pride to take your baby out in a good-looking pram'—at least according to *Good Housekeeping*.[198]

Finally, it is necessary to examine the impact of austerity on toys and treats as well as Christmas. Children of the 1940s, especially those from more affluent backgrounds, were denied many of the traditional pleasures of childhood—a 'heart-rending' experience for many parents.[199] There are plenty of touching, quaint, and oddly amusing stories about children's

---

[192] PRO, BT 64/1999 Regional Distribution Officer's Report, Region 1, 25 Sept. 1947; Region 2, 22 Oct. 1947.

[193] *Board of Trade Journal*, vol. 162, Consumer Goods Supplement, Supplies of Consumer Goods to the Home Market, 24 May 1952.

[194] PRO, BT 64/1798, Memo, 13 Dec. 1944; Hargreaves and Gowing, *Civil Industry and Trade*, pp. 83, 506, 509.

[195] *Board of Trade Journal*, vol. 162, Consumer Goods Supplement, Supplies of Consumer Goods to the Home Market, 24 May 1952.

[196] *Good Housekeeping*, Jan. 1945; GHI, *Baby Book*, 2nd edn. (London, 1946), p. 52.

[197] *Good Housekeeping*, Apr. 1948.

[198] GHI, *Baby Book*, 7th edn. (London, 1949), pp. 46–7; GHI, *Baby Book*, 9th edn. (London, 1953), p. 45.

[199] Longmate, *How We Lived Then*, p. 180.

reactions and inordinate gratitude for apparently modest gifts. Longmate provides the fullest account including the story of a small girl who, when offered her first ice-cream, handed it to her mother 'with the request "Please peel it, Mummy"'. A 10-year old girl's Christmas presents in 1941 included 'a *whole* orange'. Incidentally, the girl and her brother were 'both very lucky . . . because Mummy and Daddy don't care much for eggs, or sweets'.[200] Longmate, born in 1925, was evidently a 'sweet eater' himself and devotes several pages to vividly describing the privations suffered under sweets rationing before moving on to birthday cakes made with improvised icing and candles and Christmas—'the greatest challenge of all'—where home-made toys and decorations at least partly plugged the gap left by short-ages.[201] With regard to toys, the Board of Trade followed a policy which combined outright prohibition of the manufacture of toys using scarce raw materials, such as rubber, plastic, or synthetics, with a drastic reduction of the remainder in order to save factory space and labour. Shortages were intense until decontrol of the industry in 1948. Subsequently, domestic sup-ply figures show a rapid increase in the availability, especially of metal and plastic toys, although complaints about high toy prices and poor quality persisted until the end of the decade.[202]

There was little change in 1939 apart from the appearance of military toys, and austerity provided a great challenge to those housewives who were determined to retain as much as possible of traditional Christmas, while women's magazines were full of helpful hints for improvisation and making do.[203] There is little doubt about the importance attached to Christmas on the home front and particularly the central rituals—some sort of tree and decorations, formal Christmas dinner, and presents—above all for children. According to Mass-Observation, in 1942 just under three-quarters of pan-ellists were prepared or forced to economize on cards, presents, and food but about a quarter 'deliberately' planned 'not having an economy Christmas and trying to make it as normal as possible'. At the other extreme, a hand-ful decided to have a smaller, or no, party or to give no presents.[204] Home Intelligence weekly morale reports illustrate both widespread tension prior to Christmas, as housewives worried about not being able to get sufficient food, and parents resented toy shortages as well as gratitude and relief about a successful Christmas between 1940 and 1944. Despite 'widespread

[200] Ibid., pp. 180, 186 (my emphasis); see also pp. 180–90.   [201] Ibid., pp. 181–5.
[202] *Board of Trade Journal*, vol. 162, Consumer Goods Supplement, Supplies of Consumer Goods to the Home Market, 24 May 1952; see e.g. MO Bulletin, *Toys*, No. 39, Dec. 1950.
[203] MO, FR 17, Summary of Toys and Christmas 1939, 10 Jan. 1940; Longmate, *How We Lived Then*, p. 187; see e.g. *Woman*, 19 Dec. 1942, 15 Dec. 1945, 14 Dec. 1946; *Good Housekeeping*, Dec. 1941, 1942, and 1945; N. Walsh and B. Braithwaite (eds.), *The Christmas Book: The Best of Good Housekeeping at Christmas 1922–1962* (London, 1988).
[204] MO, FR 1514, Christmas Economies 1942, 27 Dec. 1942.

grumbling' about 'high prices and scarcity of goods', Christmas 1940 was 'a relative success' as people faced the 'New Year with optimism'—setting a pattern which was repeated throughout the war.[205] In December 1941 food morale was high following the introduction of points rationing as well as the arrival of Lend-Lease supplies and 'Woolton was praised for having done "a good job in this, the third war Christmas"'.[206] In 1942 Allied successes did not prevent widespread discontent with shortages. Nine regions complained of shortages or unequal supplies of Christmas fare but this was overshadowed by the toy situation:

From eleven Regions come complaints of the 'extortionate prices' charged for toys, disgust and anger being reported at 'the excessive cost of poor quality toys, and the extreme profiteering which is going on in the trade'. The Government is 'frequently blamed for not coping with the whole matter reasonably, fairly and in plenty of time', and for having 'made so little effort to make Christmas a happy season for children'. According to one report 'the release of further supplies of toys has caused some satisfaction', and is quoted as evidence that 'public opinion is still listened to by the Government', but some people consider it 'farcical', and are said to be even angrier because 'not one extra toy has been seen'.[207]

In the event 1942 was described as the '"most hopeful Christmas since war began" . . . "in spite of austerities, it was enjoyed as no other"'.[208] Similarly, in 1943 complaints about toy shortages, poor quality, and high prices began in late November, most people had 'little hope of a turkey, and there is much resentment at the alleged "black market" and unsatisfactory distribution' of Christmas fare.[209] Nevertheless, 'in spite of much grumbling . . . people appear to have been less dissatisfied with supplies than they expected. Shortages, too, were accepted more readily in the general expectation that this would be the last Christmas before victory over Germany'.[210] Christmas 1944 was little different, there was 'much bitter comment' especially about toys, '"parents have to get the children something, even if it does mean paying 12/6d for two bits of unplaned wood badly stuck together"', and austerity Christmases persisted into the early post-war period, judging by women's magazines.[211] Matters improved towards the end of the decade and, for instance, in 1948 *Good Housekeeping* took a traditional Christmas dinner with a turkey for granted, 'simplifying . . . here and there in accord with present-day limitations', and the magazine carried features

[205] PRO, INF 1/292, Home Intelligence Weekly Morale Reports, 11–18 Dec. 1940, 24 Dec. 1940–1 Jan. 1941.
[206] Ibid., 22–9 Dec. 1941. [207] Ibid., 15–22 Dec. 1942.
[208] Ibid., 22–9 Dec. 1942.
[209] Ibid., 23–30 Nov., 30 Nov.–7 Dec., 7–14 Dec., 14–21 Dec. 1943.
[210] Ibid., 21–9 Dec. 1943.
[211] Ibid., 5–12 Dec. and 21–7 Dec. 1944; *Good Housekeeping*, Dec. 1945; *Woman*, 14 Dec. 1946.

on toys and other gifts now available, although the following year home-made gifts and toys were again suggested.[212]

The austerity policy has to be understood from a gendered perspective. Although male consumption standards were of course also reduced, the policy particularly involved women on a number of levels. Not only were women responsible for implementing a range of economy measures on a daily basis, but the disproportionate sacrifice of housewives and mothers frequently shielded men as well as children from the full impact of the reduction in consumption. Above all housewives bore the brunt of the burden and their arduous job became more onerous as a result of rationing, shortages, and interminable shopping difficulties. Women's central role in the austerity policy was acknowledged by the government, which had to muster housewives' and mothers' co-operation in order to implement the austerity policy successfully. Women's achievement in maintaining public health and morale played a vital role in the war effort, and this achievement contributed towards raising women's status and consolidating their citizenship.

Women's relationship with the austerity policy was complex. Attitudes varied depending on the policy and also changed over time. While women welcomed the introduction of a comprehensive food policy, which included special rations and welfare foods for pregnant women and children, the difficulties of clothing children under rationing were a continuous source of grievance. During the war, housewives supported rationing and accepted sacrifice as their contribution to the war effort, and their morale remained high. By contrast, the continuation of austerity after the war was unpopular, and housewives were more worried about shortages and high prices than any other social group. A majority of housewives felt that their diet was inadequate after the war and ration cuts bore particularly heavily on housewives and mothers, who frequently gave up part of their rations to other members of the family. Women's disproportionate sacrifice, which extended well beyond the poorest income groups, provided a buffer within the family economy and was a central element of the post-war recovery policy based on domestic austerity and the export drive. Housewives did not accept this situation passively, and female support for the continuation of rationing and controls became increasingly equivocal. Housewives' problems became a focus of public debate after the war and housewife discontent had important political and electoral consequences.

A gendered analysis of the austerity policy questions the degree to which shares were genuinely fair during and after the Second World War. Rationing reduced income differentials in consumption standards but these

---

[212] *Good Housekeeping*, Dec. 1948, Dec. 1949; see also *Woman*, 9 Dec. 1950, which includes a 'present' feature.

were by no means eliminated, and class differences in vital statistics persisted virtually unchanged. In many ways austerity hit low-income households, as indicated by the growing problem of providing palatable meals on a tight budget during the late 1940s as well as the shopping difficulties of poorer housewives with regard to miscellaneous consumer goods. The introduction of welfare foods and special rations contributed to dramatic improvements in maternal and child health on average, as illustrated in mortality rates and anthropometric data. Nevertheless, the combination of rationing, food subsidies, and targeting of vulnerable groups failed to reduce class differences in vital statistics—yet again highlighting the shortcomings of the policy. Over and above these limitations, the unequal distribution of scarce resources within the household, based on long-standing gender inequalities, provided an additional element in which the aspiration of fair shares was compromised by a more complex reality. The black market, which is discussed next, provided a further factor which undermined the equity of fair shares and illustrates the limits of popular acquiescence in the reduction of consumption during the 1940s.

4
The Black Market

The black market casts doubt on the myth of shared sacrifice on the home front. This chapter aims to transcend the conventional image of 1940s Britain characterized by a commitment to the overriding principle of fair shares. According to this image, common sacrifice fostered national unity during the war. After 1945 Labour tried to harness this spirit to its reconstruction programme and particularly the export drive. The following discussion shows that the black market was extensive during and after the war. The emphasis here is not on theft and receiving of stolen goods but on endemic circumvention of the emergency legislation which confronted many citizens with the prospect of law breaking for the first time. There are countless examples of exploitation of loopholes and breaches of the legislation controlling production, distribution, and supply of consumer goods. These provide a good indication of the limits of public acceptance of the austerity policy. The black market has received insufficient attention in the literature and, in contrast with Smithies who details examples of spectacular rackets based on local newspapers or Hughes who provides an impressionistic account of the spiv in the late 1940s, this chapter examines the topic from an administrative perspective.[1] The administration had to ensure that the controls were at least reasonably well observed. There were numerous changes of the control orders, while the public had to cope with an avalanche of new laws and regulations.

The black market could be understood either as organized crime involving large-scale theft and receiving or as apparently minor infringements of the emergency legislation. In the USA in 1945, 'the term "black market" had become a recognized term to refer to all kinds of violations of OPA [Office of Price Administration, the American regulatory body] regulations'.[2] Similarly, the black market is defined here as all breaches of the emergency legislation including sale above the maximum price, imposing a condition of sale, sale of rationed goods without coupons and trade in

[1] E. Smithies, *Crime in Wartime: A Social History of Crime in World War II* (London, 1982); E. Smithies, *The Black Economy in England since 1914* (Dublin, 1984); D. Hughes, 'The Spivs', in M. Sissons and P. French (eds.), *Age of Austerity* (London, 1963), pp. 86–105. See also R. Murphy, *Realism and Tinsel: Cinema and Society in Britain, 1939–1948* (London, 1989), ch. 8, *passim*; Hopkins, *The New Look*, pp. 97–102; Addison, *Now the War is Over*, pp. 44–50.
[2] M. B. Clinard, *The Black Market: A Study of White Collar Crime* (New Jersey, 1952), p. 15.

coupons, manufacture and supply of controlled goods in breach of the regulations, false declaration, and illicit slaughter of animals or supply of agricultural produce. The focus is not on black market rackets, which were effectively an extension of ordinary criminal activity, but on non-compliance with the control orders.

According to Cairncross, it 'is generally agreed that black markets were relatively unimportant in Britain during and after the war'.[3] For Woolton this was 'because the British public disapproves of black markets'. The deterrent effect of heavy penalties, including imprisonment, was 'literally ruinous to people convicted . . . that few indeed dared to embark on' black market dealings. National character was critical and the 'fact that, in spite of all the scarcity . . . and the rigidity of rationing, there was little or no black market in Britain was a tribute to the British people which I hope the historians of this period will proudly record'.[4] The evidence amply disproves this complacency.

While there was no large-scale organized black market in Britain, it operated through widespread infringement of the regulations by producers, distributors, and retailers, ultimately sustained by public demand. The black market was also limited since the administration never lost control of distribution of any commodity through official channels. The problem was more acute elsewhere and, for instance, in the USA the majority of civilian meat was estimated to pass through black market channels or a majority of businesses investigated were found to be in violation of the regulations.[5] The question as to why the black market was less extensive in Britain than in the USA is addressed by Mills and Rockoff.[6] They conclude that the key was the degree of regimentation rather than voluntary compliance due to the more law-abiding character of the British people or the Dunkirk spirit. In Britain, controls were vertically and horizontally integrated, controlling a product at all stages from import or production of raw materials and restricting production to a limited range of commodities. Controls of production were bolstered by extensive rationing of the consumer coupled with high allocation of resources to enforcement activity.

While it is possible to construct some quantitative data of the extent of the black market for particular commodities for limited periods or to estimate changes over time in black market activity from a range of sources, ultimately the black market—in line with the black or informal economy more generally—defies the statistics. As Calder put it, 'it was in the nature of a successful black market transaction that it was left out of official sta-

---

[3] Cairncross, *Years of Recovery*, p. 351.
[4] Lord Woolton, *The Memoirs of the Rt. Hon. The Earl of Woolton* (London, 1959), pp. 230–1.
[5] Clinard, *Black Market*, pp. 30 and 37 and ch. 2, *passim*.
[6] G. Mills and H. Rockoff, 'Compliance with Price Controls in the United States and the United Kingdom during World War II', in H. Rockoff (ed.), *Price Controls* (Aldershot, 1992), pp. 78–94.

tistics and evaded the courts of law'.[7] Table 4.1 shows that convictions for offences against the defence regulations were high in mid-war, peaking in 1943. There was another high point between 1946 and 1948 which was followed by a dramatic reduction in the early 1950s. While these figures provide some indication of black market activity, they also reflect the level of enforcement action, which increased during the middle years of the war and peaked in 1947–8, as well as political decisions on whether to press charges for minor breaches which account for the reduction, particularly in 1945. These statistics are severely limited and fail to indicate the extent of black market activity, just as crime statistics generally do not provide a comprehensive measure of crimes committed.[8] The black market coincided with a dramatic increase in recorded crime, and especially property crime, during the 1940s.[9] Criminologists explained this phenomenon as a consequence of wartime disruption resulting in the

general cheapening of all values; loosening of family ties; weakened respect for the law, human life and property, especially property of the State; . . . scarcity of all consumer goods, the black market and the resulting rise in prices; rationing and the well-justified austerity policy of the government; easy accessibility of many bomb-damaged houses and ample supplies of guns and ammunition; lack of trained police officers and, finally, the activities of deserters.[10]

In these exceptional circumstances, the social composition of offenders extended well beyond the expected social groups right across the social spectrum. The 1940s saw a dramatic rise in white-collar crime and the black market involved many 'hitherto "respectable" persons' such as 'businessmen, shopkeepers and tradesmen'.[11]

The administration was certainly not deluded by lofty notions about the British character. The experience of the First World War led to the recognition that enforcement was an essential aspect of food control. The policy to ensure 'the proper observance of Orders' was based on the following principles: '(a) Wide publication. (b) A system of inspection to spread knowledge and to assist the Trade and Public in obeying it. (c) Investigation of contraventions; and finally (d) Prosecution if necessary'.[12] The requisite powers were conferred under Defence Regulation 55, which empowered the relevant minister to make orders regarding the control of food and

[7] Calder, *The People's War*, p. 469.
[8] T. Morris, *Crime and Criminal Justice since 1945* (Oxford, 1989), pp. 5–6. For a trenchant analysis of the shortcomings of crime statistics see H. Taylor, 'Rationing Crime: The Political Economy of Criminal Statistics since the 1850s', *Economic History Review* 51 (1998), pp. 569–90.
[9] Home Office, *Criminal Statistics England and Wales 1954*, Cmd. 9574 (London, 1955), p. viii.
[10] H. Mannheim, *Group Problems in Crime and Punishment* (London, 1955), p. 112.
[11] Smithies, *Crime in Wartime*, p. 4, see also p. 78; Morris, *Crime and Criminal Justice*, p. 18.
[12] PRO, MAF 72/562, Enforcement: Notes on Procedure in the Great War and Brief Recommendations for a Future Emergency, n.d. [approx. 1939].

TABLE 4.1. *Persons found guilty of offences against the defence regulations, 1940–1954*

Date	Number	Date	Number
1940	5,629	1948	20,163
1941	13,580	1949	12,640
1942	23,015	1950	7,785
1943	30,309	1951	6,049
1944	24,458	1952	5,667
1945	17,711	1953	2,397
1946	20,389	1954	642
1947	18,863		

Notes: These statistics are slightly different from the figures relating to convictions for black market offences compiled by the Ministry of Food cited in Table 4.4, since they include other breaches of defence regulations such as looting or black-out offences. There were only 20 cases in 1939. The overwhelming majority of offenders were tried by magistrates courts and fined minor sums. A small number were tried by higher courts and both levels of court occasionally imposed prison sentences.
Sources: Home Office, *Criminal Statistics England and Wales, 1939–1945*, Cmd. 7227 (London, 1947); these data are published annually from 1948 onwards, Cmds. 7428, 7528, 7733, 7993, 8301, 8616, 8941, 9199, and 9574.

consumer goods as well as to require the keeping of records and authorization of inspection of undertakings. As the head of the Ministry of Food's enforcement branch put it in 1946, the key priorities of enforcement work were 'Prevention, Detection, Prosecution—in that order of importance'. It was impossible to judge 'the success of our overall activities other than the false "yard-stick" of successful prosecutions. Real success can only be achieved by concentration on "preventive" measures—detection and subsequent prosecution being incidental thereto'.[13] Hence the key to enforcement of the controls was publicity rather than the actual policing of millions of transactions which was administratively impossible. Publicity surrounding convictions and targeted drives, for example against illicit slaughter, was to act as a deterrent by showing that something was being done. Convictions for black market activities were relatively low and a 'false "yard-stick"' of the extent of the black market because it was extremely difficult to assemble satisfactory evidence.

Comprehensive policing of literally thousands of orders and regulations was impracticable from a manpower point of view. Therefore, enforcement work focused on certain priorities, and commodities which had low priority were left to their own devices. Essentially, enforcement work was a public relations exercise that was necessary in order to maintain the credibility of the system. The real solution to the black market was not comprehensive and costly policing of an inappropriately designed scheme but devising a scheme

[13] PRO, MAF 100/52, Interim Report on Enforcement Policy and Organisation, 1 July 1946.

that would effectively enforce itself. The most frequent administrative response to extensive evasion was to recast the control orders, usually by tightening up the regulations and closing obvious loopholes. Occasionally the alternative strategy of loosening controls or even abolishing the controls altogether was adopted.

To analyse the black market it is most appropriate to concentrate on selected commodities. These are food and specifically meat, poultry, eggs, and tea; clothes and clothing coupons; cosmetics; and finally petrol as well as petrol coupons. These commodities were chosen since they were extensively sold outside official channels and effectively eluded control continuously or during certain periods until drastic measures were taken to improve enforcement. All share certain common features and, above all, severe shortage coupled with high demand. They were considered to be sufficiently significant by the authorities to result in extensive enforcement action and frequent alteration of the control orders. Other key features of these black market commodities were ease of storage and distribution. Many were neither perishable nor bulky, such as tea, clothes, or cosmetics, and the latter were easy to produce, requiring few raw materials, and of high added value. Conversely, meat, poultry, and eggs were difficult to control since meat was only partially rationed and home production by small farmers and self-suppliers accounted for a significant proportion of total supplies.

The following sections examine the extent of the black market and how it operated for each of these commodities in turn. While the black market in foodstuffs centred on unlawful supply of food stolen in transit, illicit slaughter, and home production, as well as sale without coupons, the actual trade in coupons, reuse of coupons, and forgery were prevalent with regard to clothes as well as petrol. Cosmetics were never rationed and illegal manufacture and supply fed the black market. The magnitude of the black market fluctuated, being governed by three factors. The two most important were the combination of severity of shortages and level of demand, and the structure of the control orders. Finally, patriotism contributed towards a higher level of voluntary compliance during the war, and a range of evidence suggests that public co-operation was more equivocal after 1945. The administration stoically accepted the inevitability of evasion which manifested itself in a number of ways. First, a common practice was breaking the spirit if not the letter of the law. For instance, the reduction in supplies of cosmetics was circumvented by dubious accountancy as well as packaging practices. Second, and most importantly, there were numerous breaches of the emergency legislation which were not a crime as conventionally understood, such as the use of loose coupons in contravention of the clothes rationing orders. Finally, ordinary criminal activity increased enormously since shortages offered unprecedented opportunity and reward for theft and forgery. As Chuter Ede, the Home Secretary, put it in 1945, 'No one would have thought of stealing a second-hand shirt in 1939; to-day the sight of a shirt on the clothes line has become a temptation.'[14]

While enforcement work was primarily the responsibility of the Ministry of Food and the Board of Trade, they co-operated with the police in the detection of crimes of this sort. Frequently the police, afraid to come into conflict with public opinion, were reluctant to enforce the emergency legislation; and police officers were involved in the black market, conducting themselves 'perhaps no better and no worse than the majority of the population'.[15] The focus here is on the first two forms of evasion since the chapter aims to trace how the general public responded to the extensive regulation of traditionally private economic activities which effectively prohibited the maximization of profit in the production, distribution, and exchange of consumer goods. Thus, black markets are an inevitable consequence of regulation since:

What were once perfectly innocent private transactions can be transformed into criminal activities and the increase of official surveillance and interference increases the temptation for individuals to conceal what they have previously done openly, or to switch into illegal activities, which are less visible.[16]

Confronted with the black market, the administration was not passive and reliant on public good will but rather in control of the framework within which the market operated. The response to extensive evasion was based on a considered judgement of the manpower requirements of administration and enforcement of a particular control scheme as well as the concerns of public opinion. Frequently it was neither efficient in terms of manpower nor astute with regard to morale to be overly zealous at all times. Enforcement policy had to balance legal purity with ease of administration and common sense. Priorities changed over time and as shortages were intensifying in mid-war many control schemes were tightened up and enforcement activity increased. During 1944 and 1945 the supply situation improved and a more relaxed attitude was adopted. This was again reversed between 1946 and 1948 when economy measures, coupled with high demand and low morale, resulted in increased black market dealings. The chapter traces how these boundaries were defined and re-defined throughout the period. To justify close control the black market had to be widespread and the commodity sufficiently important either because it had to be

---

[14] Quoted in Mannheim, *Group Problems in Crime and Punishment*, p. 112. For an account of the new opportunities afforded to professional criminals see R. Murphy, *Smash and Grab: Gangsters in the London Underworld* (London, 1993), pp. 82–7.

[15] R. Ingleton, *The Gentlemen at War: Policing Britain 1939–45* (Maidstone, 1994), p. 285.

[16] S. Henry (ed.), *Can I have it in Cash? A Study of Informal Institutions and Unorthodox Ways of Doing Things* (London, 1981), pp. 15–16.

paid for with precious dollars—such as petrol—or because it was seen as critical to morale, as in the case of cosmetics.

Popular attitudes to the black market are intriguing since there was an inherent conflict between vehement public condemnation and universal private indulgence. Table 4.2 reveals a high level of public awareness of the existence of the black market, concern about its increase after the war, as well as a desire for more stringent penalties and stronger measures to eliminate it. Similarly, a wartime Mass-Observation survey noted a general awareness that the black market was widespread, resulting in calls for heavier penalties, including 'the death penalty, the cat, and the abolition of the possibility of a fine without imprisonment'. Black marketeers were described as 'traitors' or 'Fifth Columnists' and there was an *under-lying* feeling ... that Black Market offences are highly anti-social and unpatriotic'.[17]

Irrespective of these attitudes, the following discussion shows that consumers, retailers, wholesalers, and manufacturers colluded in circumventing the emergency legislation. The shortages coupled with the consumer-retailer tie altered the relationship between retailers and their customers and the former were equally dependent on the good will of their suppliers. Illegal practices such as over-charging, tied sales, and under-the-counter sales were impossible to eradicate. Consumers could report a retailer's malpractices to the authorities and change retailer, but consumer satisfaction was usually better served by co-operation and evasion of the rules. Off-ration sales or barter, either among business men and traders or the general public, were illegal but in practice the wheels of the machinery were oiled by tips and favours to obtain the little extras above the ration, or not generally available in the shops, which made all the difference to life in the 1940s. The Mass-Observation archive includes a censorious account of a black market-eer operating in a Chester factory in 1942, in which apparently all employees as well as the foreman and the manager participated.[18] A member of the Enforcement Sub-Committee of the Food Control Committee in a rural area was one of a number of customers purchasing Christmas turkeys from a retailer above the maximum price, which was an offence under the food control orders. The retailer escaped with a warning and the person concerned continued to serve on the committee.[19]

Perhaps the most interesting source is reports by a Mass-Observation investigator on shopping in London during 1947.[20] These openly describe

---

[17] MO, FR 1781, Some Notes on Popular Feeling about Black Markets, 17 May 1943 (emphasis in original).

[18] MO, TC, Food Box 3F, Trade in Rationed Food in Factory, 10 Jan. 1942.

[19] PRO, MAF 67/151, Food Control Committees: Midhurst R.D., Enforcement Sub-Committee Minutes, 19 Jan. 1942.

[20] MO, TC, Food Box 6E, Black Market and Barter in London in 1947.

TABLE 4.2. *Popular attitudes to the black market, 1942, 1943, and 1947* *(per cent)*

Date	Question	Response		
		Approve	Disapprove	No opinion
Jan. 1942	Would you approve/disapprove if all persons convicted of black market dealings in food are sent to prison without option of fine?	85	10	8
		Agree	Disagree	No opinion
June 1943	Lord Woolton says that no black market exists in this country. Do you agree/disagree?	12	72	16
		Increasing	Decreasing	Don't know
Apr. 1947	Do you think in this country the black market is increasing/decreasing?	61	10	29
		Enough	Stronger measures	Don't know
Apr. 1947	Do you think the authorities are doing enough to stop the black market, or should they take stronger measures?	14	65	21

Source: G. H. Gallup (ed.), *The Gallup International Public Opinion Polls: Great Britain, 1937–1975*, I, *1937–1964* (New York, 1976).

black market dealings in which the investigator herself is involved, quoting various black market prices and referring to shops and other suppliers where coupons and rationed goods without coupons were easily obtainable. Tipping and barter were commonplace as was the '"legal" black market' (presumably under-the-counter or off-ration sales). There was also an '"illegal" black market' (presumably in stolen goods) at a higher price. One informant told the investigator about a woman who could 'get me anything I want . . . but what a price—real Black Market—however I shall certainly see her if I'm short'. Everybody seemed to know somebody who had something to sell or exchange and one woman said that 'it makes me smile when some of these people say they never have anything to do with the Black Market—just show me where it is and I'll go to it'.

The *New Statesman* lamented this state of affairs in yet another version of Marlowe's 'Passionate Shepherd':

'The Passionate Spiv to His Love'

Come spiv with me and be my spove*
And we will all the pleasures prove
That markets black and rackets bring;
Though shalt not lack for anything.

. . .

Thou shalt not queue yet shalt thou see
Food manna-like rain down on thee

. . .

Attendant spivs shall ply the barrow
Through London's streets both wide and narrow
To ease the toils of thy housewifery
With a percentage from their spivvery;

And keep us safe from rivals' raids
With their protective razor blades.
If these delights thy mind may move,
Come spiv with me and be my spove.[21]

The authorities were concerned about the corrupting effect of this growing separation between public and private morality. Ministers and civil servants feared that this division would undermine the entire rationing and controls apparatus and even threaten the rule of law and the sanctity of private property. Public condemnation of the black market may well have identified it with large-scale rackets and theft while not necessarily considering as crimes apparently trivial offences such as tipping to obtain extras, barter, or off-ration purchases. Confronted with a deluge of ever-changing rules and regulations, the public frequently did not know what was and was not legal or understand the purpose of highly technical and apparently meaningless restrictions. The inquiry into the black market in petrol in 1948, which deplored 'that the moral standards of the country in regard to rationing had dropped amazingly', noted that 'many responsible people did not think it wrong to get extra petrol'.[22] A senior official in the Ministry of Food rejected this distinction between trivial infringements and major black market activities, comparing minor rationing offences to peacetime traffic offences. If motorists were not prosecuted for exceeding the speed limit because the offence was trivial and the fines small, 'the speed limit would cease to have any significance whatever'.[23]

This analysis of the black market traces how the relationship between the individual and the state was negotiated at a time when the role of the state

---

* *The female of the species* (note in original). [21] *New Statesman and Nation*, 27 Sept. 1947. Compare with wartime version, cited in Chapter 2, p. 78.

[22] PRO, POWE 33/1440, Committee of Inquiry into Evasion of Petrol Rationing Control, Meeting, 29 Jan. 1948.

[23] PRO, MAF 100/38, Minute, 6 Mar. 1943.

expanded immensely. With extensive controls of all foodstuffs and most other consumer goods, the state became involved in the production, distribution, and exchange of consumer goods to a degree which was unprecedented in British history. These activities were now governed by a comprehensive set of regulations administered by a large and frequently distant bureaucracy. While this system was relatively easy to justify during the war, when public opinion was ready to make great sacrifices for the war effort, this readiness was less forthcoming in the post-war period when the shortcomings of the austerity policy were more obvious and its purpose less clear.

4.1. FOOD

A Ministry of Food leaflet defined the black market as:

attempts to distribute foods in short supply through abnormal or unauthorised channels with the object of securing profit out of all proportion to the services rendered. To exploit scarcity is always profitable, since in every community there are unscrupulous men ready to defy regulations by paying more than the legal price or obtaining more than their fair share of goods in short supply. The most profitable sources of profit for the 'Black Market' are the unscrupulous private individual, the trader anxious to build up stocks unfairly, and, above all . . . the hotels and restaurants.[24]

According to the Director of Enforcement, '"Black Market" activities are prevalent throughout the country, and are likely to increase or decrease in direct relation to deterioration or improvement of the food situation'. Worst affected were docks, ports, and large industrial areas where food traffic was heavy. There was:

no evidence that such activities are highly organized and centrally directed by 'master minds'. The indications are, rather, that they are widespread 'opportunist' and carried out by loosely organized gangs of 'small-time' operators and receivers which are constantly fluctuating in composition as the situation, and attractiveness of commodities, changes.[25]

The main object of the Ministry of Food was 'to secure fair shares of food for all, and the various Rules and Instruments are framed accordingly. The Enforcement Organisation has the important job of seeing that these Orders are observed'.[26] In other words, as the internal monthly review put

---

[24] PRO, MAF 83/2681, The Black Market and the Ministry of Food's Attempt to Stop it, 5 Feb. 1942.
[25] PRO, MAF 100/52, Enforcement—Policy and Organization: Interim Report, 1 July 1946.
[26] PRO, MAF 286/30, Draft Circular, 9 May 1949.

it, 'the first object of Enforcement is the prevention of food crime'.[27] This
objective was pursued by efforts to prevent serious offences, to detect major
black market dealings, and to apply persistent pressure on retailers and consumers through routine inspections.

Enforcement work at the Ministry of Food was organized on a three-tier
basis.[28] Headquarters were in charge of policy and co-ordinated activities to
ensure uniform practice across the country. Nineteen regions or divisions
supervised work within their own areas and focused on more serious
offences in close collaboration with the police. Finally, about 1,500 food
control committees, corresponding with local authorities, dealt with minor
offences committed by retailers and the general public. During the middle
of the war, this structure was considered to be unsatisfactory since it 'was
obvious that many black market operators worked on a national scale and
a co-ordinated effort was needed to defeat them'.[29] In response, a central
intelligence bureau was set up in 1942 which was to act as a 'clearing
house' collecting information on black market operations in close liaison
with the police and divisional offices as well as to work in the preventive
area of cutting the supply lines of the black market.[30] Staffing levels of the
enforcement division were presumably strengthened at this time although
no figures are available until the post-war period. Table 4.3 shows the
changes in enforcement staff between 1945 and 1952. In May 1946, the
minister was concerned that food orders were 'generally being ignored and
evaded more flagrantly now than at any time during the war' and personnel at headquarters were increased by 50 per cent.[31] Enforcement staff
peaked in 1948, a policy 'rendered necessary by the current food situation'
and particularly following the recommendations of the Bodinnar committee investigation into illicit slaughter.[32] Staff members were scaled down as
shortages subsided from 1949 onwards and stood at 567 in 1952, with
the Conservative government looking for further reductions in line with
the decontrol policy.[33]

In view of the limited manpower, even during the peak period, enforcement work had to be prioritized. This was expressed vehemently by
Strachey, the Minister of Food, in November 1947. Anticipating a tough

[27] PRO, MAF 100/61, Enforcement Review, vol. 6 (1952), Enforcement of Food Regulations, n.d.
[28] PRO, MAF 75/40, Enforcement. This file is a history of enforcement work throughout the
period of control. See also MAF 83/2681, Enforcement of Food Orders, 8 June 1943.
[29] PRO, MAF 100/30, Conference of Divisional Food Officers, 14–15 Apr. 1943.
[30] Ibid., Divisional Food Officers Conference, 10–11 Nov. 1943; on the creation of the bureau see
Divisional Enforcement Officers Conference, 1 July 1942; Circular letter, 31 July 1942.
[31] PRO, MAF 100/45, Minute, 3 May 1946; MAF 100/52, Enforcement—Policy and
Organisation: Interim Report, 1 July 1946; Minute, 23 Oct. 1946.
[32] PRO, MAF 100/57, Enforcement Review, vol. 2, no. 2 (Feb. 1948); see also MAF 75/40.
[33] PRO, CAB 129/56, C (52) 360, Enforcement of Food Controls, 24 Oct. 1952; CAB 128/25,
CC (52) 91, 29 Oct. 1952.

TABLE 4.3. *Ministry of Food enforcement staff, 1945–1949 and 1952*

Date	Headquarters	Division	Total
Nov. 1945	57	891	948
1946	112	957	1,069
Spring 1948	199	1,171	1,370
Mar. 1949	178	1,083	1,261
Oct. 1952	N/A	N/A	567

Note: The 1948 data are based on the authorized complement after the Bodinnar Committee investigation into black market activities and particularly illicit slaughter.
Sources: PRO, MAF 286/30, Operation Octopus: Third Report to the Minister, Apr. 2, 8 Apr. 1949; CAB 129/56, C (52) 360, Enforcement of Food Controls, 24 Oct. 1952.

winter and drawing attention to the difficult food situation in Europe and American concern about spending billions of dollars 'on pouring food into black markets', he emphasized that enforcement of food orders was 'of terrific importance to this country' in securing Marshall Aid as a precondition of the recovery programme. It was necessary:

to concentrate on essentials, not to waste . . . precious man hours on chasing such things as ice cream, but to spend them on illicit slaughter cases. To give an extreme example, ice cream offences would not shake the nation but, to go to the other extreme, our whole rationing system and our whole national life would be shaken if illicit slaughter caused a serious food shortage. The utter inability to control illicit slaughter has made nonsense of the whole French rationing system . . . [as cereals were drained away to fatten livestock sold on the black market]. Illicit slaughter is not only a key point but it is the 'keyest' of all key points. . . . Let us not waste our efforts on the imposition of controls of game, or frills of that sort, the total supply of which in any case makes no difference to the real level of nutrition of the country . . . Let us concentrate on real things that matter—illicit slaughter, feeding stuffs, thefts from docks . . . Let us protect these citadels of the rationing system at all costs, while letting the ice cream outposts surrender to the enemy.[14]

Accordingly, post-war enforcement work focused on meat and livestock and above all on illicit slaughter, which was targeted in special drives, as well as feeding stuffs, eggs, and poultry. Other priorities were theft of food in transit, malpractices by catering establishments, large-scale black market dealings in fruit and vegetables, along with concern about misuse of rationing documents including forgery of emergency coupons.[35]

[14] PRO, MAF 100/56, Enforcement Review, vol. 1, no. 3 (Nov. 1947), Extracts from an address to the Divisional Enforcement Officers Conference, 26 Nov. 1947.

[35] PRO, MAF 75/40, Enforcement; MAF 100/52, Enforcement—Policy and Organisation: Interim Report, 1 July 1946; MAF 100/56, Enforcement Review, vol. 1, no. 2 (Oct. 1947), Progress Report, January–August 1947; MAF 286/30, Circular, 1 Jan. 1949; MAF 100/60, Enforcement Review, vol. 5, no. 7 (July 1951); for illicit slaughter drives see MAF 100/57, vol. 2, no. 2 (Feb. 1948); and MAF 88/470.

Prosecution statistics, despite their obvious limitations, provide some indication of enforcement activity throughout the period. Table 4.4 details the number of successful Ministry of Food prosecutions between 1939 and 1951.[36] The level of prosecutions was high throughout most of the war and the sharp drop in 1944–5 was the result of the expressed preference by the minister that food control committees should 'adopt even more extensively the practice of warning suspected offenders who had not previously been convicted or warned'.[37] This period of leniency came to an end in 1946 against the background of concern about the escalation of the black market after the war. The internal history of enforcement sums up the shift from war to peace:

During the war, the determination to win, and general unselfishness resulting from patriotism, made the Enforcement Inspector's task comparatively simple and assured him of a considerable measure of co-operation from the public.

TABLE 4.4. *Ministry of Food enforcement: successful prosecutions, 1939–1951*

Date	Successful prosecutions
Oct. 1939–Aug. 1940	4,408
Sept. 1940–Aug. 1941	18,966
Sept. 1941–Aug. 1942	26,403
Sept. 1942–Aug. 1943	25,168
Sept. 1943–Aug. 1944	23,862
Sept. 1944–Aug. 1945	15,681
1945	15,756
1946	20,466
1947	24,265
1948	23,569
1949	22,517
1950	14,383
1951	12,343

Notes: The 1951 figure is for 11 months only since there are no data for December. Successful prosecutions accounted for well over 90% of prosecutions launched throughout the period. For example in 1944–5 just over half of all prosecutions were brought by Food Control Committees, 40% by Divisions, and the rest by Headquarters. According to enforcement statistics in MAF 156/289 on penalties in 1941–2, the vast bulk of prosecutions resulted in small fines of up to £5 and a small number of offenders were imprisoned. For 1945–51 yet again roughly 80% resulted in fines of up to £5; roughly 3–5% in imprisonment; the rest received larger fines.
Sources: PRO, MAF 100/45, Note on Enforcement, 7 May 1946; MAF 156/289, Enforcement Statistics,

[36] These figures are somewhat different from those in Table 4.1 which is based on persons prosecuted rather than prosecutions, since multiple charges were frequent. Moreover, Table 4.1 is not confined to offences against Ministry of Food orders. Nevertheless, both tables show roughly the same trend.
[37] PRO, MAF 100/45, Note on Enforcement, 7 May 1946.

Immediately subsequent to the war, however, the situation altered insofar as black market operators on a larger scale came into existence, and the public tired of controls and withdrew, to a great extent, their co-operation with the Enforcement inspectorates.[38]

The additional food restrictions imposed after the fuel and dollar crises of 1947 were 'inevitably encourag[ing] black market dealings in the commodities affected'[39] and hence enforcement activity peaked during 1947–8 in terms of both prosecutions and staffing levels. This policy was not without success and in 1949:

[the] increased enforcement activity which was developed as a result of the Bodinnar Report has now had time to have some preventive effect and food rackets which might otherwise have developed have not done so. It is to be hoped that we have passed through that dangerous transitional phase from war to peace-time control without the general break-up in respect for food regulations which was at one time feared. . . . [Improvements in food supplies] should render the profits of black market operations progressively less attractive. The main exception, of course, is meat.[40]

From 1950 onwards prosecutions declined markedly.

Table 4.5 indicates that, as measured by successful prosecutions, the most important offences were those against the maximum price order and, above all, illegal sale, that is supplying and obtaining foodstuffs illegally and other documentary offences. This table is based on November and December data only and the pattern might have been different at other times of the year. According to Table 4.6 the bulk of offences were committed by retailers, followed by the general public and caterers when separate data are available. A whole range of commodities was affected, as illustrated in Table 4.7. The most interesting aspects of this table are the preponderance of meat and illicit slaughter offences towards the end of the period and the high number of rationing offences committed by traders and consumers. In sum, the statistics relating to successful prosecutions suggest that the bulk of black market offences were committed by retailers, caterers, and the general public, selling and buying foodstuffs illegally or above the maximum price as well as documentary offences such as false accounting or misuse of ration documents.[41] By contrast offences such as conditions of sale or failure to display prices appear rare, although it is possible that warnings rather than prosecutions were a more likely response to such offences. Similarly, the low number of prosecutions against wholesalers and producers may well be a

[38] PRO, MAF 75/40, Enforcement.

[39] PRO, MAF 100/56, Enforcement Review, vol. 1, no. 2 (Oct. 1947), Progress Report, Jan.–Aug. 1947

[40] PRO, MAF 286/30, Operation Octopus, Third Report to the Minister, 8 Apr. 1949.

[41] This pattern of offences is much the same as during the war, see PRO, MAF 83/2681, The Black Market and the Ministry of Food's Attempts to Stop it, 5 Feb. 1942.

TABLE 4.5. *Successful prosecutions by type of offence during one month, 1945–1951*

Panel A. Successful prosecutions

Date	Total	Price[a]	Condition of sale	No price displayed	Illegal slaughter	Illegal sale[b]	No licence[c]	False declaration	Other
1945	1,300	214	10	73	46	524	103	126	204
1946	2,284	353	14	74	65	780	272	165	561
1947	1,687	205	5	22	137	1,034	25	126	133
1948	2,260	613	13	37	63	1,018	62	335	119
1949	1,326	314	4	23	39	799	22	79	46
1950	749	247	—	11	19	296	18	126	32
1951	1,519	395	4	13	35	764	66	94	148

Panel B. Index of successful prosecutions (per cent)

Date	Total	Price[a]	Condition of sale	No price displayed	Illegal slaughter	Illegal sale[b]	No licence[c]	False declaration	Other
1945	100	16.5	0.8	5.7	3.5	40.3	7.9	9.7	15.7
1946	100	15.5	0.6	3.2	2.9	34.2	11.9	7.2	24.6
1947	100	12.2	0.3	1.3	8.1	61.3	1.5	7.5	7.9
1948	100	27.1	0.6	1.6	2.8	45.0	2.7	14.8	5.3
1949	100	23.7	0.3	1.7	2.9	60.3	1.7	6.0	3.5
1950	100	33.0	—	1.5	2.5	39.5	2.4	16.8	4.3
1951	100	26.0	0.3	0.9	2.3	50.3	4.3	6.2	9.7

[a] Offences against the maximum price order.
[b] Supplying or obtaining foodstuffs without correct authority or other documentary offences.
[c] Trading without licence.
Note: The table is based on December data in 1945, 1947, 1948, 1949, and 1950 and November data in 1946 and 1951.
Source: PRO, MAF 156/289, Enforcement Statistics, 1945–51.

TABLE 4.6. *Persons prosecuted by specified group of offender in one month, 1945–1951*

Panel A. Persons prosecuted

Date	Total	Wholesalers	Retailers	Producers	Caterers	Others[a]
1945	654	8	371	66	N/A	209
1946	972	33	528	125	N/A	286
1947	728	10	341	70	73	234
1948	774	26	385	56	103	204
1949	523	20	314	33	64	92
1950	326	6	203	14	41	62
1951	509	24	311	45	51	78

Panel B. Index of persons prosecuted (per cent)

Date	Total	Wholesalers	Retailers	Producers	Caterers	Others[a]
1945	100	1.2	56.7	10.1	N/A	32.0
1946	100	3.4	54.3	12.9	N/A	29.4
1947	100	1.4	46.8	9.6	10.0	32.1
1948	100	3.4	49.7	7.2	13.3	26.4
1949	100	3.8	60.0	6.3	12.2	17.6
1950	100	1.8	62.3	4.3	12.6	19.0
1951	100	4.7	61.1	8.8	10.0	15.3

[a] General public.
Notes: The table is based on December data in 1945, 1947, 1948, 1949, and 1950 and November data in 1946 and 1951. The discrepancy between successful prosecutions in Table 4.4 and persons prosecuted in this table is explained by the fact that usually a number of charges were laid against a single individual. The sources also provide details of which type of offence was committed by particular offenders. The most significant were retailers charged with offences against the maximum price orders as well as supplying and obtaining foodstuffs without correct authority and other documentary offences. The latter was also the most preponderant offence committed by the general public. All other offences account for only a small percentage of the total.
Source: PRO, MAF 156/289, Enforcement Statistics, 1945–51.

result of the structure of enforcement work, with food control committees focusing on retailers and consumers, while the manpower limitations at divisions and headquarters allowed for little more than token investigations. With regard to penalties in 1941–2, the vast bulk of prosecutions resulted in small fines of up to £5, while at the other extreme a small number of offenders were imprisoned. After the war, four-fifths of prosecutions resulted in fines of up to £5, approximately 3–5 per cent of offenders were imprisoned, and the rest received larger fines.[42]

These statistics draw attention to catering establishments as well as retailers. Restaurants and hotels were particularly well placed to exploit black

[42] PRO, MAF 156/289, Enforcement Statistics, 1941–2, 1945–51.

TABLE 4.7. *Persons prosecuted by commodity for selected periods,*
1946–1954

Panel A. Persons prosecuted

Commodity	1946	1947	1949	1952	1953[a]	1953[b]	1954
Animal feeding stuffs	225	299	77	44	6	N/A	N/A
Bacon and ham	62	84	9	7	8	10	—
Bread, biscuits, and cake	178	97	46	—	2	—	—
Butter, cheese, and milk products	41	27	14	7	6	12	—
Chocolate and sugar confectionery	40	44	22	8	N/A	N/A	N/A
Eggs and egg products	225	173	44	23	1	—	—
Fish	152	112	21	—	—	—	N/A
Fresh fruit and veg.	366	768	33	1	N/A	N/A	N/A
Horseflesh, goatflesh, and venison	34	39	20	—	N/A	N/A	N/A
Illegal slaughter	377	436	38	18	26	9	37
Meat	267	242	74	53	40	62	33
Milk	299	385	53	5	—	—	—
Oils and fats	79	74	15	6	5	—	—
Points rationing: traders	671	620	52	26	N/A	N/A	N/A
Points rationing: consumers	107	72	24	8	N/A	N/A	N/A
Potatoes and carrots	114	215	8	13	3	16	7
Poultry	249	189	22	—	N/A	N/A	N/A
Rabbits	94	63	21	—	N/A	N/A	N/A
Rationing offences: traders	277	319	64	50	36	10	5
Rationing offences: consumers	315	1,056	169	69	62	20	—
Waste of food	289	32	4	3	—	N/A	N/A
Miscellaneous	217	267	74	29	14	2	—
Total	4,867	5,621	891	370	209	141	82

market opportunities since there was no price control on meals in restaurants until the introduction of a 5s. limit in March 1942 and even this
restriction was easily evaded, for instance by charging disproportionately
for drinks or service.[43] Smithies details the emergence of a black market
between East Anglia farmers and West End restaurants centring around
Romford and the latter featured prominently among black market offenders
in the minutes of the City of Westminster Food Control Committee.[44] False
returns by catering establishments on meals served, which formed the basis
of allocation of rationed foods, were a persistent problem. In 1952 a 'recent
special check of samples in all parts of the country showed inflation of

[43] PRO, MAF 83/2681, The Black Market and the Ministry of Food's Attempts to Stop it, 5 Feb.
1942.
[44] Smithies, *Crime in Wartime*, p. 60; PRO, MAF 67/99, 101, London: City of Westminster Food
Control Committee, 1943, 1945–6.

TABLE 4.7 *Panel B. Index of persons prosecuted (per cent)*

Commodity	1946	1947	1949	1952	1953[a]	1953[b]	1954
Animal feeding stuffs	4.6	5.3	8.6	11.9	2.9	N/A	N/A
Bacon and ham	1.3	5.3	1.0	1.9	3.8	7.1	—
Bread, biscuits, and cake	3.7	1.5	5.2	—	1.0	—	—
Butter, cheese, and milk products	0.8	0.5	1.6	1.9	2.9	8.5	—
Chocolate and sugar confectionery	0.8	0.8	2.5	2.2	N/A	N/A	N/A
Eggs and egg products	4.6	3.1	4.9	6.2	0.5	—	—
Fish	3.1	2.0	2.4	—	—	—	N/A
Fresh fruit and veg.	7.5	13.7	3.7	0.3	N/A	N/A	N/A
Horseflesh, goatflesh and venison	0.7	0.7	2.2	—	N/A	N/A	N/A
Illegal slaughter	7.6	7.8	4.3	4.9	12.4	6.4	45.1
Meat	5.5	4.3	8.3	14.3	19.1	44.0	40.2
Milk	6.1	6.9	6.0	1.4	—	—	—
Oils and fats	1.6	1.3	1.7	1.6	2.4	—	—
Points rationing: traders	13.8	11.0	5.8	7.0	N/A	N/A	N/A
Points rationing: consumers	2.2	1.3	2.7	2.2	N/A	N/A	N/A
Potatoes and carrots	2.3	3.8	0.9	3.5	1.4	11.4	8.5
Poultry	5.1	3.4	2.5	—	N/A	N/A	N/A
Rabbits	1.9	1.1	2.4	—	N/A	N/A	N/A
Rationing offences: traders	5.7	5.7	7.2	13.5	17.2	7.1	6.1
Rationing offences: consumers	6.5	18.8	19.0	18.7	29.7	14.2	—
Waste of food	5.9	0.6	0.6	0.8	—	N/A	N/A
Miscellaneous	4.5	4.8	8.3	7.8	6.7	1.4	—
Total	100	100	100	100	100	100	100

Note: The data refer to two six-months periods, namely Jan.–June 1946 and Jan.–June 1947, and subsequently individual months only, namely November 1949,[a] June 1953,[b] November 1953, and June 1954.

Sources: PRO, MAF 75/40; MAF 100/56; MAF 100/62–3.

returns in 25 per cent. of cases. The inflation ranged up to 700 per cent., with an average of 80 per cent.'[45]

The preponderance of retailers among black market offenders is not surprising given the nature of the rationing system. Under straight rationing, with the consumer-retailer tie, retailers' supplies were based on the number of registered consumers. Supplies were allocated assuming a 100 per cent uptake and it was difficult to keep registrations up to date, with the result that there were inflationary tendencies. Consequently retailers were frequently left with a margin of unclaimed rations which could be sold to favoured customers. In order to ease administration food offices merely monitored retailers' eight-weekly returns detailing opening stock,

[45] PRO, CAB 129/53, C (52) 215, Enforcement of Food Controls, 26 June 1952.

purchases, and closing stock. Since these could not be audited properly retailers were in a very strong position to be fraudulent, particularly since any 'glaring discrepancies' could be explained away as a mistake and even if 'suspicions aroused by the return were confirmed, it still remained to prove illegal disposal in court; it was not enough to demonstrate that stock was missing'.[46] In a classic case a grocer from Scotland disposed of 18 cwt. of sugar in November 1943 although his registered customers had received none. Food officers assumed a connection with an illicit whisky distillery but could only prove that 'the grocer had mislaid' the sugar but not 'what he had actually done with it. The only ground for prosecution was ... the purely technical one of failing to maintain the 14 days emergency stock.' Therefore, the retailer's licence could not be withdrawn since he had not been found guilty of a serious breach of regulations.[47] Hence, Hammond concludes that the notion that retailers were controlled by means of returns was '"sheer delusion"' since food offices could do little more than 'to exert moral pressure on retailers, even though the more intelligent might rapidly realize that a care for paper conformity was all that was necessary to escape prosecution'.[48] This lax control of retailers was easy to administer but required relatively plentiful supplies to work. These disadvantages have to be offset against the advantage of greater security of ration documents under straight rationing. Since consumers could only obtain their ration from a specific retailer, who in turn knew the consumer personally, theft and forgery of or trafficking in food ration books were rare, in marked contrast with the clothes rationing scheme where coupon control was the single out-standing enforcement problem.

Another weakness of the close tie between retailers and consumers from an enforcement point of view was that it was in the interest of both retailers and consumers to circumvent the regulations. In 1943 it was noted that as a result of

the continuous pressure exercised by the Enforcement Staff ... organised operations of the type commonly described as black market, have been driven more and more underground and are becoming more and more difficult to detect. Detection is made all the more difficult by the fact that the offences are collusive, the fixing of low maximum prices for most foodstuffs having brought into existence a host of buyers willing to pay more than the maximum price, both among traders and members of the public.[49]

Judging from the Mass-Observation reports on shopping in London in 1947, off-ration and under-the-counter sales as well as tipping and favouritism were endemic after the war. The situation during the war was little different and retailers' defence in allegations of over-charging was that

[46] Hammond, *Food Volume II*, pp. 640–1.　　[47] Ibid., p. 641.　　[48] Ibid., p. 642.
[49] PRO, MAF 83/2681, Enforcement of Ministry of Food Orders, 8 June 1943.

they themselves were forced to pay above the legal price by wholesalers. Thus the 'various branches of the distributive trades blamed one another: retailers held that wholesalers were responsible, and vice versa, though the two sides would occasionally unite to criticize the Ministry of Food ... [which] failed to attack the "real racketeers".'[50] Apart from extreme measures such as the revocation of a retailer's licence, which 'should be regarded only as a last resort' and was applied in only a handful of cases,[51] there was little that the ministry could do since it was impossible to police thousands of retailers. Complaints from the public about retailers had to be treated with care since the person concerned might bear a grudge, this evidence could rarely be used in court, and prosecutions were frequently based on offences committed in the course of test shopping. During test shopping, enforcement officers should in 'no circumstances . . . use persuasion or pressure to induce the shopkeeper to break the law'.[52] Thus, the enforcement officers' task of detecting offences was difficult particularly since they also had to retain the co-operation of the public. After the war, they were derided as 'Strachey's Snoopers' and accused of being *agents provocateurs* in the press, while an internal circular stressed the importance of courtesy, tact, and avoidance of over-zealousness in dealings with the public.[53]

Apart from retailers selling rationed and controlled foods in breach of the regulations there were two other sources of supply to the black market, namely theft of food in transit and home producers, including self-suppliers. Theft or pilferage of food throughout the distribution network, and particularly from docks, was a persistent problem despite efforts of improved liaison between the ministry's transport, warehousing, and enforcement divisions in order to tighten security.[54] In 1946 losses were thought to be 'small compared with the volumes of food handled, they are, nevertheless, substantial. Such losses, which feed the Black Market, are variously estimated at well over £1,000,000 a year.'[55] A survey concluded that the practice was pursued by 'a small and concentrated section of the community . . . a daily habit in the case of a certain number . . . and a less frequent occurrence in the case of the majority'. It was also noted that 'claims upon the Railway Companies for losses for all kinds of goods in transit appear to be some 15–20 times greater than they were before the war'.[56]

[50] Smithies, *Crime in Wartime*, p. 75, see also pp. 64–5.

[51] PRO, CAB 71/12, Lord President's Committee: Revocation of Licences, LP (43) 83, 15 Apr. 1943. Between Aug. 1941 and Mar. 1943, the licences of 70 retailers, 6 caterers, and 12 wholesalers were revoked, while warnings were issued to 82, 2, and 21 respectively.

[52] PRO, MAF 100/29, Circular, 10 June 1943.

[53] PRO, MAF 286/30, Minute, 28 Sept. 1949; Circular, 9 May 1949.

[54] PRO, MAF 83/2681, The Black Market and the Ministry of Food's Attempts to Stop it, 5 Feb. 1942; MAF 100/31, Circular, 28 Apr. 1943, Minute, 16 Jan. 1946.

[55] PRO, MAF 100/52, Enforcement—Policy and Organization: Interim Report, 1 July 1946.

[56] Ibid., app. 3, 5 Feb. 1946.

From 1947 onwards a range of statistics on this problem were compiled. These showed that losses of food, which occurred primarily at the ship's side, from docks, and from railways, amounted to a fraction of 1 per cent of total food handled. Meat and livestock were stolen most frequently, followed by tea, dried fruit and nuts, and canned fish.[57]

Tea was rationed in July 1940 when it was decided that in order to sustain morale 'the nation apparently needed not merely tea, but particular brands of tea'.[58] For this reason, along with the fact that postal trade was extensive, neither registration nor coupon replacement was to accompany rationing, and retailers' supplies were based on loose datum allocation, amounting to roughly two-thirds of pre-war consumption. This was sufficient to meet the domestic ration but it soon became clear that rationing with little more than 'the trappings of control' was 'unenforceable'.[59] Attempts to monitor retailers' sales by means of permits early in 1942 showed that 'sales had apparently amounted to 18 per cent. more than the "theoretical maximum" . . . At worst, retailers had sold a good deal of tea "off ration"; at best, they had overstated their sales in order to secure inflated permits.'[60] In February 1942, 'it was clear that the "moral pressure" on the retailer had failed. About one million pounds—eight million rations—of excess tea were being released.'[61] With supplies running short, the only solution was to reform the rationing scheme fundamentally and a coupon replacement scheme was introduced in 1942. The effect of this reform was 'remarkable' and in December 1942, retailers' sales stood at '1 per cent. *below* the "theoretical maximum" . . . [amounting to] a decrease of some 1,000,000 lb. *a week* in retailers' demands'.[62] While the black market did not disappear entirely, as indicated by the prevalence of tea among foods stolen in transit, this case study illustrates the extensiveness of evasion without genuine control and shows that the specific characteristics of a rationing or control scheme were the key to enforcement.

In view of the discontent about meat shortages, particularly among male manual workers, it is not surprising that meat was a principal black market commodity throughout the period.[63] Apart from theft in transit and sale of condemned meat to the general public, official attention to contain the black market focused on butchers, as well as breaches of restrictions relating to animal feedstuffs and illicit slaughter among domestic producers, including self-suppliers. Meat was difficult to control because it was 'intractable', 'highly perishable', and 'elusive'.[64] It was virtually impossible to monitor butchers' supplies since meat was rationed by price and not quantity, individual cuts could be presented in a way to appear to be of a

[57] PRO, MAF 100/57–61.   [58] Hammond, *Food Volume II*, p. 699.
[59] Ibid., p. 712.   [60] Ibid., pp. 726–7.   [61] Ibid., p. 728.
[62] Ibid., p. 733 (emphasis in original).   [63] See Chapter 2, section 2.1.
[64] Hammond, *Food Volume II*, p. 659, also pp. 659–96.

higher grade, and meat was also processed into unrationed foods such as sausages or pies. Against the background of initially plentiful supplies and a generous ration, the ministry combined 'under-issue of the ration with slackness in its administration' and in September 1940 the minister noted that 'meat is the only rationed article in which the rationing rules are being persistently evaded'.[65] Nothing was done until winter 1940–1 when a supply crisis resulted in local shortages, allocation became virtually arbitrary, and there was a danger that the ration could not be honoured. This episode was one of 'only three major occasions on which something went seriously wrong' in the administration of rationing.[66] The problem was addressed by the introduction of very tight control on butchers, who had to submit a weekly statement on the number of consumers and sales. This had to be supported by evidence such as counterfoils and caterers' order forms. This system apparently worked well for the remainder of the war and beyond but malpractices such as overcharging continued. According to a survey in the Lancashire area, 'overcharging by butchers was disclosed in 80 per cent. of the investigations undertaken and the average overcharge was around 18 per cent. In all there were 2,700 convictions by the Courts of overcharging for meat in the six months ended 30th April' 1952.[67]

In the agricultural industry, 'offences are common, in many cases calculated and deliberate, and on the increase. This is particularly so as regards illicit slaughter, eggs, poultry and now, feeding stuffs for animals.'[68] The head of enforcement thought in 1946 that:

[a] substantial section of the agricultural community habitually disregard the Food Orders, adopting the attitude that they are just more regulations to be 'got round'— at a profit—and not that such avoidance is fundamentally dishonest and unfair to the whole community. This attitude appears to be general in Wales, parts of Northern England and Scotland—in that order. Generally speaking, such farmers and associated dealers can afford the risk of detection, prosecution and relatively petty fines—and act accordingly.[69]

According to an auctioneer, illicit dealings and other malpractices in the sale of cattle were commonplace in 1947. Since the ministry issued orders 'which they do not police', the result was that 'a large number of normally perfectly honest people [were] breaking the law openly and seeing nothing wrong in doing it, and they [were] being turned from decent honest citizens into dishonest people'.[70] Attached to the letter is a note by a ministry official which reads, 'I cannot deal with this diatribe . . . to put an end to the practices' would require 'about a dozen qualified inspectors at each store

[65] Quoted in *Hammond, Food Volume II*, pp. 675, 665.   [66] Ibid., p. 753.
[67] PRO, CAB 129/53, C (52) 215, Enforcement of Food Controls, 26 June 1952.
[68] PRO, MAF 100/52, Enforcement—Policy and Organization: Interim Report, 1 July 1946.
[69] Ibid.   [70] PRO, MAF 88/470, Letter, 11 Nov. 1947.

sale . . . It would only require about 5,000 inspectors'.[71] At about the same time, a butcher was 'gravely disturbed by the recent volume and power of the black market' in rabbits and meat. Unless something was done about the situation, it 'will grow to such an extent that it will become increasingly difficult for the honest man to obtain a living, and remain outside the black market activities'. Butchers who did not buy black market rabbits or meat were losing registered customers and he urged that to prevent the 'break down' of control 'a system [had] to be re-established where the honest citizen can find it easy to observe the law, and at the same time to preserve his means of livelihood'.[72] In this context, Strachey made his impassioned plea against illicit slaughter, the Bodinnar committee was appointed, resulting in the strengthening of enforcement staff, and a number of drives were launched against illicit slaughter. While the number of offences detected during these drives amounted to only a fraction of inspections carried out, the associated publicity presumably had some deterrent effect.[73] A major source of black market bacon was illicit slaughter and sale by self-suppliers but even the tighter regulations introduced in 1948 'never had any demonstrable deterrent effect'.[74] While the bacon ration was reduced after the war, slaughtering by self-suppliers reached peak levels, forcing the ministry to sacrifice the principle of fair shares in the face of self-help which provided a 'net contribution to total food supplies, however ill-distributed'.[75]

The attempt to control eggs and poultry similarly failed since a large proportion of total output was produced by small-scale home producers who were actually exempt from the control scheme. These commodities illustrate public ingenuity in evading the regulations. The shortage of eggs led to an unprecedented trade in supposed hatching eggs by auction which was:

in effect a legalised black market . . . the operators of which are in a privileged position. They can obtain supplies legally and provided they obtain the declaration [that the eggs were being bought for hatching] . . . they are unconcerned with the use to which the eggs are ultimately put. . . . A large number of the declarations have been proved to contain false names and addresses and no further action was possible.[76]

A corresponding racket emerged with regard to alleged breeding poultry which was also smuggled to the mainland from Eire and Northern Ireland.[77] In 1942, 'only about two-thirds or less of the eggs that should come to packing stations were doing so. So large a black market appeared to menace the very existence of the scheme'.[78] Targeted drives, such as one in Wales

[71] Ibid., Note, 13 Nov. 1947.
[72] Ibid., Letter, 11 Nov. 1947.   [73] Ibid.; see also MAF 100/56, 59.
[74] Hammond, *Food Volume III*, p. 736; see pp. 727–36 on the self-suppliers' scheme.
[75] Ibid., p. 736.
[76] Hammond, *Food Volume II*, p. 94; see pp. 65–102 for details of the egg control scheme.
[77] Hammond, *Food Volume III*, p. 722; see pp. 721–6 on the difficulties of poultry and rabbit control.   [78] Hammond, *Food Volume II*, pp. 86–7.

which resulted in a 100 per cent increase in deliveries to packing stations had little more than a temporary effect.[79] Various attempts at tightening the regulations achieved little and in 1943 the ministry conceded defeat, since under 'the present Poultry Order, it [was] impossible to achieve any proper degree of enforcement. This order has been most troublesome and could be removed without changing the present position materially simply because it is ineffective.'[80] There were a number of reasons why the ministry was not 'prepared to admit the logic of the situation, abandon appearances, and remove control altogether'.[81] Although both poultry and eggs were considered to be of low priority in national food policy, public demand to a fair share forced the ministry to go through the motions of control. Moreover, rising prices, particularly in view of the exaggerated weight of eggs in the cost-of-living index, could not be ignored and an uncontrolled poultry industry would have depleted precious feedstuffs.

While the typical official response to the black market was to strengthen controls—with greater or lesser degrees of success—the loosening of regulations provided an alternative policy. A good example is the controversy about the legality of gifts of rationed foods. This illustrates the fundamental importance of public consent in the administration of rationing and controls. The issue made headlines in November 1942 with articles and correspondence published in the *Daily Mail, New Statesman*, and *The Times* protesting that people were denied 'their right to do as they like with their rations', which was 'silly' and 'treating people like children'.[82] The absurdity of the regulation meant that it was legal to share rationed foods within a household but not with a relative or friend living next door; to give away a cake as a present but not the ingredients it was made from; and to share a meal with a tramp but not to give him a slice of buttered bread at the door. The matter was taken up by Churchill who, in a minute to Woolton, hoped

it is not true that we are enforcing . . . vexatious regulations of this kind. It is absolutely contrary to logic and good sense that a person may not give away or exchange his rations with someone who at the moment he feels has a greater need. It strikes at neighbourliness and friendship. I should be so sorry to see the great work you have done spoilt by allowing these officials, whose interests are so deeply involved in magnifying their functions and their numbers, to lead you to strike a false note.[83]

The officials in question defended the 'considered' policy that 'the ration is a maximum and if not required . . . should not be drawn' and that it

[79] PRO, MAF 100/30, Detectives' Conference No. 6 (Southern Region), 28 July 1943.
[80] PRO, MAF 83/2681, Enforcement of Ministry of Food Orders, 8 June 1943.
[81] Hammond, *Food Volume III*, p. 725.
[82] PRO, MAF 102/147, Consumer Reaction Reports, 30 Nov. and 7 Dec. 1942; MAF 99/1184, extract from *The Times*, 21 Nov. 1942.
[83] PRO, MAF 99/1184, Minute Churchill to Woolton, 21 Nov. 1942.

'should not be transferable whether by sale, barter or gift except within . . . [the] household', in terms of the need to economize on shipping space, the fact that a 100 per cent take-up would reduce the ration of some commodities, and 'because of [the] impossibility from [an] enforcement point of view of proving that money [had been] passed'.[84] However, the legal ambiguity of, at least in theory, criminalizing an essentially harmless and common practice was also acknowledged. While proceedings under the order were extremely rare, Woolton, in his reply to Churchill, held that 'it appears to me unwise to have a law which does not meet with the consent in practice of reasonable people'.[85] He acknowledged that the supply position and danger of abuse were important but these considerations were eclipsed by

the general public sense of what is required of our laws. The first of these considerations in a democratic state is that it shall have the support of public opinion. The public would never agree that adult people should not give away their sweet ration if they were so disposed: neither would they agree that they should not make presents of surplus tea or sugar if through taste or abstinence they had some slight surplus. To maintain that the public should be reassured by telling them that they would not be prosecuted for such minor breaches of the law is in my view not sound administration. The Executive has no right to take such powers over the public. Self respecting people following the harmless practice of generous instinct ought not to be made into law breakers and they ought not to be at the mercy of any malicious informer or overzealous official who could cause them, as the law stands, to suffer the indignity of trial in a police court. From the point of view of administration the Order is bad since no sensible magistrate would penalise a delinquent and such a decision against the Order would bring it into disrepute and encourage that section of the public that like to beat the law to risk the defiance of other food laws.[86]

Hence, the rationing order was amended 'to permit gifts of rationed food by a person who has duly obtained that food from a retailer for household consumption. It should however be clearly understood that barter or trade in any rationed foods will still be an offence' and new regulations were issued to control gifts of rationed foods by self-suppliers.[87]

The complex and cumbersome nature of the regulations frequently appeared absurd and exposed the ministry to ridicule. To give just a few examples, in 1942 a jar of sweets, auctioned at the Stock Exchange to raise money for a war charity, raised £79,500.[88] Since sweets were price controlled, Ministry of Food officials went to the Stock Exchange to enquire about the transaction. Press comment suggested that either the auctioneer or the Chancellor of the Exchequer had rendered themselves liable to a fine

---

[84] Ibid., Teleprint, 23 Nov. 1942; Minutes, 21 Nov. 1942.
[85] Ibid., Minute Woolton to Churchill, 23 Nov. 1942.
[86] Ibid., Minute, Woolton, 19 Dec. 1942.   [87] Ibid., Press Notice, 23 Dec. 1942.
[88] PRO, MAF 102/147, Consumer Reaction Report, 3 Apr. 1942. The next few sentences are based on this source.

of £238,500 although the sweets were actually given away. *The Times* lamented the waste of time

spent by wise men in undoing the work of the good. . . . It reveals in official good-ness a power more dangerous even than that against which the gods themselves struggle in vain, a cold and mechanical correctness in high places which is insensi-tive to the fullest flow of national feeling and which values a rule above a great act of faith.

An explanation issued by the ministry a few days later caused further amusement, with the *Financial News* suggesting that the 'incident will go down into Stock Exchange history with inextinguishable laughter coupled with regret that the Ministry did not postpone its action until the following day, April 1st'. Another example was the 'cake crime' committed by one 'of the typical figures of our time . . . the "doughnut criminal"'.[89] A baker was prosecuted and fined for decorating doughnuts with sugar in contravention of the regulations although he had not used additional sugar but saved some that would normally have been used in the batter, leading the *Daily Mail* to deplore the 'crazy, inefficient state of society' in which 'an Order must be obeyed, no matter to what absurd results'. Churchill asked for a special report on the matter, the Minister of Food promised to amend the order and generally to have a 'stop put to these trivial and stupid little prosecutions'.[90] Churchill replied, 'Good. You will gain much credit by stamping on these little trashy prosecutions, and also by purging the regulations from petty, meticulous arrogant officialism which tends to affect the reputation of a great and successful Department'.[91] Ridicule of excessive bureaucracy and red tape mocked the control apparatus especially after the war, when Jay's dictum that 'the gentleman in Whitehall really does know better what is good for the people than the people know themselves' was taken up in the right-wing press and Conservative propaganda.[92] It certainly seems ludi-crous that enforcement officers spent their time as late as spring 1951 decid-ing whether 'chocolate snowballs'—a product 'usually made of marshmallow covered with chocolate couverture and sprinkled with coconut. A small piece of wafer or other biscuit is sometimes used as a base'—should be classified as a sweet or a cake. In discussion, it was admit-ted that the issue of classification 'had a deplorable history', particularly since 'an inter-Divisional committee had considered the classification of several products, but experts on the committee had not always been able to agree'. The absurdity of this discussion was acknowledged in a comment in

[89] PRO, MAF 286/19, Extract from *Daily Mail*, 23 Mar. 1944.
[90] Ibid., Minute, Minister of Food to Churchill, 25 Mar. 1944.
[91] Ibid., Minute, Churchill to Minister of Food, 2 Apr. 1944.
[92] D. Jay, *The Socialist Case* (London, 1937, 1947 edn.), p. 258. See Chapter 5, sections 5.3 and 5.4.

the margin: 'Nothing to be gained by our discussion . . . which is embarrassing and difficult'.[93]

4.2. CLOTHES AND CLOTHING COUPONS

Following the introduction of rationing in 1941, clothing became susceptible to black market dealings since clothing was easy to store, distribute, and manufacture, as well as high in demand. Official concern about the danger of abuse was high, as illustrated in the *Clothing Coupon Quiz*, the Board of Trade's publicity leaflet about clothes rationing. The first paragraph of the first issue appealed to the public, emphasizing the importance of fair shares to the war effort: it 'is *your* scheme—to defend you as a consumer and as a citizen. All honest people realise that trying to beat the ration is the same as trying to cheat the nation'.[94] The illegality of breaches of the regulations, which were subject to heavy penalties, was mentioned on a number of occasions in this and later editions. The Board of Trade 'were always aware that clothes rationing could not work unless the vast majority of the population helped to make it work. The system would have collapsed if there had been really wide-scale evasion'.[95] In the event, the system functioned adequately until the final months of rationing but, nevertheless, the black market was an endemic problem throughout.

The black market operated primarily through trade in coupons. Prices fluctuated and in 1944 the black market price stood at 'about £5 a book or 2/-d a coupon, whereas the forgeable 1941/2 clothing card could at one time be bought for 2/6d a card'.[96] In London in 1947, coupons could be bought for '1/6 each until the recent issue became valid then the price jumped to 2/6 and 3/-'.[97] This trade was an inevitable consequence of a rationing scheme based on coupon replacement. Since coupons could be presented to any retailer and were used as replacement for stock, it was impossible to prevent loss of coupons along the chain of distribution, there was a strong incentive to steal or forge ration books and coupons, and consumers could sell their ration book and apply for a replacement on the grounds that they had lost it. While retailers were supposed to cut coupons out of books, in practice many accepted loose coupons and it was impossible to prove after the transaction had taken place whether these coupons

[93] PRO, MAF 100/55, Letter, 21 Apr. 1951, Minutes of Annual Conference of Chief Regional Enforcement Officers, 22 May 1951.

[94] Board of Trade, *Clothing Coupon Quiz* (London, 1941) (emphasis in original).

[95] Hargreaves and Gowing, *Civil Industry and Trade*, p. 424.

[96] PRO, T 230/119, Interdepartmental Committee on Rationing, 31 Mar. [1944]; Hargreaves and Gowing, *Civil Industry and Trade*, p. 328.

[97] MO, TC Food, Box 6E, Black Market and Barter, 12 May 1947.

had been used previously or had been presented by a customer who had acquired them illegally. A comparison of losses of various documents during the 12 months ending July 1942 showed that the clothing book (416,000 losses) was well ahead of identity cards (370,000 losses) and especially of food ration books, of which only 220,000 were lost.[98] These figures illustrate the security advantages of the consumer-retailer tie as a basis of rationing. In contrast with the black market in food, that in clothing functioned not by off-ration sales but by coupon fraud, and the latter was the main focus of enforcement activity.

It is impossible to estimate the extent of the black market, and statistical data are limited. In the first months of rationing, loose coupons were used fairly extensively according to a survey of retailers in 11 towns conducted in August 1941.[99] On average 18.9 per cent of retailers were offered loose coupons by over 20 per cent of customers. The practice varied greatly between towns and the figure stood at one extreme at 50 and 39.2 per cent in Warrington and Liverpool respectively whereas it was only 1.7 and 3.3 per cent in Wolverhampton and Torquay at the other extreme. It is important to appreciate that at this time clothing coupons were in fact the unused margarine coupons from the food ration book and the main reasons for offering loose coupons were practical convenience (37 per cent) and that ration books were used for other rationed goods (22 per cent). Hence, the situation may well have been different after the introduction of separate clothes ration books from 1942 onwards.

Perhaps a better indication of the extent of the black market are statistics relating to replacement of lost ration books. It was impossible to distinguish between fictitious and genuine claims and the majority were thought to be fraudulent. According to one report, 'the officials who issue the replacement coupons consider that over 90 per cent of the applications are false, but there is no method of checking the stories told'.[100] An internal survey concluded that about 70 per cent of applications for replacement were 'unsatisfactory' since the applicant claimed that coupons were simply '"lost in street", "dropped from handbag" (nothing else lost) . . . [or] "thrown in fire"'.[101] The total number of applications was substantial, especially in the first year of rationing, 1941–2, when 781,966 were received and just under 27 million additional coupons were issued.[102] Subsequently replacement procedure was tightened up and applications fell to 482,172 and 392,510 in 1942–3 and 1943–4 resulting in the issue of 14.6 and 15.6 million coupons respectively. Officials were greatly concerned about the increase in

[98] PRO, BT 64/1921, Letter, 2 Jan. 1943.
[99] PRO, RG 23/1, Wartime Social Survey, Loose Coupons, n.s. 1, Aug. 1941.
[100] PRO, BT 64/1423, Letter, 9 July 1943.   [101] PRO, BT 64/1921, Report, 1 June 1943.
[102] PRO, BT 64/1519, Lost Coupon Replacement: Histories, statistical appendix.

applications in 1944–5 (556,832) as well as replacement coupon issues
which stood at 18.8 million for 10 months only. Unfortunately, no figures
are available for the last years of rationing.

Enforcement of Board of Trade orders was the responsibility of a special
investigation branch, staffed by ex-police officers, and an accountants'
branch with about 300 inspectors covering the whole country. The former

> investigates offences arising out of the rationing of clothing, . . . deals with some
> thousands of cases annually and institutes about two thousand prosecutions each
> year. Many of the offences are petty ones, but aggregate sentences during a year
> amount to about two hundred years' imprisonment and some thousands of pounds
> in fines. About four thousand persons are cautioned each year for trivial offences.[103]

The accountants' branch 'deals more particularly with offences by traders
in circumstances where examination of their books and records is necessary'. Work was not confined to clothes rationing and since offences tended
to be 'of a less casual nature than those dealt with by the Investigation
Branch, the prosecutions instituted are correspondingly fewer, but usually
result in much bigger fines'.[104] The observance of rationing orders by retailers was monitored by test purchases during which an officer would aim to
buy rationed goods without coupons or would offer loose coupons. In practice, a handful of investigation officers could do little in dealing with
approximately 300,000 retailers and 40 million consumers as well as
wholesalers and manufacturers.[105] Even a semblance of national coverage
was 'beyond the capacity of the available staff', policing was confined to
larger towns, leaving 'small towns, villages etc. untouched'. Setting examples was not a sufficient deterrent since 'we have information of widespread
infringement even in towns where prosecutions have taken place'. A proposal to set up a local structure similar to food control committees or to
work with them came to nothing and little was done apart from limited
reorganization and increase in staffing levels to help cope with the sheer volume of enforcement work.[106] Hence, the Board of Trade had no alternative
but to close the most glaring loopholes by tightening the regulations and to
rely on voluntary compliance. This policy was successful until the summer
of 1948 when a flood of loose coupons effectively undermined the rationing
scheme a few months before its abolition.

Before analysing the various forms of coupon fraud and how they were
dealt with, I turn briefly to the other side of the black market, namely sale

[103] PRO, BT 64/793, Swiss Questionnaire on the Black Market Report, n.d. [approx. Jan. 1946].
[104] Ibid.; see PRO BT 13/189, Committee on Accountancy and Enforcement, Report, 11 Aug.
1942 on details of accountancy and enforcement work.
[105] PRO, BT 64/1113, Note on Consumer Rationing Order: Enforcement, 4 Oct. 1941; Minutes,
Nov. 1941 until June 1942. The next few sentences are based on this source.
[106] PRO BT 13/189, Committee on Accountancy and Enforcement, Report, 11 Aug. 1942.

of rationed clothes at inflated prices and without coupons. A range of evidence suggests that this was a common practice both during and after the war.[107] The sources of supply, apart from theft, lay in the clothing industry. This was an industry that could never be controlled completely, in view of the large number of small makers-up. While the need for coupons might deplete fraudulent traders' stock it was always possible to make up the shortfall by purchasing additional coupons on the black market. Other sources of supply, particularly of silk and nylon stockings, were smuggling or diversion of output earmarked for export to the home market. The abolition of rationing in 1949 did not put an end to the black market since prices remained controlled and shortages persisted. Supplies to the home market of fully-fashioned stockings were still well below pre-war levels at the end of the 1940s and the issue was considered sufficiently significant to be raised in Parliament in spring 1950.[108] *Picture Post* reported on a 'nylon racket' in 1951. Seconds or export strays were sold at between 50 and 80 per cent above the controlled price by spiv traders in London using a public lavatory to replenish stock. Little could be done by the authorities since it was difficult to secure a prosecution, fines tended to be small and the official response sums up the underlying reason for the black market neatly: 'If only women didn't set such high store on getting nylons, if only they weren't prepared to pay extortionate prices, if only they would report overcharging to us, there wouldn't be a nylon black market'.[109]

Following the introduction of clothes rationing, coupon control along the chain of distribution was 'most unsatisfactory' since coupons or vouchers worth 500 coupons, which retailers obtained from post offices, were literally passed back with every transaction.[110] Several thousands of millions of coupons were in circulation, which would change hands up to seven times, from consumers to retailers, exchanged for vouchers by retailers, then to wholesalers, makers-up, cloth suppliers, and finally to the Board of Trade for cancellation. The task of counting and re-counting was intolerable, the post offices were not prepared to count loose coupons presented by retailers, the Board of Trade could only make spot checks, and there were many disputes over shortages at various stages. The system was open to abuse and lost coupons or vouchers 'might all too easily find their way back into circulation'.[111] Moreover, anyone could pose as a retailer at a post office and

---

[107] Smithies, *Black Economy*, pp. 74–5; Smithies, *Crime in Wartime*, pp. 73–4, 78, 80; MO, TC Food, Box 6E, Black Market and Barter, 12 May, 13 and 21 June 1947. Apart from food, clothing, and especially stockings, featured prominently in these accounts.

[108] *Board of Trade Journal*, Supplies of Consumer Goods to the Home Civilian Market, 7 May 1949; report of parliamentary questions, 18 Mar. and 6 May 1950.

[109] Quoted in *Picture Post*, 'Behind the Nylon Racket', 10 Feb. 1951.

[110] Hargreaves and Gowing, *Civil Industry and Trade*, p. 325; the remainder of this paragraph is based on pp. 312, 325–6.   [111] Ibid., p. 326.

obtain a voucher in exchange for an envelope stuffed with waste paper. A survey in November 1941 found that this practice accounted for 4 per cent of envelopes exchanged in the London area. The loophole was closed by the introduction of a coupon banking scheme in June 1942. Subsequently, all traders had to open coupon banking accounts, banking coupons as they would bank cash, and after the consumer-retailer stage all coupon transfers were conducted through these accounts with coupon cheques. The system dispensed with clerical labour in counting coupons, ended disputes over the number of coupons received, and 'immeasurably strengthened control' by eliminating an obvious source of coupons for the black market.[112]

Another source of supply of coupons to the black market was theft and forgery. Coupons were vulnerable to theft in store as well as at printers and pulpers. For example, 46,970 coupons were stolen from the Public Assistance Board, which distributed replacement coupons, in Camberwell in 1943 and in total 'about a million coupons had been reported to the Board as stolen' in 1943–4.[113] The obvious response was to tighten security. According to instructions on the counting of coupons and vouchers received from banks, 'the utmost importance of security precautions cannot be over-emphasised'. All bags received were individually numbered and to be opened only in the presence of a supervisor. Staff, who had to wear pocket-less overalls, were under constant supervision during counting and exami-nation and no one was allowed to work alone. Any discrepancies were to be reported immediately, shortages could be traced back to the individual trader, and records were kept on a '"black list"' in order 'to count all envelopes from this trader in the next consignment'.[114] Forgery, 'which had fallen into decay' earlier in the century was revived during the period since coupons initially 'were crudely designed and did not present anything like the technical problems involved in the forgery of bank notes'.[115] The threat of forgery was much reduced with the introduction of security printing from 1942 onwards when coupon design became ever more sophisticated and coupons were printed on coloured paper.[116] Concern about forgery per-sisted and the 1949–50 clothing book, which was printed but never actu-ally distributed, used special paper containing fibre. These coupons 'while not completely guaranteed against forgery, could only be reproduced by hand and, therefore, not in large quantities'.[117]

[112] Ibid.
[113] PRO, BT 64/1423, Telephone Message from East Dulwich Police Station, 10 Nov. 1943; T 230/119, Interdepartmental Committee on Rationing, 31 Mar. [1944].
[114] PRO, BT 64/465, I.M. 1—Accountants' Branch, Coupon Banking, Procedure for Dealing with Coupons and Transfer Vouchers received from Banks, 11 Oct. 1948.
[115] Smithies, *Crime in Wartime*, p. 89; see pp. 90–1 for details of major rackets.
[116] For examples of coupon design, see Board of Trade, *Clothing Coupon Quiz*, 4th edn. (London, 1943).   [117] PRO, BT 64/811, Meeting, 24 Feb. 1948.

It was considerably more difficult to prevent the illegal sale, barter, or misuse of coupons by the general public. A police report in 1944 noted:

considerable traffic in Clothing Coupons, particularly in the poorer districts, and that it is a well known fact that one has only to report the loss to the Police and get a form signed to obtain another book. Prosecutions for this type of offence are very few, because they are difficult to prove, as it is to the advantage of both parties to the transaction to keep their mouths shut.[118]

According to the Mass-Observation report on the black market in 1947, barter was commonplace and, for instance, the investigator's boss at the War Office 'would barter clothing coupons for sweet rations'.[119] The misuse of service coupons, which were restricted to certain items and to be used by service personnel only, became a cause for concern in 1944. An example of such a purchase 'without any questions being raised' was reported to the Board by a manager of Selfridges, who was able to confirm the story's veracity since the customer concerned was his son.[120] The practice could not be ignored because it was 'penalising the trader who abides by the law' and according to the Drapers' Chamber of Trade, honest traders 'get very irate when they find that although they have attempted to carry through these instructions other traders appear to ignore them with impunity'.[121] The only possible response by the Board was to add a sentence to the notice which all retailers had to display, warning against the use of loose coupons, that 'SERVICE COUPONS must NOT be used except for articles on the authorised list for the holder's personal requirements'.[122]

As the figures cited above show, replacement of lost or stolen coupons provided a threat to the entire ration system. Since 'the missing coupons so often remain in circulation, replacement has to be restricted severely in order to keep the drain on our limited supplies of civilian clothing within reasonable limits and to avoid the grave danger of coupon inflation'.[123] Replacement was a 'tiresome and delicate policy to administer', particularly since the public, forced to cope with threadbare clothing and declining rations, were 'hyper-sensitive to the way in which coupon replacement claims are handled'.[124] The official information leaflet warned about the danger of lost coupons and asserted that, 'Only in very special circumstances can they be replaced.'[125] In practice, even after the first year of rationing when replacement was effectively automatic, genuine claims could not be ignored, it was impossible to prove which claims were genuine, and

---

[118] PRO, BT 64/1423, Extract from Police Report, 11 Aug. 1944.
[119] MO, TC Food, Box 6E, Black Market and Barter, 12 May 1947.
[120] PRO, BT 64/1409, Letter, 1 June 1944.   [121] Ibid., Letters, 6 and 18 July 1944.
[122] Ibid., Notice, display of which was compulsory from 31 Mar. 1945 (emphasis in original).
[123] PRO, BT 64/799, Draft Letter, n.d. [approx. Jan. 1948].
[124] PRO, BT 64/1519, The History of the Lost Ration Document, Aug. 1948.
[125] Board of Trade, *Clothing Coupon Quiz*, 4th edn. (London, 1943).

the majority were thought to be bogus. In order to contain the problem, policy from 1942 onwards distinguished between Groups I and II applications. Group I, which accounted for about 15 per cent of the total, included applicants who had suffered from air-raids, fire, or burglary and who received an automatic replacement of coupons lost. With regard to applicants in Group II, where evidence was more doubtful, replacement was rarely made in full and based on a wardrobe test which in itself could not actually be verified. A 'couple of formidable application forms' which were 'progressively tightened' were deliberately used as a 'deterrent'.[126] The 'main object of our policy is to teach careless losers a lesson and . . . to inculcate coupon-vigilance'.[127] Thus, the *price* paid by a fraudulent claimant was the effort involved in obtaining replacement coupons and, since records of replacements were kept, 'people cannot "try it on" twice without coming under suspicion'.[128] Moreover, in doubtful applications a 'policy of delayed inaction was at first adopted' since it was assumed that 'dishonest people' would be 'reluctant to press their claims'.[129] Inconsistent applications arousing suspicion were followed up by a personal visit by an investigation officer who asked 'searching questions' and, although there was 'usually insufficient evidence for prosecution, these visits were valuable for their deterrent effect'. Finally, so-called pockets of repeated applications from within the same household, street, or neighbourhood were also followed up with the aim to 'put the cat among the pigeons'.[130]

The basic mechanism by which coupons illegally acquired entered or re-entered the distribution network was for consumers to offer and retailers to accept loose coupons. All issues of the *Clothing Coupon Quiz* stressed that this practice was illegal, with the exception of purchase by mail order, and the notice displayed by retailers stated: 'LOOSE COUPONS cut from clothing books or sheets must NOT be used except for—orders by post; quarter-coupons used to buy towels; or in other circumstances expressly authorised'.[131] Generally speaking, the clothes rationing scheme enforced itself since coupons had to be passed back in order to replace stock but ultimately the system functioned through voluntary compliance. Since it

was impossible to close every loophole and check all coupon transactions . . . rationing . . . worked for two reasons. One was bluff—that is, giving the public the impression that their activities were being checked more closely than was the case.

---

[126] PRO, BT 64/1519, The History of the Lost Ration Document, Aug. 1948.

[127] Ibid., Draft Minute, n.d.

[128] PRO, BT 64/1424, Letter, 5 Feb. 1945.   [129] PRO, BT 64/1519, The History of the Lost Ration Document, Aug. 1948.   [130] Ibid.

[131] PRO, BT 64/1409, Notice, display of which was compulsory from 31 Mar. 1945 (emphasis in original). This notice replaced an earlier version which did not include the restrictions on the use of service coupons discussed above.

Second and even more important was the goodwill of the great majority of the public.[132]

This was less forthcoming after the war.

During the summer of 1948 certain items were derationed and the issue of a special bonus crimson token, worth six coupons, which was limited in validity to mop up stocks of summer clothing, led to the erosion and finally the breakdown of this compliance. In the event, many consumers did not spend the entire token but bought small articles and received loose coupons as change, thereby converting the short-term bonus into coupons of unlimited validity.[133] Woolworth's reported that large numbers of loose coupons were issued in June, and in July another department store expressed concern that traders obeying the law in not accepting loose coupons were losing custom.[134] An article in *Men's Wear*, entitled 'Coupons playing fast and loose', called for a change in the rules.[135] The situation was summed up in a letter by the Retail Distributors' Association: 'the market has been flooded with loose coupons and . . . it would not be an exaggeration to suggest that the majority of retailers are now accepting loose coupons . . . or that the public are under the mistaken impression that this practice is now quite legal.' The situation 'has latterly deteriorated considerably', leaving law-abiding retailers in an 'extremely embarrassing' position. Official action was 'absolutely essential' since 'the stage has now been reached at which it would be impossible to retrieve the situation and that immediate removal of all restrictions on the use of loose coupons is essential if the law is not to fall completely into disrepute'.[136] According to internal minutes, exploitation of this loophole, which could 'cause us a lot of embarrassment', was anticipated in May 1948, when the crimson token was issued, although it was hoped that 'most people wanted to spend the coupons while the goods were there'. The inevitability of changing the regulations was accepted in August.[137] In order to retain the co-operation of the trade and not to disadvantage those consumers who had not converted their crimson tokens, in September the rationing order was amended to extend the validity of the tokens and, above all, to remove 'the existing prohibition on the use of loose coupons by retail customers'.[138] Subsequently the rationing scheme was no longer enforceable and it was abolished in May 1949.

---

[112] Hargreaves and Gowing, *Civil Industry and Trade*, p. 329.
[113] PRO, BT 64/819, Note on Crimson Tokens, July 1948.
[114] Ibid., Letters, 9 June and 13 July 1948.   [115] Ibid., *Men's Wear*, 14 Aug. 1948.
[116] Ibid., Letter, 11 Aug. 1948.   [117] Ibid., Minutes, 27 May, 24 June and 4 Aug. 1948.
[118] Ibid., Supplies and Services, Consumer Rationing, The Consumer Rationing (Amendment) (No. 12) Order, 1948, 13 Sept. 1948.

4.3. COSMETICS

Cosmetics or toilet preparations differed from the other commodities discussed in this chapter since they were never actually rationed. Instead, the black market operated through persistent evasion of the control orders in breach of both the spirit and the letter of the law. Control extended to perfumery and toilet preparations but certain products such as dentifrices, soap, shaving creams, deodorants, and medicinal preparations were exempt, frequently resulting in the need to classify borderline products.[139] Cosmetics are a good example illustrating the limitations of control. Legal supply was restricted to 25 per cent of the pre-war level but against the background of high demand it proved to be impossible to eradicate black market manufacture and supply in excess of the official limits.

The history of control is dominated by a cat-and-mouse relationship between the authorities, on the one hand, and manufacturers, retailers, and consumers, on the other. As one loophole was closed others were found and exploited and the official files are dominated by continuous discussion of the difficulties of enforcement and persistence of evasion. Perhaps surprisingly, at the end of 1943, 'the control over the manufacture and supply of toilet preparations was one of the most complicated of the controls . . . that had been evolved within the Board of Trade'. The purpose of these controls was not primarily to economize on labour and materials but 'to defeat the plans of unscrupulous persons who were ready to make use of every loophole in control in order to supply goods illicitly to a public willing to buy unknown goods when known varieties were not available'.[140]

In mid-war the black market had become so extensive that the question arose whether to end control or to prohibit the industry altogether. In view of the likely public outcry the latter course was not adopted. The Board of Trade had to provide for the minimum needs of the civilian population and in a long and tedious war, this minimum went beyond mere physical requirements. Apparent luxuries which might be considered as dispensable in fact 'acquired a surprising importance' in order to sustain morale and 'women must have lipstick and powder'.[141] The restrictions as a result of clothes rationing focused attention on make-up, and the overwhelming majority of younger women applied cosmetics regularly. As Doris White, a young, single engineering worker put it, 'Our aim in life seemed to concern our faces and hair'.[142] Therefore, the Board of Trade chose a middle way of increasingly tight control, both to

[139] PRO, BT 64/845, Control of Toilet Preparations, n.d. [approx. spring 1942].
[140] PRO, BT 64/1827, History of Toilet Preparations, n.d. [approx. 1945].
[141] Hargreaves and Gowing, *Civil Industry and Trade*, p. 125; see also Kirkham, 'Beauty and Duty, pp. 13–28.
[142] White, *D for Doris, V for Victory*, p. 63. See also Chapter 2, section 2.2.

protect the major manufacturers willing to observe the law from unfair competition and to safeguard the public from the potential danger of inferior products.

Legislation governing the control of cosmetics was changed eight times in six years. They were initially controlled under the Limitations of Supplies (Miscellaneous) Order, 1940, which restricted supplies of a range of consumer goods to 25 per cent of the pre-war level, in order to free labour and factory space for the war effort and to economize on raw materials.[143] This soon proved unsatisfactory and a separate Limitations of Supplies (Toilet Preparations) Order was introduced in February 1941 and amended in December 1942 in order to close obvious loopholes. Since the black market persisted, in 1943 a No. 3 Order was introduced which extended control beyond supply to the manufacture of cosmetics by means of an elaborate licensing system. At about the same time the industry went through two stages of concentration with output centred on a number of nucleus firms which were granted concessionary licences. Three additional amendments during the war aimed to eliminate further loopholes and the Toilet Preparations (Consolidation) Order of August 1946 concluded the stream of legislation governing the control of cosmetics. The 'chief object' of control after the war was 'to force as many toilet preparations as possible overseas'[144] and the industry was decontrolled in July 1948.

Control of the cosmetics industry was exceptionally difficult because of the structure of the industry and the distinctive characteristics of cosmetics coupled with growing demand. Cosmetics were easy to manufacture and required few, generally plentiful, raw materials. Neither large amounts of labour nor factory space were necessary and the final product, small in size and easy to distribute, was of high added value. While the industry was dominated by a small number of large manufacturers, at the other extreme many retail chemists, beauty salons, and hairdressers sold toiletries of their own manufacture. This practice, which provided an easy outlet for the black market, continued throughout the period with little more than a nominal restriction on turnover because the Board of Trade did not wish to deprive these traders of their livelihood. At the same time, demand for cosmetics was not only high but rising with changing social habits and increased female employment. This changing nature of demand was recognized by the Board of Trade:

a great proportion of the female population, who before the war, due to their peacetime duties, were not constant users of cosmetics are now either in the Forces or working in the war industries and have become users of the normal range of

---

[143] For details see Hargreaves and Gowing, *Civil Industry and Trade*, pp. 531–5.
[144] PRO, BT 64/1827, Letter, 4 Sept. 1947.

cosmetics to a great degree. It cannot be contended that because these people did not use toilet preparations in 1939, they should not be allowed to do so.[145]

While the black market in cosmetics was never eliminated entirely, the situation was particularly unsatisfactory early on in the war when the controls only limited supply but did not place any restrictions on the actual manufacture of toiletries. Under the Limitations of Supplies Order, 'rackets increased. As soon as one was stopped another broke out' with the result that the 'ineffectiveness of the old Order was producing what was very nearly a public scandal'.[146] To give some indication of the extent of the black market, during 1941, when supplies among registered manufacturers were supposed to be limited to 25 per cent of the pre-war level, 'the trade produced and sold 57.75 per cent of their pre-war output'. These figures illustrate what was

well known to both the trade and to the Board of Trade that during the year 1941 in spite of deterrent legislation the black market continued to prosper and increase. . . . During the year 1941 the only cosmetics that one could normally see in shops were those of very obscure and, in most cases, illegal origins, which . . . [proves] that there was a greatly increased demand for cosmetics, and that with legitimate manufacturers making [over] 50 per cent of their pre-war quota this demand was by no means met and it encouraged black market sales.

Retailers 'through whom most of the illegal manufactures are sold' also increased their own production 'over which the Board of Trade Enforcement Officers have no control whatever'.[147] In view of this situation it is not surprising that Board of Trade officials concluded that a change in the legislation would 'deal with the most important of the present abuses, but there is little doubt that the black market will merely move on to some other forms of evasion'.[148]

In the early phase of control the black market operated primarily through abuse of the quota system which restricted the value of output that could be legally supplied. Initially the most serious form of evasion was 'invoicing through', where a manufacturer sold goods directly to a retailer but invoiced them through a wholesaler. According to this 'paper transaction' supply did not count against the manufacturer's but the wholesaler's quota. There was nothing 'legally wrong' with the practice provided the latter did not exceed his quota but 'some wholesalers were tempted by the offer of large commissions to exceed their permitted quotas, sometimes by large amounts' and prosecutions proved difficult as a result of the widespread destruction of

[145] PRO, BT 64/1739, Minute, n.d. [approx. 9 Dec. 1942].
[146] PRO, BT 64/1795, Decontrol of Toilet Preparations, 22 Mar. 1944; Future Control of Toilet Preparations, n.d. [approx. Apr. 1944].
[147] PRO, BT 64/1739, Minute, n.d. [approx. 9 Dec. 1942].
[148] PRO, BT 64/1752, Minute, 10 Dec. 1942.

records during the air-raids of 1940–1.[149] This form of evasion came to an end in October 1941 when wholesalers' quotas were abolished and only registered manufacturers were allowed to supply cosmetics for resale.

Another method by which registered manufacturers could sell excessive quantities without exceeding their quota was to supply products in bulk to a packer who would repack the preparations in small containers. This was attractive since 'the cost of packing was a high proportion of the cost of production, materials valued at £1 might make £25 to £50 worth of finished goods'.[150] After August 1942, packaging was defined as part of the process of manufacture and it became illegal to supply goods for resale 'except in the same condition as they were received, that is to say in the same quantity and in the same container'.[151] This legislation probably eliminated the worst abuses but in March 1943 a further loophole was observed. Firms, including 'some reputable manufacturers', were now 'reducing the price of the contents of their jars and selling the jars separately at a much increased price'.[152]

During 1942 there was considerable debate within the Board of Trade about cosmetics policy. In the context of a general austerity drive the possibility of a 'total prohibition of the supply of cosmetics was considered . . . but was not adopted' since the industry employed relatively few workers, required little factory space, and could do without scarce raw materials. It was, 'therefore, doubtful whether the saving to be effected by prohibition would be sufficient compensation for the uproar which prohibition would evoke'.[153] The suggestion to ration cosmetics was rejected since 'rationing ought to be used only for goods that are really necessary' and the need to deal with coupons collected by 50,000 traders 'would complicate administration enormously'.[154] Likewise, the proposal to introduce a utility scheme for cosmetics came to nothing.[155] Stimulated by policy in Australia, where many cosmetics were prohibited in spring 1942, a partial ban was discussed in the autumn.[156] Under the Limitations of Supplies Order, there was no restriction on the type of cosmetics produced and many seemed 'non-essential in the fourth year of war'. The purpose of a partial ban was to economize on labour, factory space, containers, transport and 'expenditure by the consumer which might otherwise be devoted to War Saving'. Complaints by

[149] PRO, BT 64/1827, History of Toilet Preparations, n.d. [approx. 1945].
[150] Hargreaves and Gowing, *Civil Industry and Trade*, p. 533.
[151] PRO, BT 64/1827, History of Toilet Preparations, n.d. [approx. 1945].
[152] PRO, BT 64/1739, Toilet Preparations Advisory Committee, Meeting, 16 Mar. 1943.
[153] PRO, BT 64/845, Control of Toilet Preparations, n.d. [approx. spring 1942].
[154] Ibid.
[155] Ibid., Toilet Preparations, Discussions in London, 7 Apr. 1942; Toilet Preparations: Proposed Amendments to the Order, 8 Apr. 1942.
[156] PRO, BT 64/1752, Australian War Effort and Capacity: Prohibition of Cosmetics, n.d. [Mar. 1942].

manufacturers could be countered with the argument that they had 'done very much better than most luxury producers and that there is a war on'.[157] However, this proposal was rejected since the case for further economies was not sufficiently strong and 'we have always emphasised that we are not going in for austerity for its own sake'.[158] This confirmed an earlier decision by the president who 'felt that it was extremely awkward to distinguish between various vanities except purely on raw material grounds', and that the matter should be dealt with by prohibiting 'the use of exceptionally scarce raw materials in cosmetics'.[159]

By 1943 it had become 'clear that the only alternatives were decontrol or close control'.[160] The Board of Trade was reluctant to incur the additional administrative burdens associated with the control of manufacture, and trade representatives reached the 'unanimous conclusion that . . . nothing would be gained . . . by the introduction of a Manufacture and Supply Order'.[161] However, in April, trade representatives expressed 'grave concern' about black market producers who 'were trying to establish themselves as legitimate concerns'. This was due to weaknesses in the present order which did not restrict manufacture, with the result 'that there were more cosmetics about than ever'.[162] In the summer frustration at the failure of control reached a crisis point within the trade 'who were now completely up in arms'. The extent of the black market was damaging 'the fabric of the industry, which is being brought into public disrepute; the public are being swindled and even its health jeopardised'. While there were 'innumerable instances of quite needless hardship and injustice to individual manufacturers' it was 'public knowledge that fortunes have been acquired by the unscrupulous'. This was due to 'inefficient, inadequate and dilatory (not deliberate) policy drafting and general administration'. There was no longer any 'possibility of going back' since the industry had 'been turned upside down . . . To sweep away control is not the way out of the difficulty now that most of the reputable manufacturers are concentrated'. The only real alternative was to control manufacture through licences and to strengthen enforcement staff.[163] This suggestion was taken up and from September 1943 onwards cosmetics production became subject to individual licences which specified the value of controlled goods to be produced. The administration of the new system was complex and, for example, over 50 different licence forms were used in 1944.[164] The policy amounted to 'the first serious

[157] PRO, BT 64/1752, Draft Proposal for the Control of Toilet Preparations, 10 Nov. 1942; see also Minute, 17 Nov. 1942.
[158] Ibid., Minute, 28 Nov. 1942.   [159] Ibid., Minute, 8 July 1942.
[160] PRO, BT 64/1795, Decontrol of Toilet Preparations, 22 Mar. 1944.
[161] PRO, BT 64/1739, Toilet Preparations Advisory Committee, Meeting, 16 Mar. 1943.
[162] Ibid., Toilet Preparations Advisory Committee, Meeting, 22 Apr. 1943.
[163] Ibid., Toilet Preparations Advisory Committee, Meeting, 11 June 1943.
[164] Hargreaves and Gowing, *Civil Industry and Trade*, p. 535.

blow at the Black Market'. In recognition of high demand, the maximization of legal output 'dealt a second blow at the Black Market when we put up the rate of licensing from 50% [of the pre-war output] (for concentrated firms) and 20% (for unconcentrated firms) to 75% and 33 ⅓% in January 1944.[165] At the same time, an enforcement subcommittee was appointed and evasions of the order were more closely monitored with, for instance, 3,433 visits paid to small retailers during the first half of 1944.[166]

This recasting of the control scheme ended the worst abuses but the black market was by no means eliminated. One persistent form of evasion was to add medicinal properties to creams 'while advertisements, labels or descriptions on the jars showed quite clearly that they were cosmetics in disguise'.[167] The practice, which led to a continuous need to classify borderline products, was attractive as a means to evade quota restrictions until 1942 when medicinal preparations were included in the control scheme. Subsequently, differential purchase tax ratings provided the incentive. Medicinal preparations were subject to a purchase tax of only 16 ⅔ per cent while toilet preparations were rated at 33 ⅓ per cent and 100 per cent during the war and these figures were raised to 33 ⅓ per cent, 100 per cent and 125 per cent respectively after November 1947.[168] These high purchase tax rates caused great resentment within the industry. Since 'Illicit manufacture of goods of dubious quality [was] not very difficult', it was predicted that the 125 per cent tax would result in 'an epidemic of "black market" products'.[169]

A second example was the appearance of the product 'Laddastop' on the market following the prohibition of nail varnish and nail varnish remover, which required scarce solvent-based substances, from January 1943 onwards.[170] An article in the *Daily Mail*, entitled 'Girls Find New "Nail Varnish"', described the product 'marketed to stop ladders in silk stockings'. Widely sold in the London area, 'Laddastop' was pink, sold in small bottles with a brush for application, and accompanied by a preparation called 'Laddastop Remover'.[171] An internal minute lamented that 'the Black Market has defeated us' since 'all efforts . . . to get sufficient evidence to build up a case for a successful prosecution of a Ladderstop [*sic*] manufacturer had failed, partly because the manufacturers would say that they were

[165] PRO, BT 64/1795, Decontrol of Toilet Preparations, 22 Mar. 1944.
[166] PRO, BT 64/1739, Toilet Preparations Advisory Committee, Meeting, 16 Sept. 1943; BT 64/1795, Accountants' Branch IM3 Report, 29 July 1944.
[167] Hargreaves and Gowing, *Civil Industry and Trade*, p. 533.
[168] PRO, BT 64/1157, Letters, 14 Aug. 1945, 13 Feb. 1946, and 21 June 1948; see also BT 64/1794 on classification of borderline products during the war.
[169] PRO, BT 64/1157, Extract from *Chemist and Druggist*, 6 Mar. 1948.
[170] PRO, BT 64/1752, Press Notice, 21 Dec. 1942.
[171] PRO, BT 64/1795, Extract from *Daily Mail*, 12 July 1944.

producing not a toilet preparation but a preparation to stop ladders in stockings'.[172] The predicament was resolved by a Ministry of Supply order which prohibited packing of preparations containing the banned solvents in bottles of less than half a pint in size.[173]

Finally, spraying fluids or disinfectants were marketed as perfume after the war, 're-packed in miniature pyramid bottles . . . and sold under cover of a front label bearing only the name of a flower or a perfume'.[174] Officials were concerned about these fake perfumes because they evaded the 100 per cent purchase tax placed on perfume and because they 'contained formaldehyde or other disinfectants which might be deleterious to the skin'.[175] Little could be done because neither the Board of Trade nor Customs and Excise wished 'to interfere with the legitimate trade' whose association agreed to follow voluntary guidelines on packaging and labelling of disinfectants in order to curtail the practice.[176]

In conclusion, Hargreaves and Gowing ask whether 'the control in the end was successful' and 'whether the results were worth all the trouble'.[177] In view of the structure of the industry and the nature of its product it was impossible to eliminate illicit production 'however large a staff may be employed on enforcing controls. All that can be said therefore is that the restrictions on manufacture and supply made it more difficult for black market operators to escape detection'.[178] Against the backcloth of the general austerity policy, it was inconceivable that cosmetics could have escaped control entirely and, as the trade representatives stressed in 1943, once this policy and the associated concentration scheme had been operational for some time, it was impossible to turn back. Regardless of the limitations of control, the Board had little choice but to regulate output increasingly closely for two reasons. On the one hand, 'from the point of view of the buying public', the Board was obliged to endeavour to ensure 'that the toilet preparations in the shops were produced in hygienic conditions and that they did not contain materials liable to injure their health'. On the other, it was 'unfair to the honest manufacturer who was hedged in by restrictions that unscrupulous persons should build up trade connections and make large profits, in contravention both of the letter and the spirit of the law'.[179]

---

[172] PRO, BT 64/1795, Minute, 2 Feb. 1944, Letter, 5 Aug. 1944.
[173] Hargreaves and Gowing, *Civil Industry and Trade*, p. 534; PRO, BT 64/1827, History of Toilet Preparations, n.d. [approx. 1945].
[174] PRO, BT 64/1157, Letter, 13 Mar. 1946.   [175] Ibid., Minute, 8 Nov. 1946.
[176] Ibid., Letters, 13 and 21 Nov. 1946.
[177] Hargreaves and Gowing, *Civil Industry and Trade*, p. 535.
[178] PRO, BT 64/1827, History of Toilet Preparations, n.d. [approx. 1945].   [179] Ibid.

4.4. PETROL AND PETROL COUPONS

In contrast with cosmetics which were of interest primarily to younger women, the black market in petrol involved predominantly male middle-class motorists. Yet again, shortages of petrol were intense as high demand was juxtaposed with a drastic reduction in supplies, especially after the war when petrol had to be paid for in precious dollars. The black market was defined by the Russell Vick committee as 'all unlawful transactions in petrol or petrol coupons, not merely those which involve extra payment but also those which do not'.[180] The discussion, which focuses on the black market in petrol after the war, criticizes Worswick's conclusion that there 'seems no reason ... to accept the often expressed and pessimistic doctrine that rationing schemes in peace-time must inevitably be corroded and crumble away before the "natural forces of demand and supply"'.[181] The Russell Vick committee noted that the black market was 'both extensive and increasing', a judgement that led to the 'conclusion that by the time the basic ration ceased [from September 1947] those who still honoured the spirit of the regulations were a dwindling minority'.[182] Indeed, Shinwell, the Minister of Fuel and Power, had suggested in 1946 that petrol rationing should be abolished because there

> was already a considerable amount of evasion and it was impracticable to tighten up the administration of the rationing scheme. A breakdown of petrol rationing might undermine public confidence and co-operation in other rationing schemes and bring into disrepute the whole structure of the economic controls.[183]

However, the cabinet decided to continue petrol rationing in view of the dollar shortage. In 1948 Gaitskell, the new Minister of Fuel and Power, argued that 'the law and its administration were being brought into disrepute' by widespread evasion.[184] In view of the tight supply situation, a minute concluded that the 'fact is that in peace-time it is almost impossible to administer petrol rationing efficiently, with a basic ration, unless a fairly generous basic ration can be given'.[185] Thus Gaitskell might condemn black market offences as a 'social crime' which amounted, according to Morgan, to 'social sabotage', and which were 'therefore, immoral',[186] but this high moral standard conflicted with public behaviour if not public opinion. For this reason the police were reluctant to enforce the regulations since they 'were being brought into conflict with a public opinion which does not feel

---

[180] Cmd. 7372, Ministry of Fuel and Power, *Evasions of Petrol Rationing Control: Report of the Committee of Enquiry* (London, 1948), p. 5.   [181] Worswick, 'Direct Controls', p. 287.
[182] Cmd. 7372, p. 6.   [183] PRO, CAB 128/6, CM (46) 94, 4 Nov. 1946.
[184] PRO, CAB 128/12, CM (48) 24, 22 Mar. 1948; CAB 129/25, CP (48) 90, Petrol Rationing, Memorandum by the Minister of Fuel and Power, 18 Mar. 1948.
[185] PRO, PREM 8/1060, Minute to Prime Minister, 20 Mar. 1948.
[186] Morgan, *Labour in Power*, p. 297.

people are really committing an offence in evading the petrol rationing scheme'. In order to alter this state it was 'necessary to make quite clear the menace to the state involved by this attitude'.[187]

It was always obvious that petrol would be rationed in the event of a major war and by the time of the Munich crisis a rationing scheme was ready to go into operation.[188] Petrol rationing, which was based on a coupon replacement scheme, distinguished between commercial coupons for goods vehicles and private coupons for private motorists. Commercial coupons were administered through the Ministry of Transport as a means to control road haulage. Private motorists were divided into three groups, namely, essential users such as doctors, semi-essential users such as commercial travellers, and non-essential users for whom a car was simply an amenity. It would have been easiest to deny petrol to those not using it in the national interest but since pleasure motoring was perceived as part of the way of life a so-called basic petrol ration was granted to all motorists. With almost two million cars in 1939, private motoring was 'no longer seen as a luxury hobby: it had become a central factor in the lifestyle of approximately one in every five families'.[189]

Private motorists could apply for their basic ration through the post office and supplementary allocations for essential and semi-essential use were dealt with by divisional petroleum offices. In September 1939, the Motor Fuel Rationing Order

> forbade dealers in motor fuel and their customers to 'furnish or acquire' petrol or derv fuel except against the surrender of coupons, valid for the period of the transaction and for the vehicle concerned. It forbade the use of motor fuel acquired against coupons for any purpose other than that authorised by the coupons.[190]

The aim of rationing was to distribute limited supplies in a way which was perceived to serve the community best. The basic ration stood at approximately 1,800 miles per annum, with semi-essential users receiving up to 4,800 and essential users entitled to a maximum of 9,000 miles per annum.

Initially there were many complaints about delays in granting supplementary allowances and semi-essential users in particular resented the privileged position of 'basic only' motorists since the former had little, if any, petrol left for leisure purposes. Although stocks fell from the autumn of 1940 onwards, petrol allowances to non-essential consumers were not reduced; the fact that they were not was partly because the savings achieved

---

[187] PRO, MEPO 2/8793, Minutes of Meeting, 26 Feb. 1948.

[188] D. J. Payton-Smith, *Oil* (London, 1971), pp. 50–1. The next few sentences are largely based on this source, pp. 85, 89–93, 288–92; see also PRO, POWE 33/1428–9.

[189] S. O'Connell, *The Car and British Society: Class, Gender and Motoring, 1896–1939* (Manchester, 1998), p. 2.   [190] Payton-Smith, *Oil*, p. 85.

as a result of rationing were greater than expected. Indeed, in July 1940 motorists were granted a concession of 300 miles for servicemen on home leave, which continued throughout the war. In spring 1941, allowances to private and commercial motorists were cut by between 10 and 20 per cent but the basic ration was left untouched, a decision that caused fierce criticism among priority consumers. The basic ration was finally cut by one-sixth later in the year. In view of worsening shipping conditions there were further cuts early in 1942 and the basic ration was abolished from July 1942 onwards for the remainder of the war. This did not mean that all the petrol used to provide the basic ration was saved, since supplementary allowances partly made up the shortfall and a so-called domestic allowance was introduced to serve the needs of the rural population.

In 1943 total civilian petrol consumption had been reduced to about half the pre-war level, while consumption among private motorists stood at just over 10 per cent as many cars were taken off the road altogether.[191] Consumption rose again after the restoration of the basic ration in June 1945. This relaxation was short-lived and following the convertibility crisis the basic ration was abolished again from September 1947 onwards in order to economize on dollar imports.[192] The basic, now called standard allowance, was restored in March 1948 at a lower level. While motorists had been entitled to 270 miles per month (3,240 per year) in 1945, the standard allowance stood at only 90 miles per month (1,080 per year) and was also deducted from all existing allowances.[193] In view of larger than expected savings as a result of measures introduced to break the black market, this latter restriction was relaxed in October, thereby allowing some pleasure motoring to essential users.[194] Improved economic prospects, coupled with a campaign by motorists for a substantial increase in the standard allowance, resulted in the doubling of the ration during the summer months of 1949.[195] The petrol rationing scheme was terminated in May 1950 after an agreement about the allocation of earnings and dollars was concluded between the government and the principal oil companies.[196]

Enforcement of the rationing order was the responsibility of a Ministry of Fuel and Power inspectorate, which was largely staffed by former police

---

[191] Payton-Smith, *Oil*, p. 395, and tables, pp. 396, 484.

[192] PRO, CAB 128/10, CM (47) 74, 25 Aug. 1947.

[193] PRO, CAB 128/12, CM (48) 24, 22 Mar. 1948; CAB 129/25, CP (48) 90, Petrol Rationing, Memorandum by the Minister of Fuel and Power, 18 Mar. 1948.

[194] PRO, CAB 128/12, CM (48) 64, 18 Oct. 1948; CAB 129/30, CP (48) 233, Petrol Rationing, Memorandum by the Minister of Fuel and Power, 15 Oct. 1948.

[195] PRO, CAB 128/15, CM (49) 20, 17 Mar. 1949; CAB 129/33, CP (49) 41, The Petrol Ration, Memorandum by the Minister of Fuel and Power, 25 Feb. 1949.

[196] Worswick, 'Direct Controls', p. 286; *Hansard*, vol. 475, c. 2384–5.

officers, as well as the police.[197] Inspectorate staff initially stood at 40, rose to 75 in 1943, and in 1945 there were 12 regional enforcement officers and 85 inspectors responsible for enforcing Ministry of Fuel and Power regulations.[198] These officers had powers under Defence Regulation 55AA to issue warrants, enter and inspect undertakings, but not private premises, as well as to seize petrol and coupons. Enforcement work focused on three categories of abuse, namely, 'the misuse of petrol or coupons by individuals; the persistent transfer to private cars of supplies intended for commercial use, and to a much lesser extent, the use of forged, stolen or "washed" coupons'.[199] Between June 1943 and May 1945, approximately 50,000 to 60,000 cases were investigated but in contrast with Ministry of Food enforcement work the ratio between investigations and successful prosecutions was relatively poor. For example, after the war only a quarter of enquiries initiated by the inspectorate actually reached prosecution stage and a total of 7,662, 2,492, and 1,972 prosecutions were secured in 1945, 1946, and 1947 respectively.[200] This was a consequence of the availability of the basic ration before July 1942 and after the war since 'the existence of a legal supply of petrol, with no conditions as to use, made it virtually impossible to prove the misuse of petrol obtained against supplementary coupons and ... enforcement action for misuse of petrol almost disappeared'.[201] After the abolition of the basic ration this offence was easier to detect because 'the purposes for which a private car was driven could now be specifically defined and limited'.[202] The problem was particularly intense in 1946–7 and one argument in favour of abolishing the basic ration was that it 'would help us deal more effectively with the black-market in industrial petrol, which so long as there is a basic ration at all, however small, is very difficult to combat'.[203] Hence, the cabinet agreed to introduce the standard allowance only on the understanding that steps would be taken to save petrol 'by measures against the black market' which are discussed below.[204]

No figures are available until the Russell Vick committee of enquiry was set up in 1948 to investigate 'the nature and extent of the black market and the measures which should be taken to check it'.[205] The committee's report acknowledged that it was difficult to gauge the black market precisely and

[197] PRO, POWE 33/1436, Motor Fuel Rationing, 1939–50, 23 Sept. 1950. This paragraph is largely based on this internal history of petrol rationing. [198] Cmd. 7372, p. 14.
[199] PRO, POWE 33/1436, Motor Fuel Rationing, 1939–50, 23 Sept. 1950.
[200] Cmd. 7372, pp. 14, 23–4, app. II.
[201] PRO, POWE 33/1436, Motor Fuel Rationing, 1939–50, 23 Sept. 1950.
[202] Payton-Smith, *Oil*, p. 292.
[203] PRO, CAB 129/20, CP (47) 235, Balance of Payments: Abolition of the Basic Petrol Ration, Memorandum by the Minister of Fuel and Power, 22 Aug. 1947.
[204] PRO, CAB 128/12, CM (48) 24, 22 Mar. 1948.
[205] PRO, CAB 129/23, CP (48) 16, The Basic Petrol Ration, Memorandum by the Minister of Fuel and Power, 13 Jan. 1948.

estimates on its size in 1947 varied from 30 to 180 million gallons of petrol.[206] The Ministry of Transport proposed the lower figure whereas the higher was suggested by the motoring organizations based on information from garage proprietors as well as mileages indicated by information on routes given to members. Representatives of garage proprietors estimated the amount at 20 per cent of commercial coupons or 135 million gallons. The report highlighted the large surplus of coupons issued in excess of legitimate petrol consumption, namely 165 million gallons (550,000 tons), amounting to up to 15 per cent of coupons issued for commercial and other essential purposes. According to the committee the

inference is therefore that black market petrol consumption in 1947 may have amounted to some 47 million gallons (a little under 160,000 tons). . . . It would have represented rather more than 3 per cent of the total petrol consumed in 1947 by all users and about 10 per cent of the total consumption in that year in motor-cars.

While this figure might be considered as relatively low, the report maintained that the 'potential dangers' of surplus commercial coupon issues were 'far too great to be ignored', particularly if the basic ration were restored. It is interesting to note that the reduction in petrol consumption, following the introduction of measures to check the black market in spring 1948, points towards the accuracy of the higher estimates suggested by the motoring organizations and garage proprietors. The standard allowance was introduced on the understanding that the 120,000 tons of petrol a year required would be found through cuts in allowances and suppression of the black market. By October, petrol consumption had fallen at an annual rate of an additional 250,000 tons per year after the standard ration was supplied in full. The Minister of Fuel and Power now accepted the accuracy of the estimates suggested by the motoring organizations who expected that 'the savings from suppressing the Black Market . . . would turn out to be two or three times as much as I did'.[207]

Apart from misuse of petrol, the black market operated through the sale of petrol without coupons by garages to favoured customers, usually at a higher price, as well as the sale of coupons themselves. The witnesses to the Russell Vick enquiry generally agreed that the 'ultimate demand in the black market comes almost entirely from motorists'. There was no 'evidence of "master minds" at work organising a black market on a colossal scale, or of large quantities of petrol by-passing the rationing scheme. On the contrary, all the evidence points to a multiplicity of individual transactions within the coupon system.'[208] The key to black market supplies was the over-issue of

[206] Cmd. 7372, p. 6; the next sentences are based on pp. 6–7.
[207] PRO, CAB 129/30, CP (48) 233, Petrol Rationing, Memorandum by the Minister of Fuel and Power, 15 Oct. 1948.   [208] Cmd. 7372, pp. 14, 5.

commercial coupons. Lorry drivers disposed of these to garage proprietors who sold extra petrol to private motorists and used the commercial coupons to replace stock. Alternatively, commercial coupons were passed directly to motorists enabling them to purchase additional petrol. The opportunities for this 'most prevalent' offence 'lie in the fact that it is impossible to estimate a lorry's fuel consumption precisely'. Consumption 'which cannot be accurately gauged beforehand and cannot always be confirmed afterwards' could vary by up to 10 per cent. 'The driver must be given enough coupons to ensure that he can complete his journey in the worst conditions, with the inevitable consequence that he will often be left with more coupons than he actually requires'. Even

before the war it had become a practice among dishonest lorry drivers to sign or obtain receipts at garages for more fuel than was in fact put into the lorry, the price of the fictitious fuel being regarded as a perquisite of the job. To this practice the value of the coupons now adds a further incentive. In corroboration of these allegations we have had evidence that coupon-free petrol is most easily obtainable from garages on trunk routes where the goods traffic is heavy.[209]

Another source of supply to the black market was the custom of motorists to deposit coupons at a garage. If not all coupons were actually claimed, as was frequently the case, the surplus could be sold to another customer coupon free without depleting petrol stocks.[210]

By contrast, offences such as theft of petrol in transit, forgery, or theft of coupons were a continuous 'nuisance . . . but at no time did they present a serious threat to the petrol rationing scheme'.[211] Indeed, in bulk distribution theft of petrol amounted to only 0.38 per cent of total throughput in 1947, a figure which compares favourably to the estimated stock loss of 0.39 per cent by the largest distributor in 1939.[212] While several issues of forged coupons resulted in successful prosecutions in 1945–6, during 1947 there were 'few if any forged coupons in circulation'.[213] In the summer of 1948 there was a spate of forged coupons which received wide publicity in the press.[214] The administration was prepared to withdraw all coupons if necessary, but a range of decisive measures soon got the situation under control. Instructions were issued that all coupons passed back, rather than just a sample, were to be scrutinized. Forged coupons were traced back to motorists who were prosecuted since there was no legitimate reason why

[209] Ibid., p. 12. See also PRO, CAB 129/20, CP (47) 206, Reduction in Petrol Consumption, Memorandum by the Minister of Fuel and Power, 18 July 1947; CP (47) 207, Reduction in Petrol Consumption, Memorandum by the Minister of Transport, 18 July 1947.
[210] Payton-Smith, *Oil*, p. 219; Cmd. 7372, p. 12.
[211] PRO, POWE 33/1436, Motor Fuel Rationing, 1939–50, 23 Sept. 1950.
[212] Cmd. 7372, p. 11.   [213] Ibid., p. 10.
[214] PRO, POWE 33/1510, extracts from *Daily Mirror*, 10 and 26 July 1948; *Motor Trader*, 4 Aug. 1948.

they had surrendered forged coupons. If the motorist could not be traced proceedings were taken against garage proprietors, who were advised that they would receive no stock replacement for forged coupons.[215] In January 1949, the 'passing of forgeries ha[d] practically ceased', and the large number of recent prosecutions was hailed as 'a tribute to the efficacy of the measures we adopted and the co-operation of the garages in detecting offenders'.[216] There were a number of large-scale thefts of coupons which again resulted in successful prosecutions and, with serial numbers of the stolen coupons circulated to dealers, 'it can safely be said that the vast majority of stolen coupons did not get into circulation'.[217]

The final part of this section discusses how the administration responded to loopholes in the petrol rationing scheme. During the war the misuse of supplementary rations was contained by the introduction of log books in which motorists were required to log all journeys. From the autumn of 1941 a selection of logs were inspected and those motorists who did not produce them had their supplementary allowances halved. The policy was successful in reducing allowances since about half of all applicants, who failed to produce logs, accepted the cuts without protest.[218] At about the same time concern about the illegal transfer of commercial coupons to private motorists led to the suggestion to add dye to commercial petrol. The proposal was not taken up since all available dye was used by the forces to differentiate motor spirit and aviation spirit. Instead, enforcement activity was intensified and later in the war cuts in commercial coupons reduced the amount of petrol available to the black market.[219]

A dual strategy was adopted to suppress the black market after the war. On the one hand, dye was inserted into commercial petrol to break the easy transfer of commercial coupons to private motorists. On the other, the Russell Vick report recommended harsh statutory penalties as a deterrent against breaches of the new regulations. In order to ensure the success of the scheme a standard petrol allowance was introduced simultaneously. The abolition of the basic ration was 'extremely unpopular . . . It has been followed by a sustained and violent campaign that shows no signs of abating.'[220] In a later memorandum, the minister argued that it was 'imperative that we should have the fullest possible support from the Motoring public' and he did not 'think we shall obtain the support of the motoring organisations unless we can allow some small all-purpose

[215] PRO, POWE 33, 1510, Minutes, 20 and 23 July 1948; Circulars to Dealers, Aug. 1948; Forged Petrol Coupons, Note for Information of the Minister, 2 Sept. 1948.
[216] PRO, POWE 33/1511, Minute, 22 Jan. 1949.
[217] PRO, POWE 33/1436, Motor Fuel Rationing, 1939–50, 23 Sept. 1950; Cmd. 7372, p. 10.
[218] Payton-Smith, *Oil*, p. 218.   [219] Ibid., pp. 219, 292–3.
[220] PRO, CAB 129/23, CP (48) 16, The Basic Petrol Ration, Memorandum by the Minister of Fuel and Power, 13 Jan. 1948.

ration'.[221] Under the so-called 'red' petrol scheme, dye and other chemicals were added to commercial petrol which was readily distinguished from private or 'white' petrol. Coupons also differentiated between the two classes of petrol and garage proprietors were required to install separate pumps to serve commercial and private customers. The supply of commercial petrol to unauthorized vehicles became an offence and the police were responsible for carrying out roadside tests on motor cars to check whether the tank contained red petrol.[222] The Motor Spirit (Regulation) Act, in force from June 1948, introduced a number of statutory penalties. Garage proprietors found to have commercial petrol in private pumps were to be deprived of all petrol for 12 months and those who supplied commercial petrol to private motorists would receive no commercial petrol for one year. Any motorist whose car was found to contain red petrol in the tank would lose his or her licence for a year and, to prevent any further petrol being issued to the vehicle, the registration book was also withdrawn for 12 months regardless of ownership.[223] While these penalties were 'of an entirely novel character',[224] there was general agreement in cabinet 'that stringent penalties could be justified as a means of putting an end to the black market'. Cabinet ministers also hoped that 'it should be possible to secure a relatively easy passage for the Bill if it were made clear that the proposal to grant a standard allowance could not be entertained unless the Government had adequate powers to deal with the black market'.[225]

These measures eliminated the worst abuses but the experience of enforcing the red petrol scheme yet again showed that motorists were prepared to exploit any loopholes in the regulations. Due to limitations of manpower, 'enforcement by traffic patrols should be of a token character. On any large scale enforcement, the laboratory staff could not cope with the number of requests for attendance of expert witnesses . . . that would be necessary in all cases going to court'.[226] In September 1948 proceedings had been taken in a number of cases but usually the offences were 'detected only after the suspicions of the police had been aroused by some other action of the offender', who frequently held a criminal record. On the one hand, this experience

may show that it is in general only the criminal classes who are taking the risk of using commercial petrol in private motor vehicles, or on the other hand it may show that the police are not taking very energetic steps to enforce the law about the

[221] PRO, CAB 129/25, CP (48) 90, Petrol Rationing, Memorandum by the Minister of Fuel and Power, 18 Mar. 1948.
[222] PRO, POWE 33/1436, Motor Fuel Rationing, 1939–50, 23 Sept. 1950; Cmd. 7372, pp. 16–17.   [223] Cmd. 7372, pp. 18–19.
[224] PRO, PREM 8/1060, Meeting on Offences relating to Motor Fuel, 1 Apr. 1948.
[225] PRO, CAB 128/12, CM (48) 24, 22 Mar. 1948.
[226] PRO, MEPO 2/8793, Minute of Meeting, 4 Mar. 1948.

misuse of commercial petrol and are in fact only checking the petrol when they have suspicions about a motorist on other grounds.[227]

This pattern persisted and, for example, between March and September 1949 some 150,000 vehicles were checked and on average less than half a per cent were running on red petrol. The figures were much higher in tests carried out '"on information received"', 13 and 15 per cent in June and July 1949 respectively, and the 'wide variation in the number of tests carried out' showed that 'some Police Forces are clearly doing very little in this matter'.[228] Prosecutions under the Act were taken primarily against private motorists and only five dealers were prosecuted, of whom three were disqualified, indicating that the deterrent effect of the legislation was rather more powerful with regard to retailers than motorists.[229]

One early loophole was for motorists to acquire a 'shooting brake type of vehicle' which could be licensed for commercial and private use, thereby allowing red petrol in the vehicle as well as the unrestricted standard allowance available to private motorists, a practice which was prohibited after February 1949.[230] Another weakness of the red petrol scheme was the failure to insert dye into commercial petrol which, especially in smaller firms, was the responsibility of the drivers themselves.[231] Alternatively, the proportions of mixed loads could be switched, a practice for which the driver might be paid 2/- per gallon while the dealer could sell the surplus white petrol for up to 6/-. The latter was now greatly in demand by those 'who for years have been able to obtain more than adequate supplies of petrol by purchasing goods coupons, now find their source of supply . . . cut off and . . . will be on the look out for alternative methods of obtaining white petrol'.[232] The administration responded by tightening procedures within the distribution network as well as intensified enforcement activity.[233] Since it was 'a simple matter to remove the red dye', decoloured petrol was a 'growing problem'.[234] An even greater cause for concern was that roadside tests could not disclose red petrol in a dilution of less than 20 per cent and a 'mixture containing only 10% "red" . . . petrol was ordinarily safe from detection. By the end of 1949, it was evident that a number of dealers had discovered this for themselves, and cases of mixtures of red and white petrol in the pumps made an appearance'.[235]

[227] PRO, POWE 33/1507, Prosecutions for the Use of Commercial Petrol in Private Motor Vehicles, Note for Information of the Minister, 2 Sept. 1948.

[228] PRO, POWE 33/1511, Minutes, 23 Nov. 1949, 31 Aug. 1949.

[229] PRO, POWE 33/1436, Motor Fuel Rationing, 1939–50, 23 Sept. 1950.

[230] PRO, POWE 33/1507, Extracts from Quarterly Intelligence Reports, 25 Oct. 1948; Home Office Circular, 1 Feb. 1949.

[231] PRO, POWE 33/1508, Minute, 5 July 1948.   [232] Ibid., Letter, 19 July 1948.

[233] Ibid., Circular, 9 July 1948; Colouring of Commercial Petrol and Delivery of Private Petrol against Commercial Coupons, Note for the Information of the Minister, 3 Sept. 1948.

[234] PRO, POWE 33/1436, Motor Fuel Rationing, 1939–50, 23 Sept. 1950.   [235] Ibid.

This evidence points towards the limits of motorists' co-operation, for which the Russell Vick report had appealed:

Honesty cannot be universally enforced by regulations. The black market not only in petrol but in any other commodity begins *and must end* with the man in the street. It is not enough to point to flagrant cases and disclaim one's own responsibility. At no time in our history was it ever more important than it is today to conserve our resources. We believe that the proposals we have made . . . would go a long way to preserve the available petrol supplies for honest motorists; it will then remain for the motoring public to play their part to make the scheme a success.[236]

Officials who had initially 'expressed the hope, and indeed held the opinion, that very few cases would be taken' under the Motor Spirit (Regulation) Act, were soon forced to accept that they had been 'over-optimistic about the deterrent effects of the Act'.[237] The internal history of petrol rationing maintained that 'the Act was an effective weapon . . . [but] its existence was constantly threatened on all sides; and as the technique to defeat it was ever improving, it is doubtful whether its effectiveness could have been maintained indefinitely'. It concluded that: 'Experience of the enforcement of the petrol rationing system over a period of some ten years has shown that attempts at evasion are persistent and flexible. Laws which at one moment appear adequate for the purpose, quickly become ineffective as weaknesses are found and exploited.'[238]

The black market—ultimately driven by public demand—was extensive throughout the 1940s. The black market in Britain was probably less pervasive than elsewhere, but the evidence confutes any notion that wartime patriotism or support for Labour's policies after 1945 were sufficient to prevent widespread circumvention of the control orders. Black markets were an inevitable consequence of the austerity policy. Rationing, price controls, and controls on production amounted to an unprecedented degree of state interference in the economy which effectively abolished the price mechanism. In the event, this was achieved only with regard to formal or official prices and the black market effectively entailed an illegal reassertion of frequently distorted market prices. The pervasiveness of black markets for individual commodities was governed above all by the relationship between demand and supply coupled with the specific features of a particular control scheme. Some commodities were more difficult to control than others and home-produced foodstuffs or non-perishable goods such as cosmetics were among the most popular black market commodities. A recasting of the control scheme, as in the case of tea or petrol after the war, could alter the situation materially. Nevertheless, these reforms frequently had a limited

---

[236] Cmd. 7372, p. 22 (emphasis in original).
[237] PRO, POWE 33/1511, Minute, 19 May 1949.
[238] PRO, POWE 33/1436, Motor Fuel Rationing, 1939–50, 23 Sept. 1950.

shelf-life and the case studies illustrate how new loopholes were found and exploited. The black market defines the boundaries of popular consent in the reduction and regulation of consumption. These boundaries were not rigid or fixed but permeable and fluid. Altruism and commitment to the war effort contributed towards containing the black market and voluntary compliance was less forthcoming after the war, as illustrated by the failure to restrict self-suppliers or the breakdown of the clothes rationing scheme during its final months. However, there were always limits to the degree of self-sacrifice and women were not prepared to forgo lipstick, motorists petrol, or the general public the practice of barter and exchange of rationed foods. In many ways, the black market functioned as a necessary safety valve which the authorities had little option but to tolerate.

The black market embodied the dark, frequently unacknowledged, underside of fair shares. No quantitative data are available and most people probably purchased on the black market at some point, but those on low incomes would have been least able to afford extra goods at inflated prices. This inherent contradiction of fair shares, namely that the policy was flaunted by the better-off who had money to spend on black market goods, yet again shows that the aspiration of common sacrifice was subverted in practice. Regardless of fair shares propaganda, during the 1940s sacrifice was not evenly distributed between classes or between men and women and the black market provided a further element instituting inequality. Money, access to scarce goods, and a readiness to take advantage of opportunities could alter consumption patterns materially. Although public opinion vehemently condemned the black market, this denunciation coexisted awkwardly with extensive infringement of the control orders. The black market resulted in a growing division between public and private morality and between the formal economy and its informal, illegal counterpart. The unfairness of the black market and its corrupting ramifications highlight the shortcomings of the austerity policy. The Labour government paid insufficient attention to these problems, which did not, however, weaken the party's continued commitment to fair shares and economic controls. As well as by moral condemnation, the black market was kept in check by increased enforcement activity and drastic measures such as the Motor Spirit (Regulation) Act. The Conservatives believed that these policies amounted to an erosion of civil liberties which was unacceptable in peacetime. For the Conservatives, the black market could only be dealt with by the abolition of controls, increased supplies of consumer goods, and a return to the price mechanism. These differences in approach illustrate the fundamental division between the two parties with regard to the role of the state in economic management. This conflict lies at the centre of the party political debate about post-war austerity which is discussed next.

5
Party Politics

This chapter analyses the party political debate about rationing and controls and the electoral implications of the austerity policy from the end of the Second World War and Labour's landslide election victory of 1945 until the general election of 1955 when the Conservatives were returned to power with an increased majority.[1] It examines the connection between consumption and politics and illustrates the changing relationship between state and society in war and peace, in the sense that public acceptance of sacrifice in wartime did not necessarily imply that this would be equally forthcoming after the immediate transition period. Labour assumed after 1945 that the electorate shared its wider purpose of building socialism even if this required continued sacrifice. In the event, the Attlee government's failure literally to deliver the goods undermined its initial popularity and the campaign against austerity provided a focus for the Conservative recovery of the late 1940s. The issue is critical in explaining why this reforming government was finally defeated at the polls in 1951 and affluence was central to Conservative electoral dominance during the 1950s. The discussion focuses on food shortages, which were high on the political agenda from 1946 to 1948, and again in 1951, as well as wider questions of economic management and the role of controls. While the Labour government defended its economic record, full employment, and fair shares during the difficult reconstruction period, Conservative efforts to rebuild an electoral majority after 1945 were very much based on a critique of continued austerity. This appeal was directed particularly towards women and, generally speaking, housewives became an important political category fought over by both parties. In the early 1950s, Conservative propaganda celebrated the ending of austerity and a return to affluence, which goes a long way towards explaining the party's disproportionate success among women voters, especially in 1955.

Despite an extensive literature on the 1940s and 1950s, the debate about rationing, austerity, and controls has been relatively neglected. The policy was of course not the only topic of party political debate, but it was critical

[1] The following argument draws heavily on ideas first published in I. Zweiniger-Bargielowska, 'Rationing, Austerity and the Conservative Party Recovery after 1945', *Historical Journal* 37 (1994), pp. 173–97.

during the general elections of 1950, 1951, and 1955. These three elections focused on the battle over consumption, which had important implications for the role of the state in the economy and wider society. The perception of the early post-war years is central to this argument. The conventional literature emphasizes a shift to the left during the war and the emergence of 'Attlee's consensus',[2] characterized by the commitment to full employment, the welfare state, and a mixed economy which formed the basis of Labour's landslide victory in 1945. In implementing these reforms, the Attlee government provided a framework which was to dominate British politics until 1979.[3] Accordingly, Morgan's classic account portrays the Attlee government as 'without doubt the most effective of all Labour governments, perhaps amongst the most effective of any British government since . . . 1832'.[4] Recent publications range from celebratory histories[5] to short study guides and documentary readers.[6] By contrast, a revisionist literature questions the radicalization of popular attitudes during the war and highlights Labour's continued commitment to building a socialist society. This literature casts doubt upon the validity of the consensus framework.[7] The Labour party interpreted 1945 not just as an election victory but as the culmination of a long-term process indicating that the people were now ready to transform Britain into a socialist commonwealth.[8] Labour believed that it could retain this support as long as people were told the facts but in practice the Attlee governments' propaganda campaigns either fell on deaf ears or actually backfired.[9] Equally, the endeavour to make socialists was essentially unsuccessful since popular attitudes were dominated by an individualistic focus on family and personal life, a desire for privacy, and a longing for a return to normalcy—albeit without the mass unemployment of the 1930s.

[2] P. Addison, *The Road to 1945: British Politics and the Second World War* (London, 1975), p. 270.

[3] See D. Kavanagh and P. Morris, *Consensus Politics from Attlee to Major*, 2nd edn. (Oxford, 1994); D. Dutton, *British Politics since 1945: The Rise and Fall of Consensus* (Oxford, 1991); M. Pugh, *State and Society: British Political and Social History, 1870–1992* (London, 1994). For a more nuanced approach see Morgan, *The People's Peace*; P. Clarke, *Hope and Glory, 1900–90* (London, 1996).

[4] Morgan, *Labour in Power*, p. 503. See also H. Pelling, *The Labour Governments, 1945–51* (Basingstoke, 1984).

[5] Hennessy, *Never Again.*

[6] K. Jefferys, *The Attlee Governments, 1945–1951* (London, 1992); R. D. Pearce, *Attlee's Labour Governments, 1945–51* (London, 1994); S. Brooke, *Reform and Reconstruction: Britain after the War, 1945–51* (Manchester, 1995).

[7] Tiratsoo, *Attlee Years*; Fielding, Thompson, and Tiratsoo, *England Arise*; M. Francis, 'Economics and Ethics: The Nature of Labour's Socialism, 1945–1951', *Twentieth Century British History* 6 (1995), pp. 220–43; Francis, *Ideas and Policies under Labour.* For a critique of consensus see H. Jones and M. Kandiah (eds.), *The Myth of Consensus: New Views on British History, 1945–64* (Basingstoke, 1996).

[8] S. Fielding, 'Labourism in the 1940s', *Twentieth Century British History* 3 (1992), pp. 138–53.

[9] Crofts, *Coercion or Persuasion?*

Fielding highlights the significance of apathy in public opinion, which could be observed particularly with regard to the finer points of economic surveys or policies such as cement nationalization.[10] By contrast, people did care about the food they were able to eat and the importance of the austerity policy was that it translated party politics into day-to-day concerns, precisely those issues which scored highly in polls on people's personal problems. The late 1940s were an 'age of austerity' and especially during the crisis year of 1947 it appeared as if 'the home front ran on without a war to sustain it'.[11]

This situation was not accepted as inevitable by contemporaries but was controversial and central to party political debate. Thus, the Conservative recovery of the late 1940s was not just due to organizational reform and the adoption of new policies such as the *Industrial Charter* of 1947.[12] Equally in 1951, the party was not just a passive beneficiary of Labour fatigue, redistribution, and Liberal disintegration. Rather, the Conservatives were actively engaged in forging an anti-socialist coalition of consumers disaffected with austerity, rationing, and controls. Having campaigned with the slogan 'set the people free', the Conservatives in power embarked on a 'march to freedom' and the government was rewarded for its achievements with a comfortable election victory in 1955.[13] Early post-war Britain, far from being exceptionally consensual, may be viewed as a divided society, not least on the issue of consumption.

During the war controls had a positive role of allocating resources between competing claims within the war economy as well as the negative function of reducing resources available to civilian consumers. In wartime government priorities necessarily took precedence, 'leaving the minimum to be shared out in meeting civilian requirements, [but] there was no such compelling need in peacetime when the whole purpose of production was to meet those very requirements'.[14] After the war, only the negative function of controls remained and the perpetuation of restrictions on consumption

[10] S. Fielding, '"Don't Know and Don't Care": Popular Political Attitudes in Labour's Britain, 1945–51', in Tiratsoo, *Attlee Years,* pp. 106–25.

[11] Addison, *Now the War is Over,* p. 2; Sissons and French, *Age of Austerity.*

[12] J. D. Hoffman, *The Conservative Party in Opposition 1945–51* (London, 1964); T. F. Lindsay and M. Harrington, *The Conservative Party 1918–1979,* 2nd edn. (London, 1979); A. Gamble, *The Conservative Nation* (London, 1974).

[13] Ramsden, *Age of Churchill and Eden,* p. 247; see also K. Jefferys, *Retreat from New Jerusalem: British Politics, 1951–1964* (Basingstoke, 1997); J. Ramsden, '"A Party for Owners or a Party for Earners"? How far did the British Conservative Party really Change after 1945?', *Transactions of the Royal Historical Society* 5th ser. 37 (1987), pp. 49–63; H. Jones, 'The Conservative Party and Social Policy, 1942–1955', unpublished Ph.D. thesis, University of London (1992). For general histories of the Conservative party see S. Ball and A. Seldon, *Conservative Century: The Conservative Party since 1900* (Oxford, 1994); M. Francis and I. Zweiniger-Bargielowska (eds.), *The Conservatives and British Society, 1880–1990* (Cardiff, 1996); J. Ramsden, *An Appetite for Power: A History of the Conservative Party since 1830* (London, 1998); G. E. Maguire, *Conservative Women: A History of Women and the Conservative Party, 1874–1997* (Basingstoke, 1998).

[14] Cairncross, *Years of Recovery,* p. 343.

became contentious. Socialist economic policy did not limit consumer spending for dogmatic reasons and, indeed, Labour aimed to raise personal consumption in the long run, once the debts were paid off and the external balance was restored. A pamphlet of 1946 declared:

[the] only cure for shortages is to abolish them. The way to do this and to raise the standard of living is to increase production. . . . But capital investment can only take place at the immediate cost of the consumer. If electrical equipment factories turn out more electric motors for cotton mills there will be less radio sets than would otherwise be available . . . But if we are prepared to do without some of the frills in the next years, Britain's reward will be a higher standard of living in the future. Soviet Russia demonstrated this truth between the wars; only by sacrificing immediate consumption was that country's colossal industrialisation made possible.[15]

Labour demanded sacrifice now and promised jam tomorrow, but especially after 1947 the goalposts were shifting all the time and tomorrow never came. This gives rise to the question as to how long people were prepared to wait or, to be more specific, how many Labour converts in 1945, especially in seats which had returned a Labour MP for the first time, accepted replacing the free market with a command-style economy after the initial post-war problems were overcome.

There was little common ground on the issue of consumption and living standards between Labour and the Conservatives during the late 1940s and early 1950s. This debate was highly ideological and conducted in terms of competing philosophies, namely socialism versus capitalism and positive versus negative notions of freedom. Labour endeavoured to rebuild Britain as 'a socialist nation. To this end we seek freedom from the enslaving material bonds of capitalism'. 'Justice demands that fair shares should be the national rule' and:

Full employment is essential if men are to be free from fear. Full employment has been achieved and will be maintained only by asserting control over economic forces. Economic power must be responsible to the people [rather than subject to the free market] if security and a rising standard of life are to be ensured.[16]

According to the Conservatives, Britain was faced with a choice of two roads: 'One leads downward to the socialist state, and inevitably on to Communism, with all individual freedom suppressed, and living standards lowered.' Only the Conservative road would 'restore to our citizens their full personal freedom and power of initiative'. 'Socialism thrives on scarcity' but Conservatism 'flourishes in conditions of abundance' by freeing 'the pro-

[15] Labour Party, *Fair Shares of Scarce Consumer Goods*, Labour Discussion Series No. 2 (London, 1946), pp. 7, 4.

[16] Labour Party, *Labour Believes in Britain* (London, 1949), p. 3; Labour Party, *Labour and the New Society* (London, 1950), p. 4.

ductive energies of the nation from the trammels of overbearing state control and bureaucratic management'.[17] During the early post-war years, Labour remained wedded to a collectivist and producerist agenda, whereas the Conservatives favoured a return to individualism and championed the consumer.[18] This contrasting perspective had important electoral implications, particularly with regard to gender differences in voting behaviour. While Labour continued to do well among men, obtaining a clear lead among male voters throughout, Conservative propaganda was extremely well placed to exploit the low morale among women and especially housewives during the late 1940s. Indeed, by articulating a mainstream critique of austerity—in contrast with that of fringe pressure groups such as the British Housewives' League—the Conservatives not only stimulated female discontent but also provided a credible alternative to Labour's policies. This strategy was remarkably successful since the erosion of female support for Labour and the rise of the Conservative women's vote were critical factors in the electoral turnaround between 1945 and 1951 as well as 1955.

Disagreement between the parties focused on the causes of persistent shortages as well as on the most appropriate policies to adopt to increase consumption and living standards. Labour propaganda held that the government was doing a good job in difficult circumstances. Austerity was an inevitable consequence of post-war dislocation in general and the world food and dollar shortage in particular. In view of the balance of payments deficit, the first priority of economic policy was to raise exports and reduce imports. Domestic policy gave priority to investment, collective provision, and social reform rather than personal consumption. The maintenance of fair shares in the context of full employment and the welfare state was hailed as a major success and as providing a great improvement in working-class living standards, in contrast with the bad old days of the interwar years. The Conservatives did not deny that there was post-war economic dislocation but argued that austerity was largely due to Labour's incompetence, mismanagement, and socialist-inspired policies which were making matters much worse than they need have been. Controls were imposed for controls' sake, while excessive bureaucracy stifled the economy and hampered recovery. The Conservatives claimed that for the majority of the population living standards under Labour were worse than during the 1930s

---

[17] Conservative and Unionist Central Office (hereafter CUCO), *The Right Road for Britain*, popular edn., (London, 1949); CUCO, *This is the Road* (London, 1950), pp. 3, 22, 23; CUCO, *The Industrial Charter* (London, 1947), p. 14.

[18] N. Tiratsoo, 'Popular Politics, Affluence and the Labour Party in the 1950s', in A. Gorst, L. Johnman, and W. Scott Lucas (eds.), *Contemporary British History, 1931–1961: Politics and the Limits of Policy* (London, 1991), pp. 44–61; S. Brooke, 'Labour and the "Nation" after 1945', in J. Lawrence and M. Taylor (eds.), *Party, State and Society: Electoral Behaviour in Britain since 1820* (Aldershot, 1997), pp. 153–75; E. H. H. Green, 'The Conservative Party, the State and the Electorate, 1945–64', in ibid., pp. 176–200.

and that only a return to the free market and the abolition of wartime controls would restore living standards.

These arguments, which were repeated over and over again, were based on different perceptions of the interwar years. Labour's theme of 'Never again' contrasted unemployment, poverty, and hardship with great improvements, especially among the poorest sections of the working class, during the 1940s. Conversely, the Conservatives emphasized declining levels of personal consumption suffered by the majority of the population, which compared unfavourably with low prices and wide choice of consumer goods during the 1930s. Despite continued support for Labour's achievement in maintaining full employment and establishing the welfare state, the persistence of austerity was hard to bear and popular discontent was fuelled by constant Conservative criticism which was widely reported in the right-wing press.

The use of wartime emergency legislation to control consumption in peacetime entailed many problems for the Labour government. On the one hand, the vast apparatus of controls which was administered by a large bureaucracy was fraught with contradictions and petty restrictions. These were easily criticized and provided the Conservatives with ammunition in their claims that controls amounted to an erosion of civil liberties which was not justifiable in peacetime. On the other, the fuel crisis of spring 1947 and the convertibility crisis of the summer undermined the credibility of Labour's faith in the efficacy of socialist planning. Import cuts in the autumn resulting in reduced rations proved deeply unpopular. This was illustrated by Conservative gains in the local elections of November 1947, which were the first clear sign of a swing in public opinion away from the Attlee government.

While local elections and opinion polls give some indication of trends in party fortunes, it is of course the general elections that are critical. The general elections of 1950, 1951, and 1955 were fought on the theme of austerity versus affluence and the ascendancy of the Conservative vision of the role of consumption in post-war British society was only secure in 1955. Owing to the narrow result in 1951, and especially the fact that Labour polled more votes than the Conservatives, the Churchill government had little confidence in its electoral support. The economic crisis of 1952 resulting in deflation and renewed austerity contributed to a poor Conservative performance in local elections, while Labour expected that its period in opposition was little more than a brief interlude. With improved economic prospects, decontrol proceeded apace in 1953, culminating in the termination of rationing in 1954. Labour did not intend to reintroduce rationing, but there was little change in party policy, which retained its commitment to fair shares and extensive controls. Hence, political debate in 1955 still focused on the themes first articulated during the immediate postwar period—albeit from the vantage point of consumer freedom under the Conservatives in contrast with Labour's almost regretful hankering for a reintroduction of economic controls which had originated during the Second World War.

The following discussion illustrates this argument by analysing party policy and propaganda, including that specifically aimed at women, from 1945 until 1955. The chapter is divided into five sections and begins with a discussion of the 1945 general election campaign. Section 5.2 explores the post-war austerity debates, from the abolition of dried egg and the controversy over bread rationing in 1946 to the economic crises, ration cuts, and the argument about the adequacy of the diet in 1947. The third section focuses on the debate about austerity, controls, and economic management during the 1950 and 1951 general election campaigns. Section 5.4 traces the Conservatives' celebration of the ending of rationing between 1952 and 1954 as well as Labour's ambivalent response, and highlights the continued importance of austerity versus affluence during the 1955 general election campaign. The chapter concludes with an evaluation of electoral trends throughout the period which analyses regional, class, and gender differences in voting behaviour.

5.1. THE 1945 GENERAL ELECTION

Despite the undoubted success of the Churchill coalition government in conducting the war effort, the notion of a consensus between the Labour and Conservative parties has been extensively criticized, particularly with regard to plans for post-war reconstruction, economic policy, and welfare policy.[19] This ideological divide between the parties was clearly apparent during the 1945 general election campaign. The role of the state in post-war society was the central battleground and Labour's commitment to planning, continued controls, and collectivist welfare reform stood in stark contrast with Conservative advocacy of free enterprise, decontrol, reduced taxation, and sound finance.[20] The 1945 general election manifestos illustrate the contrasting positions of the parties well. *Let Us Face the Future* was firmly focused on post-war issues and demonstrates Labour's exceptional unity of purpose with regard to social reform, nationalization, and full employment.[21] By contrast, *Mr Churchill's Declaration of Policy to the*

---

[19] K. Jefferys, *The Churchill Coalition and Wartime Politics 1940–1945* (Manchester, 1991); Brooke, *Labour's War*; R. Cockett, *Thinking the Unthinkable: Think Tanks and the Economic Counter-revolution, 1931–1983* (London, 1994), ch. 2, *passim*.

[20] R. B. McCallum and A. Readman, *The British General Election of 1945* (Oxford, 1947), pp. 53–8.

[21] S. Brooke, 'The Labour Party and the 1945 General Election', *Contemporary Record* 9 (1995), pp. 1–21.

Electors stressed that Britain was still at war. Owing to internal divisions
and the relative absence of policy making within the Conservative party
during the war, the manifesto, drafted in a hurry, was little more than a per-
sonalized statement by Churchill, and was distinguished above all by a negative attack on socialism.[22]

Labour's 'distinctive socialist message' was designed as a 'reasonable
appeal to the middle ground' which placed the party 'firmly in the framework of rigorous collectivist planning, including . . . public ownership . . .
and, not least, the retention of wartime controls, which had brought the
country "nearer to making 'fair shares' the national rule than ever
before"'.[23] *Let Us Face the Future* declared: 'The Labour Party is a Socialist
Party, and proud of it. Its ultimate purpose at home is the establishment of
the Socialist Commonwealth of Great Britain—free, democratic, efficient,
public-spirited, its material resources organised in the service of the British
people.'[24] This socialism amounted to a commitment to economic planning,
limited nationalization, and the continuation of economic controls. These
policies were intended to prevent a post-war slump, preserve full employment, and maintain the greater social equality achieved during the war. For
Labour the choice was 'either sound economic controls—or smash', but the
party denied that they would 'impose controls for the sake of control'.
Decontrol would 'give the profiteering interests and the privileged rich an
entirely free hand to plunder the rest of the nation as shamelessly as they did
in the nineteen-twenties'. Labour questioned whether 'freedom for the prof-
iteer [meant] freedom for the ordinary man and woman' since 'Freedom is
not an abstract thing'. The party called for 'order, for positive constructive
progress as against the chaos of economic do-as-they-please anarchy'.
While Labour stood for freedom of worship, freedom of speech, and the
restoration of civil liberties sacrificed during the war, 'there are certain so-
called freedoms that Labour will not tolerate: freedom to exploit other people, freedom to pay poor wages and to push up prices for selfish profit;
freedom to deprive the people of the means of living full, happy, healthy
lives'.[25] Using the imagery of austerity, a cartoon suggested that popular
post-war aspirations such as decent schools, homes, health care and jobs
were available only under the counter and 'reserved for the Rich and
Privileged' in the 'Tory Peace Stores'. Labour held that the choice was
between a Labour or a Conservative government and urged electors to vote

---

[22] M. D. Kandiah, 'The Conservative Party and the 1945 General Election', *Contemporary Record* 9 (1995), pp. 22–47; Ramsden, *Age of Churchill and Eden*, pp. 39–44.

[23] Brooke, 'The Labour Party and the 1945 General Election', pp. 11–12, 13–14, quoting from *Let Us Face the Future*.

[24] F. W. S. Craig (ed.), *British General Election Manifestos 1900–1974* (Chichester, 1975), p. 127 (*Let Us Face the Future*, 1945 manifesto).

[25] Ibid., pp. 128, 124, 125.

Straight Left as the only guarantee of extensive reforms since only Labour was unequivocally pledged to 'deliver the goods' which the people had already paid for twice over—in 1914 and again in 1939.[26]

Socialism was the key election issue, but whereas for Labour socialism was 'the principal means by which reconstruction, reform and "fair shares" would be realised',[27] the Conservatives warned of the dangers of socialism in Hayekian terms. The Conservatives, very much on the defensive against the collectivist tide during the war, 'could do little but to cling to a pre-war status quo that was already discredited in the popular imagination by appeasement and unemployment', until the publication of Hayek's *Road to Serfdom* in 1944.[28] This book made a powerful polemic case against collectivism, with its central argument that there was no middle way between free-market capitalism and totalitarianism. Hayek thus helped to fill the vacuum in Conservative thinking and finally provided Churchill with a message which remained part of his rhetoric for at least a decade. The Conservative manifesto gave lukewarm support to the wartime coalition government's white papers, but the party maintained that full employment was only possible within the context of 'free enterprise' and 'sound government—mutual co-operation between industry and the State, rather than control by the State—a lightening of the burdens of excessive taxation—these are the first essentials'.[29] A case for nationalization or industrial restructuring could only be made on grounds of efficiency and, 'As against the advocates of State ownership and control, we stand for the fullest opportunity for go and push in all ranks throughout the whole nation. This quality is part of the genius of the British people, who mean to be free to use their own judgement and never intend to be State serfs'. With regard to controls:

We stand for the removal of controls as quickly as the need for them disappears. Control of labour, of materials and of prices, is necessary in war, when we have to give up much of our freedom in order to make sure that the war machine gets all that it requires. Some of these controls will continue to be needed until normal times return. As long as shortage of food remains, rationing must obviously be accepted: the dangers of inflation must also be guarded against. As long as any wartime controls have to be retained, they must be made subject to strict Parliamentary scrutiny and sanction. We must watch the interest of the consumer always. Controls, originally imposed on his behalf, tend to bind him down and injure him as soon as circumstances change. We intend to guard the people of this country against those

---

[26] Harvester, Archives of the British Labour Party, ser. 2, Pamphlets and Leaflets (hereafter Harvester Lab.), 1945/34, *Straight Left! Now is the Time to Strike a Blow for Progress*; see also McCallum and Readman, *The British General Election of 1945*, pp. 45–6.

[27] Brooke, 'The Labour Party and the 1945 General Election', p. 16.

[28] Cockett, *Thinking the Unthinkable*, pp. 76–7; F. A. Hayek, *The Road to Serfdom* (London, 1944).

[29] Craig, *British General Election Manifestos 1900–1974*, p. 115 (Mr Churchill's Declaration of Policy to the Electors, 1945 manifesto).

who, under guise of war necessity, would like to impose upon Britain for their own purposes a permanent system of bureaucratic control, reeking of totalitarianism.[30]

The most notorious incident of the election campaign, Churchill's so-called Gestapo speech, used similar rhetoric. In his first election broadcast, Churchill reiterated the central points from the manifesto and declared:

I must tell you that a Socialist policy is abhorrent to the British ideas of freedom. . . . there can be no doubt that Socialism is inseparably interwoven with totalitarianism and the abject worship of the state. It is not alone that property in all its forms is struck at, but that liberty, in all its forms, is challenged by the fundamental conceptions of Socialism. Look how even today they hunger for controls of every kind, as if these were delectable foods instead of war-time inflictions and monstrosities. There is to be one State to which all are to be obedient in every act of their lives. . . . Socialism is, in its essence, an attack not only upon British enterprise but upon the right of an ordinary man or woman to breathe freely, without having a harsh, clumsy, tyrannical hand clapped across their mouths and nostrils. A Free Parliament . . . is odious to the Socialist doctrinaire. . . . But I will go further, I declare to you, from the bottom of my heart, that no Socialist system can be established without a political police. . . . No Socialist Government conducting the entire life and industry of the country could afford to allow free, sharp, or violently worded expressions of public discontent. They will have to fall back on some form of Gestapo.[31]

This speech is generally thought to have backfired, and probably damaged the Conservatives rather than Labour, especially in view of Attlee's cool reply:

When I listened to the Prime Minister's speech last night, in which he gave such a travesty of the policy of the Labour Party, I realised at once what was his object. He wanted the electors to understand how great was the difference between Winston Churchill, the great leader in a war of a united nation, and Mr Churchill, the party leader of the Conservatives. He feared lest those who had accepted his leadership in war might be tempted out of gratitude to follow him further. I thank him for having disillusioned them so thoroughly.[32]

It is inappropriate to dismiss the speech as an aberration. The Gestapo reference was 'nothing more than a colourful and clumsily phrased extension of Hayek's critique of Socialism', and the identification of Labour's socialism with totalitarianism was fairly typical of Conservative rhetoric during the early post-war years.[33]

When the results were finally declared, it was clear that Labour had won a landslide victory gaining 240 seats, while the Conservative parliamentary

---

[30] Craig, *British General Election Manifestos 1900–1974*, pp. 119–20.
[31] Quoted in *The Times*, 5 June 1945.   [32] Ibid., 6 June 1945.
[33] Cockett, *Thinking the Unthinkable*, p. 94; M. Francis, '"Set the People Free"? Conservatives and the State', in Francis and Zweiniger-Bargielowska, *The Conservatives and British Society*, p. 61.

party was reduced by half.[34] For Labour, 1945 was a bright new dawn, particularly because victory was so unexpected, and although the election was
not the 'Waterloo'[35] of the Conservatives, the party was undoubtedly routed.
A number of factors account for this electoral turnaround.[36] Labour seemed
to represent the popular mood and the Conservatives appeared out of
touch—whether the party was punished for unemployment and appeasement of the 1930s or rejected because its Hayekian anti-planning, anti-
statist stance in 1945 was unappealing. Moreover, instead of a usual
electoral bonus in terms of superior organization and carefully orchestrated
campaign, the Conservatives approached the 1945 election with a number
of liabilities. Party organization was in a mess, it lacked a clear set of policies, and its campaign failed at all levels. By contrast, united behind a
coherent programme, Labour fought a successful, confident campaign and
its organization was in better shape than that of its opponents. Many voters had made up their minds well before 1945. During the war, a stream of
anti-Conservative propaganda, which the party failed to counter effectively,
resulted in a rejection of the Conservative hegemony of the 1930s. This
swing to the left, illustrated in opinion polls and by-elections, favoured the
Labour party which, in its identification with the Beveridge report, was able
to fashion itself as 'the people's' party.

Nevertheless, it is important to qualify this interpretation of the electoral
and political implications of 1945. The electoral system exaggerated both
the strength of Labour support and the severity of the Conservatives' defeat.
While Labour now had nearly twice as many MPs as the Conservatives, the
gap between the parties in the share of the vote was only 8 per cent and,
since turnout had been low, Labour in fact received the support of only just
over one-third of those eligible to vote.[37] Moreover, 1945 was such a transformation partly because it reversed the Conservatives' success of 1935
and, therefore, any notion that the electoral landscape had changed irre-
versibly was short-sighted to say the least.[38] For party activists 1945 was 'a
moment of triumph which vindicated over fifty years of struggle', but support for Labour's programme was rather more tenuous among many voters
and those who favoured social reform had little alternative but to vote for
Labour.[39] For the first time, Labour had been able to capture the middle
ground, but this cross-class coalition in favour of the Beveridge report dis-

[34] See Table 5.1.

[35] McCallum and Readman, *The British General Election of 1945*, p. 243.

[36] Brooke, 'The Labour Party and the 1945 General Election'; Kandiah, 'The Conservative Party
and the 1945 General Election'; Ramsden, *Age of Churchill and Eden*, ch. 2, *passim*; S. Fielding,
'What did "the People" Want?: The Meaning of the 1945 General Election', *Historical Journal* 35
(1992), pp. 623–39.   [37] Fielding, 'What did "the People" Want?', p. 639.

[38] G. K. Fry, 'A Reconsideration of the British General Election of 1935 and the Electoral
Revolution of 1945', *History* 76 (1991), pp. 43–55.

[39] Fielding, 'What did "the People" Want?', pp. 637, 629–31, 638–9.

integrated after Labour had implemented its programme resulting in the subsequent erosion of Labour's popular appeal. When the Conservatives had recovered from the initial shock of defeat, they consoled themselves by arguing that since the 'Socialist and anti-Socialist votes were approximately equal at 12 millions each, it ought not to be an impossible task—given an efficient machine for the purpose—for the Conservative Party to secure a sufficient turnover of votes to give them a majority'.[40] To achieve this goal, the party embarked upon an aggressive strategy of reorganization, fund raising, and recruitment drives, as well as policy making and propaganda. This approach soon bore fruit, not least because the Conservatives' critique of collectivism and controls was articulated in an increasingly favourable climate.

5.2. THE AUSTERITY DEBATES, 1946–1947

The austerity debates of the early post-war years are important because they established consumption as a major focus of party political controversy. The continuation and, indeed, intensification of shortages brought Labour's honeymoon to an end in the summer of 1946 and following the economic crises of 1947 and further cuts the Labour government was on the defensive. At the same time, the Conservative charge of socialist mismanagement provided the party with powerful arguments which were instrumental in its campaign to regain the political initiative and restore its electoral fortunes.

    In order to economize on dollar imports dried egg—a staple of the post-war diet—was withdrawn in February 1946, resulting in a public outcry. Press criticism of food policy focused on housewives' protests with headlines such as '700 Wives in Ration-Cut Protest: "Families Almost Under-Nourished"' (*Daily Telegraph*, 8 February 1946); 'Britain's Women Unite In Revolt Against Food Cuts: Wives Boo Sir Ben, Say "Feed Us First"' (*Daily Mail*, 8 February 1946); and 'Wives' Food Revolt Grows: Last Straw, Threat To Children, Say Angry Women, Heartbreak Letters. . . . "Britain Is At Breaking Point"' (*Daily Graphic*, 8 February 1946).[41] One housewife from Liverpool summed up the situation: 'We are suffering from mental exhaustion, irritation and frustration. . . . We are under-fed, under-washed, and over-controlled.'[42] The British Housewives' League, founded in July 1945 by a housewife frustrated with queuing and shortages, and other housewives'

---

[40] Bodleian Library, Oxford, M.S. Woolton 21, Memorandum, Apr. 1946 (in this calculation, Liberal voters were included in the 'anti-Socialist' vote).
    [41] *Royal Commission on the Press 1947–1949: Report*, Cmd. 7700 (London, 1949), pp. 324, 333, 341.
    [42] Quoted in Hinton, 'Militant Housewives, p. 133.

protest movements suddenly acquired front-page notoriety. While the right-wing press certainly exploited the housewives' anger, it did not fabricate it, since 'the cuts had touched a raw nerve and support for the BHL mushroomed'.[43] These protests contributed to the resignation in May 1946 of Sir Ben Smith, the Minister of Food, who had first considered resigning in February.[44] A Conservative leaflet mocked his resignation, 'Because he was "very tired" after 10 months as Food Minister Sir Ben resigned. British Housewives, too, are "very tired" after months of Socialist bungling. They can't resign; they have to carry on! But—next time they will know how to vote.'[45] Although the policy was reversed and dried egg again became available, the episode marked the beginning of the debate about food policy.

Of greater significance was the introduction of bread rationing in July 1946, which initiated the first concerted campaign against the Labour government on a major policy issue. This policy, which had been avoided during the war, represented the height of post-war austerity and involved a severe blow to morale. It was controversial because the entire system of food control depended on ample supplies of bread and potatoes. The government justified bread rationing as a necessary step to guarantee the bread supply and ensure fair shares in the context of the world food shortage which required sacrifice in Britain to prevent famine in continental Europe and elsewhere. During spring and summer 1946 opposition to bread rationing was led by the Conservative party, backed by the right-wing press. The Conservatives doubted that the policy was really necessary and that substantial savings in wheat could be made. The party leadership deplored the added burden placed on housewives and alleged that the government had mismanaged the supply situation.

The Labour government's principal justification for bread rationing was the precarious supply situation. Strachey, the new Minister of Food, argued that the 'pipeline of supplies' might reach 'breaking point' after the end of August. Only the introduction of rationing could prevent 'breakdowns in the supply of bread' by maintaining distribution on lower stocks. In conclusion, Strachey responded to the press campaign against bread rationing by comparing it to that preceding the 1945 general election:

Now we are told that we are rationing the bread of the people out of fun, or out of spite against them. Then we were told that we were loosing the Gestapo in Britain. I think we shall find that the results of the two campaigns in the end will be very similar. We shall find that the people of this country are a little too steady and sane to fall for an agitation of that sort. I think we shall find that the people will respect

[43] Ibid., pp. 134, 132–3; Crofts, *Coercion or Persuasion?*, pp. 99–100.

[44] British Library of Political and Economic Science, London, Hugh Dalton Papers, Diary, vol. 34, 9 and 18 Feb. 1946.

[45] Harvester, Archives of the British Conservative Party, ser. 1, Pamphlets and Leaflets (hereafter Harvester Cons.), 1946/29, *Sir Ben Smith Resigned*.

a Government which prefers the safety of the bread supply to its own immediate popularity. In any case, whatever the consequences in terms of temporary voting, we are determined to go through with this thing because we know that it is right, that it is necessary for the safety of the country.[46]

Churchill described the announcement that bread would be rationed as 'one of the gravest announcements that I have ever heard made in the House in time of peace'.[47] In a last-minute prayer for annulment of the bread-rationing order, he summed up the Conservative position. Churchill calculated a saving of 'less than three days' supply' which did not warrant all the 'inconveniences . . . of bread rationing'. He doubted that 'this petty saving [was] the true reason' and demanded reassurances that rations would not be cut later and that distribution was not already breaking down. In view of expected 'bumper harvests' in the wheat-exporting countries, he likened the policy to 'using a steamhammer to crack a nut when there is nothing in the nut'. Churchill concluded that the government had 'made no case which could justify . . . an ill thought out scheme involving a great measure of hardship on the people'.[48]

These arguments were reiterated in Conservative periodicals as well as occasional propaganda material. One pamphlet contrasted promises of bigger rations and more choice in 1945 with a succession of cuts and reductions during 1946 culminating in 'The Last Straw: BREAD RATIONING' and concluded that the 'Socialist Government has failed the nation in the first year of peace'.[49] Conversely, Labour party publications defended bread rationing as Britain's contribution to the world food crisis and the only means of guaranteeing the bread supply.[50] For example, *Two Queues* contrasted British women who 'queue to get' with European women who queued in the '*hope* to get' and emphasized the necessity of continued controls in ensuring fair shares and high nutritional standards during this difficult period of post-war reconstruction.[51]

Papers such as the *Daily Mail*, the *Daily Express*, and the *Daily Graphic* rejected the notion of a world food shortage, describing the problem as one of maldistribution. These papers, as well as the *Daily Telegraph*, saw bread rationing, 'the most hated measure ever to have been presented to the people of this country' (*Daily Mail*, 3 July 1946), as an unnecessary conse-

[46] *Hansard*, 5th ser., vol. 424, cols. 2168–2207, 3 July 1946.

[47] Ibid., vol. 424, col. 1527, 27 June 1946.

[48] Ibid., vol. 425, cols. 1448–58, 18 July 1946.

[49] Harvester Cons., 1946/34, *Food Facts* (emphasis in original); CUCO, *The Weekly Newsletter* (George E. Christ ed.), vol. 2, nos. 27–9, 33, July and Aug. 1946; Conservative Party Headquarters, *Notes on Current Politics*, no. 14, 15 July 1946.

[50] Labour Party Research Department, *Labour Party Year Book 1946–47* (London, 1947), pp. 65–7; Harvester Lab., 1946/21, *Food Shortage: The Facts*; 1946/62, *Bread Rationing* (John Strachey, MP).

[51] Harvester Lab., 1946/67, *Two Queues* (emphasis in original).

quence of government mismanagement and gave prominence to housewives' protests against the policy.[52] Labour was rattled by this campaign, as is illustrated in Attlee's New Year message to Labour women of January 1947. Stressing the inevitability of shortages, he appreciated that

many of these restrictions fall heavily on the housewife. You can be assured that the Government will ease them as soon as it is possible to do so. We have been greatly helped in the past year by the understanding and loyalty of the women of the movement. On the question of bread rationing, your knowledge and good sense was an important factor in steadying and educating public opinion in the face of the press campaign last summer.[53]

Indeed, coverage of the issue contributed towards the appointment of the Royal Commission on the Press in October 1946, and it was certainly more than a coincidence that bread rationing was one of the topics chosen for analysis of political bias. Since pro-Labour papers such as the *Daily Herald* and the *Daily Mirror* emphasized the seriousness of the world food shortage, for which the government was not held responsible, considered bread rationing as essential, and minimized opposition to the policy, the Commission concluded that 'the treatment of bread rationing indicates political bias to a greater or lesser degree on the part of almost all the national papers'.[54]

Public disapproval was epitomized by angry housewives, whose plight was highlighted in the parliamentary debate. Conservative backbenchers took up the housewives' case, for instance in a petition signed by 514 housewives from Llangollen, who viewed 'with grave concern the further difficulties and restrictions about to be imposed upon them by bread rationing'. A petition from Ruislip described the policy as striking 'a cruel blow at the housewives of this country' and 11,890 housewives from Blackpool prayed 'that bread shall not be rationed'.[55] At this time petitions against bread rationing, carrying between 200,000 and 300,000 signatures, were cited in the press.[56] Hudson, Conservative Minister of Agriculture and Fisheries during the wartime coalition, claimed that the 'real burden is going to fall on the housewife. After seven years' hardship and shortage . . . she does not deserve this added tribulation.'[57] By contrast, the pro-Labour press cited examples of women supporting bread rationing, as in a *Daily Herald* headline, 'Women Back Food Policy', refering

[52] *Royal Commission on the Press 1947–1949: Report*, pp. 322–47.
[53] *Labour Woman*, January 1947.
[54] *Royal Commission on the Press 1947–1949: Report*, p. 110.
[55] *Hansard*, 5th ser., vol. 425, col. 1191, 17 July 1946, cols. 1354–5, 18 July 1946.
[56] *The Times*, 9 July 1946, quoted in Crofts, *Coercion or Persuasion?*, p. 101; *Daily Express*, 14 July 1946, quoted in *Royal Commission on the Press 1947–1949: Report*, p. 329.
[57] *Hansard*, 5th ser., vol. 424, col. 2207, 3 July 1946.

to the Women's Co-operative Guild in Torquay.[58] Labour backbenchers denied that housewives would suffer under bread rationing, described the Conservatives' sudden interest in housewives as hypocritical, and rejected the notion of widespread discontent.[59]

Temporarily passions ran deep on the issue, with opinion very much split along party lines. Bread rationing had an impact on the Bexley, Monmouthshire Pontypool, and Battersea North by-elections held in July 1946.[60] Whereas all registered a swing to the Conservatives, it was about 4 per cent in the latter two seats which Labour held with large majorities. However, in the Kent constituency of Bexley the swing was 11 per cent, reducing Labour's lead to only 5 per cent, and the seat was won for the Conservatives by Edward Heath in 1950.[61] In the event bread rationing entailed no hardship and the issue soon disappeared off the agenda. Nevertheless, the episode represented an initial drawing of battle lines in the debate about consumption and indicated that Labour's honeymoon was already over during Dalton's *annus mirabilis*.[62] Indeed, Dalton himself acknowledged that the controversy over bread rationing, 'illustrates vividly . . . the inescapable reasons for our gradual loss of backing in the country'.[63]

The dollar economy measures introduced during 1947—in the wake of the fuel and convertibility crises—included savage food import cuts. Many rations, especially of popular items such as meat, bacon, and ham, as well as fats, now fell to their lowest ever level (that is, below wartime) and calorie consumption also declined.[64] These cuts were supplemented by other restrictions such as a reduction in the clothes ration, the abolition of the basic petrol ration, and the suspension of foreign currency for pleasure travel, and ushered in the harsh austerity of the Cripps era.[65] Consumption was very much at the heart of the debate about the economic crisis and food shortages were the most important problem for the public during this period.[66] The crisis was politically devastating for the government since it undermined the credibility of Labour's claim of the effectiveness of socialist planning. Simultaneously, the Conservative charge that austerity was largely a consequence of government mismanagement rather than an inevitable consequence of the war became increasingly convincing. Public opinion was above all divided, but none the less the crisis had important electoral consequences, since the beginning of the Conservative recovery can be traced back to the local elections of November 1947.

[58] Quoted in *Royal Commission on the Press 1947–1949: Report*, p. 332 (26 June 1946).

[59] *Hansard*, 5th ser., vol. 424, cols. 2215–17, 2250–2, 2261–4, 3 July 1946.

[60] F. W. S. Craig (ed.), *British Electoral Facts 1885–1975* (London, 1976), table 2.02, p. 52.

[61] F. W. S. Craig (ed.), *British Parliamentary Election Results 1950–1970* (Chichester, 1971), p. 62.

[62] H. Dalton, *High Tide and After: Memoirs 1945–1960* (London, 1962), p. 91.

[63] Ibid., p. 144.   [64] See Figure 1.2 and Table 1.5.

[65] See Chapter 1, section 1.3; Chapter 4, section 4.4. For details of the cuts see Labour Party, *ABC of the Crisis* (London, 1947).   [66] See Figures 2.1 and 2.2.

According to the Labour government, this crisis was the inevitable consequence of post-war economic dislocation. The cuts, coupled with an export drive, were necessary to restore Britain's external balance. Indeed, the government, with slogans such as 'We're up against it. We work or want. A challenge to British grit', actually highlighted the severity of the crisis by invoking the danger of national collapse if export targets were not achieved.[67] Basically,

[the] degree to which the home consumer will go short will depend upon the degree to which production can be raised. . . . Reductions of home supplies need therefore be no more than temporary; it depends on the efforts of British producers. . . . In those conditions, all public-spirited citizens will need to take action to suppress any possible extension of black market dealings in scarce goods.[68]

Despite the present hardships, Labour stressed the government's achievements, above all the maintenance of full employment which stood in stark contrast with the bad old days of unemployment and inequality under the Tories. The government called for loyalty and national unity to help Britain pull through in this battle for the peace:

The grimness of the [Conservative] alternative is all the more reason why we must make Labour's plan a success. Full employment must be preserved. The economic fabric must be restored. Both depend on higher production. It is a formidable task, and the consequences of failure would be terrible. But there is no doubt the job can be done if the people exert themselves to save themselves.[69]

The government was defended vigorously in the *Daily Herald*:

the reason for the cuts, as the country well understands, is that they are unavoidable. They must be made because we have not yet had time to build up our production sufficiently to pay our way in the world . . . Obviously it is impossible to expect that the government should have been able to forecast the whole world food situation and our ability to buy following the end of convertibility of £ . . . Immediately this harsh news should act as a fresh summons to hard work and patriotic action . . . That appeal . . . has been met with great response in defiance of the dirges preached in the Tory press.[70]

By contrast, the Conservatives held the government responsible for the economic crisis. The *Industrial Charter*, published in May 1947, called for a return to free enterprise, reduced taxation, decontrol, and the 'ultimate restoration of freedom of choice . . . to the consumer' as the key 'to a better standard of living'.[71] The Conservative critique of Labour's socialism restated the themes of 1945:

[67] Crofts, *Coercion or Persuasion?*, p. 45.   [68] Labour Party, *ABC of the Crisis*, p. 10.
[69] Ibid., p. 15.   [70] *Daily Herald*, 28 Aug. 1947.
[71] CUCO, *The Industrial Charter: A Statement of Conservative Industrial Policy* (London, 1947), p. 4.

Where men are free they do not allow their Government to be master of their lives. That only happens under dictatorship. Socialists may not wish to be dictators but they become so because they believe that the Government should direct all business and lay down most of the conditions of life. Conservatives know that in a free country there is a limit to what a Government can do in directing the affairs of the people. A Government should be like a watchful parent. It should not be a jailer.[72]

Current shortages were 'due to the incompetence of this Government' since 'rationing one article, like bread, makes it all the more likely that the substitute for that article, like potatoes, will become scarce and be rationed in their turn. Controls breed like rabbits.'[73] Excessive controls contributed to a swollen bureaucracy which was 'wasteful of manpower and a brake on production'. While the Conservatives did not intend to abolish all controls immediately and pledged that '*We will not remove the control from any necessity of life until we are certain that it is within the reach of every family*', they believed that 'hundreds of orders and regulations . . . could be cancelled' and that 'some risks for freedom must be taken'. Thus, the 'speed with which controls can be dispensed with depends upon the success with which abundance can overtake scarcity. *Socialism thrives upon scarcity because it believes in concentrated power. On the other hand, delegated power, the Conservative aim, flourishes in conditions of abundance.*'[74]

Not surprisingly, the right-wing press responded to the cuts with anger and dismay. The *Daily Express*, under the headline, 'Less–Less–Less: The Reckoning', lamented, 'The nation that used to be proud and strong . . . suffers a new humiliation from its rulers. For do not doubt it—the cuts and restrictions . . . are not to be counted some natural disaster . . . They are the result of wrong thinking and wrong policy on the part of the group of men in power.'[75] Similarly, the *Daily Telegraph* noted 'a grim irony in the reflection that in the third year of peace a victorious country is condemned to revert to a war-time footing in respect alike of the necessities and amenities of life'.[76] The Conservative case against the government was summarized by Churchill—for whom the government was not merely incompetent but fundamentally mistaken. Under the slogan 'Set the people free', he declared in his reply to the King's Speech:

No long-term scheme for keeping a community alive can be based on an export scheme alone . . . The conception that any community could make its living without a healthy and vigorous home market and strong domestic consuming power [is] a fallacy . . . I do not believe in the capacity of the state to plan and enforce . . . economic productivity upon its members . . . No matter how numerous are the com-

---

[72] CUCO, *The Industrial Charter: Popular Edition* (London, 1947), p. 1.
[73] This prediction was confirmed by later events, namely the potato control scheme of the autumn and winter of 1947–8.
[74] CUCO, *The Industrial Charter*, pp. 13–15 (emphases in original).
[75] *Daily Express*, 28 Aug. 1947.   [76] *Daily Telegraph*, 28 Aug. 1947.

mittees ... or the hordes of officials ... they cannot approach the high level of internal economic production which, under free enterprise, personal initiative, competitive selection and the profit motive ... constitute the life of a free society.

He concluded: 'I am sure that this policy of equalising misery and organising scarcity, instead of allowing diligent self-interest and ingenuity to produce abundance, has only to be prolonged to kill this British island stone dead.'[77]

Following the ration cuts, the nutritional adequacy of the post-war diet was hotly debated. The first shot in the battle over calories was fired by Dr Franklin Bicknell in an article published in *The Medical Press* in May 1947. Under the headline, 'Dying England', Bicknell argued that rationed and unrationed foods combined amounted to less than 2,100 calories per day, 'Yet the average moderately active man must eat 3,000 calories daily and the average housewife 2,500 calories daily in order to provide the energy used up in a full day's work. . . . In other words, everyone in England is suffering from prolonged chronic malnutrition.'[78] The article received extensive press coverage and its publication coincided with a Lords' debate on food policy in which Lord Woolton, the Conservative party chairman, quoted from Bicknell's article and expressed great concern, 'because, as every housewife in the country knows, the food position is gradually getting worse'.[79] While the government claimed that adults, on average, consumed about 2,900 calories a day, this assumed regular access to canteens or restaurants and, for example, housewives who relied primarily on meals at home probably fell below this average. Despite the tight calorie situation, vital statistics registered considerable improvements as a result of greater equality in consumption coupled with targeting of vulnerable groups such as children. The Labour government took pride in this achievement and much was made of the healthy and rosy-cheeked children of the late 1940s compared with the poverty and deprivation, especially among large families, during the inter-war years.[80]

In an Opposition debate about food policy in July 1947, Strachey denied that there was a food crisis and defended government policy since housewives had the assurance that they would be able to afford the basics which 'for the poorer housewives was a new assurance'.[81] He admitted that there was little surplus but maintained that the diet was nutritionally adequate and well balanced. Strachey categorically dismissed claims by those involved in 'calorie-mongering' that the diet had deteriorated drastically since the

---

[77] Ibid., 29 Oct. 1947. [78] Quoted in Crofts, *Coercion or Persuasion?*, p. 102.
[79] Ibid., pp. 102–3.
[80] Labour Party, *Proud Heritage* (London, 1949); see also Central Office of Information, *Something Done: British Achievement 1945–47* (London, 1948).
[81] *Hansard*, 5th ser., vol. 439, 1 July 1947, cols. 1174–6, 1183.

war and that Britain was 'starving to death', and stressed that in contrast
with the interwar years, calorie intake 'today is very largely according to
need instead of according to class'. Michael Foot took on the charge that
'there has been a disastrous fall in the standard of life of the people of this
country . . . That is the charge of Dr Franklin Bicknell, who . . . says that we
are dying of starvation'. Drawing attention to improvements in vital statistics, he stressed that despite wartime dislocation children were 'healthier,
tougher, stronger than any breed of children we have ever bred in this country before. This is a fact of which we ought to be proud, and we are proud.'[82]

This optimistic assessment of the post-war diet was rejected by
Conservative politicians. For example, James Reid denied that Britain was a
well-fed nation and rejected the notion of fair shares since some people had
access to ample canteen foods whereas others had to make do with meagre
rations. While some people were 'better off today than they were prewar . . .
the great majority of people who were not in the lowest income class before
the war . . . are very much worse off than they were prewar'. Calories 'tell
only half the story' since, 'weight for weight, there are more calories in
bread than in stewing steak' but there had been a 'falling off in the quality
of our diet'.[83] According to Lady Grant, there were 'a great number of people in this country who cannot understand why the standard of our living is
falling now in the open seas of peace. We know perfectly well that since
1945 there have been cuts in several of our vital rations' which meant that
'while we may not be dying of starvation, we are undergoing a famine in
quality'. This 'lack of quality . . . is having a grave effect upon our people's
will to work' and 'a very great number of the people of this country consider not only that we are worse fed than before the war, but that our standard of living is declining and, therefore, that they lack confidence in . . . the
present administration'.[84]

At this time both features and correspondence in the *British Medical
Journal* and the *Lancet* frequently expressed concern about food shortages
which might lead to malnutrition. There was a general agreement among
general practitioners that the post-war diet was monotonous and unap-
petising. Ration cuts and especially the low fats ration were thought to
cause fatigue and irritability, with negative repercussions for morale. Not all
correspondents were pessimistic, since vital statistics were improving and
there was no hard evidence that public health was deteriorating. Regardless
of this, the nutritional situation was perceived to be precarious.[85] In view of
this concern, the Hunterian Society debated the motion that 'our present

[82] *Hansard*, 5th ser., vol. 439, 1 July 1947, cols. 1190–1, 1193.   [83] Ibid., cols. 1155–6.
[84] Ibid., cols. 1208–9.
[85] See *British Medical Journal*, 1947, vol. 1, pp. 235, 525, 863; vol. 2, pp. 422, 696–7, 882–4,
926, 1011–12; 1948, vol. 1, pp. 27, 73–4, 476, 619; vol. 2, pp. 231–2, 397; *The Lancet*, 1947,
vol. 1, p. 196; vol. 2, pp. 41, 60, 67, 72, 391, 407–8, 660, 768–70, 775–6, 848. From 1949

diet is undermining the nation's health' in November 1947.[86] Dr Franklin
Bicknell defended the motion in view of ration cuts and the decline in calorie consumption. Nutritionists such as Sir Jack Drummond and Magnus
Pyke stressed that limited malnutrition was extremely difficult to detect,
acknowledged that the situation was tight, but defended the post-war diet
and particularly the fact that sacrifice was now equally shared—compared
with the inequalities in food consumption during the interwar years. Despite
the fact that little, if any, concrete evidence was produced to indicate that
health was deteriorating, doctors were concerned about recent ration cuts
resulting in a decline in calories as well as signs of fatigue and weariness
among the adult population. The motion was carried by a majority of three
to one. Whatever the doctors' motives in supporting the motion it provides
further evidence of low food morale and lack of faith in government policy.[87]

Women and, above all, housewives were disproportionately affected by the
ration cuts. As argued above, the flexibility of female consumption standards
served as a buffer in the family as well as the national economy during this
period and female morale was low.[88] Conservative women deplored this situation, for example in a resolution debated at the Conservative party women's
conference which coincided with the Commons food debate discussed above:

This Conference views with the most profound concern the ever-increasing burden
placed on the already weary shoulders of the housewives of this country because of
the gross mis-management and absence of practical foresight exhibited by the present Government, resulting in continued lack of food, fuel, housing, clothing and
household goods, and calls on the members of the Conservative Opposition to
protest to the Government by every legitimate means against the intolerable burdens
imposed upon housewives.[89]

This resolution was passed unanimously by over 2,700 delegates, representing between four and five million Conservative women voters.[90]
Woolton, in his address to the conference, returned to 'the subject of malnutrition' and 'recalled his earlier quotations from an article by Dr Bicknell
... that "England was dying from starvation"'. He drew attention to the
fact that calorie consumption in Ministry of Food surveys had declined
from 2,360 calories per day in 1941 to 2,325 in 1947[91] and highlighted the

---

onwards, when the worst shortages were over, discussion on food issues was less prominent and
more favourable to the government's point of view.

[86] *British Medical Journal*, 1947, vol. 2, pp. 882–4.

[87] It is of course only possible to speculate about GPs' motives and whether opposition to government policy on the National Health Service may have prejudiced GPs' attitudes towards food
policy. [88] See Chapter 3, section 3.1.

[89] Harvester Cons., Committee Minutes, Central Women's Advisory Council, General Purposes
Committee, Meeting, 6 May 1947. [90] *Daily Telegraph*, 2 July 1947.

[91] These surveys were based on domestic food consumption and excluded food consumed outside
the home such as canteen or restaurant meals.

reduction of the meat, cheese, sugar, and, above all, the fats ration. Recalling his experience as wartime food minister, he believed that:

when we got the country down to 8 oz. of fat we were at the lowest point at which we dared to go, if we were going to maintain the nation's health and productive capacity. I told the Prime Minister that I could not take responsibility of keeping the nation properly fed on less than 8 oz. a week. Now we are down to 7 oz. I say that's a dangerous position.[92]

Emphasizing that women were the majority of the electorate, a resolution calling for special prominence to be given to women's problems in the party programme was also passed unanimously and the Conservative conference of October 1947 carried a resolution: 'That this Conference condemns the persistent attitude of the Government in ignoring the claims of the house-wife to a fair deal, and calls upon the Government to take steps to increase the available supplies of food and household commodities'.[93]

To counter such criticism, Labour issued a pamphlet in the form of a 'message from the Prime Minister . . . To the housewives of Britain'. Attlee acknowledged that the 'housewife today has a difficult task', but argued that shortages and economic problems were beyond government control and he defended Labour's record by stressing the benefits of welfare reforms to women and that the 'Government by rationing, by food subsidies and by price control is preventing excessive prices and is seeking to give a fair deal to all'. A photograph showed Mrs Attlee talking to 'the housewives of blitzed East London who remember the grim days of Toryism and compare them thankfully with the Fair Shares policy of the Labour Government'. In conclusion, the prime minister appreciated the 'loyal support we have had from you in the past and [is] . . . confident that we can claim it in the future'.[94] Labour women defended government policy and warned of rising prices if controls were lifted and that this 'would mean the end of fair shares and a return to the hungry thirties for many families'.[95] The editor of *Labour Woman* expected that:

[the] Tories will certainly try to exploit the position, but they will have no more suc-cess than they had in their campaign against bread rationing a year ago, if Labour women are active in their propaganda and educational work. . . . The preoccupa-tions of the Government are the preoccupations of the ordinary housewife . . . The Government's policy of fair shares is her protection. She may well look askance at her new Tory or Tory-sponsored 'champions;', who have suddenly discovered she is a harassed and over-worked member of the community, and who are trying to enlist

---

[92] *Daily Telegraph*, 3 July 1947.
[93] F. W. S. Craig (ed.), *Conservative and Labour Party Conference Decisions 1945–1981* (Chichester, 1982), p. 3.   [94] Harvester Lab., 1947/5, *To the Housewives of Britain.*
[95] *Labour Woman*, May 1947. The following quotations are based on this source. See also Harvester Lab. 1947/2, Agenda for 25th Annual Conference of Labour Women, for resolutions supporting government policy along similar lines.

her support in a campaign to get rid of controls and rationing, without attempting to explain how, if controls were scrapped, she could be sure of getting bread for her family at a price within her means. Their propaganda is neither responsible nor well-informed, and Labour women have an effective answer to it.

This answer basically was that:

With a determined co-operative effort on the part of the whole community ... the immense difficulties and dangers which confront us can be overcome and economic recovery assured. The necessary co-operation will be forthcoming if the people knew the facts; and the facts can be explained in straight and simple terms.

By the autumn, *Labour Woman* held that the import cuts of the summer were accepted by the 'great majority of women ... with common-sense and courage' since, as one correspondent put it, '"it does make a difference to the way we look at things when we know that with the rations, everybody has a fair share"'.[96]

The political costs of the crisis are exemplified by the local elections of November 1947. Reversing the losses of 1945 and 1946[97] the Conservatives made sweeping gains in what Morgan Phillips, the Labour party general secretary, described as 'a food and basic petrol election'.[98] He rejected suggestions that the results implied a political landslide since Labour had consolidated a high proportion of recent gains 'in the face of a high-pressure Tory attack, which was deliberately aimed at exploiting popular discontent over inevitable shortages and restrictions'. By contrast, Churchill rejoiced at this 'splendid victory over the inept and wrong-headed forces which have already led us far along the road to ruin. ... The result deprives the Socialist government of any mandate they obtained at the general election. Hence forward they will govern without the moral support and against the will of the people.'[99] Bolstered by this result the *Daily Express* claimed that the 'Socialist government does not command the confidence of the people' and endorsed Conservative calls for a general election under the slogan 'Set the people free'.[100] For the *Daily Herald* the elections were the 'climax of a campaign of misrepresentation unparalleled in British political history'. Highlighting constant criticism of the government, the editorial continued: 'Such an incessant and indefatigable barrage of slanders was bound to make some impression, especially when fullest opportunity was taken to exploit for political ends the sacrifices made necessary by the economic crisis'.[101] The political temperature remained high until Labour's success in holding the Gravesend by-election at the end of the month. Although there was a swing of 6.8 per cent to the Conservatives, Labour held the seat by a

[96] *Labour Woman*, Sept. 1947. [97] See Table 5.2.
[98] *Keesing's Contemporary Archives: Weekly Diary of World Events* (15–22 Nov. 1947), p. 8941.
[99] Ibid. [100] *Daily Express*, 3 Nov. 1947. [101] *Daily Herald*, 3 Nov. 1947.

margin of 3.6 per cent. However, the Conservative share of the vote increased by 13 per cent compared with 1945, primarily due to Conservative success in capturing the Liberal vote in the absence of a Liberal candidate.[102] This victory was hailed as a triumph for Labour and clearly was a bitter blow for the Conservatives. Gravesend indicated the limits of the Conservative recovery but also showed how much the government was now on the defensive and how vulnerable Labour had become during Dalton's '*Annus Horrendus*'.[103]

5.3. THE 1950 AND 1951 GENERAL ELECTIONS

The supplies situation improved from 1948 onwards and the salience of food and other shortages declined. Simultaneously, rising prices became the most important problem for the public. The cost of living was a central issue in party policy and propaganda during the general election campaigns of 1950 and 1951. This debate raised wider arguments with regard to controls and the role of the state in economic management. Despite economic recovery, there were further crises, namely devaluation in 1949 and the outbreak of the Korean war in 1950 which contributed to high inflation and the balance of payments crisis of 1951. By the end of the 1940s, the tide of popular opinion was turning away from Labour and towards the Conservative party, as indicated in local election results, by-elections, and above all opinion polls.[104] An interesting example of this transformation was an article entitled, 'Why I do not support Labour', by Edward Hulton, editor of *Picture Post* and one of the government's strongest erstwhile supporters, published in July 1948.[105] Hulton, had been 'delighted' that Labour won in 1945. Concerned about the 'very perilous' condition of the country and rejecting 'anything resembling a totalitarian Communist Government of the Russian type', he now argued that Labour's socialism and especially the 'panacea' of nationalization was 'just not working'. Hulton felt 'that at the next general election the Conservative Party ought to be allowed another chance' because:

it looks as if there is an inescapable drabness and sadness, to say nothing of austerity, about the whole Socialist way of life, as at present evolved. . . . It has become pretty generally realised that too many controls must stifle all joy in work and kill essential spontaneity. Another important aspect is that too many restrictions are bound to lead to a gradual lowering of the political morality of the people, and the

---

[102] Craig, *British Electoral Facts 1885–1975*, table 2.02, p. 53. It is worth noting that Gravesend was another Kent constituency comfortably won by the Conservatives in 1950, see Craig, *British Parliamentary Election Results, 1950–73*, p. 412.

[103] Dalton, *High Tide and After*, p. 187.   [104] See Figures 5.1 and 5.2 and Table 5.2.

[105] *Picture Post*, 17 July 1948.

too great tolerance of the Black Marketeer which we are beginning to see all around us.

Although Labour won the general election of February 1950, the party's majority was reduced to single figures. This result was generally perceived as inconclusive, indicating the need for a further general election in the near future. The Conservatives won the general election of October 1951 with a small, but workable, majority, although Labour obtained a slightly higher share of the vote and, indeed, its highest share ever. Since the case put forward by each party changed little between these elections, the following paragraphs analyse Labour and Conservative party policy and propaganda produced between 1949 and 1951. However, two important issues which arose after February 1950 require attention, namely the debate about Labour's policy of introducing permanent controls in the autumn of 1950 and the argument about the lowest ever meat ration in 1951, which catapulted the food issue back on to the agenda.

Labour propaganda expressed pride in the Attlee government's successes in contrast with the Tories' broken promises after the Great War and the unemployment and hardship of the interwar years. Labour's central achievement was the maintenance of full employment which, coupled with rationing, food subsidies, and social reform, had transformed working-class living standards. Thus, according to the 1951 election manifesto: 'To-day, after six years of Labour rule and in spite of post-war difficulties, the standard of living of the vast majority of our people is higher than ever it was in the days of Tory rule. Never have the old folk been better cared for. Never had we so happy and healthy a young generation.'[106] Labour argued with 'such tenacity about full employment and fair shares' because 'we Socialists have a grand human aim. We want to make the world a happier place'. Labour aimed to wipe out 'avoidable unhappiness' by establishing 'a new kind of life in which everyone is free from fear of unemployment, preventable disease and poverty'.[107] Labour's aims went beyond material improvement. Ultimately, the party wanted to establish a 'new moral order':

Socialism is not bread alone. Economic security and freedom from the enslaving material bonds of capitalism are not the final goals. They are means to the greater end—the evolution of a people more kindly, intelligent, free, co-operative, enterprising and rich in culture. They are means to the greater end of the full and free development of every individual person. We in the Labour Party . . . have set out to create a community that relies for its driving power on the release of all the finer constructive impulses in man.[108]

[106] Craig, *British General Election Manifestos, 1900–1974*, p. 176.
[107] Harvester Lab., 1950/37, *Good to be Alive*.
[108] Craig, *British General Election Manifestos, 1900–1974*, p. 153 (*Let Us Win Through Together*, 1950 manifesto).

In order to contain inflation under full employment as well as to maintain fair shares, permanent controls were a central feature of Labour's economic policy. 'Only by price control and rationing can fair shares of scarce goods be ensured'. 'Food subsidies, rationing, price control of essentials, rent control . . . these are all helping to keep down the cost of living' and Tory proposals to abolish controls and cut food subsidies would be 'disastrous' and would mean 'dearer' food.[109] Despite rising prices, most people were better off than before the war since average working-class family income had increased more than prices. Moreover, 'the fair shares policy has helped to raise the standard of living still more. Today every member of the community has a "social wage". While food subsidies have helped to keep the cost of living down, the expansion of social services has removed more and more items from the family budget.' Though subsidies and social services were of course paid for by taxation, taxes fell 'most heavily on those best able to pay'.[110] Hence, Labour remained committed to economic planning, food subsidies, along with bulk purchase, and proposed an extension of price controls and the utility scheme. Labour argued that the Tory 'promise to "set the people free from controls"', by scrapping bulk buying, removing price controls, cutting subsidies, and ending the utility scheme, 'would cause a catastrophic rise in the cost of living'.[111] Labour's policy for consumers aimed to 'bring down excessive prices, by increasing the efficiency of production and distribution', by nationalizing some areas of wholesale trade, and by establishing an independent consumer advice centre to ensure quality. The fundamental question facing the electorate was whether Britain should 'continue along the road of ordered progress' or whether 'reaction, the protectors of privilege and the apostles of scarcity economics . . . [should] take us back to the bleak years of poverty and unemployment'.[112]

According to the Conservatives the recurring economic crises were due to the failure of Socialist planning and government mismanagement as well as excessive controls and bureaucracy. Government policy was the prime cause of persistent shortages and rising prices. Only a return to the free market would result in lower prices and a wider choice of consumer goods. The Conservative critique of Labour's policies consisted of four main arguments. In the first place, the party deplored the meagre rations and other shortages, which compared unfavourably with pre-war and even wartime consumption standards. The Conservatives denied allegations that starvation was rife during the interwar years, stressed that pre-war urban working-

[109] Craig, *British General Election Manifestos, 1900–1974*, pp. 154, 157.

[110] Harvester Lab., 1950/24, *Campaign Notes, General Election 1950*, no. 24 (Feb. 1950).

[111] Ibid., 1951/8, *Campaign Notes, General Election 1951*, no. 1 (Oct. 1951); see also 1951/76, *What Price the Tories? Straight from the Horse's Mouth* . . .; Craig, *British General Election Manifestos, 1900–1974*, p. 175 (1951 manifesto).

[112] Craig, *British General Election Manifestos, 1900–1974*, pp. 157, 161 (1950 manifesto).

class consumption of many foodstuffs exceeded ration scales in 1949 as well as in 1951, and highlighted Woolton's success as minister of food during the war in maintaining rations at a higher level.[113] Second, the high number of controls regulating rationing, prices, raw materials, production, and labour were depicted as an erosion of civil liberties. These included 'over 8,500 new Statutory Rules and Orders' introduced since 1945, 'the great majority of which became operative without reference to Parliament'.[114] In Churchill's words, 'while shortages persist some controls are inevitable, but . . . wartime controls in time of peace [are] a definite evil in themselves'.[115] Third, the Conservatives opposed the large bureaucracy administering the control apparatus along with high taxes which were an integral part of the socialist state. To quote Churchill again: 'Seven hundred thousand more officials . . . have settled down upon us to administer 25,000 regulations never enforced before in time of peace', supported by a 'rate of wartime taxation . . . [which] has hampered . . . recovery in every walk of life'.[116] This 'crushing burden of taxation amounting to eight shillings in every pound earned' was 'a grave evil'; 'to lower taxes and the high cost of living we must cut down Government spending'.[117] Finally, the Conservatives highlighted examples of mismanagement such as the fuel and convertibility crises of 1947 along with projects such as the groundnuts scheme, which were said to have cost £500 m., and ridiculed unconventional foods such as snoek or whale meat.[118] In 1951 one pamphlet, showing photographs of a reindeer, a horse, and a whale, proclaimed: 'see what a wide choice of food you have under the Socialists'.[119] At the same time, another publication displayed drawings of these and other animals under the caption, 'Can you guess what these are?' A 'clue' was 'something in common', namely 'they are being used to provide food for the British public because the Socialist Government has so mismanaged our fresh meat supplies'.[120]

Conservative propaganda was not entirely negative. The party's alternative policies had to tread a thin line between reassertion of the traditional philosophy of freedom, enterprise, and opportunity, on the one hand, and reassurance, on the other. While the Conservatives endeavoured to restore

[113] CUCO, *The Campaign Guide 1950* (London, 1949), pp. 225–7; Conservative Research Department (hereafter CRD), *All the Answers*, 2nd edn. (London, 1949), pp. 39–42; CRD, *All the Answers to 100 Vital Issues* (London, 1951), p. 26; CRD, *Six Years of Socialist Government* (London, 1951), pp. 105–10.
[114] CUCO, *The Campaign Guide 1950*, p. 654.
[115] CRD, *Six Years of Socialist Government*, p. 58.
[116] Harvester Cons., 1948/17, *Set the People Free* (a broadcast talk by Winston Churchill).
[117] Craig, *British General Election Manifestos, 1900–1974*, pp. 140–2 (*This is the Road*, 1950 manifesto).
[118] Harvester Cons., 1949/83, *Mr and Mrs John Everyman . . . in Account with Messrs C. R. Attlee & Co.* This pamphlet was reissued in 1950, ibid., 1950/109, with 'Final demand' printed in bold across the page.   [119] Harvester Cons., 1951/43, *Home Truths*, March 1951.
[120] Ibid., 1951/47, *Popular Pictorial*, n.s., no. 9, Mar.–Apr. 1951.

'full personal freedom and power of initiative', the party vowed 'to serve the nation as a whole' and to foster 'a spirit of unity for a common purpose in industry'.[121] Ultimately, the Conservatives promised 'To denationalise wherever practicable, to decentralise as much as possible, to encourage and reward personal responsibility, to give enterprise and adventure their heads'. With regard to food, 'As soon as we have been able to ensure that the prime necessities of life are within the reach of every family . . . we shall abolish the existing rationing system'. Food supplies would be increased by encouraging domestic production, terminating bulk buying, and reopening commodity markets. These measures, coupled with lower taxes, reduced subsidies, and more efficient management, would restore incentives and enable 'the British people to save themselves now and win lasting prosperity for the future'.

Following the 1950 general election, Labour plans to make the emergency powers permanent were outlined in the King's Speech of October 1950:

'In order to defend full employment, to ensure that the resources of the community are used to best advantage and to avoid inflation, legislation will be introduced to make available . . . on a permanent basis . . . powers to regulate production, distribution and consumption and to control prices.[122]

Wartime emergency powers, which provided the legal basis for economic controls, were extended temporarily under the Supplies and Services Acts of 1945 and 1947. The Conservatives opposed the 1947 Act, which made emergency powers applicable to purposes such as 'fostering and directing exports and reducing imports', as well as 'generally for ensuring that the whole resources of the community are available for use . . . in a manner best calculated to serve the interests of the community'.[123] For Churchill, this Act amounted to 'a blank cheque for totalitarian Government'. All emergency legislation was due to expire in December 1950. According to Woolton, Labour's policy to make these powers permanent would introduce:

government by Ministerial decree. . . . It perpetuates the war-time system when we put the constitution into cold storage. . . . I urge the public to remember in particular this threat to their freedom—the Supplies and Services Act, the S.S. Act, the instrument whereby the public will be kept under perpetual control.

Similarly, Butler described the proposals as 'wrong economically' as well as 'sinister constitutionally', and amounting to 'the Reichstag method of

---

[121] Craig, *British General Election Manifestos, 1900–1974*, pp. 139, 152 (1950 manifesto). The following quotations are based on this source, pp. 152, 144, and 140.

[122] F. W. S. Craig (ed.), *The Most Gracious Speeches to Parliament 1900–1974: Statements of Government Policy and Achievements* (London, 1975), p. 134. For details of Labour's policy see Rollings, '"The Reichstag Method of Governing"?', pp. 15–36.

[123] CUCO, *The Campaign Guide 1951* (London, 1951), p. 97. The following quotations are based on this source, pp. 97–102.

government'. The Conservatives demanded an annual renewal of emergency legislation and held that useful controls should be transferred to the statute book. The remainder should be reduced to a minimum and abolished as soon as possible:

To make such powers permanent . . . is a confession by the Government that they believe the emergency itself will be permanent: that supplies will always be scarce; that ration-books and identity cards will never disappear . . . Conservatives hold that a perpetual emergency is a contradiction in terms, and that, if the liberty of the subject is to be preserved . . . the State cannot be granted, as a normal and everlasting part of its authority, powers of government by decree originally conceived at a time of impending military peril.

Finally, the Conservatives tried to exploit the reduction of the meat ration to its lowest ever level during 1951, a reduction which pushed the question of food shortages back on to the agenda.[124] Labour explained the drastic cut in the ration, which was due to the breakdown of negotiations of a new contract with Britain's major supplier, Argentina, as part of the government's anti-inflationary policy in the context of world shortages. The government was not prepared to pay the price demanded by Argentina, and it was 'only by holding out, even if it means going without meat for a time, that we can hold prices for the future' and thereby strike 'a blow against exorbitant world prices'.[125] The episode did not weaken Labour's commitment to bulk buying but, not surprisingly, it provided ammunition for the Conservative opposition to government purchasing.[126] Early in 1951, *Home Truths*' housewife Winnie Welcome agonized over what to cook for husband Jim, and *Popular Pictorial* showed a photograph of 'your weekly meat ration [which] is not much bigger than a matchbox'.[127] In the summer, the Conservatives mocked Labour's policy since Britain, under a new contract, in fact did pay a higher price for Argentine meat; 'all the brave talk . . . about "holding out" for lower prices was sheer humbug! Socialist State-buying has failed again. Conservatives believe in letting men who are professional at the job, buy the nation's food.'[128]

Both parties courted female voters with policy and propaganda specifically addressed at women, but there were significant differences in approach.[129] The Conservative charter for women, *A True Balance: in the*

[124] See Figures 1.2, 2.1, 2.2, and 2.3.   [125] Harvester Lab., 1951/75, *What Price Meat?*
[126] CRD, *All the Answers to 100 Vital Issues*, pp. 27–31; CRD, *Six years of Socialist Government*, pp. 113–20.
[127] Harvester Cons., 1951/42, *Home Truths*, Feb. 1951. *Home Truths* was a periodical aimed at housewives, which regularly featured the problems of Winnie Welcome, an average, but fictitious, housewife. Ibid., 1951/47, *Popular Pictorial*, n.s., no. 9, Mar.–Apr. 1951.
[128] Ibid., 1951/50, *Popular Pictorial*, n.s. no. 12, June–July 1951.
[129] See Zweiniger-Bargielowska, 'Explaining the Gender Gap', pp. 194–223; A. Black and S. Brooke, 'The Labour Party, Women and the Problem of Gender, 1951–1966', *Journal of British Studies* 36 (1997), pp. 419–52; Francis, *Ideas and Policies under Labour*, ch. 8, *passim*.

Home, in Employment and as Citizens, went beyond the consumption agenda and appealed to women by building on the traditions of the women's movement.[130] *True Balance* contained feminist demands such as equal pay in the public sector and equal citizenship, policies which were incorporated into the election manifesto of 1950 and other party literature.[131] The section on women in the home emphasized the importance of family life and demanded adequate housing, more plentiful food, and labour-saving devices to ease 'the heavy burden of the housewife today'.[132] By contrast, the Labour Party produced nothing of the status of *True Balance* during the period and the demand in *Labour Woman* for a 'charter' for housewives and mothers in 1944 was never followed up.[133] Labour's *Is a Woman's Place in the Home?*, published in 1946, advocated equal pay and equal opportunities for women as well as better welfare provision to improve the position of women in the home.[134] However, this pamphlet was only intended for use by constituency discussion groups and its arguments were not translated into official policy statements. While Labour supported equal pay in principle, the government did not implement equal pay since the policy was considered to be inflationary. Labour propaganda aimed at women generally focused on women's roles as wives and mothers, as in a 1949 leaflet which declared that 'no government has done more for women in such a short period', citing family allowances, the NHS, food subsidies, and fair shares, as well as full employment.[135]

Two examples further illustrate how the Conservatives attempted to exploit Labour's paternalist and gender-blind attitudes and propaganda. *True Balance* argued that the housewife was 'the best judge of how to run her home' and rejected the 'ridiculous doctrine' postulated by Douglas Jay by quoting from his *The Socialist Case*:

Housewives as a whole cannot be trusted to buy all the right things, where nutrition and health are concerned. This is really no more than an extension of the principle according to which the housewife herself would not trust a child of four to select the week's purchases. For in the case of nutrition and health just as in the case of education, the gentleman in Whitehall really does know better what is good for the people than the people know themselves.[136]

A Conservative leaflet, entitled *Housewives' Choice*, contrasted an abridged version of this quotation with Woolton's homely 1941 Christmas broad-

---

[130] CUCO, *A True Balance: In the Home, in Employment and as Citizens* (London, 1949).

[131] Craig, *British General Election Manifestos 1900–1975*, p. 143 (1950 manifesto); CUCO, *The Right Road for Britain* (London, 1949), pp. 42–4; CUCO, *The Campaign Guide 1950*, pp. 663–4.

[132] CUCO, *A True Balance*, pp. 7–10.   [133] *Labour Woman*, Feb. 1944.

[134] Labour Party, *Is a Woman's Place in the Home?*, Labour Discussion Series No. 9 (London, 1946).

[135] Harvester Lab., 1949/40, *There is a Place for Every Woman in the Labour Party*.

[136] CUCO, *A True Balance*, p. 10.

cast, 'Drink . . . a toast to "The Mothers of Britain" whose cooking know-ledge and shopping skill has [*sic*] kept the people fighting fit' and claimed that 'the Socialists have no real understanding or sympathy with the house-wives' lot'.[137] Churchill, speaking in Plymouth during the 1950 general elec-tion campaign, again used the quotation in full, deriding 'our Socialist masters [who] think they know everything. They even try to teach the housewife how to buy her food.'[138] Similarly, Labour's slogan, 'Ask your Dad!', which was countered by 'Ask their Mums' in a *Daily Mail* cartoon picturing queuing women, was taken up by the Conservatives.[139] Alleging that Labour 'forgot to ask about Mum', the party highlighted mothers' memories of plentiful food and consumer goods at low prices during the 1930s.[140]

Morrison, however, appreciated that 'especially the women in the home, have their special difficulties and problems which command our sympa-thetic understanding' and stressed the need to counter 'the Tories who [were] laying themselves out to exploit' these problems.[141] A typical example was *Housewives' Choice*, which highlighted the government's success in 'winning the fight against poverty' as a result of fair shares and full employ-ment coupled with better health care, housing, and education.[142] Similarly, *To All Women* acknowledged that women bore 'the burden of the country's difficulties' since they had 'to cope with shortages and rising prices . . . to stretch the rations . . . to queue, contrive, work and worry'. In these difficult circumstances, Labour's policies helped the housewife 'through rent and price controls, rationing and subsidies', as well as 'the really important thing . . . a regular wage packet'.[143] Hence, Labour disparaged Tory claims to '"Set the housewives free"', by asking:

Free for what? Freedom for the few to winter in Monte Carlo and buy their mink coats and pearls? Freedom for the many to face the threat of unemployment and insecurity? No woman in her senses would deliberately endanger her children's health, her husband's job and her own happiness by choosing the Tory road for Britain. The *really* smart woman will vote Labour again.[144]

The Conservatives, in a leaflet picturing food, toys, and household goods, urged housewives to vote Conservative because government 'can preserve or destroy, slowly but surely, the little things that make up your happiness. It

---

[137] Harvester Cons., 1950/125, *Housewives' Choice*.

[138] Quoted in W. S. Churchill, *His Father's Son: The Life of Randolph Churchill* (London, 1996), p. 294.

[139] *Mass-Observation Bulletin*, n.s., no. 25, Feb. 1949.   [140] CRD, *All the Answers*, 2nd edn., Apr. 1949.

[141] Labour Party, Research Department, RD 175, Memorandum by H. Morrison, Oct. 1948.

[142] National Library of Wales, Aberystwyth, miscellaneous Labour party pamphlets, *Housewives' Choice* (1949).

[143] Ibid., *To All Women* (1950).   [144] Ibid., *The Thinking Voter* (Feb. 1950) (emphasis in original).

can keep the cost of them down ... or allow their price to rise ... It can leave you free from interference or it can make your life a burden with more and more restrictions and controls.'[145]

Austerity was, of course, not the only issue dividing the parties or determining votes, but there were genuine policy choices and both parties, influenced by their respective ideologies, had very different priorities with regard to rationing, controls, and consumption. This controversy was central to political debate during the period and the electorate was deeply divided, as indicated by the close result of both the 1950 and 1951 general elections. Record party membership and high turnouts point towards powerful disagreement between the parties and among the electorate, not least on the issue of consumption and controls. There was no general repudiation of Labour's policies and the party remained strong, especially in its heartlands, with Labour polling a small majority of votes in 1951. Nevertheless, the Conservative party was the main beneficiary in the battle for the votes. The Conservatives recovered from their apparent 'Waterloo' in 1945 to a neck-and-neck position by exploiting popular dissatisfaction with austerity and controls. Victory in 1951 was based on constructing a broad coalition of consumer interests which was strengthened in subsequent elections when affluence became the byword of Conservative success.

5.4. THE END OF AUSTERITY AND THE 1955 GENERAL ELECTION

Following the Conservative election victory—in the context of more favourable international economic conditions—wartime controls on consumption were finally abolished, culminating in the termination of food rationing in the summer of 1954. In the run-up to the 1955 general election, Conservative propaganda celebrated rising living standards and the return of freedom of choice: 'Austerity has gone the way of shortages, black markets, controls, power cuts, identity cards and ration books.' The government took pride in the restoration of 'general prosperity' since 'To-day the British people are earning, eating, producing, buying, building, growing and saving more than they ever did under the Socialists.'[146]

By contrast, Labour retained its commitment to controls and condemned the Conservative policy of *laissez-faire*, tax cuts, and reduced food subsidies: 'Socialists and Tories differ fundamentally. ... Labour knows that the economy cannot be kept at full employment and full output without Government planning, controls and fair taxation.' Hence, Labour intended

---

[145] Harvester Cons., 1950/22, *The Little Things in Life.*
[146] CRD, *Three Years' Work: Achievements of the Conservative Government* (London, Dec. 1954), pp. 39, 7, see also pp. 9–11, 36–41.

to 'restore powers of control which have been abandoned by the Tory Government' and planned to 'introduce legislation to place the necessary powers for ensuring full employment on a permanent basis'.[147] Labour disparaged the re-emergence of inequalities which put an end to fair shares. As Attlee put it in 1955:

> [the] Conservative government, by the abolition of subsidies, has brought about untold difficulties. I realise that the rationing of foodstuffs was not popular, but at least it enabled people to obtain fair shares at reasonable prices. Nowadays . . . the shops [are] filled with articles at prices which the ordinary man and woman cannot afford.[148]

There is no evidence of an emerging consensus in party policy during the early 1950s, and the role of the state in economic management remained a principal theme of political debate. The Conservative victory in 1955 was by no means a foregone conclusion and the party's tenuous hold on power, owing to its small majority, was a cause of anxiety throughout the Churchill government. The government got off to a bad start in 1952 when deflation and renewed austerity, introduced to tackle the balance of payments crisis, contributed to poor Conservative performance in opinion polls and local elections. The subsequent economic upturn helped to restore the government's fortunes and Conservative morale was bolstered by winning Sunderland South in May 1953, the first government gain in a by-election since 1924.[149] As decontrol accelerated food consumption finally returned to pre-war levels, and by the mid–1950s the post-war consumer boom was well under way, while the public gave a cautious welcome to derationing— despite the fact that it was accompanied by rising prices. Most by-elections in the second half of 1954 and 1955 registered a swing towards the government but in opinion polls and local elections Labour's lead was reversed only in 1955, suggesting that the electorate continued to be deeply divided. Despite the fact that the 1955 general election is generally described as quiet and low key, consumption and controls were vigorously debated— albeit within the context of Conservative affluence and decontrol.

After the 1951 election, many in the Labour party believed that the Conservatives 'would soon reveal their true colours', reverse the Attlee governments' achievements, and 'face nemesis at the next general election'.[150] Arguably, Labour had 'fallen victim to its own mythology', both with regard to its portrayal of the Conservatives as the party of unemployment and poverty during the interwar years and in its view of 'history as leading ineluctably towards the socialist millennium' which was merely halted

---

[147] Harvester Lab., 1953/6, *Challenge to Britain* (London, June 1953), pp. 6, 19.
[148] *Labour Woman*, Jan. 1955.
[149] D. E. Butler, *The British General Election of 1955* (London, 1955), p. 12.
[150] A. Thorpe, *A History of the British Labour Party* (Basingstoke, 1997), p. 136.

temporarily in 1951.[151] For example, according to *Labour Woman*, there was 'no cause to be disheartened by the General Election result' since the Tories were in office 'without a majority of votes in the country' and Labour should be 'justly proud' of the 'highest vote ever achieved by any political party'.[152] Labour lost because many people had been 'fooled by the false Tory election promises', which were soon shown to be 'empty and dishonest'.[153] Tory promises of lower prices had proved hollow in the face of the cut in food subsidies, which bore particularly heavily on housewives. This policy was 'dictated by purely sectional interests', namely 'to redistribute the national income in favour of the well-to-do'.[154]

A rare attempt to question Labour's complacency was a resolution debated at the 1952 women's conference which suggested that Labour's defeat in 1951 was due to inadequate education and propaganda in the face of the Tory campaign aimed at housewives since: 'Everyone knew that the last election was lost mainly in the queue at the butcher's or the grocer's.' However, the resolution was defeated because it was 'unfairly critical' of the party which had polled the largest number of votes and thereby earned a moral victory.[155] Labour's difficulty in coming to terms with defeat was compounded by the aged leadership—Attlee stayed on as party leader until after the 1955 general election—internal divisions, and the failure to develop new policies. Thorpe describes the period 1951 to 1955 as 'one of the most dismal' in the party's history and, according to Jefferys, after 1951 Labour showed 'every sign of having pushed the self-destruct button'.[156] The party, having implemented its traditional programme, was divided about its future direction, and the battle between fundamentalists and revisionists continued throughout the 1950s. Tension was high, particularly during the 1952 party conference, and the truce of 1953 came to an end with Bevan's resignation from the shadow cabinet in 1954. Therefore, despite record membership and union density coupled with substantial electoral support at local and national level, Labour appeared on the defensive—especially in the face of an increasingly confident Conservative government whose record belied Labour's worst predictions.

The Conservatives claimed that rationing and austerity had been accepted as inevitable under Labour and that the 'combination of Socialist State planning, inflation and rigid controls had proved an infallible recipe for disaster'. By contrast, the Conservatives had achieved economic recovery

---

[151] Throrpe, *History of the British Labour Party*, p. 136.   [152] *Labour Woman*, Nov.–Dec. 1951.   [153] Ibid., Jan. 1952.

[154] Ibid., May 1952; quoting from the address of the chairman to the National Conference of Labour Women.

[155] Harvester, Labour Party Women's Organisation, Women's Conference, 22–4 Apr. 1952, pp. 12–13.

[156] Thorpe, *History of the British Labour Party*, p. 137; Jefferys, *Retreat from New Jerusalem*, p. 21.

'from near bankruptcy to solvency and prosperity'. This transformation was a consequence of sound financial policy, an increase in the bank rate, cuts in taxation, the abolition of controls and rationing, the termination of bulk buying, and the revival of commodity markets. With record levels of employment, the standard of living had increased, since wages had risen faster than prices and, in particular, food consumption had expanded dramatically.[157] Butler summed up the situation in July 1954:

In the past three years we have burned our identity cards, torn up our ration books, halved the number of snoopers, decimated the number of forms and said good riddance to nearly two-thirds of the remaining war-time regulations. This is the march to freedom on which we are bound. And the pace must quicken as we go forward. . . . Within the limits of law and social justice, our aim is freedom for every man and woman to live their own lives in their own way and not have their lives lived for them by an overweening State.[158]

Following the abolition of rationing in the summer of 1954, the party produced an avalanche of propaganda aimed at housewives with slogans such as, 'Ration Book "Good-bye-ee!"' and 'Housewives' Heyday', accompanied by pictures of smiling women, torn ration books, and full shopping baskets.[159] Drawing on a comment in 1946 by Edith Summerskill, parliamentary secretary to the Ministry of Food under Labour, that, '"Housewives will have their Victory Day when they can throw their ration books on a bonfire"', the Conservatives rejoiced at having 'made a Socialist dream a reality' by giving 'housewives their "Victory Day"' after 14 years.[160] The end of rationing was celebrated with a 'big blaze' at Heathfield, Sussex:

Headed by the local undertaker, who came to see that ration books were properly disposed of, the procession shows a 14-year-old boy who has lived through only rationing—then came two shoppers followed by a butcher, a baker . . .—somewhere lurking in the back is a Ministry of Food 'official'. . . . Amid cheers all round the 14-year-old boy touches the torch and up they all go in flames—books, coupons, forms, and with them the memory of 14 years of queues, waiting, shortages and empty shelves. As a final touch the people of Heathfield collared the Ministry of Food 'official' to throw him on the fire, umbrella and all, and he enjoyed the fun, too.[161]

---

[157] CRD, *Three Years' Work: Achievements of the Conservative Government*, pp. 6–13, 36–41; on Conservative economic policy see Ramsden, *Age of Churchill and Eden*, pp. 247–9; Rollings, '"Poor Mr Butskell: A Short Life, Wrecked by Schizophrenia"?', pp. 195–202.

[158] CUCO, *The Campaign Guide 1955* (London, 1955), p. 68.

[159] Harvester Cons., 1954/33, *Ration Book 'Good-bye-ee!'*; 1954/6, *Food Rationing Ends!*; 1954/7, *Food Rationing Ends! The Conservatives Get Things Done!*; CUCO, *Onward*, Apr. and Sept. 1954.

[160] Harvester Cons., 1954/7, *Food Rationing Ends! The Conservatives Get Things Done!*; 1954/24, *Westminster News no. 15: End of Rationing, Final Extra.*

[161] CUCO, *Onward*, Sept. 1954.

The party was concerned about the higher prices that had accompanied derationing but stressed the advantage of greater choice, better quality, and better value. Under the slogan, 'bigger shares for all', the Conservatives emphasized that 'the rise in prices has been less than the rise in wages'. Moreover, the 'end of rationing has been a major factor in the rise in the standard of living . . . [since] people can now spend their money how they like on an increasing variety of better quality food and other goods, unrestricted by ration books, shortages or controls'. This leaflet also invoked the language of austerity, 'those everyday expressions of the Socialist era— short supply, bottlenecks, black markets, spivs, registered customers, under the counter, utility, pool, queues, coupons, crisis and cuts' which were 'almost forgotton'.[162] Another leaflet warned that although

freedom has returned . . . it does not mean that it would remain under another Labour Government. Already the Socialists are hinting at the return of controls. Housewives know that controls did not stop high prices but only led to scarcity, the Black Market and near-bankruptcy. Yet the Socialists admit that they would do it again—only this time even more extensively.[163]

There is no evidence of a substantial change in Labour's economic policy during the early 1950s, and many in the party were ambivalent about or actually suspicious of affluence throughout the decade.[164] *Challenge to Britain*, which was approved by the 1953 party conference and reissued in December with the subtitle, *A Programme of Action for the Next Labour Government*, rejected the Tory government's policies: 'the country has been encouraged to relax, to dream of "back-to-normal". That dream is vain.' Britain could only

win the peace . . . [if] we face the harsh facts of life and take the drastic Socialist measures which alone can prevent catastrophe. The Plan for Britain . . . will involve sacrifices not only of material benefits but of many cherished habits and traditions. We are convinced that the British people will accept these sacrifices once it is realised that only by so doing can we regain our economic independence, defend our living standards and play our full part in saving the peace.

On top of permanent economic controls to guarantee full employment, Labour proposed an 'extension of Socialist planning and public ownership' and to 'reorganise and strengthen . . . the planning machinery within the Civil Service' to achieve the 'rapid expansion of the economy in the particular directions required'. Further policies included the reintroduction of bulk buying, standardisation and long production runs to lower prices of

---

[162] Harvester Cons., 1954/38, *Pocket Politics no. 11: Standard of living.*
[163] Ibid., 1954/24, *Westminster News no. 15: End of Rationing, Final Extra.*
[164] Rollings, '"Poor Mr Butskell: A Short Life, Wrecked by Schizophrenia"?', p. 192; Tiratsoo, 'Popular Politics, Affluence and the Labour Party in the 1950s', pp. 44–61.

consumer goods, along with 'subsidies and other means' to restore fair shares and 'bring the basic foodstuffs within reach of all'.[165] In contrast with the barrage of Conservative propaganda marking the end of rationing, Labour for obvious reasons produced no comparable material and, generally, published very little aimed at housewives. Labour's critique of Tory policy focused on rising prices and the return of inequality as a result of cuts in food subsidies, the abolition of the utility scheme, and, of course, the termination of food rationing.[166] Under the slogan, 'Fight for fair shares', one leaflet agreed that: 'Everyone would welcome the end of rationing if it maintained the principle of fair shares at fair prices'. The party deplored that, 'For Labour's system of fair shares the Tories are substituting rationing by the purse—a system where the rich benefit and the not-so-rich suffer'.[167] This was one of many leaflets itemizing the increase in prices under the Tories. In 1955 one of few pamphlets addressed directly at the housewife again detailed price increases and compared her experience to that of 'Old Mother Hubbard [since] she has a lean time of it when she goes to the cupboard but Old Mother Hubbard wasn't the victim of "true blue" politics'.[168]

The Conservatives moved ahead in the opinion polls in the spring of 1955 and the popular Eden, who became prime minister on Churchill's resignation in April, bolstered by a tax-cutting budget, immediately announced a general election to be held in May. Foreign policy issues, peace, and security received a great deal of attention during the campaign but, apart from housing, controls and consumption were again the principal focus of domestic policy debate. The Conservatives fought on their 'highly defendable domestic record' which was detailed, for example, in the party's *Campaign Guide*.[169] Much was made of the rise in the standard of living, evidenced by booming sales in Co-operative Societies, multiple shops, and small retailers, a more than three-fold increase in television licences since 1951, a 25 per cent increase in cars and motorbikes, along with a dramatic rise in ownership of washing machines, vacuum cleaners, and refrigerators.[170] The manifesto contrasted the 'regular cycle of crises' under Labour, which had 'spent most of their time in Opposition quarrelling with one another', with the government's economic success: 'We have proved, by reestablishing confidence in our currency, by maintaining full employment, by

[165] Harvester Lab., 1953/6, *Challenge to Britain* (London, June 1953), pp. 1, 7, 9, 28–31; 1953/7, *Challenge to Britain: A Programme of Action for the Next Labour Government* (London, December 1953); this document included amendments but there was no change in the passages quoted here.

[166] Ibid., 1953/19, *People's Pictorial*; 1954/15, *The Food Fraud: We can't Afford the Tories no. 4*; see also *Labour Woman*, Mar. and Apr. 1952, Oct. 1953 and Apr. 1954.

[167] Harvester Lab., 1954/18, *Is it Really Good-bye to Rationing? We can't Afford the Tories no. 9*.   [168] Ibid., 1955/4, *And so the Poor Housewife Has None!*

[169] Ramsden, *Age of Churchill and Eden*, p. 275.

[170] CUCO, *The Campaign Guide 1955*, pp. 181–3.

restoring housewives' choice and by smashing housing records, that Conservative freedom works'. There were few specific policy commitments, but the Conservatives aimed to 'double our standard of living in twenty-five years' and to develop a 'property-owning democracy'. The manifesto again criticized Labour's policy of planning and controls which had

led, despite heavy food subsidies, paid for out of taxation, to a 40 per cent. rise in the cost of living in six years and to the perpetuation of shortages and queues, ration-books and black markets, snoopers and spivs. All these things will inevitably come back if the Socialists get their way. They seem to think that the British house-wife is incapable of deciding for herself; we are sure that it is the customer, and not "the gentleman in Whitehall", who knows best.[171]

The 'gentleman in Whitehall' who gave the 'housewife her shopping orders' appeared on a number of occasions in Conservative propaganda.[172] Not only were housewives mentioned in the manifesto but the party again produced a number of pamphlets appealing to women voters. According to one leaflet, the 'Housewives' choice . . . [was] control under Labour or freedom under the Conservatives'. Next to a picture of queuing women and details of the various bread ration scales, the caption read, 'Queuing for bread and pota-toes in peacetime—will you ever forget it?' The leaflet continued:

Why remind you of the misery of rationing? Only because the Socialists' food plans involve the return of some form of rationing again. . . . If Labour were returned to office they would 'rationalise' food supplies. In plain English this means they would control supplies to the shop—and the housewife. . . . this spells rationing under another name. . . . The housewife will also realise that when Labour hint at 'con-trol' of prices this must also mean some form of rationing for controls and rationing are twins.[173]

The Conservative charge that Labour would reintroduce rationing if they were elected was repeated over and over again and certainly raised the tem-perature of the election campaign.[174] In the final example, Wilson's comment in a television broadcast of 16 May that, '"We are not going to . . . reintro-duce rationing . . . we are going to introduce . . . price controls"', was dis-missed as 'Labour's big election bluff to catch the housewife. . . . We

[171] Craig, *British General Election Manifestos, 1900–1974*, pp. 184, 189, 192, 195 (*United for Peace and Progress*, 1955 manifesto).

[172] Harvester Cons., 1955/5, *Conservative Key Points: Standard of living*; 1955/20, *Westminster News no. 19: Labour's 'Back to Queues'*; 1955/35, *Pocket Politics no. 2: Labour's New Policy: Shopping Orders to the Housewife*.

[173] Ibid., 1955/128, *Popular Record: Voters' Choice*.

[174] Examples include ibid., 1955/20, *Westminster News no. 19: Labour's 'Back to Queues'*; 1955/35, *Pocket Politics no. 2: Labour's New Policy: Shopping Orders to the Housewife*; 1955/83, *Under Labour: Rationing—under the Conservatives: Freedom of Choice*; 1955/84, *Is this Honest?*; 1955/92, *Socialists Impose Controls*; 1955/119, *Three Black Spots Among the Many in Labour's Policy*; 1955/123, *Coming Back?*, which pictured a ration book on the front cover.

repeat: Labour's policy must lead to some form of rationing. . . . You just can't trust Labour.'[175]

Labour responded to these allegations by issuing an angry denial. Under the title *Nail this Tory Lie*! a leaflet, picturing a crossed-out ration book, declared, 'The last-minute scare, Tory weapon in many elections is being used in the 1955 election. . . . This is a lie. Labour says in its manifesto: "The charge that Labour would reintroduce rationing is a deliberate Tory lie".' A cartoon depicting Attlee as 'Winston's "Socialist Gestapo" bogey' was captioned with, '1945: The stunt that failed. Winston Churchill went to the microphone for the Conservatives and suggested that if a Labour Government was returned Britain would have to accept "some kind of Gestapo". The electors refused to believe him and the Tories were resoundingly defeated.' A second cartoon on the theme of Tory ministers' ration book scare in 1955 described this 'latest stunt' as 'unscrupulous' but 'characteristic' and asked 'the electors to defeat this Tory trickery'.[176] In the manifesto, Labour defended the Attlee governments' achievements in difficult circumstances and rejected Tory claims of greater prosperity, since recent economic improvements were mostly due to a shift in the terms of trade in Britain's favour.[177] Despite these fortunate circumstances, prices had gone up, demonstrating that the Tories were 'clearly unfit to rule' because the combined effect 'of cutting subsidies, of ending price control—in general of reducing government intervention in the economic sphere—has been to raise needlessly the cost of living'.[178] Labour pledged to keep prices 'steady' with policies such as long-term purchase agreements, modernization of food distribution, and by 're-imposing price-controls on essential goods'. Labour would reintroduce planning, extend public ownership, and restore fair shares by using 'the Budget as an instrument for the twin purposes of remedying social inequality and increasing production'.[179] Labour reiterated its ethical commitment to the 'brotherhood of man' as well as its aim to 'make men more truly free', and stressed that the differences between the parties were 'sharp and clear'.[180] While the Tories were the party of privilege, Labour was dedicated to the struggle for the underdog. With regard to economic policy, the issue was:

whether to have a plan-for-all or a free-for-all. Labour believes that we cannot afford to have a free-for-all and that we must plan for the future. The Tories believe

[175] Ibid., 1955/127, *Labour's Bluff*.
[176] Harvester Lab., 1955/51, *Nail this Tory Lie!*
[177] Craig, *British General Election Manifestos, 1900–1974*, p. 204 (*Forward with Labour*, 1955 manifesto).
[178] Harvester Lab., 1955/74, 3 *Wasted Years: The Record of the Tory Government*.
[179] Craig, *British General Election Manifestos, 1900–1974*, pp. 204, 206.
[180] Ibid., p. 208; Harvester Lab., 1955/21, *Campaign Notes General Election 1955* no. 13 (19 May).

the reverse. . . . Another five years of Tory rule will mean a further retreat from fair shares. . . . The Tories say they believe in providing a minimum standard of living for the poorest. But Labour will ensure that everybody gets better standards as the nation's wealth increases. No section of the community must monopolise or take to itself an unfair share of the rewards.[181]

Hence, the 1955 general election campaign was rather more interesting than conventionally understood. Local elections and opinion polls suggest that a Conservative victory was by no means inevitable, and party fortunes were closely associated with economic performance and, particularly, consumption trends. The election was plainly not an almost meaningless ritual in which both parties subscribed to a consensus in economic management with only marginal, if any, differences in policy. The decisive Conservative victory with an increased majority 'finally laid the ghost of 1945' and, according to Butler, 'destroyed for ever the myth that 1945 represented the beginning of some irreversible revolution'.[182] This victory enshrined the predominance of the Conservative approach to economic management—whatever the long-term consequences for Britain's economic performance—despite internal divisions in the party which came to the surface in the later 1950s. Eden's honeymoon was certainly short-lived and shattered by the Suez crisis which forced his resignation. Conservative fortunes were restored under Macmillan, who led the party to a third successive election victory with an increased majority in 1959.

For Labour, which had fought a defensive and backward-looking campaign, defeat in 1955 belied the complacency evident after 1951. It signalled the need to change, a process begun under Gaitskell, who took over as party leader on Attlee's retirement. The party continued to be dogged by internal divisions and, above all, by the battle between revisionists and fundamentalists until after the 1959 general election. This third successive election defeat heralded a major overhaul of policy and the party became revitalized only from the early 1960s onwards.

Arguably, the post-war period came to an end in the mid-1950s and 1955 was the last general election dominated by policies and rhetoric which originated during and immediately after the Second World War. The Conservatives continued to underline their achievement of affluence by invoking the language of austerity until the early 1960s.[183] However, by this time the theme had become tired and dated, especially in the face of a rejuvenated Labour party led by the dynamic Wilson, who cloaked himself in the image of modernization and harnessing the white heat of technology.

---

[181] Harvester Lab., 1955/21, *Campaign Notes General Election 1955* no. 13 (19 May).
[182] Quoted in Ramsden, *Age of Churchill and Eden*, p. 281.
[183] See, e.g., Harvester Cons., 1958/35, *More Liberty for You: Conservative Government Means*

5.5. ELECTORAL TRENDS, 1945–1955

The study of British general elections was pioneered in 1945 by the Nuffield team which has produced a volume for every general election since the war, with David Butler taking the lead from 1951 onwards.[184] Drawing on post-war social science, their so-called electoral sociology approach was based on the premise that voting behaviour was essentially a barometer of social change and, therefore, the rise of Labour was an inevitable consequence of electoral reform and the emergence of organized working-class institutions in the twentieth century. The high level of class voting during the early post-war period was taken as the norm, despite the fact that the relationship between class and party has been at best complex during the Edwardian and interwar periods as well as since the 1970s. A recent critique of the electoral sociology model points towards fluctuation rather than secular decline in class voting and emphasizes the importance of political factors rather than social change in explaining changing voting patterns since the 1970s and, above all, the declining support for Labour.[185] Similarly, Lawrence and Taylor reject the notion of parties as 'passive beneficiaries of social change or electoral reform'.[186] While:

[the] need for parties to mobilise and forge stable coalitions of interests is not an idea which is absent from the electoral sociology model . . . all too often electoral sociology has assumed that voter interests and identities are predetermined and self-evident, *only* requiring recognition and expression by the parties.

They argue that, 'Interests are only effective signposts for political behaviour in so far as language allows them to be described and articulated' and call for more attention 'to the ways in which political parties have themselves defined and been forced to redefine the social identities and audiences to which they address their politics'. Therefore, 'Instead of being interpreted simply as signs of a well-tuned organization, party propaganda and rhetoric should be studied for the evidence they provide of parties' attempts to construct viable forms of political and social identity'.[187] This emphasis on historical context, in which the parties are recognized as active agents in the battle for the votes—utilizing policies and propaganda as a means to create and mobilize support—has informed the above discussion. The following

---

Freedom for All; 1958/39, *This Was Your Life . . . Seven Years Ago*; 1961/116, *Do You Remember Life Ten Years Ago?*; 1964/121, *Prosperity—Just Look Around You*.

[184] McCallum and Readman, *The British General Election of 1945*; H. G. Nicholas, *The British General Election of 1950* (London, 1951); D. E. Butler, *The British General Election of 1951* (London, 1952); Butler, *The British General Election of 1955*.

[185] J. Curtice, 'Political Sociology 1945–92', in J. Obelkevich and P. Catterall (eds.), *Understanding Post-war British Society* (London, 1994), pp. 31–44.

[186] Lawrence and Taylor, *Party, State and Society*, p. 18; for a summary of the literature on electoral behaviour in modern Britain see ibid., pp. 1–26.

[187] Ibid., p. 18 (emphasis in original).

paragraphs detail the changes in party fortunes during the early post-war period by discussing the general election results as well as trends in public opinion indicated by Gallup polls, by-elections, and local elections. These trends are then analysed by focusing on three factors, namely regional changes between elections as well as class and gender differences in voting behaviour.

Table 5.1, which shows the general election results between 1935 and 1959, illustrates the magnitude of Labour's landslide in 1945 and the severity of the Conservatives' defeat. Between 1935 and 1945 there was a swing to Labour of about 12 per cent and the party gained 240 seats, while the Conservative parliamentary party was reduced by half and its share of votes was down by 14 per cent. The two major parties accounted for the overwhelming majority of seats and, although the Liberals improved on their performance of 1935 and polled 9 per cent of the vote, the party won only 12 seats. The turnout was low by post-war standards but actually slightly higher than in 1935. In 1950, Labour's majority was reduced to single figures and the party's share of the vote fell slightly, while the Conservatives, who benefited disproportionately from the redistribution of 1948, managed to narrow the gap in terms of seats with an average swing of 2.9 per cent in their favour. The Liberals' share of the vote was virtually unchanged although the party won only 9 seats in 1950. In 1951, Labour polled its highest share of the vote ever, improving on its 1945 performance by 1 per cent. Due to the high turnout, 1951 also marked an all-time high in the number of votes cast for Labour. Nevertheless the party narrowly lost, in the face of the Conservatives' dramatic recovery from the position of a poor second in 1945 to almost close the gap in terms of share of votes. Despite polling fewer votes, the Conservatives won a small majority of seats on a uniform swing of 1.2 per cent. They achieved this because of the bias in the electoral system due to the redistribution and, above all, by being the main beneficiary of the Liberal collapse. In 1955, the Conservatives consolidated their hold on power with an increased majority, by polling almost half of all votes cast. Labour's share of the vote fell by 2.4 per cent and there was virtually no change in the Liberal vote. Although turnout had fallen arguments that voters had become apathetic in the face of affluence should not be exaggerated since turnout in 1955 was higher than in 1945 and again recovered in 1959. In 1959, the Conservative share of the vote was virtually unchanged, and the party achieved a record third successive election victory with an increased majority, as a result of a further reduction in support for Labour. The Liberals accomplished a modest revival.

The early post-war elections are interesting not only because of the dramatic transition from Labour landslide to Conservative ascendancy and the highly ideological battle between the two parties discussed above, but also because they stand out from twentieth-century general elections in a num-

TABLE 5.1. *General election results, 1935–1959*

Election	Conservative	Labour	Liberal	Other
Nov. 1935 (turnout: 71.2%)				
MPs	432	158	21	5
per cent	53.7	38.6	6.4	1.3
July 1945 (turnout: 72.7%)				
MPs	213	393	12	22
per cent	39.8	47.8	9.0	2.8
Feb. 1950 (turnout: 84.0%)				
MPs	298	315	9	3
per cent	43.5	46.1	9.1	1.3
Oct. 1951 (turnout: 82.5%)				
MPs	321	295	6	3
per cent	48.0	48.8	2.5	0.7
May 1955 (turnout: 76.7%)				
MPs	344	277	6	3
per cent	49.7	46.4	2.7	1.2
Oct. 1959 (turnout: 78.8%)				
MPs	365	258	6	1
per cent	49.4	43.8	5.9	0.9

Source: D. Butler and G. Butler, *British Political Facts 1900–1985*, 6th edn. (London, 1986), pp. 226–7.

ber of aspects. On the one hand, 1950 and 1951 were not only unusually close but exceptional because of the record turnout which, at well over 80 per cent, was higher than at any election since 1918. The only comparable episode, albeit in the context of an exclusive electorate, were the elections of 1906 and 1910. On the other hand, 1951 and 1955 were unique since they marked the high point of the two-party system in terms of votes, with Labour and Conservatives accounting for over 96 per cent of votes cast.[188] While the two major parties held about 98 per cent of seats between 1950 and 1970, their share of the vote was less than 90 per cent in all these elections, apart from 1959, and over 96 per cent only in 1951 and 1955. Twentieth-century Britain is usually perceived as possessing a two-party system, but this approach is inappropriate with regard to the interwar years and questionable for the period since 1974 when Labour and the Conservatives frequently accounted for only about three-quarters of votes cast. From this longer-term perspective, the post-war elections and particularly those of the early 1950s were exceptional, and the period was also marked by record levels of party membership. This evidence should not be

[188] F. Conley, *General Elections Today*, 2nd edn. (Manchester, 1994), p. 4, fig. 1.

interpreted as indicating a consensus across the party divide. Rather it suggests a picture of Britain as a highly partisan and relatively divided society.

The trend in public opinion between general elections is indicated in Gallup polls, by-elections and local elections (see Figures 5.1 and 5.2 and Table 5.2). Opinion polls on voting intention were first conducted in Britain in 1939 and were carried out on a regular basis after the war.[189] The Gallup poll was a lone voice in predicting Labour's landslide in 1945[190] and showed a strong Labour lead until 1946. Subsequently, this lead was eroded and, significantly, the two parties were level during the fuel crisis in March 1947. The Conservative ascendancy reached its climax in November 1947 following the announcement of Draconian import cuts. During 1948–9 opinion fluctuated, but generally the Conservatives maintained a lead. This was eroded when party battle intensified in anticipation of the 1950 general election, and Labour stayed just ahead for the remainder of the year. Conservative support increased sharply at the beginning of 1951, coinciding with rearmament and the cut in the meat ration, and this lead was main-

FIGURE 5.1. *Voting intention, as reported in Gallup polls, January 1945–May 1955 (per cent)*

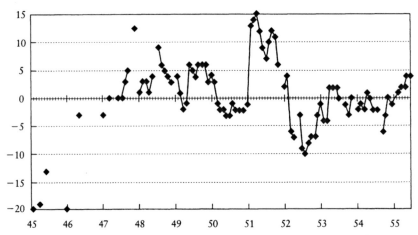

Note: This figure shows the Conservative lead over Labour in percentage terms; negative values indicate a Labour lead. The figure excludes support for the Liberal party and other parties as well as 'don't knows'.
Source: D. Butler and G. Butler, *British Political Facts 1900–1985*, 6th edn. (London, 1986), pp. 254–7.

[189] Gallup polls, the only poll available throughout this period, were fairly accurate in the early post-war years. The average error of polls at general elections was 1.4 per cent between 1945 and 1970 and the winner was always forecast correctly. The record of opinion polls deteriorated after 1970, when the margin of error increased and polls predicted the wrong result, for instance, in 1970 or February 1974. See F. W. S. Craig (ed.), *British Parliamentary Election Statistics 1918–1970*, 2nd edn. (Chichester, 1971), pp. 67–8; D. Butler, *British General Elections since 1945* (Oxford, 1989), pp. 106–7.
[190] McCallum and Readman, *The British General Election of 1945*, pp. 242–3.

FIGURE 5.2. *Contested by-election swings from Conservative to Labour, 1945–1955 (per cent)*

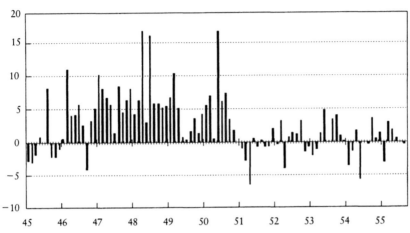

Notes: This graph shows the swing between Conservative and Labour in contested by-elections between 1945 and 1955. The swing details the average of the Conservative percentage gain and Labour percentage loss between the previous general election and the by-election—a negative value indicating a swing to Labour. Swing figures are only given where Conservative and Labour candidates shared the top two places in the poll at both the previous general election and the by-election.
Source: F. W. S. Craig, *British Parliamentary Election Statistics 1918–1970,* 2nd edn. (Chichester, 1971), pp. 27–31.

TABLE 5.2. *Local election results, 1945–1955*

	Nov. 1945	Nov. 1946	Nov. 1947	May 1949	May 1950	May 1951	May 1952	May 1953	May 1954	May 1955
Cons.	−489	+4	+625	+536	+210	+103	−420	−241	−290	+311
Lab.	+988	+159	−652	−453	−79	−3	+641	+354	+414	−341
Lib.	−134	−20	−1	−21	−22	−15	−17	−4	+3	+8
Ind.	−357	−138	+37	−60	−109	−85	−187	−102	−125	+24

Notes: The data, net gains (+) and net losses (−), refer to county and municipal borough council election results in England and Wales, excluding London. The London County Council and municipal borough elections, held every three years, followed a similar trend.
Source: Keesing's Contemporary Archives: Weekly Diary of World Events, pp. 7535, 8257, 8941, 9951, 10001, 10720, 11489, 12221, 13076, 13609, and 14208.

tained until just after the 1951 general election. Labour moved decisively in 1952 as the new Conservative government introduced deflationary measures and cuts to deal with the balance of payments crisis. Labour held on to its lead, although much reduced, for most of 1953 and 1954. The Conservatives moved ahead in the polls only from the beginning of 1955 onwards.

With regard to by-elections, the fact that Labour did not lose a single by-election between 1945 and 1951 is frequently interpreted as proof of the continuing popularity of the government. Without doubt, this fact demonstrates the limitations of the Conservative recovery. Nevertheless, this is not the only interpretation of by-elections during the period. While there was little movement between the parties, in terms of swing the trend was clearly in favour of the Conservatives during the late 1940s, roughly coinciding with opinion poll findings. There were a handful of spectacular swings of between 10 and 17 per cent, and the majority of by-election results moved towards the Conservatives. There were only eight, largely modest swings to Labour and all but one occurred during Labour's first year in office. The pattern was rather different between 1952 and 1955, when both parties performed about equally in terms of swing. While Conservative morale was boosted by gaining Sunderland South from Labour in May 1953, the only seat to change hands during the period, erratic swings in both directions gave little indication of a clear trend in public opinion, with perhaps a slight advantage in Conservative performance towards the end of the parliament.

The local election results tie in well with opinion polls and by-election swings. In line with the 1945 general election success, Labour made sweeping gains in November 1945, a trend which continued in 1946. However, in November 1947 the Conservatives achieved widespread gains at the expense of Labour, which also lost seats to Independents. This success was followed by further Conservative advances, particularly during 1949. In 1951, Labour's position was similar to the party's standing before the war, whereas the Conservatives had made considerable gains at the expense of Liberals and Independents. This Conservative ascendancy was reversed during the early 1950s, when Labour registered extensive gains, largely at the expense of the Conservatives, particularly in 1952. The Conservatives regained some of this lost ground only in 1955, when Labour's recent advances were reversed with losses to the Conservatives as well as Independents and Liberals.

Generally speaking, public opinion, which was strongly pro-Labour in 1945 and 1946, began to move away from the party in 1947, a trend which continued largely uninterrupted until 1949. Labour's revival in 1950 was undermined by the consequences of the Korean war, which ushered in renewed shortages. The Conservatives achieved a dramatic recovery during the height of post-war austerity and surpassed Labour during the years 1947 to 1949 and again in 1951. However, following the election of the Conservative government, public opinion swung back towards Labour, a trend which was particularly marked in 1952, and there is little evidence of a sustained upturn in Conservative fortunes until the beginning of 1955. These data further confirm the divisions in public opinion and indicate that the Conservative victory in the 1955 general election was less of a foregone conclusion than is generally assumed.

Labour's landslide in 1945 was the result of a substantial increase of the party's representation in England, from 116 seats in 1935 to 332 seats in 1945, as well as some advances in Scotland and Wales.[191] The major difference between 1945 and 1929, Labour's previous peak performance when the party came close to an overall majority, was an increase in Labour representation in the South-east and especially the London suburbs. In 1945 Labour, for the first time, won predominantly middle-class seats such as Mitcham and Wimbledon as well as agricultural seats such as Cambridgeshire and Sudbury. Most seats with a very high swing to Labour of between 17 and 22 per cent, compared with a national average of 12 per cent, were 'either middle-class residential areas, or long-time Conservative strongholds, or both. On the other hand, nearly all places with relatively low swings to Labour had had a high Labour vote in 1935, or else they had had a high Liberal vote in 1945'.[192] Above all, 'the high swing to Labour in the London suburbs in 1945 produced the large Labour majority . . . [while] the high swing to the Conservatives in 1950 deprived Labour of their working majority'.[193] The narrow result in terms of seats in 1950 was partly a consequence of the fact that, while the national swing to the Conservatives was 2.9 per cent, 92 seats in eight predominantly middle-class areas in England, and especially the South-east and Home Counties, experienced swings exceeding 7 per cent. This was critical and, indeed, 'the Labour recession in the suburbs of London was by far the most striking thing about the election'.[194] By contrast, four areas in Wales, Scotland, and the North-east, accounting for 48 seats, registered swings towards Labour. There was a uniform swing to the Conservatives in 1951, but the party benefited disproportionately from the Liberal collapse. The Conservatives gained more seats even though Labour won more votes partly because 'Labour won very large majorities in mining and slum seats . . . while the Conservatives won many suburban seats with small but comfortable majorities'.[195] This bias in the electoral system, exaggerated by a further redistribution in 1954, continued to favour the Conservatives in 1955, when the party won about 20 predominantly English seats from Labour on a uniform swing of 1.6 per cent. By 1955 Labour had lost just over a third of its English seats of 1945. In comparison, there was relatively little change in either Scotland or Wales. In sum, Labour held on to the gains of 1945 in its heartlands but, above all, English suburbia gradually became disillusioned with the party. The

---

[191] The following paragraph is based on M. Kinnear, *The British Voter: An Atlas and Survey since 1885* (London, 1968), pp. 52–63. For further details on regional voting patterns see the Nuffield election studies cited above.

[192] Ibid., p. 55.   [193] Ibid., p. 56.   [194] Ibid., p. 58.   [195] Ibid., p. 60.

Conservative advances between 1950 and 1955 were based on recapturing middle-class waverers, attracting stranded Liberals, and generally making inroads in areas where conversions mattered most.

Class was a major determinant of voting behaviour during the early post-war period, as illustrated in Figure 5.3. Excluding support for the Liberals, which was roughly similar between classes in 1945 and 1950 and very low thereafter, about three-quarters of the middle and upper-middle classes supported the Conservatives while Labour won the votes of over half of the working class.[196] However, there were significant variations between elections. The Conservatives won only 61 per cent of the middle-class vote in 1945, when one in eight middle-class voters supported the Liberals, and middle-class Conservative voting peaked at 77 per cent in 1955. This transformation was partly a consequence of a decline in middle-class Labour support, but above all due to Conservative successes in attracting former Liberal voters. With regard to the working class, Labour was ahead of the

FIGURE 5.3. *Class differences in voting behaviour, 1945–1959 (per cent)*

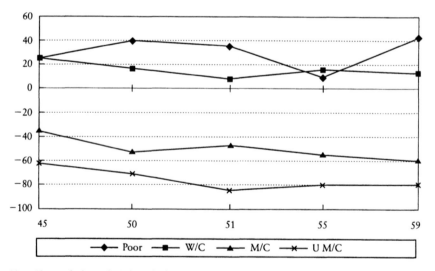

Note: The graph shows the Labour lead over the Conservatives in percentage terms; negative values indicate a Conservative lead. The figure excludes support for the Liberal party, but note that for U M/C the Liberals were the second party in 1950 and 1959. 'U M/C' represents the upper middle class (approx. 5% of the population), 'M/C' the bulk of the middle class (21% of the population), 'W/C' most of the working class (59% of the population), and 'Poor' the poorest 15% of the population, including the very poorest manual workers and a disproportionate number of poor pensioners. In 1945 no distinction was made between 'W/C' and 'Poor'.
Source: Based on Gallup poll data; see Gallup Poll, 'Voting Behaviour in Britain, 1945–1974', in R. Rose (ed.), *Studies in British Politics: A Reader in Political Sociology*, 3rd edn. (London, 1976), p. 206.

[196] See Gallup Poll, 'Voting Behaviour in Britain, 1945–1974', in R. Rose (ed.), *Studies in British*

Conservatives by 25 per cent in 1945, a figure which was reduced to 8 per cent in 1951. While Labour maintained a substantial lead among the lowest-paid manual workers and pensioners in every election apart from 1955, the party's support among the bulk of the working class was rather less solid. Labour retained a majority of the working-class vote throughout but this was reduced to only 52 per cent in 1951. Simultaneously, Conservative working-class support increased from about a third in 1945 to 44 per cent in 1951 and remained above 40 per cent until 1959. Among working-class voters Labour support between 1945 and 1959 remained fairly stable, fluctuating between 57 and 52 per cent, while the Conservatives improved their share of the vote by benefiting disproportionately from the collapse of the Liberals. These figures show that electoral success depended on attracting voters across the class divide. While Labour's appeal as the people's party produced a cross-class coalition in 1945 this was subsequently eroded and during the 1950s the Conservatives' success was based on attracting substantial support from both the middle and working classes.

Beyond identifying these fluctuations, class-based analysis is problematic for a number of reasons. In the first place, classification is difficult since class, a 'most elusive concept',[197] could be defined in terms of 'income, occupation or ownership of capital'[198] as well as 'consciousness' and 'collective identity'.[199] Conventionally, occupation is used to define classes, with salary earners counted as middle class and wage earners included in the working class; the respective percentages in the 1951 census among occupied males were 22 and 78.[200] There were considerable differences in income and status within these strata and it is virtually impossible to define the boundaries between middle and working class. There was also a marked disparity between objective and subjective class identities. According to a Gallup poll conducted in 1948, 47 per cent described themselves as middle class and only 46 per cent as working class.[201] These ambiguities might explain the extent of working-class Conservative voting, which is difficult to account for within a class-based framework. Finally, women do not fit easily into essentially male categories based on income and employment patterns, and the

Politics: A Reader in Political Sociology, 3rd edn. (London, 1976), p. 206, table, for details on class differences in voting behaviour.

[197] A. M. Carr-Saunders, D. Caradog Jones, and C. A. Moser, *A Survey of Social Conditions in England and Wales* (Oxford, 1958), p. 115.

[198] P. Summerfield, 'The "Levelling of Class"', in Smith, *War and Social Change*, p. 179.

[199] R. S. Neale, *Class in English History, 1680–1850* (Oxford, 1981) quoted in Summerfield, 'The "Levelling of Class"', pp. 179–80.

[200] Carr-Saunders *et al.*, *Survey of Social Conditions*, p. 114.

[201] Lewis and Maude, *The English Middle Classes*, pp. 17–18; A. Marwick, *British Society since 1945* (London, 1982), p. 48.

practice of classifying women with the male head of household is highly questionable.[202]

An analysis of male and female voting behaviour does not suffer from these definitional problems and associated sampling difficulties. Of course, the gender gap was much smaller than the class gap but it was sufficient to make a difference, especially when the results were close and the political implications of narrow majorities were further exaggerated by the first-past-the-post electoral system. Figure 5.4 shows a gap of up to 17 per cent in male and female voting during the early post-war elections.[203] While Labour obtained a small lead among women in 1945, probably for the first time, especially from 1951 onwards there was a strong female preference for the Conservative party. By contrast, men continued to favour the Labour party and if women had been disenfranchized Labour would have won every general election during the period. These data suggest that Labour needed the female vote to win a working majority and that the Conservatives were able to offset their poor performance among men with a disproportionate share of the female vote during the 1950s. In 1950 Labour lost 8 per cent among men and only 2 per cent among women, but it was perhaps more significant that this deterioration in the female vote obliterated Labour's lead whereas the male Labour lead at 5 per cent remained secure. In 1950 the Liberal vote remained stable at about 12 per cent among men and women and the erosion of male Labour voting was largely at the expense of the Conservatives. In 1951 there was a large swing towards the Conservatives among women, primarily as a result of substantial Conservative gains at the expense of the Liberals as well as a small reduction in the female Labour vote. By contrast, the collapse of the Liberal vote among men benefited the Conservatives and Labour equally and the Labour party actually increased its male vote by 5 per cent. Therefore, the female Conservative preference in 1951 goes a long way towards explaining the Conservative victory. Similar factors were at work in 1955 when Labour held on to its share of 51 per cent among men but this lead was offset by a further rise to 55 per cent among women supporting the Conservative party.

Gender differences in voting behaviour are a critical and neglected factor in understanding the general election results of the early post-war period. These differences were not static, indicating a mechanical predilection among women towards Conservatism and among men towards the Labour

---

[202] See, e.g., Zweig, *Women's Life and Labour*, pp. 121–3. His respondents who disliked being labelled 'working class' emphasized respectability and status rather than occupation and income.

[203] See Gallup Poll, 'Voting Behaviour in Britain, 1945–1974', p. 211, table, for details on gender differences in voting behaviour. This topic is discussed in more detail in Zweiniger- Bargielowska, 'Explaining the Gender Gap', pp. 194–223. See also Black and Brooke, 'The Labour Party, Women and the Problem of Gender, 1951–1966', pp. 419–52; Francis, *Ideas and Policies under Labour*, ch. 8, *passim*.

FIGURE 5.4. *Gender differences in voting behaviour, 1945–1959 (per cent)*

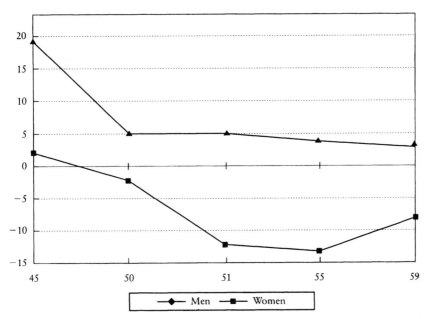

Note: The graph shows the Labour lead over the Conservatives in percentage terms; negative values indicate a Conservative lead. The figure excludes support for the Liberal party.
Source: Based on Gallup poll data; see Gallup Poll, 'Voting Behaviour in Britain, 1945–1974', in R. Rose (ed.), *Studies in British Politics: A Reader in Political Sociology*, 3rd edn. (London, 1976), p. 211.

party, but rather contingent and historically determined.[204] Labour's social reform and full employment programme attracted overwhelming support from both men and women in 1945 but subsequently Labour's collectivist and producerist agenda continued to be favoured predominantly by men while women moved away from the party. As a consequence of Labour's 'essentially masculinist' culture and ideology,[205] the party was 'at best, a reluctant attendant to women's concerns, whether they were feminist or traditional in nature . . . possibly at great political cost to itself'.[206] By the same token, female preference for the Conservatives was the result of a sustained effort by the Conservative party to appeal to the female electorate with a set of policies which recognized the importance of gender difference. The politics of affluence appealed to women in their role as homemakers and

[204] It is worth noting that Labour again polled the largest share of the female vote in 1966 and, more generally, that the gender gap was much reduced after 1970, see Zweiniger-Bargielowska, 'Explaining the Gender Gap', p. 195.
[205] Francis, *Ideas and Policies under Labour*, p. 202.
[206] Black and Brooke, 'The Labour Party, Women and the Problem of Gender, 1951–1966', p. 452.

consumers and the Conservative party also called for equality for women as workers and citizens.[207] The Conservatives were rewarded for their efforts by attracting a majority of the female vote which was critical in the 1951 and 1955 general elections. Hence women and, especially, housewives were a significant political force under austerity, and Labour's failure to accommodate their grievances enabled the Conservative party to reconstruct an electoral majority which, if initially fragile, was consolidated following the abolition of rationing and return to prosperity.

Consumption and the role of the state in economic management were central to party political debate after the Second World War. The clash between Labour's commitment to socialist planning and collectivism and Conservative calls for decontrol and a return to the free market signified a fundamental conflict between the parties with regard to the role of the state in the economy and wider society. While Labour continued to take pride in its achievement of full employment, fair shares, and social reform, which were hailed as a great improvement in working-class living standards, the Conservatives maintained that living standards were declining and that increasingly austerity resulted from government mismanagement rather than post-war economic dislocation. The debate about fair shares and consumer freedom, controls and decontrol, austerity and affluence continued with little modification for a decade following the end of the war, and its associated rhetoric and imagery were used by both Labour and the Conservatives until the mid-1950s. Consumption and living standards were of course not the only issue dividing the parties, but this topic carried particular resonance with the public. The issue was important because people cared deeply about the food they were able to eat and in this sense party politics was translated into day-to-day concerns. Apprehension about the persistence of shortages was widespread particularly among women, but the public was divided as to the most appropriate solution to these problems and opinion shifted over time.

This debate provided a focus for both parties in their efforts to mobilize support and construct coalitions of interests. The changes in party popularity and voting behaviour during the early post-war period correspond neatly with consumption trends and Labour and Conservative rhetoric and policies. In 1945 Labour's reformist appeal to 'the people' for the first time enabled the party to forge a cross-class alliance supported by both men and women in which Labour became the party not only of industrial, urban Britain but also of English suburbia. Labour's vision of democratic socialism characterized by economic planning and controls to ensure full employment and maintain fair shares remained popular with Labour's core

[207] The Conservatives introduced equal pay by increments in the public sector in 1954, see Zweiniger-Bargielowska, 'Explaining the Gender Gap', pp. 213–14.

constituency and, above all, male manual workers in the industrial North and West as well as the big cities. However, the gradual loss of backing by the middle ground deprived Labour first of a working majority and subsequently of its hold on power. From the late 1940s onwards the Conservative critique of austerity and promise of consumer freedom and affluence allowed the party to create a broad coalition of consumer interests which restored the Conservatives' former hold on 'the "public"' destroyed during the Second World War.[208] The Conservatives' skilful exploitation of popular dissatisfaction with rationing, austerity, and controls deprived Labour of its landslide majority in 1950 when the party lost support among women and middle-class voters, especially in south-eastern suburban seats, to the Conservatives. The renewed shortages following the outbreak of the Korean war, the prospect of permanent economic controls, and public discontent with the lowest-ever meat ration further strengthened the Conservative critique of Labour's policies in 1951. In this context, the Conservatives were able to broaden their appeal across the class divide by capturing the bulk of former Liberal voters. The party also won a majority of the female vote. This suggests that the appeal to housewives in particular brought extensive rewards in terms of electoral support. This broad-based coalition was sufficient to return the Conservatives to power despite the fact that the party won fewer votes than Labour. Although Conservative popularity after the 1951 election initially declined while Labour's rose, by 1955 the government's celebration of the ending of rationing and a return to prosperity further strengthened Conservative support among all social classes and women, allowing the party to consolidate its hold on power with an increased majority.

---

[208] R. McKibbin, *The Ideologies of Class: Social Relations in Britain 1880–1950* (Oxford, 1991), pp. 292–3.

Conclusion

Rationing, austerity and fair shares were essential components of the British war effort and post-war reconstruction. The policy was the principal means by which the government facilitated the dramatic reduction of civilian consumption and reallocation of resources for mobilization in a total war. Rationing and controls were never just a straightforward response to scarcity but comprised a major element of external and internal economic policy which, after the war, came to be associated with a distinctive ideological perspective. Domestic austerity was a response to balance of payments constraints both during and after the war by economizing on imports, especially from the dollar area, as well as contributing to the export drive. Simultaneously, rationing and controls of and subsidies on basic goods were an integral element of anti-inflationary policy under full employment. Over and above these policy objectives, ideological considerations came to the fore after 1945. Labour's continued commitment to socialist planning and fair shares accounts for the fact that the policy was retained until the early 1950s and consumption was not simply decontrolled as the supply situation improved. Rather, controls of consumption were an integral part of Labour's approach to post-war reconstruction which prioritized exports, investment, and collective provision. This policy was controversial during the late 1940s and the continuation of austerity became a major predicament of the Attlee government and the underlying reason for the erosion of its popular support and ultimately Labour's loss of power.

The austerity policy resulted in the establishment of a large and frequently remote bureaucracy and the regulation of consumption became a central element of the relationship between the state and British society. The public accepted reduced consumption as a necessary sacrifice for the war effort but the continuation and, indeed, intensification of austerity after the war was unpopular. On the one hand, the erstwhile justification of austerity—winning the war—was no longer applicable. On the other, there was little readiness to tolerate further hardships, and the continued restrictions of consumption conflicted with widespread expectations of a gradual return to pre-war consumption standards. Rationing and controls reduced the great disparity in consumption standards between classes or income groups of the 1930s but these did not disappear. In many ways, gender differences in the experience of and attitudes towards austerity were more important than those between classes; and women in their role as housewives and mothers were responsible for the implementation of rationing and controls. The notion of fair shares was central to wartime propaganda and Labour's ethical commitment to establishing a more egalitarian society after the war but the practical application of this policy was problematic and in the event sacrifice was not equally shared.

Material factors and particularly the availability of food and other consumer goods were intimately linked to the state of morale during and after the war. Shortages were a leading public concern early in the war and again in the late 1940s. Morale was determined not just by actual consumption levels but also by attitudes towards the austerity policy in the sense that uncertainties of supplies were more damaging than stability and the perception of unequal sacrifice caused resentment. During the war the fair shares policy was welcomed in principle, but support for rationing was neither universal nor unqualified. While food policy was generally popular from 1942 onwards, attitudes to clothes rationing and miscellaneous shortages were rather more ambivalent. Despite some areas of discontent, morale remained high during the war as the public acquiesced in the need for sacrifice for the duration. By contrast, the continuation of austerity after the war contributed to low morale—as illustrated by widespread discontent with persistent shortages, the erosion of voluntary compliance with controls (indicated by the expansion of the black market), and growing disillusionment with the Labour government. The very success of wartime food policy contributed to high confidence, post-war demand for consumer goods was high, and victory only served to reinforce general expectations of improved consumption standards. These expectations were undermined by the intensification of austerity after the war coupled with unprecedented levels of taxation in peacetime. When the shortages receded at the end of the 1940s, the remaining hopes of a gradual return to pre-war consumption standards were dashed in the face of the high rate of inflation. Pre-war consumption standards were only surpassed during the consumer boom from the mid-1950s onwards after inflation had been reduced and rationing and controls had been abolished.

Low food morale after the war was a consequence of small and volatile rations which amounted to a traumatic experience in contrast with wartime stability. The ration levels of protein foods and fats dropped below the already sparse wartime levels and the psychological effect of these cuts undermined the faith in the adequacy of the diet among the majority of the population. While the post-war diet was nutritionally adequate, it was also monotonous and ration cuts eroded many traditional elements of the diet, making it increasingly difficult to provide palatable meals. In this context food policy became a prominent and contentious issue of public debate and housewives, who bore the brunt of the burden of post-war austerity, emerged as the most dissatisfied social group in the early post-war years. Labour's recovery policy, which continued to curtail domestic consumption, was one solution to Britain's post-war economic difficulties, but the policy was problematic since shortages undermined workers' incentives, and the lack of variety in the diet as well as the widely held perception of its inadequacy impaired the ability to work, especially during the difficult years of 1947 to 1949.

The reduction in and regulation of consumption was administered by a large bureaucracy which considerably expanded the role of the state since the austerity policy touched everyone and the state now laid down what and how much the civilian population could consume. The policy resulted in the creation of the Ministry of Food, which was established immediately on the outbreak of war, and greatly increased the functions of the Board of Trade. These two ministries, which were mainly responsible for administering the austerity policy, were charged with the complex task of implementing domestic economies, rationing, and controls in a way which ensured that public health and morale were maintained. This bureaucracy was retained after the war and its functions remained essentially unchanged during Labour's period in office, despite some derationing and relaxation during the government's final years. The new Conservative government, committed to decontrol and restoration of the price mechanism, rapidly dismantled this bureaucracy in the early 1950s, culminating in the termination of rationing and the abolition of the Ministry of Food in 1954.

Food policy and, particularly, rationing based on the consumer-retailer tie were influenced by the experience of the Great War but there was no precedent with regard to rationing and control of clothing and miscellaneous consumer goods. Pre-war planners perceived rationing and control of food as an essential element of a total war and the policy was introduced soon after the outbreak of war in 1939. The magnitude of the reduction in consumption of food, clothing, private motoring, and miscellaneous goods in the 1940s was unprecedented in British history in terms of both extent and duration. The austerity policy, which included the introduction of a comprehensive food policy as well as wide-ranging controls of consumer goods, continued for almost a decade after the end of the Second World War. The implementation of these policies was difficult and the imperative to retain public support and maintain morale resulted in a radical departure in food rationing policy, namely a coupon replacement scheme which reversed most of the basic principles of rationing based on the consumer-retailer tie. This scheme was applied to processed and packaged foods and points rationing, launched in December 1941, soon became one of the major government successes on the home front and contributed to high food morale during the war.

The implementation of controls on consumption was not an unqualified success, as illustrated by the emergence of the black market, which was an inevitable consequence of the austerity policy. The pervasiveness of the black market with regard to individual commodities was governed by the relationship between supply and demand coupled with the specific features of a particular control scheme. Some commodities, such as home-produced eggs or poultry as well as cosmetics or petrol, were extremely difficult to control and tightening of the regulations had a limited effectiveness, as new loopholes were found and exploited. The extent of the black market was also determined by voluntary compliance, which was less prevalent after the war, as demonstrated by the breakdown of the clothes rationing scheme during its final months. The black market highlights the limitations of the austerity policy, which resulted in a growing division between public and private morality and the formal, controlled economy and its informal, illegal counterpart. The regulation of consumption was to some extent frustrated in the face of collusion between producers, distributors, and retailers in circumventing the emergency legislation. The public response to the black market was characterized by vehement condemnation coupled with widespread private indulgence. This corrupting effect of the regulation of consumption was a major weakness of the austerity policy which became increasingly apparent in the early post-war years.

The development of a comprehensive food policy distinguished by rationing, food subsidies, and increased consumption of brown bread and milk amounted to a major turning-point in the history of the British diet. As a result of this policy, the substantial class or income differences in food consumption observed until the 1930s were considerably reduced. Perhaps more importantly, these long-standing inequalities in dietary standards never returned and from the 1940s onwards no social group was significantly deficient in terms of basic nutrients and calories. Food policy went beyond narrowing income differentials in consumption, and included the targeting of vulnerable groups, namely pregnant and nursing women and children, who received additional rations and benefited under the welfare foods scheme. The combined effect of food policy, the welfare state, and full employment resulted in material improvements in public health and especially vital statistics which were highlighted as a major achievement by the Attlee government. Maternal and infant mortality rates declined significantly during the 1940s and early 1950s and anthropometric data similarly point towards notable improvements in child health and physique. Nevertheless, this positive interpretation requires qualification and the limitations of food policy have to be highlighted. All social groups registered gains in vital statistics but, at the same time, the disparities between the highest and lowest income groups remained essentially unchanged. Rationing and fair shares failed to eliminate these inequalities for a number of reasons. Over and above environmental factors food consumption was never genuinely equal and take-up of welfare foods was well below entitlement, particularly among the lowest income groups. Moreover, there was no guarantee that the additional allowances made available to vulnerable groups were actually consumed by the official recipients rather than shared within the household.

The austerity policy amounted to a dramatic reduction in consumption of clothing, household goods, and private motoring but in contrast with food, the policy had little more than a temporary effect and wartime innovations such as the utility schemes were abolished in the early 1950s. During the 1940s consumption of clothing became somewhat more equal, supplies of furniture were confined to priority groups, and private motoring virtually disappeared. The clothes rationing scheme was unpopular for much of its duration, shortages of petrol resulted in an extensive black market especially after the war, and limited supplies and high prices of household goods caused frustration particularly among women. Nevertheless, consumption trends which had begun to emerge during the interwar years resumed and, indeed, accelerated from the early 1950s onwards, when Britain witnessed a rapid diffusion of durable goods associated with the post-war consumer boom.

The diet of the poorest sections of the working class undoubtedly improved as a result of rationing of and subsidies on basic foods, but the impact of the austerity policy on classes or income groups was complex. The middle and better-off working classes gave up most and income differentials in consumption patterns were reduced. However, these did not disappear and consumption standards were never genuinely equal. In many respects the very wealthy, who possessed large stocks and could afford expensive unrationed goods along with frequent restaurant meals, were least affected by the reductions in consumption. At the same time austerity also touched the poorest. With low stocks of clothing and household goods as well as limited funds, the lowest-paid sections of the working class were least able to buy the more desirable unrationed foods, high quality clothing or a range of consumer goods in short supply. This is illustrated by the difficulty of providing appetizing meals on a tight budget during the late 1940s or the problems of poorer housewives trying to purchase household goods. Moreover, fair shares were bypassed in the black market and those on low incomes were least able to afford scarce goods at inflated prices. These inequalities caused indignation, and class tension during the war focused on anger about the continuation of luxury feeding, high prices, and uneven distribution of unrationed goods, along with the failure of clothes rationing to distinguish between quality and quantity. The notion of common purpose on the home front has to be qualified in view of the widely held opinion that sacrifice affected some more than others and that the rich could still get what they wanted. The continuation of austerity after the war led to disillusionment and discontent among the middle classes whose expectations of a gradual return to the comfortable living of the interwar years were dashed in the face of persistent shortages and the high rate of inflation at the end of the 1940s. Although Labour's policy of full employment, social reform, and fair shares remained popular among the party's core constituency frustration with post-war austerity extended well beyond the middle classes, and gender differences in attitudes were more significant than those between income groups.

Women in their role as housewives and mothers were central to the austerity policy since they were responsible for putting it into effect on a daily basis, although male consumption standards were also reduced. Women had to adjust their housewifery skills and child-rearing techniques to the altered circumstances. They did most of the queuing, contriving, and making do in order to preserve as much as possible of customary culinary traditions and domestic rituals. This disproportionate sacrifice frequently shielded men as well as children from the full impact of the reduction in consumption. The government recognized the pivotal female contribution—as illustrated by the unprecedented outpouring of propaganda intended to help women cope and to maintain their morale. The successful implementation of the austerity policy which was vital in maintaining civilian health and morale contributed to raising women's status and consolidated their citizenship. Women's attitudes to the austerity policy were complex. While women welcomed the introduction of a comprehensive food policy and, particularly, additional rations for mothers and children, clothes rationing was widely resented and the difficulties of clothing children under rationing became a continuous source of grievance. Female morale was generally high during the war and women accepted the necessity of sacrifice for the duration. Conversely, men were disproportionately dissatisfied with food policy during the war and male manual workers stand out as the most discontented social group. They considered flat-rate rations to be unfair, and the expansion of industrial canteens and the introduction of a special cheese ration were insufficient compensation. A majority of male manual workers deemed their diet to be inadequate, and discontent focused on the small size of rations and, above all, insufficient meat.

Men and women responded differently to the continuation of austerity after the war when a majority of the entire population thought that their diet was insufficient to maintain good health and that lack of food adversely affected their ability to work. Among women there was little readiness to tolerate further hardships but housewives' situation became more arduous as a result of ration cuts and continuous shortages. These cuts bore particularly heavily on women, who frequently gave up some of their rations to other members of the family. During this period of crisis, the flexibility of female consumption standards served as a buffer in the family economy, and a disproportionate share of the burden resulting from the recovery policy based on domestic austerity and the export drive was borne by women, and especially housewives. This sacrifice extended well beyond the poorest income groups, many women were fatigued, and female morale was generally low. Women did not accept this situation passively. The problems of the housewife became a major issue of contemporary debate as women registered their dissatisfaction in protests and, more importantly, through the ballot box. Labour's collectivist, producerist agenda remained popular among men, whose discontent about shortages and low rations was outweighed by an appreciation of gains such as full employment and higher wages. These gains were not necessarily translated into increased housekeeping money, and women were greatly concerned about the high rate of inflation during the late 1940s and early 1950s. Labour's appeal to women, which highlighted fair shares, food subsidies, and welfare reform, was not without support but these policies failed to arrest the erosion of female support for the Attlee government. Many came to support the Conservative party, which fashioned itself as the champion of the female consumer by recognizing the burden borne by women under post-war austerity and promising relief in the form of decontrol, restoration of the price mechanism, and increased supplies of consumer goods.

Fair shares was a compelling slogan but the implementation of this policy, which essentially allocated the same quantity to each person regardless of need, preference, or capacity to secure alternatives was in many ways unequal. Rationing and controls were more fair to some than to others and this inherent flaw of the policy resulted in at times extensive doubts in the system, causing resentment among certain groups. Male manual workers believed themselves to be discriminated against by flat-rate rations, and the post-war ration cuts bore particularly heavily on housewives, who had no access to canteens and rarely consumed meals outside the home. The policy could not control the allocation of scarce resources within the household and, regardless of formal entitlement, many women in practice consumed less than their fair share. The black market, which embodied the dark, frequently unacknowledged underside of fair shares, further highlights the intrinsic limitations of the aspiration of common sacrifice. In the face of formal equality and official condemnation, the principle of fair shares was flaunted by those with money to spend on black market goods while the lowest income groups were least able to supplement their consumption standards through informal, illegal channels. These inherent contradictions in the attempt by the state to regulate consumption contributed to class tension during the war but the problem became far more acute in the post-war period, when the continuation of the policy became increasingly difficult to justify. The Labour government paid insufficient attention to these shortcomings, which did not weaken the government's continued commitment to controls and fair shares. The unfairness of the black market and its corrupting influence were dealt with by increased enforcement activity and drastic measures such as the legislation introduced to break the black market in petrol after the war. By contrast, the Conservative party argued that these policies amounted to an erosion of civil liberties which was unacceptable in peacetime. The Conservative solution to the black market was to abolish controls, increase supplies, and restore free market prices.

These differences in approach amounted to a fundamental disagreement between Labour and the Conservatives about the role of the state in economic management and British society. The debate about rationing, controls, and consumption was central to the party political battle in the early post-war years, and Labour's commitment to socialist planning and controls to ensure full employment and maintain fair shares clashed with the Conservatives' advocacy of decontrol and a return to the free market. This issue was not the only topic of party political controversy but it was important since it held particular resonance with the public. The Attlee government took pride in its achievement of economic recovery, welfare reform, full employment, and fair shares, which were hailed as a great improvement in working-class living standards compared with the poverty and unemployment during the interwar years. By contrast, the Conservatives argued that the living standards of the majority of the population were declining and that post-war consumption levels compared unfavourably with low prices and wide choice of consumer goods during the 1930s. The Conservatives claimed that continued austerity was increasingly due to government mismanagement rather than post-war dislocation and that Britain's economic problems were largely the result of socialist policies which were not only misguided but fundamentally mistaken.

The debate about consumption and its associated rhetoric provided a focus for both parties to mobilize support and construct coalitions of interests, and changes in party popularity correspond neatly with consumption trends. Labour's landslide of 1945 was based on a reformist appeal to the people, which allowed the party to forge a cross-class coalition supported by both men and women—in which Labour became the party not only of urban, industrial Britain but also of English suburbia. This coalition was eroded in the face of post-war austerity from the public outcry over the abolition of dried egg and the controversy over bread rationing in 1946 to the ration cuts and calorie debate in the wake of the economic crises of 1947. The Conservative critique of collectivism and controls which had appeared out of tune in 1945 was now articulated in an increasingly favourable climate and the party's skilful exploitation of widespread dissatisfaction with persistent shortages and ration cuts was instrumental to its electoral recovery. The condemnation of austerity and promise of consumer freedom and affluence enabled the Conservatives to recapture the middle ground by forging a broad coalition of consumer interests. This coalition was supported disproportionately by women voters, indicating that the Conservatives' appeal to housewives brought extensive rewards in terms of electoral success. Labour's vision of democratic socialism remained popular among the party's core constituency, above all male manual workers, but extensive dissatisfaction with austerity, especially among women and middle-class voters, initially deprived Labour of its landslide majority and subsequently of its hold on power. There was no general repudiation of Labour's policies, and public opinion was above all divided—as illustrated by the close results of the 1950 and 1951 general elections. The Conservative celebration of decontrol, the abolition of rationing, and the onset of the consumer boom enabled the government to consolidate its electoral support by winning a second general election with an increased majority. The Conservative approach to consumption was only secure in the mid-1950s, and the 1955 general election marked the end of the battle between socialist economic controls and the restoration of the free market, and between fair shares and consumer freedom, which dominated British politics for a decade following the end of the Second World War.

The rationing episode of the 1940s and 1950s is therefore a critical site on which to explore the relationship between state and society in twentieth-century Britain. The imperative to control and reduce consumption was initially conceived as an emergency response to the pressures of total war, but its continuation after 1945 owed as much to the strictures of Labour's vision of democratic socialism as to economic and structural factors. The implementation of the austerity policy draws attention to the limitations of fair shares in practice—whether in terms of the failure to achieve genuine equality between classes or men and women or with regard to the inherent shortcomings of controls exemplified by the black market. These flaws were increasingly obvious after the war, when the purposes of the policy were less clear and it became politically controversial. The post-war history of the austerity policy illustrates that extensive controls of consumption by the state were not sustainable in peacetime, partly because the inherent contradictions of the policy were more apparent but most of all because it proved impossible to sustain politically.

Bibliography

ADDISON, P., *The Road to 1945: British Politics and the Second World War* (London, 1975).

——*Now the War Is Over: A Social History of Britain 1945–1951* (London, 1985).

ALFORD, B. W. E., LOWE R., and ROLLINGS, N., *Economic Planning 1943–1951: A Guide to the Documents in the Public Record Office* (London, 1992).

ALLEN, M., 'The Domestic Ideal and the Mobilisation of Womanpower in World War II', *Women's Studies International Forum* 6 (1983).

BALFOUR, M., *Propaganda in War 1939–1945: Organisations, Policies and Publics in Britain and Germany* (London, 1979).

BALL, S., and SELDON, A., *Conservative Century: The Conservative Party since 1900* (Oxford, 1994).

BALLASTER, R., *et al.*, *Women's Worlds: Ideology, Femininity and the Woman's Magazine* (Basingstoke, 1991).

BANKS, O., *Faces of Feminism: A Study of Feminism as a Social Movement* (Oxford, 1981).

BEVERIDGE, W. H., *British Food Control* (London and New Haven, Conn., 1928).

BLACK, A., and BROOKE, S., 'The Labour Party, Women and the Problem of Gender, 1951–1966', *Journal of British Studies* 36 (1997).

BLACKFORD, C., 'Wives and Citizens and Watchdogs of Equality: Post-war British Feminists', in J. Fyrth (ed.), *Labour's Promised Land? Culture and Society in Labour Britain, 1945–51* (London, 1995).

Board of Trade, *Make Do and Mend* (London, 1943).

BOCK, G., and THANE, P. (eds.), *Maternity and Gender Policies: Women and the Rise of the European Welfare States, 1880s–1950s* (London, 1991).

BOOTH, A., 'Economists and Points Rationing in the Second World War', *Journal of European Economic History* 14 (1985).

BOURKE, J., *Husbandry to Housewifery: Women, Economic Change and Housework in Ireland, 1890-1914* (Oxford, 1993).

——'Housewifery in Working-class England 1860–1914', *Past and Present* 143 (1994).

——*Working-class Cultures in Britain, 1890–1960: Gender, Class and Ethnicity* (London, 1994).

BOWDEN, S., and OFFER, A., 'Household Appliances and the Use of Time: The United States and Britain since the 1920s', *Economic History Review* 47 (1994).

——'The Technical Revolution that Never Was: Gender, Class and the Diffusion of Household Appliances in Interwar England', in V. de Grazia and E. Furlough (eds.), *The Sex of Things: Gender and Consumption in Historical Perspective* (Berkeley and Los Angeles, Calif., 1996).

BOYD ORR, J., *Food, Health and Income* (London, 1936).

BRADY, R. A., *Crisis in Britain* (London, 1950).

BRAYBON, G., and SUMMERFIELD, P., *Out of the Cage: Women's Experiences in Two World Wars* (London, 1987).

BREWER, J., and PORTER, R. (eds.), *Consumption and the World of Goods* (London, 1993).

British Medical Association, *Report of the Committee on Nutrition* (London, 1950).

BROAD, R., and FLEMMING, S. (eds.), *Nella Last's War: A Mother's Diary 1939–45* (Bristol, 1981).

BROOKE, S., 'Problems of "Socialist Planning": Evan Durbin and the Labour Government of 1945', *Historical Journal* 34 (1991).

——*Labour's War: The Labour Party during the Second World* (Oxford, 1992).

——'The Labour Party and the 1945 General Election', *Contemporary Record* 9 (1995).

——*Reform and Reconstruction: Britain after the War, 1945–51* (Manchester, 1995).

——'Labour and the "Nation" after 1945', in J. Lawrence and M. Taylor (eds.), *Party, State and Society: Electoral Behaviour in Britain Since 1820* (Aldershot, 1997).

BRULEY, S., '"A Very Happy Crowd": Women in Industry in South London in World War Two', *History Workshop Journal* 44 (1997).

BURNETT, J., *A Social History of Housing 1815–1970* (Newton Abbot, 1978).

——*Plenty and Want: A Social History of Diet in England from 1815 to the Present Day*, 2nd edn. (London, 1979).

——'The Rise and Decline of School Meals in Britain, 1860–1990', in J. Burnett and D. J. Oddy (eds.), *The Origins and Development of Food Policies in Europe* (London, 1994).

BUSS, D. H., 'The British Diet since the End of Food Rationing', in C. Geissler and D. J. Oddy (eds.), *Food, Diet and Economic Change Past and Present* (Leicester, 1993).

BUTLER, D. E., *The British General Election of 1951* (London, 1952).

——*The British General Election of 1955* (London, 1955).

——*British General Elections since 1945* (Oxford, 1989).

——and BUTLER, G., *British Political Facts 1900–1985*, 6th edn. (London, 1986).

Cairncross, A., *Years of Recovery: British Economic Policy 1945–51* (London, 1985).

——*The British Economy since 1945: Economic Policy and Performance 1945–90* (Oxford, 1992).

——and WATTS, N. *The Economic Section 1939–1961: A Study in Economic Advising* (London, 1989).

CALDER, A., *The People's War: Britain 1939–45* (London, 1969).

——*The Myth of the Blitz* (London, 1991).

CAMPBELL, B., *The Iron Ladies: Why Do Women Vote Tory?* (London, 1987).

CAPIE, F. H., and WOOD, G. E., 'Anatomy of Wartime Inflation: Britain 1939–45', in G. T. Mills and H. Rockoff (eds.), *The Sinews of War: Essays on the Economic History of World War II* (Ames, Ia., 1993).

CARR-SAUNDERS, A. M., CARADOG JONES, D., and MOSER, C. A., *A Survey of Social Conditions in England and Wales* (Oxford, 1958).

CARRUTHERS, S. L., '"Manning the Factories": Propaganda and Policy on the Employment of Women 1939–1947', *History* 75 (1990).

CHESTER, D. N. (ed.), *Lessons of the British War Economy* (Cambridge, 1951).

CHURCHILL, W. S., *His Father's Son: The Life of Randolph Churchill* (London, 1996).

CLARKE, P., *Hope and Glory, 1900–90* (London, 1996).

CLINARD, M. B., *The Black Market: A Study of White Collar Crime* (New Jersey, 1952).

COCKETT, R., *Thinking the Unthinkable: Think Tanks and the Economic Counter-revolution, 1931–1983* (London, 1994).

COLEMAN, D. A., 'Population', in A. H. Halsey (ed.), *British Social Trends since 1900*, rev. edn. (London, 1988).

——and SALT, J., *The British Population: Patterns, Trends, and Processes* (Oxford, 1992).

CONLEY, F., *General Elections Today*, 2nd edn. (Manchester, 1994).

COOPER, S., 'Snoek Piquante', in M. Sissons and P. French (eds.), *Age of Austerity* (London, 1963).

CORLEY, T. A. B., *Domestic Electrical Appliances* (London, 1966).

CRAFTS, N. F. R., and WOODWARD, N. (eds.), *The British Economy since 1945* (Oxford, 1991).

CRAIG, F. W. S. (ed.), *British Parliamentary Election Results 1950–1970* (Chichester, 1971).

——*British Parliamentary Election Statistics 1918–1970*, 2nd edn. (Chichester, 1971).

——*British General Election Manifestos 1900–1974* (Chichester, 1975).

——*The Most Gracious Speeches to Parliament 1900–1974: Statements of Government Policy and Achievements* (London, 1975).

——*British Electoral Facts 1885–1975* (London, 1976).

——*Conservative and Labour Party Conference Decisions 1945–1981* (Chichester, 1982).

CRAWFORD, W., and BROADLEY, H., *The People's Food* (London, 1938).

CROFTS, W., *Coercion or Persuasion? Propaganda in Britain after 1945* (London, 1989).

CROSS, G., *Time and Money: The Making of Consumer Culture* (London, 1993).

CURTICE, J., 'Political Sociology 1945–92', in J. Obelkevich and P. Catterall (eds.), *Understanding Post-war British Society* (London, 1994).

DALTON, H., *The Fateful Years: Memoirs 1931–1945* (London, 1957).

——*High Tide and After: Memoirs 1945–1960* (London, 1962).

DAUNTON, M. J., 'Housing', in M. F. L. Thompson (ed.), *The Cambridge Social History of Britain 1750–1950* (Cambridge, 1990).

DAVIDOFF, L., 'The Rationalisation of Housework', in L. Davidoff, *Worlds Between: Historical Perspectives on Gender and Class* (Cambridge, 1995).

——*Worlds Between: Historical Perspectives on Gender and Class* (Cambridge, 1995).

DAVIDSON, C., *A Woman's Work is Never Done: A History of Housework in the British Isles, 1650–1950* (London, 1982).

DAVIES, J., *The Wartime Kitchen and Garden: The Home Front 1939–45* (London, 1993).

DE GRAZIA, V., and FURLOUGH, E. (eds.), *The Sex of Things: Gender and Consumption in Historical Perspective (Berkeley and Los Angeles, Calif., 1996).

DE GROOT, G. J., '"I Love the Scent of Cordite in Your Hair": Gender Dynamics in Mixed Anti-Aircraft Batteries during the Second World War', *History* 82 (1997).

DE V. WEIR, J. B., 'The Assessment of the Growth of Schoolchildren with Special Reference to Secular Changes', *British Journal of Nutrition* 6 (1952).

DIGBY, A., 'Poverty, Health and the Politics of Gender in Britain, 1870–1948', in A. Digby and M. J. Stewart (eds.), *Gender, Health and Welfare* (London, 1996).

DILNOT, A., 'The Economic Environment', in A. H. Halsey (ed.), *British Social Trends since 1900*, rev. edn. (London, 1988).

DONNELLY, P. (ed.), *Mrs Milburn's Diaries: An English Woman's Day-to-Day Reflections, 1939–45* (London, 1979).

DOVER, H., *Home Front Furniture: British Utility Design 1941–1951* (Aldershot, 1991).

DOW, J. C. R., *The Management of the British Economy, 1945–60* (Cambridge, 1965).

DRIVER, C., *The British at Table, 1940–1980* (London, 1985).

DRUMMOND, J. C., and WILBRAHAM, A., *The Englishman's Food: A History of Five Centuries of English Diet*, rev. edn. (London, 1957).

DUTTON, D., *British Politics since 1945: The Rise and Fall of Consensus* (Oxford, 1991).

FERGUSON, M., *Forever Feminine: Women's Magazines and the Cult of Femininity* (London, 1983).

FIELDING, S., '"Don't Know and Don't Care": Popular Political Attitudes in Labour's Britain, 1945–51', in N. Tiratsoo (ed.), *The Attlee Years* (London, 1991).

——'Labourism in the 1940s', *Twentieth Century British History* 3 (1992).

——'What did "the People" Want?: The Meaning of the 1945 General Election', *Historical Journal* 35 (1992).

——THOMPSON, P., and TIRATSOO, N., *England Arise: The Labour Party and Popular Politics in 1940s Britain* (Manchester, 1995).

FILDES, V., MARKS, J., and MARLAND H. (eds.), *Women and Children First: International Maternal and Infant Welfare, 1870–1945* (London, 1992).

FINE, B., and LEOPOLD, E., *The World of Consumption* (London, 1993).

FLOUD, R., WACHTER, K., and GREGORY, A., *Height, Health and History: Nutritional Status in the United Kingdom, 1750–1980* (Cambridge, 1990).

FORTY, A., *Objects of Desire: Design and Society, 1750–1980* (London, 1986).

FRANCIS, M., 'Economics and Ethics: The Nature of Labour's Socialism, 1945–1951', *Twentieth Century British History* 6 (1995).

——'"Set the People Free"? Conservatives and the State', in M. Francis and I. Zweiniger-Bargielowska (eds.), *The Conservatives and British Society, 1880–1990* (Cardiff, 1996).

——*Ideas and Policies under Labour, 1945–1951: Building a New Britain* (Manchester, 1997).

——and ZWEINIGER-BARGIELOWSKA, I. (eds.), *The Conservatives and British Society, 1880–1990* (Cardiff, 1996).

FRIEDAN, B., *The Feminine Mystique* (London, 1963).

FRY, G. K., 'A Reconsideration of the British General Election of 1935 and the Electoral Revolution of 1945', *History* 76 (1991).

FYRTH, J. (ed.), *Labour's Promised Land? Culture and Society in Labour Britain, 1945–51* (London, 1995).

GALLUP, G. H. (ed.), *The Gallup International Public Opinion Polls: Great Britain, 1937–1975*, vol. I, 1937–1964 (New York, 1976).

Gallup Poll, 'Voting Behaviour in Britain, 1945–1974', in R. Rose (ed.), *Studies in British Politics: A Reader in Political Sociology*, 3rd edn. (London, 1976).

GAMBLE, A., *The Conservative Nation* (London, 1974).

GARSIDE, W. R., *British Unemployment, 1919–1939: A Study in Public Policy* (Cambridge, 1990).

GEISSLER, C., and ODDY, D. J. (eds.), *Food, Diet and Economic Change Past and Present* (Leicester, 1993).

GERSHURY, J. I., 'Time Budgets as Social Indicators', *Journal of Public Policy*, 9 (1989).

GILES, J., 'A Home of One's Own: Women and Domesticity in England 1918–1950', *Women's Studies International Forum* 16 (1993).

GLEDHILL, C., and SWANSON, G. (eds.), *Nationalising Femininity: Culture, Sexuality and British Cinema in the Second World War* (Manchester, 1996).

GLUCKSMANN, M., *Women Assemble: Women Workers and the New Industries in Interwar Britain* (London, 1990).

GOW, A. F. S., *Letters from Cambridge* (London, 1945).

GRANT, M., *Propaganda and the Role of the State in Inter-war Britain* (Oxford, 1994).

GREEN, E. H. H., 'The Conservative Party, the State and the Electorate, 1945–64', in J. Lawrence and M. Taylor (eds.), *Party, State and Society: Electoral Behaviour in Britain since 1820* (Aldershot, 1997).

HALL, C., 'The History of the Housewife', in C. Hall, *White, Male and Middle-class: Explorations in Feminism and History* (Cambridge, 1992).

——*White, Male and Middle-class: Explorations in Feminism and History* (Cambridge, 1992).

HALL, M., 'The Consumer Sector', in G. D. N. Worswick and P. H. Ady (eds.), *The British Economy in the Nineteen-Fifties* (Oxford, 1962).

HALSEY, A. H. T. (ed.), *British Social Trends since 1900*, rev. edn. (London, 1988).

HAMMOND, R. J., *Food Volume I: The Growth of Policy* (London, 1951).

——*Food and Agriculture in Britain 1939–45: Aspects of Wartime Control* (Stanford, Calif., 1954).

——*Food Volume II: Studies in Administration and Control* (London, 1956).

——*Food Volume III: Studies in Administration and Control* (London, 1962).

HANCOCK, W. K., and GOWING, M. M., *British War Economy* (London, 1949).

HARDYMENT, C., *From Mangle to Microwave: The Mechanization of Household Work* (Cambridge, 1988).

HARGREAVES, E. L., and GOWING, M. M., *Civil Industry and Trade* (London, 1952).

HARRIS, B., 'Health, Height and History: An Overview of Recent Developments in Anthropometric History', *Social History of Medicine* 7 (1994).

——'The Height of Schoolchildren in Britain, 1900–1950', in J. Komlos (ed.) *Stature, Living Standards, and Economic Development: Essays in Anthropometric History* (Chicago, 1994).

——*The Health of the Schoolchild: A History of the School Medical Service in England and Wales* (Buckingham, 1995).

HARRIS, J., 'War and Social History: Britain and the Home Front during the Second World War', *Contemporary European History* 1 (1992).

HARRISON, B., 'Women's Health and the Women's Movement in Britain: 1840–1940', in C. Webster (ed.), *Biology, Medicine and Society 1840–1940* (Cambridge, 1981).

HARRISSON, T., *Living through the Blitz* (London, 1976).

——and C. Madge (eds.), *War Begins at Home* (London, 1940).

HAYEK, F. A., *The Road to Serfdom* (London, 1944).

HENNESSY, P., *Never Again: Britain 1945–1951* (London, 1992).

——'The Attlee Governments, 1945–1951', in P. Hennessy and A. Seldon (eds.), *Ruling Performance: British Governments from Attlee to Thatcher* (Oxford, 1987).

HENRY, S. (ed.), *Can I Have it in Cash? A Study of Informal Institutions and Unorthodox Ways of Doing Things* (London, 1981).

HILL, C., *Wise Eating in Wartime* (London, 1943).

HINTON, J., 'Women and the Labour Vote, 1945–50', *Labour History Review* 57 (1992).

——'Militant Housewives: The British Housewives' League and the Attlee Government', *History Workshop Journal* 38 (1994).

HODGSON, V., *Few Eggs and No Oranges* (London, 1976).

HOFFMAN, J. D., *The Conservative Party in Opposition 1945–51* (London, 1964).

HOLLINGSWORTH, D., 'Rationing and Economic Constraints on Food Consumption in Britain Since the Second World War', in D. J. Oddy and D. S. Miller (eds.), *Diet and Health in Modern Britain* (London, 1985).

HOLMANS, A. E., *Housing Policy in Britain: A History* (London, 1986).

HOPKINS, H., *The New Look: A Social History of the Forties and Fifties in Britain* (London, 1963).

HOWLETT, P., 'The Wartime Economy, 1939–1945', in R. Floud and D. McCloskey (eds.), *The Economic History of Britain since 1700*, 2nd edn., (Cambridge, 1994), vol. 3.

HUGHES, D., 'The Spivs', in M. Sissons and P. French (eds.), *Age of Austerity* (London, 1963).

INGLETON, R., *The Gentlemen at War: Policing Britain 1939–45* (Maidstone, 1994).

INSTONE, S., 'The Welfare of the Housewife', *The Lancet*, 4 Dec. 1948.

JAY, D., *The Socialist Case* (London, 1937 and 1947).

JEFFERYS, K., *The Churchill Coalition and Wartime Politics 1940–1945* (Manchester, 1991).

——*The Attlee Governments, 1945–1951* (London, 1992).

——*Retreat from New Jerusalem: British Politics, 1951–1964* (Basingstoke, 1997).

JONES, H., 'The Conservative Party and Social Policy, 1942–1955', unpublished Ph.D. thesis, University of London (1992).

——and KANDIAH, M. (eds.), *The Myth of Consensus: New Views on British History, 1945–64* (Basingstoke, 1996).

JONES, H., *Health and Society in Twentieth-Century Britain* (London, 1994).

JONES, T. G., *The Unbroken Front: Ministry of Food, 1916–1944* (London, 1944).

KANDIAH, M., 'The Conservative Party and the 1945 General Election', *Contemporary Record* 9 (1995).

KAVANAGH, D., and MORRIS, P., *Consensus Politics from Attlee to Major*, 2nd edn. (Oxford, 1994).

KINNEAR, M., *The British Voter: An Atlas and Survey since 1885* (London, 1968).

KIRKHAM, P., 'Beauty and Duty: Keeping up the Home Front', in P. Kirkham and D. Thoms (eds.), *War Culture: Social Change and Changing Experience in World War Two Britain* (London, 1995).

——'Fashioning the Femimine: Dress, Appearance and Femininity in Wartine Britain', in C. Gledhill and G. Swanson (eds.), *Nationalising Femininity: Culture, Sexuality and British Cinema in the Second World War* (Manchester, 1996).

——and THOMS, D. (eds.), *War Culture: Social Change and Changing Experience in World War Two Britain* (London, 1995).

KOMLOS, J. (ed.), *Stature, Living Standards, and Economic Development : Essays in Anthropometric History* (Chicago, 1994).

LAWRENCE, J., and TAYLOR, M. (eds.), *Party, State and Society: Electoral Behaviour in Britain since 1820* (Aldershot, 1997).

LEWIS, J., *The Politics of Motherhood: Child and Maternal Welfare in England, 1900–1939* (London, 1980).

——*Women in England 1870–1950: Sexual Divisions and Social Change* (Brighton, 1984).

——*Women in Britain since 1945* (Oxford, 1992).

LEWIS, R., and MAUDE, A., *The English Middle Classes* (London, 1950).

LINDSAY, T. F., and HARRINGTON, M., *The Conservative Party 1918–1979*, 2nd edn. (London, 1979).

LIVESEY, A. (ed.), *Are We at War? Letters to The Times, 1939–45* (London, 1989).

LONGMATE, N., *How We Lived Then: A History of Everyday Life during the Second World War* (London, 1971).

——*The Home Front: An Anthology of Personal Experience 1938–1945* (London, 1981).

LOUDON, I., 'On Maternal and Infant Mortality 1900–1960', *Social History of Medicine* 4 (1991).

——*Death in Childbirth: An International Study of Maternal Care and Maternal Mortality 1800–1950* (Oxford, 1992).

LOWE, R., *The Welfare State in Britain since 1945* (Basingstoke, 1993).

LYTTELTON, O. (Viscount Chandos), *The Memoirs of Lord Chandos* (London, 1962).

McCallum, R. B., and Readman, A., *The British General Election of 1945* (Oxford, 1947).

McCarty, E., 'Attitudes to Women and Domesticity in England, c. 1939–1955', unpublished D.Phil. thesis, University of Oxford (1994).

McKendrick, N., Brewer, J., and Plumb, J. H., *The Birth of Consumer Society: The Commercialisation of Eighteenth-century England* (London, 1982).

McKibbin, R., *The Ideologies of Class: Social Relations in Britain 1880–1950* (Oxford, 1991).

McLaine, I., *Ministry of Morale: Home Front Morale and the Ministry of Information in World War II* (London, 1979).

Macnicol, J., 'The Evacuation of Schoolchildren', in H. L. Smith (ed.), *War and Social Change: British Society and the Second World War* (Manchester, 1986).

Maguire, G. E., *Conservative Women: A History of Women and the Conservative Party, 1874–1997* (Basingstoke, 1998).

Mannheim, H., *Group Problems in Crime and Punishment* (London, 1955).

Marks, L., 'Mothers, Babies and Hospitals, "The London" and the Provision of Maternity Care in East London, 1870–1939', in V. Fildes *et al.* (eds.)., *Women and Children First: International Maternal and Infant Welfare, 1870–1945* (London, 1992).

Marwick, A., *British Society since 1945* (London, 1982).

Mechling, J., 'Advice to Historians on Advice to Mothers', *Journal of Social History* 9 (1975/76).

Mills, G., and Rockoff, H., 'Compliance with Price Controls in the United States and the United Kingdom during World War II', in H. Rockoff (ed.), *Price Controls* (Aldershot, 1992).

Milward, A. S., *War, Economy and Society 1939–1945* (London, 1977).

Ministry of Agriculture, Fisheries and Food, *Studies in Urban Household Diets 1944–49* (London, 1956).

Ministry of Food, *Food Consumption Levels in the United States, Canada and the United Kingdom* (London, 1944).

Ministry of Food, *How Britain Was Fed in War Time: Food Control 1939–1945* (London, 1946).

Ministry of Food, *The Urban Working-Class Household Diet 1940 to 1949* (London, 1951).

Ministry of Food/Ministry of Agriculture, Fisheries and Food, *Domestic Food Consumption and Expenditure 1950, 1951, 1956 and 1959: Annual Report of the National Food Survey Committee* (London, 1952, 1953, 1958, and 1959).

Mitchell, B. R., *British Historical Statistics* (Cambridge, 1988).

Morgan, D., and Evans, M., *The Battle for Britain: Citizenship and Ideology in the Second World War* (London, 1993).

Morgan, K. O., *Labour in Power 1945–1951* (Oxford, 1984).

——*The People's Peace: British History 1945–1989* (Oxford, 1990).

Morris, T., *Crime and Criminal Justice since 1945* (Oxford, 1989).

Murphy, R., *Realism and Tinsel: Cinema and Society in Britain, 1939–1948* (London, 1989).

——*Smash and Grab: Gangsters in the London Underworld* (London, 1993).

NELSON, M., 'Social class trends in British diet, 1860–1980', in C. Geissler and D. J. Oddy (eds.), *Food, Diet and Economic Change Past and Present* (Leicester, 1993).

NICHOLAS, H. G., *The British General Election of 1950* (London, 1951).

NICHOLAS, S., and OXLEY, D., 'The Living Standard of Women During the Industrial Revolution, 1795–1820', *Economic History Review* 46 (1993).

NICHOLAS, S., *The Echo of War: Home Front Propaganda and the Wartime BBC, 1939–45* (Manchester, 1996).

NICOLSON, H., *Diaries and Letters 1939–1945* (London, 1967).

NOAKES, L., *War and the British: Gender, Memory and National Identity, 1939–1991* (London, 1998).

OAKLEY, A., *Housewife* (London, 1974).

——*The Sociology of Housework* (Oxford, 1974).

OBELKEVICH, J., 'Consumption', in J. Obelkevich and P. Catterall (eds.), *Understanding Post war British Society* (London, 1994).

——and CATTERALL, P. (eds.), *Understanding Postwar British Society* (London, 1994).

O'CONNELL, S. *The Car in British Society: Class, Gender and Motoring, 1896–1939* (Manchester, 1998).

ODDY, D. J., 'The Health of the People', in T. Barker and M. Drake (eds.), *Population and Society in Britain 1850–1980* (London, 1982).

——'Food, Drink and Nutrition', in F. M. L. Thompson (ed.), *The Cambridge Social History of Britain 1750–1950* (Cambridge, 1990).

——and MILLER, D. S. (eds.), *Diet and Health in Modern British* (London, 1985).

OREN, L., 'The Welfare of Women in Laboring Families: England, 1860–1950', *Feminist Studies* 1 (1973).

ORWELL, G., *1984* (London, 1949).

PARKER, J., and MIRLEES, C., 'Housing', in A. H. Halsey (ed.), *Britain Social Trends since 1900: A Guide to the Changing Social Structure of Britain*, rev. edn. (London, 1988).

PARTINGTON, A., 'The Days of the New Look: Consumer Culture and Working-class Affluence', in J. Fyrth (ed.), *Labour's First Promised Land? Culture and Society in Labour Britain, 1945–51* (London, 1995).

PATTEN, M., *We'll Eat Again: A Collection of Recipes from the War Years* (Twickenham, 1985).

PAYTON-SMITH, D. J., *Oil* (London, 1971).

PEARCE, R. D., *Attlee's Labour Governments, 1945–51* (London, 1994).

PELLING, H., *The Labour Governments, 1945–51* (Basingstoke, 1984).

PERETZ, E., 'The Costs of Modern Motherhood to Low Income Families in Interwar Britain' in V. Fildes *et al.* (eds.), *Women and Children First: International Maternal and Infant Welfare, 1870–1945* (London, 1992).

PERKIN, H., *The Rise of Professional Society: England since 1880* (London, 1989).

PIMLOTT, B., *Harold Wilson* (London, 1992).

PUGH, M., 'Domesticity and the Decline of Feminism 1930–1950', in H. L. Smith (ed.), *British Feminism in the Twentieth Century* (Manchester, 1990).

——*Women and the Women's Movement in Britain 1914–1959* (London, 1992).

PUGH, M., *State and Society: British Political and Social History, 1870–1992* (London, 1994).

RAMSDEN, J., '"A Party for Owners or a Party for Earners"? How far did the British Conservative Party really Change after 1945?', *Transactions of the Royal Historical Society* 5th ser. 37 (1987).

——*The Age of Churchill and Eden, 1940–1957* (London, 1995).

——*An Appetite for Power: A History of the Conservative Party since 1830* (London, 1998).

REDDAWAY, W. B., 'Rationing', in D. N. Chester (ed.), *Lessons of the British War Economy* (Cambridge, 1951).

RHODES JAMES, R. (ed.), *Chips: The Diaries of Sir Henry Channon* (London, 1967).

RILEY, D., 'War in the Nursery', *Feminist Review* 2 (1979).

——*War in the Nursery: Theories of Child and Mother* (London, 1983).

ROBERTS, E., *A Woman's Place: An Oral History of Working-class Women, 1890–1940* (Oxford, 1984).

——*Women and Families: An Oral History, 1940–1970* (Oxford, 1995).

ROLLINGS, N., 'British Budgetary Policy 1945–1954: A "Keynesian Revolution"?', *Economic History Review* 41 (1988).

——'The Control of Inflation in the Managed Economy: Britain, 1945–53', unpublished Ph.D. thesis, University of Bristol (1990).

——'"The Reichstag Method of Governing"? The Attlee Governments and Permanent Economic Controls', in H. Mercer, N. Rollings, and J. Tomlinson (eds.), *Labour Governments and Private Industry: The Experience of 1945–1951* (Edinburgh, 1992).

——'"Poor Mr. Butskell: A Short Life, Wrecked by Schizophrenia"?', *Twentieth Century British History* 5 (1994).

——'Butskellism, the Postwar Consensus and the Managed Economy', in H. Jones and M. Kandiah (eds.), *The Myth of Consensus: New Views on British History, 1945–64* (Basingstoke, 1996).

ROSS, E., *Love and Toil: Motherhood in Outcast London, 1870–1918* (New York, 1993).

SAYERS, R. S., *Financial Policy 1939–45* (London, 1956).

SCHWARZ COWAN, R., *More Work for Mother: The Ironies of Household Technology from the Open Hearth to the Microwave* (New York, 1983).

SCOTT, J. W., *Gender and the Politics of History* (New York, 1988).

SCOTT, R., *The Female Consumer* (London, 1976).

SEERS, D., 'National Income, Production and Consumption', in G. D. N. Worswick and P. H. Ady (eds.), *The British Economy 1945–1950* (Oxford, 1952).

SELDON, A., *Churchill's Indian Summer: The Conservative Government, 1951–55* (London, 1981).

SHAMMAS, C., *The Pre-industrial Consumer in England and America* (Oxford, 1990).

SINCLAIR, A., *The War Decade: An Anthology of the 1940s* (London, 1989).

SISSONS, M., and FRENCH, P. (eds.), *Age of Austerity* (London, 1963).

SLADEN, C., *The Conscription of Fashion: Utility Cloth, Clothing and Footwear 1941–1952* (Aldershot, 1995).

SMITH, D., *Harold Wilson: A Critical Biography* (London, 1964).

SMITH, H. L., 'The Womanpower Problem in Britain during the Second World War', *Historical Journal* 27 (1984).

——'The Effect of War on the Status of Women', in H. L. Smith (ed.), *War and Social Change: British Society and the Second World War* (Manchester, 1986).

——'The Politics of Conservative Reform: The Equal Pay for Equal Work Issue, 1945–1955', *Historical Journal* 35 (1992).

——(ed.), *War and Social Change: British Society and the Second World War* (Manchester, 1986).

——*Britain in the Second World War: A Social History* (Manchester, 1996).

SMITHIES, E., *Crime in Wartime: A Social History of Crime in World War II* (London, 1982).

——*The Black Economy in England since 1914* (Dublin, 1984).

SPRING RICE, M., *Working-class Wives: Their Health and Conditions* (London, 1939).

STACEY, M., *Tradition and Change: A Study of Banbury* (Oxford, 1960).

STEVENSON, J., *British Society 1914–45* (London, 1984).

——and COOK, C., *The Slump* (London, 1977).

SUMMERFIELD, P., 'Women, Work and Welfare: A Study of Child Care and Shopping in Britain in the Second World War', *Journal of Social History* 17 (1983/84).

——*Women Workers in the Second World War: Production and Patriarchy in Conflict* (London, 1984).

——'The "Levelling of Class"', in H. L. Smith (ed.), *War and Social Change: British Society and the Second World War* (Manchester, 1986).

——*Reconstructing Women's Wartime Lives: Discourse and Subjectivity in Oral Histories of the Second World War* (Manchester, 1998).

TAYLOR, H., 'Rationing Crime: The Political Economy of Criminal Statistics since the 1850s', *Economic History Review* 51 (1998).

THOMAS, M., 'Labour Market Structure and the Nature of Unemployment in Interwar Britain', in B. Eichengreen and T. J. Hatton (eds.), *Interwar Unemployment in International Perspective* (London, 1988).

THOMPSON, F. M. L. (ed.), *The Cambridge Social History of Britain 1750–1950* (Cambridge, 1990).

THORPE, A., *A History of the British Labour Party* (Basingstoke, 1997).

TIRATSOO, N., 'Popular Politics, Affluence and the Labour Party in the 1950s, in A. Gorst,' L. Johnman, and W. Scott Lucas (eds.), *Contemporary British History, 1931–1961: Politics and the Limits of Policy* (London, 1991).

——(ed.), *The Attlee Years* (London, 1991).

TITMUSS, R. M., *Problems of Social Policy* (London, 1950).

TOMLINSON, J., 'The Attlee Government and the Balance of Payments, 1945–51', *Twentieth Century British History* 2 (1991).

——'Planning: Debate and Policy in the 1940s', *Twentieth Century British History* 3 (1992).

——'"Liberty with Order": Conservative Economic Policy, 1951–64', in M. Francis and I. Zweiniger-Bargielowska (eds.), *The Conservatives and British Society, 1880–1990* (Cardiff, 1996).

——*Democratic Socialism and Economic Policy: The Attlee Years, 1945–51* (Cambridge, 1997).

——'Marshall Aid and the "Shortage Economy" in Britain in the 1940s', Department of Government Brunel University, Discussion Paper Series no. 97/2 (1997).

WADSWORTH, E., 'Utility Cloth and Clothing Scheme', *Manchester Statistical Society* (1948).

WALLER, J., and VAUGHAN-REES, M., *Women in Wartime: The Role of Women's Magazines 1939–1945* (London, 1987).

WALSH, N., and BRAITHWAITE, B. (eds.), *The Christmas Book: The Best of Good Housekeeping at Christmas 1922–1962* (London, 1988).

WEATHERILL, L., *Consumer Behaviour and Material Culture in Britain, 1660–1760* (London, 1988).

WEBSTER, C., 'Government Policy on School Meals and Welfare Foods 1939–1970', in D. F. Smith (ed.), *Nutrition in Britain: Science, Scientists and Politics in the Twentieth Century* (London, 1997).

WELSHMAN, J., 'Evacuation and Social Policy during the Second World War: Myth and Reality', *Twentieth Century British History* 9 (1998).

WHITE, C. L., *Women's Magazines 1693–1968* (London, 1970).

WHITE, D., *D for Doris, V for Victory* (Milton Keynes, 1980).

WHITESIDE, N., 'The Politics of the "Social" and "Industrial" Wage, 1945–60', in H. Jones and M. Kandiah (eds.), *The Myth of Consensus: New Views on British History, 1945–64* (Basingstoke, 1996).

WILSON, E., *Women and the Welfare State* (London, 1977).

WINTER, J. M., 'Unemployment, Nutrition and Infant Mortality in Britain, 1920–50', in J. M. Winter (ed.), *The Working Class in Modern British History* (Cambridge, 1983).

——'The Demographic Consequences of the War', in H. L. Smith (ed.), *War and Social Change: British Society and the Second World War* (Manchester, 1986).

WOOLTON, Lord, *The Memoirs of the Rt. Hon. The Earl of Woolton* (London, 1959).

WORSWICK, G. D. N., 'Direct Controls', in G. D. N. Worswick and P. H. Ady (eds.), *The British Economy 1945–1950* (Oxford, 1952).

——and ADY, P. H. (eds.), *The British Economy 1945–1950* (Oxford, 1952).

————*The British Economy in the Nineteen-Fifties* (Oxford, 1962).

YOUNG, M., 'Distribution of Income within the Family', *British Journal of Sociology* 3 (1952).

ZMROCZEK, C., 'The Weekly Wash', in S. Oldfield (ed.), *This Working-day World: Women's Lives and Culture(s) in Britain 1914–45* (London, 1994).

ZWEIG, F., *Women's Life and Labour* (London, 1952).

ZWEINIGER-BARGIELOWSKA, I., 'Bread Rationing in Britain, July 1946–July 1948', *Twentieth Century British History* 4 (1993).

——'Rationing, Austerity and the Conservative Party Recovery after 1945', *Historical Journal* 37 (1994).

——'Explaining the Gender Gap: The Conservative Party and the Women's Vote,

1945–1964', in M. Francis and I. Zweiniger-Bargielowska (eds.), *The Conservatives and British Society, 1880–1990* (Cardiff, 1996).

——'Women under Austerity: Fashion in Britain during the 1940s', in M. Donald and L. Hurcombe (eds.), *Gender and Material Culture: Representations of Gender from Prehistory to the Present* (Macmillan, 1999).

Index

Page references in **bold** indicate figures/tables.

LaVergne, TN USA
18 December 2009
167536LV00002B/60/A